Forms of Fellow Feeling

What is the basis of our capacity to act morally? This is a question that has been discussed for millennia, with philosophical debate typically distinguishing two sources of morality: reason and sentiment. This collection aims to shed light on whether the human capacity to feel for others really is central for morality and, if so, in what way.

To tackle these questions, the authors discuss how fellow feeling is to be understood: its structure, content and empirical conditions. Also discussed are the exact roles that relevant psychological features – specifically: empathy, sympathy and concern – may play within morality. The collection is unique in bringing together the key participants in the various discussions of the relation of fellow feeling to moral norms, moral concepts and moral agency. By integrating conceptually sophisticated and empirically informed perspectives, *Forms of Fellow Feeling* will appeal to readers from philosophy, psychology, sociology and cultural studies.

NEIL ROUGHLEY is Chair for Philosophical Anthropology and Ethics at the University of Duisburg-Essen. His systematic areas of specialisation lie in ethics, action theory, philosophical psychology and the theory of human nature. His historical interests concern the classical figures of ethical sentimentalism, particularly Adam Smith and David Hume, as well as the history of action theory. He is the author of *Wanting and Intending: Elements of a Philosophy of Practical Mind* (2015) and coeditor of the German-language volume *Wollen. Seine Bedeutung, seine Grenzen* (2015).

THOMAS SCHRAMME is Chair in Philosophy at the University of Liverpool. His background is in philosophy, but he has often worked in interdisciplinary projects. He has published widely in the philosophy of medicine and psychiatry, mainly on the concepts of health and disease. He also specialises in moral psychology and political philosophy. Most recently he has published the *Handbook of the Philosophy of Medicine* (coedited with Steven Edwards, 2017). He has edited several collections of essays, for instance *Being Amoral: Psychopathy and Moral Incapacity* (2014).

Roughley and Schramme have coedited *On Moral Sentimentalism* (2015).

Forms of Fellow Feeling

Empathy, Sympathy, Concern and Moral Agency

Edited by

Neil Roughley
University of Duisburg-Essen

Thomas Schramme
University of Liverpool

CAMBRIDGE
UNIVERSITY PRESS

University Printing House, Cambridge CB2 8BS, United Kingdom

One Liberty Plaza, 20th Floor, New York, NY 10006, USA

477 Williamstown Road, Port Melbourne, VIC 3207, Australia

314-321, 3rd Floor, Plot 3, Splendor Forum, Jasola District Centre, New Delhi - 110025, India

79 Anson Road, #06-04/06, Singapore 079906

Cambridge University Press is part of the University of Cambridge.

It furthers the University's mission by disseminating knowledge in the pursuit of education, learning and research at the highest international levels of excellence.

www.cambridge.org
Information on this title: www.cambridge.org/9781107521636
DOI: 10.1017/9781316271698

© Cambridge University Press 2018

This publication is in copyright. Subject to statutory exception and to the provisions of relevant collective licensing agreements, no reproduction of any part may take place without the written permission of Cambridge University Press.

First published 2018
First paperback edition 2020

A catalogue record for this publication is available from the British Library

ISBN 978-1-107-10951-3 Hardback
ISBN 978-1-107-52163-6 Paperback

Cambridge University Press has no responsibility for the persistence or accuracy of URLs for external or third-party internet websites referred to in this publication, and does not guarantee that any content on such websites is, or will remain, accurate or appropriate.

Contents

Notes on Contributors   *page* vii

I Introduction

1 Empathy, Sympathy, Concern and Moral Agency   3
NEIL ROUGHLEY AND THOMAS SCHRAMME

II Empathy, Sympathy and Concern

2 Empathy, Altruism, and Helping: Conceptual Distinctions, Empirical Relations   59
DAN BATSON

3 Self-Recognition, Empathy, and Concern for Others in Toddlers   78
DORIS BISCHOF-KÖHLER AND NORBERT BISCHOF

III Understanding Empathy

4 Self-Simulation and Empathy   109
HEIDI L. MAIBOM

5 Empathy as an Instinct   133
MICHAEL SLOTE

6 A Moral Account of Empathy and Fellow Feeling   142
LAWRENCE BLUM

IV Fellow Feeling and the Development of Prosociality

7 Empathy-Related Responding and Its Relations to Positive Development   165
NANCY EISENBERG

Contents

8　An Interdisciplinary Perspective on the Origins of Concern for Others: Contributions from Psychology, Neuroscience, Philosophy, and Sociobiology　184
CAROLYN ZAHN-WAXLER, ANDREW SCHOEN, AND JEAN DECETY

9　Sophisticated Concern in Early Childhood　216
AMRISHA VAISH

V　Empathy and Morality

10　Is Empathy Required for Making Moral Judgments?　245
JOHN DEIGH

11　The Empathy in Moral Obligation: An Exercise in Creature Construction　265
NEIL ROUGHLEY

12　Empathy and Reciprocating Attitudes　292
STEPHEN DARWALL

13　The Role of Empathy in an Agential Account of Morality: Lessons from Autism and Psychopathy　307
THOMAS SCHRAMME

Author Index　327
Subject Index　332

Notes on Contributors

DAN BATSON, Professor emeritus in Social Psychology, Department of Psychology, University of Kansas, USA

NORBERT BISCHOF, Professor emeritus in Psychology, Department of Psychology, Ludwig Maximilians University Munich, Germany

DORIS BISCHOF-KÖHLER, Professor of Psychology, Department of Psychology, Ludwig Maximilians University Munich, Germany

LAWRENCE BLUM, Professor of Philosophy, Department of Philosophy, University of Massachusetts, Boston, USA

STEPHEN DARWALL, Andrew Downey Orrick Professor of Philosophy, Department of Philosophy, Yale University, USA

JEAN DECETY, Irving B. Harris Distinguished Service Professor of Psychology and Psychiatry, Department of Psychology, University of Chicago, USA

JOHN DEIGH, Professor of Philosophy and Law, School of Law, University of the Texas at Austin, USA

NANCY EISENBERG, Regents' Professor of Psychology, Department of Psychology, Arizona State University, USA

HEIDI L. MAIBOM, Professor of Philosophy, Department of Philosophy, University of Cincinnati, USA

NEIL ROUGHLEY, Professor of Philosophical Anthropology and Ethics, Department of Philosophy, University of Duisburg-Essen, Germany

ANDREW SCHOEN, Center for Healthy Minds, University of Wisconsin–Madison, USA

THOMAS SCHRAMME, Professor of Philosophy, Department of Philosophy, University of Liverpool, UK

MICHAEL SLOTE, UST Professor of Ethics, Department of Philosophy, University of Miami, USA

AMRISHA VAISH, Professor of Psychology, Department of Psychology, University of Virginia, USA

CAROLYN ZAHN-WAXLER, Professor of Psychology, Center for Investigating Healthy Minds at the Waisman Center, University of Wisconsin–Madison, USA

I

Introduction

1 Empathy, Sympathy, Concern and Moral Agency

Neil Roughley and Thomas Schramme

Humans frequently act and react in line with what they take to be *morally* right or wrong. Humans are also animals with strong *prosocial* behavioural tendencies, that is, tendencies to benefit others. Both facts cry out for explanation. Historically, the first kind of explanation has been seen as the province of philosophy, whereas the second has primarily been the object of research in social, developmental and – more recently – neuropsychology. This division of labour is unfortunate, not least because neither question is likely to be answered satisfactorily without consideration of the relationship between morality and prosociality. Moreover, the tools of both disciplines – conceptual analysis, stringent argument and controlled experiment – are equally germane to both questions. Finally, and key for the topic of this volume, there are good reasons to think that certain kinds of emotional connection between human agents are crucial for the explanation of both forms of behaviour. Here, we group together the kinds of emotional connection that appear the best candidates for such a role – empathy, sympathy and concern – under the label *forms of fellow feeling*. The question uniting the contributions to this volume concerns the roles that these forms of feeling have in explaining moral thought, moral action and even moral norms, roles they may in part have as a result of their contribution to prosociality.

Forms of fellow feeling have been of central interest for both psychology and philosophy. One of the most prominent psychological claims in this area has been Dan Batson's 'empathy-altruism hypothesis'. According to the hypothesis, where an agent's welfare is threatened or impeded, an observer's coming to feel a *valence-congruent emotion* for the agent generates motivation in the observer, the ultimate goal of which is the removal of that threat or impediment (Batson 2011, 29). If the hypothesis were correct, then valence-congruent affect would be a highly important motivator of prosocial behaviour. It would be particularly important because the motivation it tends to generate is intrinsic motivation to contribute to another's welfare. Such motivation is in turn plausibly at work in a fairly large set of cases that fulfil a condition frequently taken to be decisive for moral motivation by moral philosophers: that is, action for others out of intrinsic reasons.

Psychologists have further made the case that comparable forms of prosocial motivation may also be generated in an agent by their coming to feel emotions as a result of *adopting another person's emotional perspective* (Hoffman 2000, 30ff.). Negative emotional reactions grounding both directly in concern for another's threatened welfare and in forms of perspective taking – generally distinguished as 'sympathy' and 'empathy' – thus look to be good candidates for a mediating, perhaps even constitutive role in moral agency. That is, it seems that the dispositions to sympathy and empathy might be essential features of any person who qualifies as a moral agent.

This hypothesis is advanced in no uncertain terms by the psychologist Frans de Waal (de Waal 2006) and the philosopher Michael Slote (Slote 2004; 2007; 2010), both of whom see empathy as decisive for morality in its entirety. Slote in particular delineates structures according to which empathy is not only central to forms of moral motivation, but also to the functioning of moral judgement and even as the criterion of morally right action. A less radical position has been advanced by Lawrence Blum, who takes it that central areas of the moral life, if not its entirety, ground in empathy and sympathy (Blum 1980; 1988). Nel Noddings has advanced a structurally similar position, according to which the key emotional dimension of morality is a feature of what she calls 'care' (Noddings 1984). Such conceptions are related to positions in the history of philosophy, broadly known as 'sentimentalist', in particular those of David Hume, Adam Smith and Arthur Schopenhauer. However, philosophers since Kant have repeatedly criticised conceptions of morality grounding in such emotional mechanisms, arguing that they are unreliable, biased towards friends, family and in-groups and unable to track important morally relevant properties other than welfare (Kant 1785, 398f.; Prinz 2011a; 2011b).

Present-day conceptions of morality as based in some form of fellow feeling or, more modestly, as requiring fellow feeling at some significant point in their structure are advanced in a context in which there is burgeoning social, developmental and neuropsychological work on empathy, sympathy and concern (Eisenberg and Strayer 1987; Zahn-Waxler et al. 1992; Preston and de Waal 2002; Singer and Lamm 2009; Bischof-Köhler 2012; Decety 2012; Maibom 2014). It seems that any assessment of the viability of moral conceptions that place such mechanisms at centre stage should do so on the basis of an understanding of what the empirical literature tells us about their functioning. This is particularly important in view of the very specific philosophical frameworks within which the original 'sentimentalist' theories were developed: Hume's and Smith's discussions are framed by an empiricist philosophy of mind and Schopenhauer's by a rather extravagant metaphysics. Moral sentimentalism today, or any ethical theory in which sympathy, empathy or concern plays a significant role, ignores the exciting empirical work on these topics at its peril.

The following introductory discussion has two parts. In the first, we examine various phenomena of fellow feeling, from the point of view of their conceptual structures, the conditions of their development and their import in social interaction. In the second part, we turn to the question of the role of these phenomena within various conceptualisations of the moral life.

The *first part* of the introduction begins with a proposal as to how we should best narrow down the field marked by our somewhat archaic umbrella term *fellow feeling*. We use it to pick out above all positive affective relationships between the emoter and some other sentient being, in particular affective relationships that seem possible without presupposing the existence of moral norms. This specification raises the question of the status of what is often called 'cognitive empathy', which appears necessarily to involve neither a positive relationship nor an affective component. In discussing this question, we summarise Heidi L. Maibom's instructive contribution to the volume (1.1). We then go on to look in some detail at the variations in the parameters that allow the conceptualisation of the various emotional phenomena covered by the terms 'empathy', 'sympathy' and 'concern', as well as of closely related states and mechanisms. This is especially pertinent, as both the mechanisms involved in the relevant affective phenomena and their relationship to motivation differ in various ways. We focus on two decisive parameters. The first is the extent to which there is a correspondence between the valence of a fellow feeling and the valence of that feeling's target (1.2). The second is the question of whether playing host to the relevant fellow feeling depends on a mechanism of affect transfer (1.3). Both parameters help to draw a line between empathy and what is frequently labelled 'emotional contagion', on the one hand, and sympathy and 'personal distress', on the other. They also help us to provide a suggestion as to how concern and 'care' should be conceived.

With these distinctions in hand, we then turn to the two central affective phenomena at issue in the volume, *sympathy* and *empathy*. We argue that for an understanding of both, as of their relationship, it is essential to be clear on their intentional structures, that is, on the way in which they conceive, refer to, or are 'directed at' other agents and their mental states. To this end, we introduce a set of terms that pick out different dimensions of the intentionality of the states and processes involved. On this basis, sympathy can be analysed as an emotion, or group of emotions, whose 'target' is another sentient being and whose 'formal content' concerns an impediment to the welfare of the being thus picked out, where the particular type of impediment is specified by the emotion's 'focus' (1.4). Whereas sympathy's structure, thus understood, is fairly transparent, the same cannot be said for empathy, which, as a phenomenon grounding essentially in an affect transfer mechanism, may appear to have as its target either another agent or merely her mental states. It is here that it seems imperative to distinguish different affective phenomena that may be called 'empathy', only some of which involve the positive take on the other that makes a form of feeling a feeling for one's fellow. Transfer or mirroring of emotional states of another is insufficient for such a take. This feature only enters where the empathiser 'goes along with' the relevant emotion, that is, where her emoting becomes genuinely vicarious. We offer a proposal as to how this should be understood (1.5).

The last section of part 1 of the introduction looks at the *causal environment* of the various feeling forms. The questions of both their evolutionary status and of their proximate causal conditions are discussed, as are their causal and conceptual relations to other morally relevant phenomena. Here, proposals developed in several contributions to the volume – those of Batson and Slote, as well as of Doris Bischof-Köhler and Norbert Bischof – are summarised and set into relation to one another (1.6).

The *second part* of the introduction goes on to ask what the import of the emotion concepts distinguished might be in differing conceptions of moral agency. The likelihood that they will be of moral import derives from the fact that moral action, which is at least primarily a kind of action for other-regarding reasons, is likely to ground in natural capacities to transcend one's own self-interest. Such capacities seem to be at work where someone sympathises with, empathises with, or is concerned about some other or others. Three empirically based contributions to the volume that discuss the relationship of fellow feeling and prosociality, particularly in ontogeny, are discussed at the beginning of part II of the introduction. Here, we present the findings and conclusions of Nancy Eisenberg, Amrisha Vaish and Carolyn Zahn-Waxler and her coauthors Andrew Schoen and Jean Decety (2.1).

From here, we move on to the question of the significance of fellow feeling for an understanding of morality, where morality is taken to substantially overlap, but not to be identical with, prosociality. If we take it that moral agents are particularly concerned with moral reasons, we need to hone in on competing conceptions as to how *moral reasons* might be generated or grasped. Section 2 of this second part of the introduction therefore begins by outlining two distinctions among moral theories which provide some clarity as to the role forms of fellow feeling might be assigned. The first distinction is established on the basis of competing answers to either the metaphysical question as to how moral reasons are constituted or to the epistemic question as to how agents come to grasp moral reasons. In either case, the answer can refer essentially to emotions. Where emotions are taken to be essential either to the constitution or understanding of moral reasons, the corresponding theory can be labelled *sentimentalist*; where no such affective features are thought to be essentially involved, the theory can be labelled *rationalist*. Clearly, forms of fellow feeling can only be thought decisive for moral agency if the relevant moral theory is sentimentalist in at least this undemanding sense.

A second distinction divides theories along the lines of *how* emotions are thought to fulfil their constitutive or epistemic function. According to one kind of approach, moral values or reasons might be constituted through the adoption of a perspective on the weal and woe of others that takes them as the object of sympathy, concern or care. In this perspective, the fate of the relevant beings is registered in terms of their effects on an observer's own sympathetic dispositions. Such an approach can be labelled a third-personal sentimentalism. This can be contrasted with second-person approaches, according to which reasons are constituted in two-way interaction between moral agents, rather than in a one-way receptive process. In a second-personal sentimentalism, empathy, understood as a mode of adoption of others' affective perspectives, might be taken to be decisive for the constitution of moral reasons (2.2).

The paradigmatic construction of a *third-personal* sentimentalism is provided by the eighteenth-century philosopher Francis Hutcheson, for whom value is constructed from the point of view of a sympathetic or benevolent angel. Hutcheson takes this metaethical model to lead naturally to a utilitarian normative ethics, according to which the morally right is determined by the relative level of well-being that would result from the realisation of competing behavioural options. In contrast, a *second-personal* sentimentalism is naturally associated with the generation of what, in philosophical parlance, are known as agent-relative reasons. These are reasons for actions owed by agents to specific others, independently of the overall good, which is identifiable from a view from nowhere. Stephen Darwall's second-personal account of morality belongs here; accordingly, his contribution to this volume is presented at this point. There may appear, then, to be a close relation between empathy understood as vicarious emoting and a deontological ethics that specifies agent-relative duties, on the one hand, and sympathy, understood as a third-personal reaction to the well-being of others, and utilitarianism on the other. The third section of part 2 of this introduction discusses the plausibility of such a mapping and defends a more differentiated understanding of the possible relations (2.3).

With these clarifications in place, we turn in the final section of the introduction to the question of the roles various normative ethical theories might assign to forms of fellow feeling in their conceptions of *moral agency*. Moral agency plausibly involves a number of key susceptibilities and capacities: a sensitivity to moral reasons; an ability to deliberate appropriately on their basis; a propensity to be motivated by the perception of or deliberation on moral reasons and a capacity to act correspondingly. If one were to take it that morally appropriate behaviour is necessarily mediated by deliberation, it may appear that the primary agential capacity required is that of the application of the criteria of right action. Such an intellectualist conception of moral agency would leave little room for fellow feeling. However, such a conception is implausible, as moral agency in many cases works spontaneously, generating right action without the need for deliberative mediation. This point motivates a distinction between criteria of the right and forms of morally appropriate moral motivation. One way to elaborate this point involves assigning a secondary role to abstract criteria of the right, instead focussing primarily on situation-specifically appropriate motivation. Such a theoretical move is characteristic of virtue ethics. A second, consequentialist way of fleshing the point out is to see those forms of everyday moral motivation as desirable that happen to contribute to the realisation of what is right all in all, even if everyday moral agents are completely unaware of the connection. Conceptions of this latter kind might see forms of fellow feeling as contingent components of moral agency, perhaps components whose role needs strengthening by susceptibility to sanctions.

More interesting for the purposes of this volume are conceptions for which fellow feeling is an essential feature of moral agency. This might be so if local forms of sympathetic motivation are taken to be necessary substitutes for the universal benevolence that structures the contours of the right, but which is beyond everyday agents (Hutcheson). Alternatively, it might be so if the expression of 'full empathy' is taken to be the criterion of the right (Slote). And it might be so if respect is taken to be dependent on vicarious emoting (Darwall). At the end of this section of the introduction, we present the views of those contributors to the volume that centrally involve claims as to the role of fellow feeling in moral agency, that is, the views of Thomas Schramme, Lawrence Blum, John Deigh and Neil Roughley (2.4).

As will have become clear even at this stage, many of the authors of this volume have already contributed significantly to the key issues to be discussed here. Indications of such contributions will be woven into the following discussion. Where the articles the authors have penned for this volume are focussed on, the relevant paragraphs will be introduced by their names set in bold typeface.

1. Forms of Fellow Feeling

There appear to be a number of different emotional mechanisms that relate moral agents and moral 'patients' and that can lay claim to a central role in moral agency.[1] The psychological and philosophical literature has produced a wide range of terms with overlapping meanings to pick out these and related mechanisms. As is to be expected, the parameters employed in different terminological coinages depend on the varying interests of the authors. As is also to be expected, there are a number of confusions that result both from a somewhat uneven use of the relevant parameters as well as from the collision of only slightly, but significantly different terminological stipulations. Here, we attempt to order the field and at the same time situate the contributions of the authors of this volume to the decisive conceptual questions. Obviously, it is not the words used that are important, but the phenomena we should be picking out. As we need to be able to pick them out reliably and unambiguously, conceptual clarification is of the utmost importance.

1.1 *Fellow Feeling*

Let us begin with the rather old-fashioned formulation that gives this volume its title: 'fellow feeling'. And let us begin with a wide explication, that is, by naming fairly broad necessary conditions, which we can narrow down as we progress. For a psychological state or mechanism to be a form of fellow feeling in the umbrella sense in which we are using it here, it has, firstly, to be or involve an affective component and it has, secondly, in some significant way to relate its bearer to some other sentient being. In order to further narrow the range of affective states covered by the term, two additional moves seem appropriate. The connection to the relevant other should, thirdly, involve some sort of positive take on the other. Anger, for instance, is an emotion involving a significant relation to another, but does not belong here. Fourthly, the emotion should not be one that can only be made sense of if one presupposes the existence of normative standards. Moral respect is a

---

[1] Moral patients are those affected or intended by moral actions. Patiency hence refers to 'the other side of agency' (Reader 2007).

matter of a positive relation to another or others, but seems to require the acceptance of moral standards. In contrast, the attitudes, mechanisms and practices picked out by terms such as 'empathy', 'sympathy', 'concern', 'compassion' and 'care' are generally thought to be features of human life that are natural in the sense that they have at least basic variants that do not presuppose morality, but to which they may contribute substantially.

Alongside the terms just mentioned, the psychological literature makes use of the related locutions 'emotional contagion' and 'distress' as well as working with various compounds such as 'empathic concern', 'empathic distress', 'sympathetic distress' and 'personal distress'. The latter three of these compounds tend to be thought of as designating phenomena that should not be subsumed under the umbrella term, as they entail no positive take on others. Finally, various authors distinguish different variants, particularly developmental variants of empathy, picked out by qualifying adjectives such as 'egoistic', 'quasi-egoistic', 'veridical' and 'full' or 'full-blown'.

Before embarking on a discussion of these varying faces of fellow feeling and their relatives,[2] a word is in order about a phenomenon that seems infelicitously grouped together with the affective states and processes just listed, although it is picked out by one of the fellow-feeling terms. 'Empathy' is sometimes used to refer to a specific variant of so-called theory of mind, mind reading or social cognition, the variant known as 'simulation'. As the procedure is carried out in order to achieve cognitive aims, it is sometimes known as 'cognitive empathy'.[3] In simulation, mental states of another are, in Goldman's terms, 'enacted' by the agent on the basis of the other's situation in order to enable ascription of those states or the products of decision making. Simulated beliefs and desires, for instance, generate 'pretend-intentions', which in turn cause genuine beliefs as to the contents of the other's intention. 'Simulated' or 'pretend' mental states are frequently characterised by simulation theorists as 'offline', that is, they are quarantined off from the mental states that might interfere with the agent's taking on the perspective of the other (Goldman 2006, 20). For these cases, characterising the process

---

[2] A number of the contributions to this volume contain suggestions as to how we should differentiate between various related concepts. Cf. Batson this volume, 60ff.; Blum this volume, 151ff.; Darwall this volume, 291ff.

[3] James Blair uses the compound expression as a synonym for 'Theory of Mind' (Blair 2005; 2007; 2009). Other authors, for instance Alvin Goldman and Karsten Stueber, simply talk of 'empathy', but make it clear that they are using the term to pick out simulationist variants of social cognition (Stueber 2006, 111ff.). Goldman specifies that mind reading as simulation is 'an extended form of empathy (where this term's emotive and caring connotation is bracketed)' (Goldman 2006, 4).

that generates the relevant beliefs as 'empathy', even of a cognitive kind, is potentially misleading. It is potentially misleading because the core of the term's etymology is the Greek 'pathos', that is, 'feeling' or 'affect'. Of course, semantics is not a slave to etymology. Nevertheless, there are two important questions regarding the precise relationships between affect and cognition here, and so it seems sensible to keep the relevant phenomena as terminologically distinct as possible.[4]

The first question concerns the role of 'mindreading' in (emotional) empathy. Some authors take it that the former is a necessary precondition of the latter (cf. Blair 2005, 700; Blair 2007, 5; Blair and Blair 2009, 146). Moreover, as Goldman has pointed out, certain conceptualisations of empathy or empathising – particularly that developed in Baron-Cohen's early theory of autism (Baron-Cohen 2003, 21ff.) – work with cognitive, affective and motivational components without differentiating their roles (Goldman 2006, 203f.). Doing so is problematic in view of the separability of the relevant phenomena, both conceptually and neurologically. The point appears particularly important in view of the disputed extent to which autism involves an impairment not just of mindreading, but also of the affective processes picked out by talk of empathy (Blair 2005, 706ff.; Blair and Blair 2009, 146ff.; Baron-Cohen 2011, 82f.; Schramme, this volume).

The second point at which distinguishing between cognitive and affective mechanisms is paramount here concerns a very specific kind of mind reading, one which, if it really is something humans do, would merit an etymologically accurate description as 'cognitive empathy': it would be a form of social cognition that is itself essentially affective. Certain authors take this to be the case where the mental phenomena generated in the mind reader are themselves affective, for instance, where the simulation of beliefs and desires leads the simulator to 'enact' the sadness of another. Here, it seems that the cognitive process of simulation must itself involve playing host to an affective state. This is plausibly what Batson is claiming when he says that taking on 'the imagine-other perspective' on another's emotional state involves 'not simply understanding, but *sensitive* understanding' (Batson 2009, 267, emphasis in original; cf. this volume, 63f.).

There is, however, a serious question here as to how we should precisely understand an agent's playing host to an affective state in a purely 'pretend' manner, that is, in a way that does not involve the agent having the emotion in a full sense. In his classic discussion, Max Scheler

---

[4] Stueber, however, argues that there are decisive historical reasons why the term 'empathy' should primarily be used for the cognitive phenomenon (Stueber 2006, 26ff.).

attempts to provide a phenomenological description of such cases. According to Scheler, there is an affective feature involved that is absent in mere knowledge or in judgement, but which nevertheless does not amount to the experience of the 'real emotion' of the other. There is, he claims, a form of 'feeling the other's feeling, not just of knowing it', that is essentially cognitive, an affective grasping of a feeling's quality, which does not actually attain the status of an emotion of the agent herself (Scheler 1923a, 5). It is difficult to suppress doubts as to whether the idea of feeling the quality of an affect without feeling the affect itself is coherent.[5]

Scheler sees this affective-cognitive phenomenon as a capacity necessary for novelists, dramatists and historians – independently of whether they feel *for* their fellows, such that, for instance, thus 'enacting' the suffering of another leads to suffering on their own part. The simulationist explanation, according to which the affect in question is quarantined from other relevant mental states, may help to explain why such kinds of affective-cognitive experience need have no consequences for an agent's motivation. However, they do not in themselves explain why simulating the affect involved in suffering is not itself a form of suffering.

In her contribution to this volume, an extended discussion of the structure and status of simulationist accounts of perspective taking, **Heidi L. Maibom** points out that 'enacted' emotions are, unlike simulated beliefs, extremely difficult to keep 'quarantined' (Maibom this volume, 110f.). Such emotions, she says, have the tendency to linger. Indeed, she claims that feeling the relevant emotion for the person whose mental life was simulated ('affective empathy') is the default result of such affective-cognitive enactment. That is, according to Maibom, 'enacted affect' seems subject to three forms of spread: temporal spread, as it tends to linger; mental network spread, as it tends to overcome the mechanisms of mental quarantine; and personal spread, as it tends to focus on the person whose mental life was simulated. This raises the question of how these forms of spread might be explained. The first and second forms might be explained in terms of the difficulty of feeling an affect as one that is not

---

[5] Scheler uses two German compound terms to pick out this phenomenon: 'Nacherleben', which literally means 'experiencing-after', and 'Nachfühlen', literally 'feeling-after' (Scheler 1923a, 4f.). Although the latter term is an everyday German term used without any such necessary affective dimension, meaning simply 'understanding', Scheler is clearly employing it terminologically to pick out a form of affective simulation that he takes to have a purely cognitive function. He compares it to episodic visual or auditory memory, which involves episodes of seeing or hearing 'in one's mind's eye' or 'ear' and can thus be contrasted with forms of propositional memory. The comparison may have persuaded the translator of the 1959 English version of the book to render 'Nachfühlen' as 'visualized feeling' (Scheler 1923b, 9).

one's own. However, it seems somewhat more mysterious that the third transition might be the default process.

Maibom's central concern is, in any case, to raise a series of doubts as to whether the initial cognitive step, as conceived by the simulationists, can do the work that is frequently assigned to it, particularly whether it is indeed the most frequent or effective route to vicarious emoting. She argues that simulation is extremely likely to go epistemically wrong, for the same kinds of reasons that we tend to be mistaken in both our predictions and our memories of our own reactions of affective, but also nonaffective kinds. Where the simulationists see perspective taking at work, she claims, the mechanisms really doing the work involve a hybrid of inferential and normative processes. We don't need to get inside the heads of others; instead, we look for varying, particularly fine-grained descriptions of another's situation and regulate our predictions by what we take to be the most reasonable reaction in the situation thus described. According to Maibom, then, what we take to be affective-cognitive perspective taking is structured by normative considerations. If she is right, this spells trouble for any theory that attempts to ground normativity in some form of prenormative perspective taking.

1.2   *Affect Valence*

Return now to fellow feeling itself: starting from our stipulation that all fellow feeling involves affect, a first parameter is the affect's valence. There are two questions to be posed here. The first is whether the feeling in question is for conceptual reasons necessarily of a specific valence. The second concerns the extent to which the valence of the fellow feeling has, again for conceptual reasons, to correspond to the valence of some feature – affective or other – of the being in the focus of the affective state. The question of the relation between the valence of the relevant psychological state of the bearer and the valence of the condition of the state's object or target is particularly significant for the family of phenomena at issue.

Clearly, *distress* is a state it is unpleasant to be in. This is going to be true independently of how one got there or what the distress may be focussed on. There is nothing in the everyday concept that specifies its causation by anything specifically related to others. Where it is caused by witnessing another's positive experiences, as in extreme envy or jealousy, it is going to be a form of 'antagonistic', rather than 'fellow', feeling. In empirical psychology, distress qualified as 'personal' is not merely self-focussed distress, but self-focussed distress triggered by taking the other to be distressed or in a distressing situation (Batson et al. 1987; Eisenberg et al. 1988; Batson 1991, 117; 2009, 269; 2011, 19). It is thus necessarily congruent in negative valence. The satisfaction of such a congruence condition also applies to other terminological variants such as 'sympathetic distress' and 'empathic distress' (e.g., Hoffman 2000, 30ff.).

In contrast, processes of *emotional contagion*, which also deliver affective states congruent with the triggering states, or at least with represented affective states whose representation triggers the process, can deliver states of either a positive or a negative valence, depending on the trigger. The much-cited experiments of Sagi and Hoffman of taped infant crying triggering infant crying, which are generally seen as evidence for early emotional contagion (Sagi and Hoffman 1976; but see Batson this volume, 62f.; Zahn-Waxler et al. this volume, 195f.), concern negative affective states. But examples of emotional contagion can involve either pleasant or unpleasant feelings, as in the subtle phenomenon of being affected by the mood of others in a room one enters and the rather less subtle cases of mass hysteria (cf. Scheler 1923a, 12f./1923b, 14f.).

We also only talk of *compassion* where the entity with which compassion is felt is either suffering or in a situation typically associated with suffering. The concept entails that the affective state generated by the relevant intentional relation to suffering is itself negative, that is, itself a form of suffering. This is the precise meaning of the German term *Mitleid* ('suffering with') used by Schopenhauer (Schopenhauer 1840, §16, 737ff.), of which 'compassion' is the standard translation (cf. Cartwright 1988).

Sympathy in turn also tends to be used when we are thinking of a person's affective reaction to suffering, pain or discomfort. According to Eisenberg, sympathy involves 'feelings of sorrow or concern for the other' (Eisenberg this volume, 166). However, there are uses of 'sympathy' and 'sympathise' that don't have any such negative experiential or evaluative dimension. We talk of sympathising with an argument, with someone's aspirations, with the devil, or being a sympathiser with some cause. As, perhaps with the exception of 'aspirations', the objects of 'sympathising' here are neither affective states nor necessarily the bearers of affective states, we may actually be dealing with a completely different concept. Etymologically, 'sympathy with an argument' would be better labelled as a form of *syndoxa* or *synlogos*. However, in all those cases in which sympathy's target can be construed as mental or representational, 'sympathy' involves congruence between the mental state generated and the state or item with which sympathy is entertained, whether that be a congruence of thought, aim or affect. In what follows, we will focus exclusively on the primary, affective concept.

Whereas, depending on precise usage, sympathy tends to be, or is even necessarily a feeling involving negative affect, talk of '*empathy*', in contrast, is open for positive or negative evaluative or experiential valence. It seems to be a feature of everyday language that we can empathise with someone whether they are feeling frustrated or delighted at having either failed or passed some exam. As has frequently been pointed out, this difference between sympathy and empathy is a product of a semantic shift. In the eighteenth century, both Hume and Smith used 'sympathy' to pick out processes as a result of which affect congruence on either the positive or negative side of the spectrum is established (Hume 1739–40, III.3. i.; Smith 1759/90, I.1. i.). Both authors provide numerous examples of both valences. Today, the phenomena they discuss would rather be referred to as cases of empathy.

Finally, 'concern' and 'care' are also primarily directed at – real or potential – negatively valued states. Both tend to be thought of as forms of worry or mild anxiety, at least where the verbs or nouns are used without any prepositional object. Someone who is 'carefree' has no such worries, and when someone says, 'It really is a concern', they are telling you about a source of their disquiet. There is a fairly well circumscribed concept of concern along these lines in empirical psychology. Here the term is used with a clear affective tenor, as when 'concerned facial expressions' of children are taken as experimental indicators that the children have been negatively affected by witnessing unpleasant experiences of another (cf. Vaish et al. 2009, 540f.; Vaish this volume, 229). Eisenberg's characterisation of the affective component of sympathy in terms of 'feelings of . . . concern' and Bischof-Köhler's construal of 'an expression of concern and compassion' as indicative of empathy with someone suffering (Bischof-Köhler and Bischof this volume, 84) are other such uses.

But again, both 'concern' and 'care' are also used in other ways. Being concerned to get something done may be no more than an interest in doing so. And 'care' has sometimes been used – at least in philosophy – to indicate merely a form of interest that is particularly well shored up in terms of a person's identity and motivation (cf. Frankfurt 1988, 82ff.; 1999, 159ff.). Note, though, that even where 'care' is used with an affective dimension and is construed as involving assistance for those whose incapacities are a source of discomfort, much of care thus understood is a matter of nurture, helping valuable capacities to come to fruition, a process which may be highly rewarding and felt to be so.

In neither of the latter uses does talk of 'concern' or 'care' entail or imply negative experiential states on the part of the concerned person or carer. In contrast to the primarily affective terms 'sympathy', 'empathy' and 'compassion', which seem first and foremost to pick out states that are felt, 'concern' and 'care' may be thought to be primarily terms for dispositions.

'Care' in particular is likely to be a term picking out a whole set of dispositions, some of which involve affective sensitivities, whereas others concern attention, thought patterns and motivation (cf. Noddings 1984, 30ff.; Darwall 2002, 2; Slote 2007, 10ff.). Moreover, it seems plausible that the relevant affective dispositions will either be, or strongly overlap with, dispositions to empathise and sympathise. If this is correct, care will necessarily involve emotional episodes congruent with the situation or feelings of the object of care, as construed by the carer. However, it also seems likely that a carer will feel tender feelings for the being cared for, feelings that will have a certain level of stability and thus independence from the other's assumed feelings. Indeed, caring seems to involve so many facets that it may plausibly be thought of as a practice sustained by a suite of attentional, motivational and emotional mechanisms. In this respect, care is perhaps similar to love. Where care is thus conceived, the questions of affect valence and valence congruence will only be selectively applicable. As we will see, 'concern for others' can also be understood in this network sense, as in the contribution of Zahn-Waxler and her coauthors in this volume.

1.3 Affective States and Transindividual Affect Transfer Mechanisms

If care or concern, understood in this broad sense, are complex practices, then they are situated on a different conceptual level to the concepts that are primarily at issue here. Thus understood, care or concern can be seen as forms of fellow feeling, if 'form' is taken to mean the vehicle – here, the network of attentional, motivational, identity-related and agential features – within which the fellow feeling plays a role. However, in the following, we shall understand 'form' more narrowly, only using it to pick out cases of occurrent or dispositional *emotion*. Once we hone in on these more local cases, we can see that there is one very basic difference between the key concepts. The difference is brought out by asking whether the relevant terms designate specific emotion kinds, or perhaps groupings of emotion kinds. The answer is that certain terms do, whereas others pick out mechanisms for the genesis of emotions.

There is a considerable amount of terminological variety here and thus potential for serious confusion. It is important to be clear that there are two categorically different phenomena, or groups of phenomena, which we need to keep terminologically distinct. What Hume and Smith labelled 'sympathy' are at core mechanisms of emotion transfer. In contrast, many contemporary authors understand 'sympathy' as picking out a specific emotion, or at least as a generic term for a set of affectively related emotions. Correlatively, 'empathy' has generally been assigned the role of denoting the relevant mechanisms of emotion transfer originally targeted by Hume and Smith.

It is this difference that determines the openness of empathy for different affective valences, whilst what we have called the primary use of 'sympathy' necessarily picks out a state involving negative affect. Similarly to Eisenberg (see Section 1.2), Michael Slote says that sympathy involves feeling 'sorry, or bad' for someone (Slote 2010, 15; cf. this volume, 133) and according to Heidi L. Maibom, in the negative case,[6] sympathy involves feeling 'sad' (Maibom 2014, 3). Dan Batson provides a longer list of terms that he takes to belong in the same family[7]: he names feelings reported as 'empathy', 'concern', 'sympathy, compassion, softheartedness, tenderness, pity, sorrow, sadness, upset, distress, grief' (Batson this volume, 60). Batson seems to assume that the subjects of his experiments who used these predicates associate them with a specific phenomenology. It is, however, unclear whether the subjects are simply using different terms to pick out the same type of feeling or whether the reports should be taken to indicate that different kinds of negative affect were registered. The impression that these reports involve fairly vague or imprecise ascriptions is supported by the fact that the list includes all of 'empathy', 'sympathy' and 'concern'. Whereas the use of 'empathy' to pick out a specific feeling is incompatible with the framework we are developing here, 'concern' does, as indicated previously, have a central use to pick out a particular kind of affective state.

The distinction between transindividual transfer process on the one hand and individual mental state on the other is also at work in the difference between the mental features designated by the terms 'emotional contagion' and 'distress'. The former is a mechanism of emotion transfer, whereas the latter picks out what looks to be a specific set of negative affects. Someone who is distressed is, according to an early formulation of Dan Batson, 'alarmed, upset, worried, disturbed, distressed, troubled' (Batson, Fultz and Schoenrade 1987, 19). Distress may be a generic term for a family of unpleasant feelings, but not all unpleasant feelings that can be directed at others are members of the family. The feelings involved in sadness, sorrow or resignation would presumably not

---

[6] Compare note 11.
[7] To add to the confusion that looms as a result of Hume's and Smith's use of 'sympathy' where we would use empathy today, Batson, who has conducted some of the most important empirical work in this area, uses 'empathy' or 'empathic concern' (cf. section 1.6) to pick out what most authors – including the authors of this article – call 'sympathy'. As Batson agrees that it is not the words, but the psychological phenomena that are important, we take it he would be unconcerned by this difference.

normally be taken to qualify because they lack the component of agitation that seems necessary for distress.

In addition, things are complicated by the fact, mentioned previously, that 'distress' in the empirical contexts at issue is usually supplemented by a qualifier such as 'personal', 'empathic' or 'sympathetic'. The first predicate suggests and the latter two entail that the distress in question has been brought about by a transindividual processes of affect generation.

1.4 Content, Target, Object and Focus: The Case of Sympathy

Empathy, then, essentially involves an affect transfer mechanism, whereas sympathy is a particular kind of emotion.[8] Nevertheless, we talk of 'empathising with' someone, just as we talk of 'sympathising with' someone. A key puzzle involved in understanding empathy therefore concerns the connection between the relationship of an empathiser to an empathisee, on the one hand, and the empathiser's relationship to the empathisee's affective states, on the other.

A first step towards solving this puzzle is to hold onto the fact that neither empathy nor sympathy has a propositional content. Instead, their contents are 'substantival', that is, the framing of their contents is a matter of the representation of particulars, specifically of other sentient beings, agents or perhaps their mental states (cf. Darwall 2002, 68f.).

In the case of sympathy, this is easily explained. Alongside the emotions that take propositional contents, such as sadness and resentment, there are a group of emotions whose contents are irreducibly nonpropositional.[9] These include jealousy, admiration and sympathy. Just as someone can be jealous of, or admire someone else, they can sympathise with or feel sympathy for her. Let us call the real item represented by the content of an emotion the emotion's *object*. The objects of emotions with propositional contents are realised states of affairs or facts, whereas the objects of emotions with substantival contents are particulars, such as sentient beings or agents. For our purposes, it will also be helpful to have a term for the particulars *as represented* within attitudinal contents, whether those contents are propositional or substantival. Call these the *targets* of emotions. Targets are identical with substantival contents, but

---

[8] The analysis of the features of the intentionality of emotions laid out in the following is strongly indebted to the seminal work done by Ronald de Sousa in chapter 5 of *The Rationality of Emotion* (de Sousa 1990, 107ff.). For reasons related to the methodology of the respective approaches – de Sousa's derives from a commitment to Millikan's biosemantics – our typology and use of the terms differ significantly.

[9] There are plausibly also affective states that can take either kind of object, without the substantival variant being reducible to the propositional variant or vice versa. For arguments that this is the case with enjoyment, cf. Davis 1982.

are only one component of propositional contents. So *B* can be the target (complete content) of *A*'s jealousy, or the target (component of the propositional content) of *A*'s schadenfreude on hearing that *B* has had an unfortunate accident. Emotions can also have targets to which no objects correspond (such as, someone might claim, Father Christmas or God).

In order to understand the structure of the emotional states involved in fellow feeling, we need to add two further concepts. The first is the feature that the emotion's bearer takes the target to have and that she sees as explaining or justifying her emotion. We can pick this feature out by means of the term *focus*. If *A* feels sympathy with *B*, the focus of *A*'s sympathy may be *B*'s suffering, *B*'s frustration or *B*'s having lost her job. The focus of sympathy can thus be either another's emotional state or their situation. Where sympathy's focus picks out a real property in the world, this can be labelled sympathy's *focal feature*. Sympathy's focus is thus the feature of its target that the sympathiser takes to realise sympathy's *formal content*, where an emotion's formal content is the way the world must be construed if the emotion is to be appropriate. Where the emotion is appropriate, it can be said to have a *formal object*.[10] Just as the formal content of fear is danger, the formal content of sympathy is an impediment to the well being of the emotion's target (cf. Darwall 2002, 51; Batson 2011, 11; this volume, 59).[11]

Sympathy, then, seems best understood as a nonpropositional emotion, or group of emotions, with a specific kind of target, that is, a sentient being, and with a formal content according to which the welfare of that being is impeded, an impediment picked out by the emotion's focus. Whether sympathy is one particular emotion and whether it involves one specific type of affect, or whether the term pulls together a group of emotions with related but distinguishable affective features, are questions we can leave open here.

[10] Here, we deviate not only from de Sousa's (1990) idiosyncratic terminology, but also from the terminological usage that has become prevalent in the theory of emotions since Anthony Kenny, according to which our formal content is an emotion's 'formal object'. The difference is explained by the fact that we have reserved the term 'object' for items in the real world, not for items in the world as represented in the emotion. Endangerment of or impediments to welfare are essentially features of the world as emotionally construed in sympathy. Mistaken sympathy thus has a formal content, but no formal object. It should also be noted that, in contrast to the assumption made by many authors, we are not assuming that all emotions necessarily have a formal content. What is important for our purposes here is that sympathy does.

[11] Batson sees the decisive feature of the target as his or her being in 'need'. The way he elucidates this point seems to make it clear that what he takes to be 'needed' are positive contributions to the target's well-being. Maibom would disagree that sympathy's formal object must be an impediment to well being, as she claims that sympathising involves taking it either that 'something bad' or 'something good' has happened to the target (Maibom 2014, 3).

1.5 The Obscure Target of Empathy

Return to empathy, of which we have said both that it is essentially a mechanism of affect transfer and that it in some sense also has a substantival content. How can an affect transfer mechanism even have a content?

Note, first, that we have ways of speaking that emphasize either one or the other way of understanding empathy. We might describe someone as empathising with another's sorrow or desperation or as empathising with the sorrowful or desperate person. Are these merely linguistic variants, by means of which the same kind of emotional process is described with a differing emphasis, or are they descriptions of significantly different psychological phenomena? (For the latter suggestion, see Blum this volume, 151–7) We wish to suggest that these locutions can be used to pick out distinct psychological phenomena – although this will no doubt rarely be what individuals are doing when they use the words in these ways, as the phenomena can easily be fused or confused. The basic point is that the empathic transfer process can be run either with a view to the significance of the empathically felt emotion for the other or independently of any such attitudinal framework. There also seem to be phenomena located between these two which are also sometimes described as empathic. Whether all the phenomena we discuss in the following paragraphs should be called 'empathy' and, if not, where the line should be drawn and why are questions we shall not try to adjudicate.

In order to delineate a scale of cases in which the other comes ever more strongly into view, it is helpful to begin with the contents of the attitudes involved. In general, lesser levels of accuracy in the transfer of an emotion will involve lesser attention to the other as the real or potential bearer of the relevant affect.

A transfer of affect may involve a transfer of contents, but it need not. In the most minimal case, a mood, for instance of melancholy, may be transferred. Here, no contents are part of the package passed on, because moods, not being 'about' anything, don't have contents. Contents of emotions, so it seems, can also get lost on the way, as when A's jubilation at the performance of her football team simply leads to a general cheerfulness in B.

Where emotion transfer from A bequeaths B an emotion with content, it is still possible that, as in Chinese whispers, the content undergoes a distortion in the process of the transfer. A may pick up on the worry of her father, B, as a consequence of behavioural features such as B's tone of voice, eye movement and posture and, as a result, herself begin to worry about her mother, C, whose health is not too good, when in fact B's worry concerns the question of whether his boss will find his new suit too flashy. Content distortion can be more subtle, resulting from a form of indexical slippage, as when A's worry about his daughter is transmitted to B as the worry about his$_B$ daughter, rather than as a worry about A's daughter.

Importantly, loss or distortion of content can result either from non-cognitive processes or from the misidentification of the content of another agent's affect. The latter is a social cognitive failure, perhaps specifically of 'cognitive empathy'.[12] Processes of the first kind seem to be those that are properly understood as resulting from contagion, which presumably need only be operative at the level of affect. How much content such contagion carries with it looks to be an open question. Note that these noncognitive mechanisms, by means of which the emotions of others are 'caught', may but need not lead to such loss or distortion of content.

At this juncture, the terminological question is naturally raised as to whether we should refrain from talking of 'empathy' in such cases of the loss or distortion of content during affect transfer. Whoever chooses to be conceptually restrictive in this way should be clear on whether the reason is the purely noncognitive transfer mechanisms or whether the loss or distortion of contents is the decisive criterion. If the first reason is taken to be decisive, then one consequence is that certain forms of emotion mirroring that include the matching of complex contents, but which result from high levels of familiarity rather than from explicit cognitive efforts, will not count as empathic.

If, on the other hand, the reason for a restrictive ascription of empathy lies in the loss or distortion of the relevant emotion's content, then the conception sets high standards of accuracy for empathy's ascription. X may try very hard to understand what Y is feeling, whether by simulative efforts or by attempts to remember Y's reactions in comparable situations. Yet X may still end up ascribing and feeling an emotion whose content is fairly close, but still significantly different from (for instance, more retributive than) Y's. Again, some authors may feel that we should refrain from talking of empathy in such cases – or at least in cases in which the content is significantly less close to that of the other person. There does indeed seem to be a demanding everyday use of 'empathy', according to which it is a success term. Failure of precision in one's inferences about

---

[12] Social psychological research on 'empathic accuracy' focuses on the purely cognitive question of agent's capacities deliberately to impute mental states to others in laboratory situations. This is done, for instance, in the dyadic interaction paradigm, in which participants attribute 'thoughts' or 'feelings' to others they have interacted with whilst watching a video of the interaction after the event. The attributions are compared with the participants' own ex-post self-reports and evaluated by trained raters (cf. Ickes 2001; Ta and Ickes 2017).

another or limits to one's affective capacity to feel what one takes it that the other is feeling – perhaps because of lack of experience or lack of imagination – would then be a sufficient reason to withhold the ascription of empathy.

Bringing this line of thought back to our question of what it means to empathise with another agent: mere affect contagion, resulting in an unnoticed change of one's own mood, or the taking on of an emotion whose content undergoes indexical slippage are not processes that bring the other person into, or keep them in, view. In addition, even precision in emotion mirroring, including an accurate adoption of the content of the other's emotion, need not involve what we in everyday terms would think of as empathy with the other *person*. In spite of Maibom's scepticism about our capacities for simulative success, certain people are plausibly good at 'getting into the heads' of others for strategic reasons. People with the gift of selling things may, for instance, have an ability to simulate the thought and emotion processes – the hopes, aspirations, worries and concerns – of their interlocutors in a way that affords their sales strategy a point of attack. Although such strategists would not be described as empathising with the buyers, it seems that they may be employing a capacity for emotion transfer that is subtle and accurate, perhaps locally as subtle and accurate as the capacity Scheler attributes to novelists and historians (see section 1.1).

What prevents us from seeing the buyers as objects of genuine empathy – rather than of the sales strategy – is, so it seems, the effect of the wider mental framework within which the salespeople run the mechanisms of emotion transfer. Here, specific pregiven aims dictate that the results of the emotion transfer mechanisms are cognitively isolated. There is an important sense in which, although the salesperson may affectively simulate the emotion that her prospective buyer is feeling, she doesn't, as Adam Smith put it, 'go along with' or 'adopt' the emotion (Smith 1759/90, 9, 17, 35, 44, 70ff.). It is the component thus described that is necessary for at least one central everyday notion of empathising with an agent, rather than merely with an agent's affective states.

This component appears not only to be incompatible with self-distancing from the simulation of the emotion or 'quarantining' its product; it appears to require its own specific attitudinal framing. The dissolution of the mechanisms quarantining some 'quasi-emotion' is surely only going to bring the agent to have the emotion itself, not to her having it on behalf of another. The relevant form of attitudinal framing plausibly involves a willingness on the part of the empathiser to take on the other's emotional and motivational perspective. Such willingness need not be actively brought about, that is, it need not involve a corresponding intention; it may simply be a matter of the triggering of an optative disposition towards the target. Thus understood, empathy with another person also requires the involvement of the empathiser as a person in a way that engages further-reaching emotional and motivational features of the empathiser. Not only are the modular barriers required for strategic 'affective cognition' absent; now, the transfer process and its product are strongly integrated within the holistic practical perspective of the person empathising.

There seem to be various reasons why such integration might take place. Often it will be a matter of a prior affective bond between friends or family. In other contexts, that bond may be predicated on the simple classification of another as a member of some in-group. Alternatively, it might result from a deliberate attempt to understand the other – deriving, for instance, from a desire to help, a desire itself perhaps morally generated. Finally, it might be the effect of a particularly developed sensitivity. Conversely, such holistic integration processes cannot only fail to take place in the absence of such enabling factors. They can, so it seems, also be inhibited or suppressed by other emotional or cognitive phenomena, or by physiological phenomena such as exhaustion on the part of the would-be empathiser.

Further, it should be noted that the empathic processes thus enabled can be more or less complex and hence demanding. On the one hand, there are fairly local happenings, responses to which are easily divined and gone along with. On the other hand, there are also events or processes whose understanding can require extensive narrative knowledge of the other. Responding emotionally in such complex cases can be a matter of correspondingly complex and challenging processes that involve deep levels of the responding person's personality. Cases of this latter kind can motivate the sort of sceptical view of empathy argued for by Peter Goldie (Goldie 2011), who concluded that genuine empathy is impossible. Yet, although such complex cases are clearly important, they are certainly not the only important ones.

There is plenty of evidence for the widespread belief that people can empathise with each other in the Smithian sense of going along with their emotions. Smith himself claims that 'nothing pleases us more than to observe in other men a fellow-feeling with all the emotions of our own breast', where such fellow feeling 'enlivens joy' and 'alleviates grief' (Smith 1759/90, I.i.2., 13f.). It ought to be clear that the mere mirroring of affect, independently of how the agent attitudinally frames this mirroring, need have no such effect at all. It is the going along with or adopting an emotion that we tend to experience as a form of support.

Where X reacts to Y's emotions in this way, X plays host to an emotional process that, at least in paradigmatic cases, involves, a relation between emotions. Yet, the process gains its interpersonal significance from the attitude toward the other agent through which the emotional process is framed. The running of processes of emotion transfer in such a way that one comes to 'enter into' the emotion thus transferred (Smith 1759/90, I.3. i., 44) involves playing host to an attitude for which another is the target. That, we suggest, is why it is possible to empathise *with someone*, as it is possible to sympathise with her. Understood in this way, empathising involves, first, playing host to a transferred emotion that will have, qua emotion, some propositional or nonpropositional content and, second, doing so whilst volitively endorsing the perspective of the agent to whom the emotion primarily belongs. This attitude, whose nonpropositional content corresponds to the empathisee's personal perspective on the emotion's content, makes the empathisee the target of the process.

Smithian empathising involves genuinely vicarious emoting, that is, not just playing host to an emotion that the other happens to have, knowledge or perception of which causes analogous processes in oneself. An emotion felt as a result of Smithian empathic processes is an emotion generated in view of another and felt on behalf of that other. The capacity to do so is perhaps curious, but no less familiar for that. Indeed, it seems plausible that the capacity for attuned vicarious emoting may have had an evolutionary function within kin groups and in the context of shared activities, for instance, hunting and self-defence. It is not implausible that vicarious emotion may have controlled vicarious action in such evolutionary contexts.

There is a final feature of the intentionality of empathy, as conceived by certain authors, which moves it even further away from mere emotional mirroring. The modern *locus classicus* is Martin Hoffman's characterisation of empathy as involving 'psychological processes that make a person have feelings more congruent with another's situation than with his own situation' (Hoffman 2000, 30; cf. Bischof-Köhler and Bischof this volume, 95ff. and Blum this volume, 155ff.). In this point, Hoffman follows Adam Smith, for whom 'sympathy' is primarily a process of emotion generation in view of another's situation, rather than a process of emotion transfer (Smith 1759/90, I. i.1., 12). Moreover, both Smith and Hoffman are clear that the importance of the other's situation is not merely epistemic – in view of the difficulty in accessing what the other is precisely feeling. On the contrary, both make it clear that empathy may be felt in spite of the belief, or indeed the fact, that the other is playing host to no such emotion. So the emotion assigned to the other and felt by the empathiser on her behalf need be neither felt, nor thought to be felt, by the other herself.

For instance, a woman who is humiliated by her husband, but who believes that such treatment is woman's lot and therefore has no particular averse feelings, may be the object of empathic anger or resentment. And a child who thinks it fun that his parents are persuading him not to take his schooling seriously can also be the object of his teachers' empathic frustration or worry. The emotions taken on by the empathiser on behalf of the empathisee in such cases are emotions the latter takes it that the former would feel were she to be informed of the possibilities and risks attending her situation and to be able to gain clarity on what the focal features of her situation mean for her life in view of these factors.

Building this counterfactual twist into the concept of empathy brings it structurally closer to sympathy. Both emotional phenomena have a personal target, frequently targeted because of a property of the person's situation, although quite possibly also because of some emotion they are taken to feel. In both sympathy and empathy thus understood, features of the target's situation constitute the affective attitude's focus.

Not everyone would agree. For instance, Jesse Prinz has rejected the claim that empathy's content may have such a counterfactual dimension, as, he claims, doing so 'tends to blur the distinction between empathy and sympathy' (Prinz 2011b, 212). Indeed, if one is interested in defining phenomena in as disjunct a fashion as possible, in order to discuss them separately – Prinz is dismissive of empathy's importance for morality – then one may want to reject a conception of empathy that allows for counterfactual features of its content. But if the aim is, instead, to understand the psychological phenomena that play a role in our everyday lives, before going on to investigate their importance, there is no reason to worry about such overlap between empathy and sympathy. Empirical psychologists have indeed often felt that the distinctions here are less important than their commonalities (cf. Eisenberg this volume, 170, 175; Vaish this volume, 216).

Actually, accepting the counterfactual move causes no problems at all for differentiating between empathy and sympathy. Sympathy as feeling bad or sorry for someone whose welfare is vitiated requires no perception or construal of what the other either is feeling or would be feeling under certain circumstances. Empathy requires such a perception or construal. What is empathically felt is determined by the content of such cognitive or protocognitive processes, whereas what is felt in sympathy is more or less clear in advance. It is clearer if sympathy is one single emotion; it is somewhat less clear, but nevertheless clearly restricted, if 'sympathy' is a generic term for closely related forms of affect. More generally, sympathy is, as Darwall puts it, a third-person emotion directed at individuals, whereas empathy is 'second-personal', requiring the (attempted) adoption of another's point of view (cf. Darwall 2002, 54) – even where the other does not herself adopt it. So, in conclusion, we can distinguish between empathy and sympathy without losing sight of the commonalities.

1.6 Consequences, Preconditions and Aetiology

This analysis shows that there is something superficial, or at least partial, about one way in which sympathy and empathy are sometimes distinguished. Various authors have claimed that, whereas empathy is felt *with* another, sympathy is felt *for* her (Slote 2007, 13; 2010, 5; Klimecki and Singer 2012, 371). Obviously, just about everything depends on the interpretation of the two prepositions. What is usually meant by feeling 'with' here is the parallel hosting of an emotion, supplemented by some causal connection. What is meant by feeling 'for' is generally the hosting of an emotion whose nonpropositional content represents a real sentient being, where that being is construed as impaired in her well-being and where that construal generates motivation in the emoter to reduce, eradicate or compensate for that impairment. As has been repeatedly pointed out (Batson 2011, 12ff.; this volume, 63, 65; Prinz 2011a, 225ff.; 2011b, 218ff.; Bischof-Köhler and Bischof this volume, 100; Blum this volume, 151ff.), mere isomorphic emoting entertains no necessary connection to motivation that will benefit the being 'with' – or alongside – whom the emotion is being felt.

Where, however, empathy is conceived as genuinely vicarious emoting, the contrast can no longer be drawn so simply. Indeed, there is an important sense in which it is empathy, not sympathy, which involves feeling *for* the other. This is the case if 'for' means 'on behalf of': an empathiser feels on behalf of another, as a proxy agent acts on behalf of another. One might say that this is a second-personal, rather than a third-personal, 'for'. Like the sympathetic 'for', the 'for' of Smithian empathy seems necessarily to involve some corresponding form of motivation. This follows from our earlier claim that the endorsement of the – perhaps counterfactual – perspective involved in another's simulated emotion is essentially a matter of its holistic integration with other emotional and motivational features of the empathiser.

One way to put this is to say that both sympathy and Smithian empathy involve a form of *concern*. Here, 'concern' is taken to be essentially a conative feature: a desire for the well-being of the other. Perhaps it is taken to be an affectively modified desire, but where this is the case, it will presumably be difficult to draw any affective distinctions between the empathy or sympathy component, on the one hand, and the concern component on the other. Moreover, as empathy can be triggered by events that are desirable for the empathisee and thus involve positively valenced affect, 'concern' could only stand for the generic motivational feature if it were taken to be affectively and hedonically neutral.

The difference in affect valence and corresponding motivation between ways of feeling for is captured by **C. Dan Batson**'s distinction between what he calls mere 'empathy', on the one hand, and 'empathic concern' (what we are calling 'sympathy'), on the other. (What we are calling) sympathy is other-oriented and congruent with the assumed welfare of the other; where the other is 'in need', the term 'concern' is added (Batson this volume, 59). Batson's important work on the 'empathy-altruism hypothesis' in turn concerns the precise relationship between what we are calling 'sympathy' and motivation. According to the hypothesis, 'other-oriented' emotions 'elicited by, and congruent with' what is taken to be the welfare of another ('empathic concern') cause motivational states that have the ultimate goal of increasing the other's welfare ('altruism').

This hypothesis actually contains something of a conundrum for the conception just developed, according to which the 'for' of sympathy (a fortiori of both Batson's empathy and empathic concern) is the 'for' of motivation. The empathy-altruism hypothesis is precisely the claim that there is a causal connection between the relevant 'other-oriented' emotion and intrinsic motivation to improve the other's welfare. However, if the relevant motivation is already a component of (what we are calling) sympathy, then the connection between sympathy and motivation cannot be causal. It seems that Batson must therefore understand the 'other-orientation' entailed by the 'for' of sympathy in a nonmotivational manner. In order to do this coherently, talk of other-orientation must be interpreted merely in terms of the structure of the emotion's intentionality, without requiring any motivational component. Batson seems to be making this point in his specification that it is the welfare-related fate of the other, not of herself, that is at issue for the emotion's bearer (Batson this volume, 60). Such a formulation in turn raises the question *in virtue of what* it is the other and not oneself that is at issue in sympathy. The answer is presumably a matter of the emotion's affective component. Perhaps the conceptual disentanglement required here is a matter of counterfactual variation, such that the specific aversive affect would no longer be felt if the relevant impediment to welfare were to be inflicted on the emoter, rather than on the other agent. Batsonian 'concern' would then be an exclusively affective matter.

In his article in this volume, Batson distinguishes his notion of empathic concern from various other psychological phenomena that might be described as forms of 'fellow feeling'. The primary contrasting phenomenon that enables the distinction of other-oriented affect is that of (personal or empathic) distress, which is essentially self-oriented. As Batson reports, affective phenomena such as anxiety on perceiving another's misfortune can decrease the probability of altruistic behaviour and even increase the probability of behaviour that harms the other.

It should be noted that the routes from perceiving another's misfortune to one's own personal distress can vary significantly. Either of the imaginative procedures that Batson distinguishes from sympathy – imagine-self and imagine-other processes – can inhibit the generation of altruistic motivation. One way in which this may be the case is if the imaginative procedure leads to feeling distress involving a focus on oneself, a causal process more likely if the imagining pertains to how one would feel in the other's situation, rather than how the other must be feeling. However, personal distress can also result from processes that proceed via emotions that involve genuine motivation to help the other. What is sometimes called 'compassion fatigue' can come about as a result of the depletion of an agent's psychological capacity to remain affectively and emotionally focussed on another, or on others, when severe demands are placed on that capacity (cf. Klimecki and Singer 2012). Such processes presuppose the generation of genuine altruistic motivation, a form of motivation that under certain circumstances can require too much. Similarly, children with emotionally distressed caregivers may as a result of empathy or sympathy develop genuine motivation to help, but, because of the natural inability to accomplish the role reversal that appears necessary, develop pathogenic guilt and tendencies to depression (Zahn-Waxler and Van Hulle 2012; Zahn-Waxler et al. this volume, 198ff.).

In his contribution to this volume, **Michael Slote** argues explicitly that empathy is a form of 'receptivity that has a motivational aspect'. He argues against Batson that both empathy and sympathy are, for conceptual reasons, motivational mechanisms: because empathy involves 'taking in' the intentionality of another's emotion, Slote claims, it will also involve taking on their motivation where that emotion is aversive (Slote this volume, 141; cf. 2015, 130f.). The claim that empathy is a form of receptivity is central to Slote's conceptual argumentation, according to which a Humean conception of empathy that does not rely on mindreading or imagination is nevertheless not a mere passive mechanism. It is, rather, more like listening than hearing, involving what Hume calls an 'embracing' of the other's presumed affect. This move raises the question of the relationship of such Humean receptivity to the feature Smith describes as 'going along with' the emotion of the other.

Alongside such conceptual reflection, Slote also speculates on both the phylogenetic preconditions of empathy's emergence and on the ontogenetic role of empathy in the development of altruistic motivation. First, he claims that empathy's evolutionary preconditions are likely to involve the two dispositions to 'flocking', or life in groups, and to imitation, a capacity normally taken to be a relation between forms of overt behaviour, but which should, at least in humans, also be seen as a relation between forms of mentalising. Second, he suggests that the ontogenesis of sympathy or altruistic motivation may result from a child's natural empathy with the sympathy his or her parents feel towards him or her. This proposal works with the claim that empathy involves 'taking in' not only the affect, but also the intentional and moitvational structure of another's emotion. Slote claims that the capacity to feel for and be motivated to help others may be generated as a result of experiencing just such an emotional state on the part of the caregiver. The argument seems to rely on the claim that the indexical component of the emotion's content, according to which the parent's sympathy is directed to the child herself, tends to undergo a kind of slippage, such that a general disposition to the other-directed emotion of sympathy is also communicated empathically. Slote claims that the kinds of Humean osmotic processes he describes can be understood as empathic in children as young as two years of age, once they have a clearer sense of their identity as distinct from those around them.

Doris Bischof-Köhler and **Norbert Bischof** develop an empirically based model of empathy's functioning that claims to pick out the mechanisms whose development is the decisive cognitive precondition for the empathy's genesis. Those mechanisms are, they argue, driven by two modules that generally develop from the middle of the second year. One they name the 'boundary module', which enables demarcation of oneself from another; the other they call the 'identity module', which enables agents to think of what is represented at one time and place as being the same as an object with a different spatio-temporal location. This second module is, they claim, a prerequisite of forms of problem solving that involve thinking through one's own possible role in future events. It was plausibly selected for because it bequeathed a fitness advantage over competitors that rely on behavioural trial and error.

According to the model, the capacity for 'identification' thus generated is a completely different kind of mechanism from that involved in contagion, which the authors, like Slote, see as manifest in the experiments of Sagi and Hoffman. Unlike Slote, however, they see no good reason to think of empathy itself as having been selected for. Rather, they argue, it is more plausibly the capacity for identification that has resulted from the pressures of selection, a capacity that then feeds into the mechanisms responsible for empathic emotion. The primary evidence for the model is the relationship between the reaction patterns shown by fifteen-to-twenty-four-month-old children in two separate experiments designed to test, on the one hand, empathy and, on the other, the capacity for self-recognition in a mirror.

The motivational consequences of empathising, they also argue, depend on the empathiser's attitude to the empathisee. For what they call 'concern' to be generated, that attitude must be 'positive'. This is presumably the same attitude described by Batson as the valuing of the other's welfare (Batson 2011, 41ff.; volume, 69ff.). It looks as though 'concern' here means prosocial motivation, a form of motivation which may stop short of leading to altruistic behaviour if the costs of thus behaving appear too high. Bischof-Köhler and Bischof also argue that empathy can lead to malevolent behaviour or be a key feature of sadism.

This claim once again raises the question of the relationship between the form of affective cognition postulated by Scheler that stops short of genuine emotion and the taking on of a genuine emotion in view of another's situation (cf. section 1.1). It is the former that Scheler takes to be compatible with cruelty. According to Scheler, it is true of the sadist that 'in the process of *feeling* the pain or suffering of his victim increase, his original pleasure at, and enjoyment of the other's pain *grows*' (Scheler 1923a, 11; our translation, emphasis in the original). What the sadist presumably does not feel is the psychological suffering on the part of his victim. Were he to feel this, he would necessarily be suffering himself. As already mentioned, Scheler's solution, that the feeling is an 'unreal' emotion – perhaps related to the 'quasi-emotions' that Kendal Walton thinks we feel in the cinema (Walton 1990, 241ff.) – raises suspicions of incoherence. However, the claim that what the sadist feels is the full emotion looks to be simply implausible. Thus understood, sadism would be a form of masochism.

A further possibility is that the form of 'cognitive empathy' of which sadists are capable is no empathy at all, but a form of mindreading that works with the capacity to understand the meaning of expressions of suffering, without requiring any affective component. Jean Decety has shown that psychopaths, when attempting to imagine the perspective of another who is feeling pain, fail to recruit the neural circuits (amygdala–orbitalfrontal cortex [OFC] coupling) activated in nonpsychopaths in the task (Decety et al. 2013). This would appear to indicate that psychopaths are missing an experiential feature that characterises normal responses to the pain of others. If this is correct, it looks like an argument for the claim that the access psychopaths have to the suffering of others is standardly, but not affectively cognitive.

2. Fellow Feeling and Moral Agency

Even if empathy is understood as a mechanism of mere emotion mirroring, it can trigger processes that motivate its bearers altruistically. Sympathy is frequently described as being more likely to generate altruistic or prosocial motivation; indeed, if the claim is true that the pro-feature of sympathy is motivational, then the connection will be a necessary one. This may also be the case for Smithian empathy. Concern, finally, may be thought of as an emotion that involves precisely the kind of prosocial motivation that fellow feeling brings about; alternatively, it may simply be thought of as prosocial motivation, independently of affective accompaniment; or it may be thought of as a suite of attentional, affective, cognitive and prosocial motivational features. These connections of various strength and structure between forms of fellow feeling and altruistic motivation suggest that we should take fellow feeling to be a significant moral phenomenon. In as far as being moral involves transcending one's own self-interest, the emotions brought together under this heading would appear to be plausible generators of at least one key feature of the moral point of view.

This claim could be made at various levels: it might focus on the importance of occurrent fellow feeling for moral motivation or for specific features of moral reasoning in particular cases; it might be a phylogenetic claim about the evolution of the moral life form (de Waal 2006, 21ff.; Tomasello 2016, 28ff.); or it might be a claim about the ontogeny of moral thought and motivation (Tomasello and Vaish 2012, 241ff.). Three empirically oriented chapters in this volume are significant contributions to the discussion of the third version of the claim, approaching it specifically in terms of the relationship between fellow feeling and prosocial behaviour.

2.1 *Fellow Feeling and Prosociality*

In his global rejection of the significance of empathy for morality, the philosopher Jesse Prinz has argued that a meta-analysis of early studies conducted by Underwood and Moore (1982) shows that there is no correlation between empathy and prosocial behaviour (Prinz 2011b, 219). In her contribution here, **Nancy Eisenberg** clarifies that the early studies reviewed by Underwood and Moore worked with methodologically problematic and unreliable measures and thus don't justify a conclusion such as Prinz's. Much work that has been done by Eisenberg and her colleagues has focussed on the extent to which the 'empathy–altruism' connection argued for by Batson has, first, a developmental correlate and is, second, subject to modification by individual differences, particularly in relation to emotion regulation. Eisenberg concludes that empathy and, more clearly, sympathy correlate significantly with both prosocial behaviour, including reduced aggression, and with what she calls 'prosocial moral reasoning'.

One important result of Eisenberg's work is to flag a complexity in the explanation of these correlations. The most intuitive explanation might appear to be in terms of sympathy's causal involvement in the production of prosocial behaviour. However, there are also good empirical reasons to see emotion regulation via effortful control as decisive, as it facilitates both prosocial behaviour and developed sympathy. Capacities for emotion regulation in young children are reliable predictors of sympathy at a later age. This, Eisenberg claims, is likely to be because, without such regulative capacities, empathic overarousal can lead to personal distress and the resulting self-focus.

Studies found only a modest correlation between sympathy and justice-related reasoning, but a substantial association of sympathy and 'prosocial moral reasoning', that is, reasoning about conflicts between the needs or desires of participants in a social conflict. Eisenberg argues that, here again, the causal relations are probably complex, running in part from sympathy to this form of moral reasoning and being partly bidirectional, as certain moral principles may direct attention to other people's needs.

Finally, with respect to the question of sympathy's ontogenesis, Eisenberg claims that there are various reasons why supportive parenting tends to be correlated with development of children prone to sympathy. A supportive parental environment tends to foster capacities for emotion management, to provide models for sympathetic behaviour and to lead to receptivity on the children's part to parental inputs. This latter point may go some way to supporting Slote's contention that sympathy may be generated in children through their empathy with their parent's sympathy (see section 1.6).

In their interdisciplinary article, **Carolyn Zahn-Waxler, Andrew Schoen** and **Jean Decety** focus on the network of affective, cognitive and behavioural features that they call 'concern for others'. On the one hand, they argue that these components can develop to different degrees in different individuals, generating individually distinct varieties of concern.

On the other hand, they take it that patterns of these components' combination, brought together under the terms 'concern' or 'care', constitute a particularly productive unit of analysis. Where Slote claims that empathy is a biological adaptation, a claim contested by Bischof-Köhler and Bischof, for whom the logic of evolution works at the level of empathy's preconditions, Zahn-Waxler and her coauthors see the capacity for concern or care for others – a capacity realised in various mammalian species – as the trait selected for.

The authors focus specifically on the development of empathy, arguing that various results of psychological and neurological research raise serious questions about the viability of Martin Hoffman's influential four-stage model of empathy's development (Hoffman 2000, 63ff.). In particular, they cast doubt on the claim that the first months of life are characterised by a confusion between self and other, a cognitive failing that would explain early forms of emotion contagion. Rather, they claim that what is missing here is the capacity for emotion regulation. Indeed, they go further, proposing that contagion of the kinds reported by Sagi and Hoffman is the result not of a protoform of empathy, but rather of a separate affective response system, which signals the need for caregiving. In this, it contrasts with empathy, which signals the potential for providing such care. The authors also raise questions as to whether the emotional responsiveness that develops towards the end of the first year of human life should be thought of as mere 'egocentric empathy', rather than a form of genuine concern that grounds in phylo- and ontogenetically primitive neurological features.

In contrast to much of the empirical work on empathy, Zahn-Waxler and her collaborators also follow Adam Smith in emphasising the significance of positive empathic phenomena. These are of two basic types: first, empathic concern with someone in distress might itself also involve positive feelings of tenderness. Second, empathy with another's pleasure or joy results not in concern, but in empathic happiness, mediated through affective resonance or 'mirroring' and goodwill towards the other. Interestingly, goodwill is here also taken to involve a 'feeling'. The authors also distinguish 'empathic cheerfulness', which seems to be a mood rather than an emotion and thus to lack content.

The last part of the contribution addresses three (presumably socially, rather than evolutionarily) 'maladaptive' responses to others' distress: a surfeit of concern that can lead to guilt or depression, alongside what the authors label 'active' and 'passive' deficits. Active deficits are associated with callous social behaviour and early in development appear as a precursor to psychopathy. Passive deficits are taken to be characteristic of autism, which is seen as resulting at least in part from deficiencies in capacities not only for cognitive, but also for affective response.

Amrisha Vaish's article emphasises a feature of Hoffman's conception of empathy that she claims has thus far been underrepresented: the variety of its determinants (Hoffman 2000, 36ff.). Together with the variety of ways in which cognitive processes both modulate and generate 'empathic responding', this constitutes a significant level of sophistication of the relevant processes. Vaish uses 'empathic responding' as Eisenberg uses 'empathy-related responding' to cover both empathy and sympathy.

Like Zahn-Waxler et al., Vaish emphasises the importance of basic forms of affect resonance that require no sophisticated cognitive processing such as explicit perspective taking. These perception-driven, 'bottom-up' information-processing mechanisms do employ 'implicit social-cognitive tools', such as implicit forms of self-recognition not catered for in the models of Hoffman or Bischof-Köhler. Vaish describes these processes as involving genuine concern, but not 'true empathy', thus marking a point at which empathy enters into concern for others, whilst rejecting the claim that such concern only arises once functional integration of the prefrontal cortex has been established.

Vaish describes the way that top-down activity then comes both to modulate perceptually triggered processes and to independently generate more complex episodes of empathic responding. Cases that demonstrate the former role include contextual assessment of reasons for distress, but also plausibly moral judgements as to the situation of a distressed other. Cases that demonstrate the latter include responses to harm where the victim shows no distress. The latter kinds of response may be generated either as a result of perspective taking or of following social 'scripts'. The factors that influence the development of flexible empathic responding in ontogeny are various. These include the increase in children's own emotional repertoires, the improvement in their capacities for effortful control and executive attention, as well as the development of their imagination, their linguistic abilities and their capacities for metacognition and meta-emotion. On this evidence, then, the importance of emotional processes for prosociality itself depends on those processes being permeated by the workings of other mental systems, at least some of which are cognitive.

Now, in spite of the substantial overlap between prosocial and moral motivation, the two are clearly not to be identified. An agent who is both socially competent and lacks, or can regulate, any aggressive dispositions need not enlist these capacities in the service of moral aims. There are, rather, plausibly ways of keeping the social peace that don't qualify as moral, indeed may be immoral, depending on questions such as the aetiology of a socially volatile situation and its pacification or the question of who is included in or excluded from social agreement. Prosociality may well also be a local matter, whereas we at least tend to think of morality as being of a much broader, possibly universal scope. Moreover, prosociality may overlook considerations of justice, as these can concern statistical matters and thus fail to directly mobilise motivational resources.

Nevertheless, the substantial overlap between prosociality and morality strongly suggests that mechanisms responsible for the former will also be significantly involved in the latter. This suggestion has been challenged in various ways, both historically and recently, in full view of the relevant empirical findings. In order to gain clarity both on the strength of such challenges and on the precise ways in which fellow feeling can feed into morality, it is helpful to draw two distinctions among types of moral theories.

2.2   Two Distinctions in Accounts of Morality

Begin with the obvious fact that certain things matter to moral agents that don't matter to nonmoral agents, that is, that moral and nonmoral agents take themselves to have different reasons. Starting from this datum, we can ask both the *epistemic* question as to how agents come to grasp moral reasons and, assuming the possibility of epistemic success, the *metaphysical* question as to how moral reasons are constituted. The first relevant distinction between moral theories is established on the basis of competing answers to these two questions. In either case, it can be claimed that the correct answer involves reference to emotions: emotions are sometimes taken to be essential either to the constitution or understanding of moral reasons. Competing accounts claim that there is no such necessity. Such accounts may involve the claim that the decisive mechanisms are entirely a matter of – unemotional – reason. Theories with the former feature are sometimes labelled *'sentimentalist'*; theories with the latter feature are frequently called *'rationalist'*. It should, however, be noted that such labelling makes most moral theories at least a little bit 'sentimentalist' – leaving 'rationalism', the position that denies emotions any significant role, a minority view. In truth, most theories of the moral life, particularly theories of moral agency, are going to be situated somewhere on a continuum on which both reason and emotions are at work to some degree.[13] Obviously, only theories that are sentimentalist

---

[13] If moral rationalism were the doctrine that reason is the only human capacity required for the adoption of the moral point of view, there would not be many moral rationalists. As we will see in a moment, not even Kant eschews emotions completely. By the same

in this undemanding sense have room for the claim that fellow feeling might have some essential role to play in morality.

A second distinction divides theories along the lines of *how* the relevant features picked out by 'sentimentalism' or 'rationalism' are thought to fulfil their constitutive or epistemic function. Beginning with the metaphysical question: moral reasons might, on the one hand, be explained in terms of those features of the world to which either our reason or our relevant emotional dispositions react in some specified way. On the other hand, moral reasons might be thought to be, at least in part, generated by forms of two-way interaction between agents. For the rationalist, that interaction might be a form of rational discourse under specific conditions, whereas for the sentimentalist, it might be a matter of reciprocal emotional reactivity. The first set of approaches might be labelled '*third-personal*', because the constitutive relation is one of observation of those features of the world taken to be central for morality. The second group can be labelled '*second-personal*', because the relation taken to be constitutive is one of participatory involvement.

The resulting four-place matrix can equally be applied to the epistemic question, enabling us to conceive access to moral reasons in four competing ways: first, as a matter of rational insight, perhaps on the basis of the application of some criterial procedure or perhaps by means of direct rational 'intuition'. Second, moral insight might be something achieved through certain forms of emotional experience, in the way that appropriate fear reveals danger. An understanding of what is morally right or wrong might, third, be thought to come about through rational discussion or, finally, as a result of putting oneself in the emotional shoes of affected others.

A particular theory might answer both the metaphysical and the epistemic question in the same way, but there is no necessity to this. Indeed, construing the answers to the metaphysical and epistemic questions too similarly poses problems for the construal of epistemic failure: we sometimes take a certain action to be, for instance, morally required, but are

---

token, if moral sentimentalism were the converse claim that reason plays no essential role in morality and that all that is required for moral agency are certain emotional dispositions, it is difficult to see how sentimentalism could take on the shape of a plausible moral theory. If fellow feeling is taken to be decisively involved, this follows from the importance of emotion regulation and executive attention for mature 'empathic responding', as shown by the contributions of Eisenberg and Vaish in this volume. Hume makes substantial appeals to rationality in delineating the mechanisms that bring the emotional reactions constitutive of the 'natural virtues' into line with 'stable and general points of view' (Hume 1739–40, III. iii.1., 581f.) and in his construction of the 'artificial virtues' on the basis of insight into human interdependence (Hume 1739–40, III. ii.2., 484ff.). The former is clearly an achievement of emotion regulation (cf. Kauppinen 2014).

wrong to do so. Moreover, there is in principle room for pluralism in answering either question, although the usual strictures against overly complicated theories hold.

Although we have sketched the distinctions here with rather broad brushstrokes, they nevertheless enable us to pinpoint the places at which fellow feeling, in one or the other form, may be thought to play a necessary role, as well as to identify those accounts that can assign fellow feeling at most a contingent function.

First, a pure *third-person rationalist* account might take moral agency to flow from the capacity to trace the workings of the rational procedure that generates moral reasons – a capacity that works without engaging any affective features of the moral agent. It is perhaps unclear whether there is anyone who seriously takes such a global view. Even Kant ends up outlining the importance of a feeling of 'respect for the moral law' for moral agency (Kant 1788, 75ff.). Although Kant insists that emotions have no place in constituting or even in understanding the criteria for moral rightness, he comes round to the view that the criterion he deduces by means of pure reason must be attitudinally framed in a certain way by (human) moral agents, an attitudinal framing that involves an emotion he calls 'respect'. This emotion, which it seems we should distinguish from the attitude of respect for persons (see Section 2.3), might perhaps be more pertinently referred to as 'awe' (cf. Kant 1788, 161). At any rate, coopting emotion for his account of moral agency looks to be an afterthought for Kant, as both the metaphysical and epistemic levels of the theory remain steadfastly emotion-free.

A *second-person rationalist* conception might, for instance, along the lines of Habermas' discourse ethics assign the intersubjective practice of giving, justifying and accepting reasons both criterial and epistemic centrality. In such a conception, the core of moral agency appears to be the capacity to enter into open and unconstrained discussion, a capacity that may have certain emotional preconditions – such as the capacity for emotion regulation – but which is essentially an ability to appreciate arguments (Habermas 1983a). Habermas argues extensively that his moral theory can be seamlessly connected to Kohlberg's stage theory of moral development. For Habermas as for Kohlberg, genuine moral agency is only attained on the 'postconventional' level, where an agent has developed the capacity for pure argumentative justification in terms of universalist principles (Habermas 1983b). Habermas claims that Kohlberg's schema needs supplementing by a seventh stage, at which individuals no longer 'monologically' apply a universalist principle, but have recourse to intersubjective procedures of 'redeeming validity claims' (Habermas 1979, 90).

Neither kind of (more or less) pure rationalist conception is able to countenance the claim that fellow feeling is a key feature of moral agency. In contrast, variants of moral sentimentalism can make use of its forms in different ways.

A *third-person sentimentalist* theory of morality can in principle conceive any of a number of emotions as the key responses in which either our axiological or normative relationship to the world or our epistemic relationship to value or reasons grounds. There are a number of proposals that cast emotions as epistemic capacities which take on a role analogous to that of our perceptual capacities relative to empirical facts (Brentano 1889; Tappolet 2000; Roeser 2011). What is pertinent for our purposes here, however, is the possibility of a sentimentalism according to which moral values or reasons are constituted through the adoption of a perspective on the weal and woe of others that takes them as the object of sympathy, concern or care. In such a perspective, the fate of the relevant beings is registered in terms of their effects on an observer's sympathetic or caring dispositions. As we shall see in a moment, this was the conception at work behind the original formulation of utilitarianism; it may also be at work in certain versions of care ethics.

In contrast, a *second-person sentimentalism* might see empathic processes as either constitutive of or as providing access to moral reasons. Empathy, understood as emoting on behalf of others, is not primarily a way of reacting to others' well-being or lack of it. Rather, it focuses on – real or counterfactual – first-personal reactions of others, seeing these as in some sense worth adopting for the empathiser. A theory of moral agency that assigns empathy a key role takes it that the experiential perspective of other agents is of ethical importance, independently of whether the empathically transferred emotions pick out what really is good for those agents.

2.3 Fellow Feeling, the Good and the Right

Let us focus, then, on possible differences between third-person and second-person sentimentalist moral theories, or components of moral theories.

There is a particularly prominent historical theory of the former kind that appears instructive here. According to this account, the moral point of view essentially focuses on the well- or ill-being of others. According to the eighteenth-century Irish philosopher Francis Hutcheson, moral goodness is motivation by 'benevolence', the disinterested calm desire for the happiness of another. On Hutcheson's view, an agent is good in proportion to the extent of his benevolence. Universal benevolence is thus the highest form of moral good, a form that is expressed by action that 'procures the greatest Happiness for the greatest Numbers' (Hutcheson 1725–38, II.iii.7.). Hutcheson thus moves from a conception of moral agency or 'virtue' to a – utilitarian – criterion of moral rightness, where the relevant notion of moral agency is at core the possession of a kind of desire.

Hutcheson classifies the calm desires as 'affections', that is, as sensations dependent on reflection, but distinguishes them from those affections he calls 'passions' that involve 'confused sensation' attended by 'violent bodily motions' (Hutcheson 1728, II. i.). His notion of benevolence as a calm desire may share the ambiguous status of talk of 'concern', which, as we noted (section 1.2), sometimes simply picks out motivational dispositions, but sometimes clearly involves an affective component. As 'affections', all of Hutcheson's motivational concepts involve an element of affect, that is, of 'sensation'. However, the calm desire of benevolence is a form of affect that is highly purified through regulation by reflection. As it appears to be the motivational rather than the affect component that is decisive – he generally sees the passions as a disturbing factor – moral agency in Hutcheson is only in a restricted sense a matter of fellow feeling.

Nevertheless, Hutcheson's conception does provide a model for the third-person role of fellow feeling in structuring a strongly sentimentalist conception of moral agency. The standpoint taken on by a moral agent is essentially external to human interaction, a standpoint that enables the agent to calculate the weal and woe of the morally relevant sentient beings and, in distanced reflection, come to a conclusion about what is to be done. Hutcheson encapsulates this in his claim that universal benevolence could be instantiated by 'a superior nature or angel, who had no particular intercourse with any part of mankind' (Hutcheson 1728, II. ii.).

Hutcheson's benevolence involves the positive valuation of the wellbeing of others. This corresponds to the condition that various authors (Darwall 2002, 3; Batson, this volume, 69ff.; Bischof-Köhler and Bischof, this volume, 100) see as a necessary condition of sympathy or empathy generating altruistic motivation. In spite of Hutcheson also using the term to cover local forms of motivation relative to specific individuals, 'benevolence' naturally connotes a more extensive attitude, perhaps even the universal attitude that Hutcheson sees as the moral idea. More local variants that involve the affectively laden desire for the good of another for her own sake are more naturally picked out by talk of 'concern' or, as has been terminologically exploited in feminist ethics, by talk of 'care' (Noddings 1984).

Care, like benevolence, is primarily a one-way emotional and practical relation that, although it is frequently dependent on responsiveness on the part of its object (Noddings 1992, 17), nevertheless involves the carer taking the well-being or what is good for the other as the criterion for her behaviour. Children, the infirm and the elderly are paradigmatic recipients of care, as they can in some circumstances be pure moral 'patients'. Importantly, these paradigmatic caring situations are contexts in which paternalistic action is generally seen as most obviously unproblematic. As Stephen Darwall has argued, care – which he uses synonymously with 'sympathetic concern' – aims at the good for another, independently of what the other takes to be good for her (Darwall 2002, 2ff.).

In contrast, the tendency to paternalism is severely undercut by second-personal accounts of moral reasons, whether such accounts are rationalist or sentimentalist. As Darwall points out (Darwall 2002, 14f.), this is a point at which the contrast between sympathy and empathy appears crucial for sentimentalist conceptions. The basic difference is that, whereas sympathy or care involves a positive evaluation of the well-being, or – more to the point – a negative evaluation of the ill-being of others, empathy involves the positive evaluation of the subjective point of view of its relevant target. Importantly, these can come apart and it is with respect to this difference that normative moral conceptions are likely to differ where they make essential reference to fellow feeling. Of course, in as far as empathy is taken to be mere emotional mirroring, it cannot be empathy itself that assigns importance to its object's subjective perspective. This changes where empathy is conceived in Smithian fashion as a matter of genuinely vicarious emoting. You can't, so it seems, take on an emotion on behalf of another – where doing so involves taking on the relevant affective and motivational stand on the content in question – without assigning value to the other (cf. Deigh 1995, 760ff.).

Darwall has argued that the shift of perspective involved in taking on the emotion of another is intimately related to the attitude of respect for persons (Darwall 2002, 14ff.). Respect for persons, like Smithian empathy, involves assigning other agents value in a way that differs essentially from the valuing presupposed by sympathy, concern or care (Darwall 2006, 126ff.). In these latter cases, taking impediments to others' welfare as reasons to sympathise requires seeing their welfare as of a value thus diminished. Darwall adds that the value thus presupposed is agent-neutral, that is, it is not a matter of what is good-for-the-sympathisee, but what is good-full-stop. This corresponds to a natural reading of Hutcheson's claim that the attitude could be taken on by a 'superior being or angel' positioned outside the back and forth of human interaction. The benevolent or sympathetic angel sees what is absolutely good, independently of which individuals happen to be its bearer. From here it may seem like a small step to the claim that the primary moral aim should be the promotion, even maximisation, of welfare, independently of who realises it.

In contrast, respect, like Smithian empathy, involves assigning value to the practical perspective of individual others, and thus taking their desires or reasons as, at least *pro tanto*, generating reasons for behaviour that potentially affects them. Such reasons appear doubly agent-relative, in that they are reasons to treat a particular person in a specific way and reasons that are given for specific agents. These reasons are taken to be independent of the extent to which the behaviour for which they are reasons would contribute to the good as registered from a view from outside the interactive context.

In his contribution to this volume, **Stephen Darwall** argues that respect is to be understood in terms of the relation of holding responsible, a relation which, because of its second-personal structure, requires a variant of Smithian empathy, or what Darwall calls 'proto-sympathetic empathy' (Darwall this volume, 292; cf. Darwall 2002, 63ff.). Respect, according to Darwall, is at core a matter of playing host to dispositions to hold both other agents and oneself responsible for relevant actions (Darwall 2006, 140ff.; 2013, 22ff.). The dispositional attitudes that do the work are essentially 'reciprocating', that is, they essentially direct a form of demand to relevant others. The crucial role of empathy here is to enable the uptake of the address on the part of the agent blamed. Paradigmatically, this happens in feeling guilt, where an agent accepts the appropriateness of the perspective from which blame is directed at them. As others have argued, the repudiation of blame on the basis of counterreasons is plausibly also a part of the structure of the regulative relations constitutive of mutual respect (cf. McGeer 2013, 179ff.).

There is, then, a certain rationale for an association between sympathy-based conceptions of morality and a welfare-oriented, agent-neutral consequentialism, on the one hand, and empathy-based conceptions and deontology that emphasises agent-relative reasons of respect, on the other. There are, however, a number of reasons why such connection need not hold.

First, if empathy is conceived in terms of affect contagion rather than in terms of Smithian on-behalfness, the connection with consequentialism may appear just as close. Certainly, this corresponds to Rawls' classic critique of conceptions of impartiality based on what in the eighteenth century was labelled 'sympathy', viz. what we now call 'empathy'. The impartial observer thus conceived takes on the relevant attitudes of all agents involved, fuses them all in his bloated psychology and comes down on the side of the course of action for which the positive attitudes he has acquired outweigh in intensity the negative ones (Rawls 1972, 184ff.).

Rawls characterises the form of empathy that does the work here as a 'universalised' version of the everyday mechanism. However, there is a serious question as to whether such an extension would be recognisable as a version of the standard human phenomenon. Empathy looks to be essentially individual-regarding. This is the case if the concept of empathy at work here is the one expressible in locutions that refer to empathy with, or empathising with, persons or agents. The conceptualisation according to which empathy is a mechanism that transmits emotional states without a view to whom their bearers are is perhaps well suited to a construction of the kind Rawls uses, but it is far removed from both our everyday conception and that developed by Smith (cf. Roughley this volume, 284). It does, however, appear as a normative construction both in Hume's notion of 'sympathy with the public interest' (Hume 1739–40, III. ii.3., 500) and in the conception of universalisation developed by Richard Hare in his *Moral Thinking* (Hare 1981, 87ff.)

A second reason why it would be overly simplistic to map sympathy onto consequentialism and empathy onto deontology is suggested by Darwall himself when he states that sympathy is also 'an individual-regarding emotion' (Darwall 2002, 68). This follows from the intentional structure of sympathy, in particular, from the character of its target and formal content (cf. section 1.4). Sympathy at the impediment of the welfare of some entity grounds, then, in the concern for the individual herself and not in the impersonal desire whose content is the proposition that the world be such as to include nonimpediments of individuals' welfare. If this is correct, then sympathy, like empathy, contains internal restrictions to forms of transindividual extension that lose sight of the identity of the bearers of the relevant quantities of welfare. In this respect, sympathy may be radically distinct from benevolence (cf. Slote 2001, 79ff, 136f.).

Both reasons just sketched tie in with a third point, which undercuts the claim that either form of fellow feeling may be intimately connected with either of the classical conceptions of consequentialism or deontology. The point is that both sympathy and empathy are naturally partial attitudes. This has been given both negative and positive twists in discussions of the possible roles of fellow feeling in morality. Kant argued that the constitutive partiality of sympathy makes it eminently unsuited to play any central role in morality (Kant 1785, 398f.), and contemporary authors of both sentimentalist and rationalist orientations have argued that the same is true of empathy. As Hume claimed, empathy's strength appears, to a large extent, to be a function of perceived similarity, including group identity, or contiguity, under which he includes 'relations of blood' (Hume 1739–40, II. i.11., 318). Jesse Prinz and Jeanette Kennett have both emphasised that in-group/out-group mechanisms also play a highly significant role in modulating fellow feeling (Prinz 2011a, 227ff.; 2011b, 226f.; Kennett 2016, 5; cf. Vaish this volume, 230). These points raise large question marks as to whether sympathy might be taken to ground a universalist conception such as consequentialism. They equally raise doubts as to whether a universalist deontology of Kantian inspiration can draw on empathy.

There are positive variants of these doubts. Feminist care ethics has emphasised the ethical significance of relatedness, dispositions to highly selective attention to the needs of specific others and a corresponding motivational focus (Noddings 1984, 32ff.). All these features are covered by a notion of care that, both because of its contextual nature and intensity, is necessarily restricted in its applicability. Lawrence Blum has repeatedly argued that such particular forms of concern are at least in part constitutive of the ethical and stand in some sense alongside those moral spheres that are best seen as regulated by universal principles (Blum 1980, 1988). Finally, Michael Slote has gone beyond Blum in claiming that all forms of moral rightness derive from a form of fellow feeling, what he calls 'fully developed empathy' (Slote 2007, 31; 2010, 93) and which he at one point equates with 'caring motivation' (Slote 2007, 31). More precisely, he claims that the wrongness of actions lies in their 'reflecting' a lack of such empathy or caring motivation. Slote claims that we should embrace the consequence that our moral duties are to a significant extent partial (Slote 2007, 21ff.; 2010, 21ff.).

2.4 Sympathy, Empathy and Moral Agency

There are, then, various ways in which the relationship between fellow feeling and normative criteria could be conceived. The conceptualisation of these relations is frequently decisive for an understanding of moral agency. However, this need not be so. Moral agency is a multilayered capacity that plays out on the level of sensitivity, deliberation, motivation and action. It plausibly involves sensitivities to moral reasons or to morally relevant features of the world; the ability to deliberate on their basis in a morally appropriate manner; the disposition to be motivated by the perception of, or deliberation on moral reasons; and the capacity to guide or control one's behaviour in line with one's responses to relevant reasons.

In as far as deliberative capacities are taken to be central, it may seem natural to assume that moral agency essentially involves the aspiration to judge in accordance with whatever is the correct standard for moral judgement. After all, moral deliberation aims at judgements as to what would be the right or best action in some situation. So, if morally right actions are taken to be actions whose description is produced by the application of some impartial procedure, moral agency would essentially involve the capacity to step back both from one's own interests and the interests of those to whom one has emotional connections and to apply the procedure oneself. The procedure may be that of a maximising welfare function or something akin to the categorical imperative. Either way, it may seem that moral agency will consist at core of the cognitive capacity to apply such standards and the motivational capacity to realise them. There are, however, two points at which this picture can be questioned.

First, it seems clear that sensitivities to moral reasons or to morally decisive features of other agents need not always be manifest in the medium of moral deliberation and judgement. We surely often do what is right as a result of action-guiding sensitivities, specifically emotional or otherwise motivational mechanisms. These don't necessarily require the mediation by judgements or deliberation. Indeed, there are plausibly cases in which taking the circuitous route to action via judgement may itself appear morally problematic. This is so in examples in which we feel, as Bernard Williams put it, that the agent has 'one thought too many', for instance, where someone only decides to save his wife from drowning, rather than others, after coming to the conclusion that to do so would be morally permissible, perhaps even required (Williams 1981, 17f). This looks like a case in which the agent judges correctly – let us assume on the basis of correct criteria – and then carries out the correct action, but in which he nevertheless displays a defect in moral agency.

This critical move is frequently taken to point in the direction of virtue ethics, for which the evaluation of agents is generally assigned some kind of priority over the evaluation of action. The point can be put by insisting on the evaluative significance of the *way* in which the action is carried out, for instance, hesitantly or spontaneously (Hursthouse 1999, 11). This fits together naturally with the claim that taking a consideration as a reason in acting on the basis of that consideration does not require the deployment of the concept of a reason (Setiya 2007, 71). These points can be combined with the claim that the priority of the evaluation of agents over that of their actions is criterial, that is, that there are no criteria for right action other than what the good or virtuous person would do in the situation (NE 1105a5). Such an account of moral agency may appear to be independent of a metaphysics of good or right action. It may also be at work in care ethics, as where Noddings criticises what she sees as an overemphasis in moral theory on judgment, claiming that 'the moral impulse or moral attitude' should be given more prominence (Noddings 1984, 28).

A second reason why it may be thought that moral agency requires no explicit orientation in deliberation to criteria of right action is at home in the consequentialist tradition. For a conception of the morally right that derives from evaluations of states of affairs as maximally good, there are good reasons to doubt whether there are any deliberative features that are conceptually necessary for moral agency. In his most reductionist moments, John Stuart Mill appears to claim that moral agency may to a large extent primarily involve the sensitivity to sanctions installed so as to channel behaviour in the direction of the morally right (Mill 1861, ch. 4). A related move is made by Hare in developing his two-level theory. According to Hare, everyday judgement works with *prima facie* principles that diverge significantly from the true criterion of the right. He takes their application by most people to be the most effective way of securing the realisation of the true criterion – whose direct application would be overdemanding for the majority of moral agents most of the time (Hare 1981, 25ff.). In such a conception, moral agents don't need to represent the criterion of moral rightness; they may not need access to it; indeed, it may even turn out to be morally bad if they do have access to it, as that could undermine their moral behaviour.

There is thus no necessity that the metaphysical, epistemic and agential dimensions of morality align. Hence, if some form of fellow feeling is decisive as a feature of moral agency, this need not be inherited from the metaphysics of moral rightness and passed on through the epistemic features of moral judgement. Its importance might derive from the latter without implicating the former. It could also conceivably be simply a sensitising and motivating feature of moral agency, independently of either the constitutive characteristics of moral judgement or the metaphysics of moral rightness. The three possibilities thus marked in turn generate differing structures when consequentialist or deontological, universalist or partialist normative claims are fed into them. However, the second possibility just mentioned – fellow feeling as decisive for the structure of moral judgement without any constitutive metaphysical role – has had few explicit defenders.

Pure models – of empathy all the way down – seem most plausibly ascribable to Hutcheson, Schopenhauer and Slote. According to Hutcheson, universal concern (benevolence) is the third-person attitude the natural results of which mark the criterion for moral rightness. Although universal benevolence appears most likely to be taken on by some angelic observer, the motivation of everyday agents is to be assessed according to its approximation to the criterion instantiated by the universally concerned angel: 'with the common rate of men their virtue consists in intending and pursuing particular absolute Good not inconsistent with universal absolute Good' (Hutcheson 1728, I.ii.3.). The model seems likely to require the same prominence of fellow feeling ('benevolence') at all three levels, whether or not the common 'men' thus evaluated are aware that the particular good they are aiming at is merely an inferior substitute for the universal good.

Schopenhauer follows Kant in insisting that moral evaluations are essentially evaluations of moral worth. Moral worth is, moreover, tied to an action's motive. As Schopenhauer claims that compassion is the only source of actions with moral worth, the theory is built around an elegant – or simplistic – equivalence between the criterion of the good and the right on the one hand and the core feature of moral agency on the other. Not only 'love of mankind' ('Menschenliebe'), manifest in positive acts of helping (Schopenhauer 1840, §17), but also what he calls 'justice', manifest in omissions of malicious acts (Schopenhauer 1840, §18), necessarily expresses compassion. This monolithic ethics grounds in a metaphysical dualism of agential identity, according to which the 'immediate participation' in another's suffering that is the mark of compassion involves an experience of the 'true identity' of the empathiser with the empathisee, and indeed with all sentient nature (Schopenhauer 1840, 143f.). Because empathy all the way down is here fulfilling a deep metaphysical need, Schopenhauer rides roughshod over any attempt to provide an empirical explanation, rejecting for instance an explanation of compassion in terms of imagining being in the shoes of the other: 'we suffer *with* him and hence *in* him; we feel our pain as *his* and hence do not imagine it is ours' (Schopenhauer 1840, 147).

Michael Slote's empirically informed care ethical variant of virtue theory is a third model which foregrounds fellow feeling at all three – metaphysical, epistemic and agential – levels. The 'full empathy' that Slote takes to be the criterion for right action is also decisively at work at the level of the motivation of everyday moral agents. He argues that natural empathic concern is able to do just about all the work that has been claimed to require orientation by principles. This applies even in cases of negligence or indifference resulting from compassion fatigue (Slote 2010, 97ff.). As a virtue ethicist, he thinks morally right behaviour need by no means be mediated by moral judgement. Nevertheless, he argues that both moral judgement and moral understanding in some way involve empathy. Although he offers no analysis of moral judgement, Slote claims that moral judgements 'involve' approval, which he in turn believes is essentially dependent on empathy (Slote 2010, 53).

In each of these views, fellow feeling tracks the right because it feeds into moral judgement in those cases in which moral judgement works with the correct criterion of moral rightness. As it also tends to motivate, fellow feeling can be seen as the core of moral agency in such conceptions. These accounts contrast with consequentialist conceptions that don't found their criterion or criteria of right action in affect, but, for instance, in intuitions about what counts morally and why it thus counts (Sidgwick 1907, XIII, §3, 382). Such conceptions might take some form of fellow feeling to be a useful, even an empirically necessary mediator of the moral judgements of everyday folk that lead with sufficient frequency to morally correct action. If people allow their moral judgements – and corresponding behaviour – to be shaped by their empathy and sympathy, they might often get it right, in spite of the false positives and negatives that are generated now and again. Such a structure would assign empathy a contingent role in moral agency, one that might be realisable in other ways.

Finally, conceptions of moral agency might be developed without an eye to any specific conceptions of moral rightness or even moral judgement. This could be so for one of two reasons. One such reason would be the assumption that the central cases of moral behaviour are of types that are covered by just about any reasonable conception of the right. Another would be the particularistic belief that there are no criteria of the right independent of specific contexts of moral action. This second option is likely to be accommodating to claims that fellow feeling guides the action of moral agents to a significant extent independently of their moral judgements, judgement only coming into play where the largely reliable orientation provided by emotional mechanisms gives out.

Thomas Schramme's contribution to this volume is of the first kind. His strategy, in arguing for what he calls a constitutive role of empathy for moral agency, is not to focus on substantial features of morality, but to take his lead from cases in which it may seem clear that the agents in question suffer from defects that exclude them from, or at least restrict their participation in moral agency. Both autists and psychopaths, he argues, tend to be defective in their moral agency for reasons relating to mechanisms usually taken to be picked out by the term 'empathy'. Schramme's explanation takes a slightly different tack to that of Zahn-Waxler and her coauthors (section 2.1). On the one hand, being situated on the autism disorder spectrum generally involves an inability or significantly restricted ability to ascribe others mental states, that is, it involves a limitation of 'cognitive empathy'. Psychopathy, on the other hand, involves a severe restriction or complete lack of affective empathy. What both kinds of agents are missing, for different reasons, he claims, is the capacity to understand what it means for other agents to be subject to specific kinds of negative states. This capacity, he takes it, is an important step on the way to developing moral concern for others. Schramme suggests that, where a lack of affective empathy may prevent an agent understanding what it means for another to be harmed, a lack of cognitive empathy may drastically limit the capacity to appreciate another's subjective point of view and thus to respect her.

One might, then, derive from Schramme's contribution a suggestion that there are reasons for mapping 'cognitive empathy' onto deontological and affective empathy onto consequentialist reasons. This suggestion would be orthogonal to the proposal discussed in section 2.3 that we derived from Darwall. Neither proposal would have to be understood as calling for a decision between two sorts of overarching theory. Rather, they may be thought compatible with a pluralism of the sources of moral reasons. A view of this kind is proposed by **Lawrence Blum** in his *Friendship, Altruism and Morality* (Blum 1980), where he argues against the comprehensiveness of a duty-based conception of moral agency, claiming that actions aimed at helping or benefiting others are morally good. In his contribution to this volume, Blum discusses the parallel roles of 'fellow feeling' and what he calls the 'recognitional attitudes', such as respect, appreciation and recognition. Both kinds of attitude, he claims, entail motivation, dispositions to relevant forms of action and, decisively, a moment of affirmation of the attitude's target. In this latter point, he sees his notion of fellow feeling as going beyond the concept of empathy generally employed in both the psychological and philosophical literature. A moral agent, Blum argues, will be the bearer both of fellow feeling, in the course of experiencing which it is the other's welfare that is in focus, and of recognitional attitudes, which pick out other morally significant features of persons, such as their status. He further strengthens the case for a plurality of moral motive types by emphasising the importance of three further kinds of example: action out of principle; emotionally unmediated dispositions to help in simple everyday cases; and cases of humanity in extreme situations for which talk of 'sympathy' appears too weak.

John Deigh approaches the topic of moral agency explicitly via a discussion of moral judgement. Here, he revisits the claims of his article 'Empathy and Universalizability' (Deigh 1995), where he argued for a specific role of what he called 'mature empathy' in judgements of right and wrong that express 'deep' or 'sophisticated' knowledge. By this he meant knowledge of right and wrong based on an understanding of the reasons for the assignment of these deontic statuses. Mature empathy he understood as involving not just the mirroring of the affective states of others, but as also locating those states in structures of purposes that are themselves taken to be worthwhile. Only agents who engage an empathic capacity thus construed can, he argued, draw appropriate moral conclusions from the application of a criterial procedure that requires consistency in deontic judgements about the weight of reasons across persons. Without such a capacity, what are taken as patterns of relevant similarities between different persons' situations will be biased in a way that distorts the outcome of the criterion's application. According to Deigh, only deontic knowledge supported by recognition of reasons thus mediated by empathy might plausibly motivate the knower to act appropriately, that is, explain an internalism condition on deontic judgement. This connection, Deigh insisted, is purely psychological. Whether these and only these judgements count as moral judgements is, he concluded, a further question that can be left to metaethics. In other words, he took mature empathy to be central for a certain form of agency, where that agency grounds in deontic judgements, but he remained agnostic as to whether the relevant form of agency should be understood as moral.

Returning to his earlier claims, Deigh now comes to the conclusion that the separation of psychology and metaethics should be much more thoroughgoing than it appeared to be in his 1995 article. There are, he argues, different mechanisms that lead to moral judgements and which are appropriate objects of psychological research. Picking up a central distinction from Piaget, Deigh claims that a key difference between ways of understanding moral norms – as inflexible dictates of some authority or as the products of cooperative negotiation – is not a difference between inability and ability to make moral judgements. This is true in spite of the fact that, according to Piaget, the former understanding ('moral realism') only corresponds to the first stage of moral development, characteristic of children aged five to nine or ten (Piaget 1932, 28). The capacity to make a moral judgement is, Deigh argues, just the capacity to make any judgement. The relevant judgements are then simply those with a moral content. The difference in ways of understanding morality is comparable to different – more 'visual' and more abstract – ways of representing the truths of geometry, which, as shown by Hilbert, are equally valid and have differing strengths. The more mature understanding of moral judgements, which presupposes the 'visual' capacity for empathy, involves a more 'visualised', concrete understanding of a rule's import. Metaethics, however, should confine itself, Deigh believes, to a formal representation of the logic of moral judgements and reject the orientation to psychological matters raised by Hume's question as to whether our moral capacities are rooted in reason or emotion.

In contrast, **Neil Roughley**'s contribution assumes that metaethics can learn from empirical psychology. His focus is, however, not on motivational internalism or indeed primarily on moral judgement. Rather, proceeding from the assumption that morality is the product of the phylogenesis of certain kinds of psychological structure, before the development of which moral categories quite simply had no purchase, he argues that the construction of a psychology capable of supporting moral obligation can clarify the nature of moral obligation itself. In his exercise in 'creature construction', he makes use of data from psychopathology and comparative psychology in order to support the claim that the psychological features on which moral obligation builds are indeed conceivable in nonnormative form.

Roughley's first level of construction bequeaths a creature disposed to what he calls 'resentment*'. The term picks out an emotional reaction of a specific kind to manifestations of ill will or indifference on the part of others, forms of behaviour whose omission the creature dispositionally demands. Roughley argues that, although the disposition to resentment* may in normal humans be difficult to disentangle from normative preconditions (and thus from resentment), it is plausibly manifested by both psychopaths and primates. The disposition is supplemented on the second level by the capacity for Smithian empathy, that is, the capacity to take on emotions on behalf of another. The conjunction of these two capacities generates the disposition to indignation*, that is, to vicarious resentment*. Moral obligation can, Roughley argues, be constructed with these materials, as it corresponds to the indignation* that would be felt by an impartial empathiser. If the construction is successful, then moral judgement itself requires the capacity for Smithian empathy, as the concept of impartial indignation is only available to an agent capable of vicarious emoting. This means that, although there are plausibly a whole set of moral judgements which, for reasons concerning their content, require no occurrent empathy, the disposition to empathy may be a necessary condition of making deontic judgements that count as genuinely moral.

3. Conclusion

In spite of certain sceptical objections,[14] there can be no doubt that empathy, sympathy and concern all contribute significantly to prosocial

---

[14] Alongside the objections historically pressed by Kant and the newer worries of Prinz and Goldie all mentioned in this introduction, the psychologist Paul Bloom's recent *Against Empathy* (Bloom 2016) has expressed that scepticism most prominently.

behaviour. How much they contribute, in what ways they do so and with what degree of probability all depend on the precise ways in which the concepts are analysed. The present volume brings together a series of proposals as to how these questions should be answered from scholars at the forefront of research in psychology and philosophy, answers which, as we hope to have shown, profit from being set into relation to one another.

The degree and type of importance of the forms of fellow feeling for morality, in particular for moral agency, can likewise only be determined on the basis of answers to questions concerning an adequate understanding of morality, in particular, of the way its metaphysical, epistemic and agential dimensions are related. There is, fairly obviously, no necessity that individual moral acts be motivated by empathy, sympathy or concern. However, the contributions to this volume make it clear that there are a whole set of different ways in which fellow feeling might be involved in the constitution and recognition of, as well as in action that responds to moral considerations or reasons. Convincing answers to the questions thus raised will require that metaethical and ethical theory be supported by both conceptual clarity as to the relevant fellow-feeling concepts and empirical evidence as to the causal roles of the phenomena they single out.[15]

Literature

Aristotle. NE. *Nicomachean Ethics*. In: J. Barnes (ed.), *The Complete Works of Aristotle*. Princeton, NJ: Princeton University Press 1984, 1729–1867.
Baron-Cohen, S. 2003. *The Essential Difference. The Truth about the Male and Female Brain*. New York: Basic Books.
  2011. *Zero Degrees of Empathy. A New Theory of Human Cruelty*. London: Penguin.
Batson, C. D. 1991. *The Altruism Question: Toward a Social Psychological Answer*. Hillsdale, NJ: Lawrence Erlbaum Associates.
  2009. Two Forms of Perspective Taking: Imagining How Another Feels and Imagining How You Would Feel. In: K. D. Markman, W. M. P. Klein and J. A. Sur (eds.), *Handbook of Imagination and Mental Simulation*. New York and Hove, UK: Psychology Press. 267–79.
  2011. *Altruism in Humans*. New York: Oxford University Press.
Batson, C. D., J. Fultz and P. A. Schoenrade. 1987. Distress and Empathy. Two Qualitatively Different Vicarious Emotions with Different Motivational Consequences. *Journal of Personality*, 55, 19–39.

---

[15] Versions of most of the contributions to this volume were discussed at the conference of the same name held at the University of Duisburg-Essen in March 2013. The editors would like to thank Helga Bachert, Dennis Hille, Taha Laraki, Stefan Mandl and Moritz Buetefuer, whose assistance facilitated a successful conference and who provided invaluable help in preparing the final manuscript. Karina Derpmann deserves special thanks for her energetic support of the conference organisation, as does Yannick Weinand for his meticulous proof reading of the manuscript.

Bischof-Köhler, D. 2012. Empathy and Self-Recognition in Phylogenetic and Ontogenetic Perspective. *Emotion Review*, 4, 40–8.

Blair, R. J. R. 2005. Responding to the Emotions of Others: Dissociating Forms of Empathy through the Study of Typical and Psychiatric Populations. *Cognition and Consciousness*, 14, 698–718.

2007. Empathic Dysfunction in Psychopathic Individuals. In: Tom F. D. Farrow and Peter W. R. Woodruff (eds.), *Empathy in Mental Illness*. New York: Cambridge University Press, 3–16.

Blair, R. J. R. and K. S. Blair. 2009. Empathy, Morality and Social Convention: Evidence from the Study of Psychopathy and Other Psychiatric Disorders. In: J. Decety and W. Ickes (eds.), *The Social Neuroscience of Empathy*. Cambridge, MA: MIT Press, 139–52.

Bloom, P. 2016. *Against Empathy. The Case for Rational Compassion*. New York: Ecco/Harper Collins.

Blum, L. 1980. *Friendship, Altruism and Morality*. London: Routledge and Kegan Paul.

1988. Gilligan and Kohlberg: Implications for Moral Theory. *Ethics*, 98, 472–91.

Brentano, F. 1889. *The Origin of Our Knowledge of Right and Wrong*. London: Routledge and Kegan Paul 1969.

Cartwright, D. E. 1988. Schopenhauer's Compassion and Nietzsche's Pity. *Schopenhauer-Jahrbuch*, 69, 557–67.

Coplan, A. and P. Goldie. 2011. *Empathy. Philosophical and Psychological Perspectives*. New York: Oxford University Press.

Darwall, S. 2002. *Welfare and Rational Care*. Princeton, NJ: Princeton University Press.

2006. *The Second-Person Standpoint. Morality, Respect and Accountability*. Cambridge, MA: Harvard University Press.

2013. Respect as Honor and as Accountability. In: *Honor, History and Relationship. Essays in Second-Personal Ethics II*. Oxford University Press, 11–29.

Davis, W. 1982. A Causal Theory of Enjoyment. *Mind*, 41, 240–56.

Decety, J. (ed.). 2012. *Empathy. From Bench to Bedside*. Cambridge, MA/London: MIT Press.

Decety, J., C. Chen, C. Harenski and K. A. Kiehl. 2013. An fMRI Study of Affective Perspective Taking in Individuals with Psychopathy: Imagining Another in Pain Does Not Evoke Empathy. *Frontiers in Human Neuroscience*, 7, 1–12.

Deigh, J. 1995. Empathy and Universalizability. *Ethics*, 105, 743–63.

de Sousa, R. 1990. *The Rationality of Emotion*. Cambridge, MA: MIT Press.

de Waal, F. B. M. 2006. *Primates and Philosophers. How Morality Evolved*. Princeton, NJ, and Oxford: Princeton University Press.

Eisenberg, N. 2005. The Development of Empathy-Related Responding. *Nebraska Symposium on Motivation*, 51, 73–117.

Eisenberg, N. and J. Strayer (eds.). 1987. *Empathy and Its Development*. Cambridge: Cambridge University Press.

Eisenberg, N., M. Schaller, R. A. Fabes, D. Bustamente, R. M. Mathy, R. Shell and K. Rhodes. 1988. Differentiation of Personal Distress and Empathy in Children and Adults. *Developmental Psychology*, 24, 766–75.

Frankfurt, H. G. 1988. The Importance of What We Care About. In: *The Importance of What We Care About*. Cambridge: Cambridge University Press, 80–94.

———. 1999. On Caring. In: *Necessity, Volition and Love*. Cambridge: Cambridge University Press, 146–80.

Goldie, P. 2011. Anti-Empathy. In: A. Coplan and P. Goldie (eds.), *Empathy. Philosophical and Psychological Perspectives*. New York: Oxford University Press, 302–17.

Goldman, A. I. 2006. *Simulating Minds. The Philosophy, Psychology and Neuroscience of Mindreading*. Oxford: Oxford University Press.

Habermas, J. 1979. Moral Development and Ego Identity. In: *Communication and the Evolution of Society*. Boston: Beacon Press, 95–129.

———. 1983a. Discourse Ethics: Notes on a Program of Philosophical Justification. In: *Moral Consciousness and Communicative Action*. Cambridge, MA: MIT Press, 43–115.

———. 1983b. Moral Consciousness and Communicative Action. In: *Moral Consciousness and Communicative Action*, Cambridge, MA: MIT Press, 116–94.

Hare, R. M. 1981. *Moral Thinking. Its Levels, Method and Point*. Oxford: Clarendon Press.

Hoffman, M. L. 2000. *Empathy and Moral Development. Implications for Caring and Justice*. Cambridge: Cambridge University Press.

Hume, D. 1739–40. *A Treatise of Human Nature*, edited by L. A. Selby-Bigge. Oxford: Clarendon Press 1978.

Hursthouse, R. 1999. *On Virtue Ethics*. Oxford: Oxford University Press.

Hutcheson, F. 1728. *On the Nature and Conduct of the Passions with Illustrations on the Moral Sense*. Manchester: Clinamen Press 1999.

———. 1725–38. *An Inquiry into the Original of Our Ideas of Beauty and Virtue*. Indianapolis, IN: Liberty Fund 2004.

Ickes, W. 2001. Measuring Empathic Accuracy. In: J. A. Hall and F. J. Bernieri (eds.), *Interpersonal Sensitivity*. Mahwah, NJ: Lawrence Erlbaum, 219–41.

Kant, I. 1785. *Grundlegung zur Metaphysik der Sitten. Kants gesammelte Schriften*, ed. Königlich Preussische Akademie der Wissenschaften. Berlin: Georg Reimer 1911, Vol. IV, 385–463.

———. 1788. *Kritik der praktischen Vernunft. Kants gesammelte Schriften*, ed. Königlich Preussische Akademie der Wissenschaften. Berlin: Georg Reimer 1908, Vol. V, 1–163.

Kauppinen, A. 2014. Empathy, Emotion Regulation and Moral Judgement. In: H. Maibom (ed.), *Empathy and Morality*. Oxford University Press, 97–121.

Kennett, J. 2002. Autism, Empathy and Moral Agency. *Philosophical Quarterly*, 52, 340–57.

———. 2016. Morality and Interpretation. Commentary on Jonathon Glover's *Alien Landscapes? Journal of Applied Philosophy*. doi:10.1111/japp.12209

———. 2017. Empathy and Psychopathology. In: H. L. Maibom (ed.), *The Routledge Handbook of Philosophy of Empathy*, London: Routledge, 364–76.

Klimecki, O. and T. Singer. 2012. Empathic Distress Fatigue Rather than Compassion Fatigue? Integrating Findings from Empathy Research in

Psychology and Social Neuroscience. In: B. Oakley et al. (eds.), *Pathological Altruism*. New York: Oxford University Press, 368–83.
Maibom, H. (ed.). 2014. *Empathy and Morality*. Oxford University Press.
McGeer, V. 2013. Civilizing Blame. In: D. J. Coates and N. A. Tognazzini (eds.), *Blame. Its Nature and Norms*. New York: Oxford University Press, 162–88.
Mill, J. S. 1861. *Utilitarianism. Collected Works of J. S. Mill*, gen. ed. J. Robson. Toronto and London: University of Toronto Press and Routledge, Vol. X, 203–59.
Noddings, N. 1984. *Caring*. Berkeley and Los Angeles: University of California Press.
  1992. *The Challenge to Care in Schools. An Alternative Approach to Education*. New York: Teachers College Press.
Piaget, J. 1932. *The Moral Judgement of the Child*. New York: Free Press 1997.
Preston, S. D. and F. B. M. de Waal. 2002. Empathy: Its Ultimate and Proximate Bases. *Behavioral and Brain Sciences*, 25, 1–72.
Prinz, J. 2011a. Against Empathy. *Southern Journal of Philosophy*, 49, 214–33.
  2011b. Is Empathy Necessary for Morality? In: A. Coplan and P. Goldie (eds.), *Empathy. Philosophical and Psychological Perspectives*. New York: Oxford University Press, 211–29.
Rawls, J. 1972. *A Theory of Justice*. Oxford: Oxford University Press.
Reader, S. 2007. The Other Side of Agency. *Philosophy*, 82, 579–604.
Roeser, S. 2011. *Moral Emotions and Intuitions*. Palgrave: Basingstoke.
Roughley, N. and T. Schramme (eds.). 2015. *On Moral Sentimentalism*. Newcastle upon Tyne: Cambridge Scholars.
Sagi, A. and M. L. Hoffman. 1976. Empathic Distress in Newborns. *Developmental Psychology*, 12, 175–6.
Scheler, M. 1923a. *Wesen und Formen der Sympathie*. Bonn: Verlag Friedrich Cohen.
  1923b. *The Nature of Sympathy*. English translation by P. Heath, of Scheler 1923a. London: Routledge and Kegan Paul 1954.
Schopenhauer, A. 1840. *On the Basis of Morality*. Oxford: Berghahn, 1995.
Setiya, K. 2007. *Reasons without Rationalism*. Princeton, NJ, and Oxford: Princeton University Press.
Sidgwick, H. 1907. *The Methods of Ethics*, Indianapolis, IN: Hackett 1981.
Singer, T. and C. Lamm. 2009. The Social Neuroscience of Empathy. *Annals of the New York Academy of Sciences*, 1156, 81–96.
Slote, M. 2001. *Morals from Motives*. New York: Oxford University Press.
  2004. Moral Sentimentalism. *Ethical Theory and Moral Practice*, 7, 3–14.
  2007. *The Ethics of Care and Empathy*. Abingdon: Routledge.
  2010. *Moral Sentimentalism*. New York: Oxford University Press.
  2015. Reply to My Commentators. In: N. Roughley and T. Schramme (eds.), *On Moral Sentimentalism*. Newcastle upon Tyne: Cambridge Scholars, 128–69.
Smith, A. 1759/1790. *The Theory of Moral Sentiments*, edited by D. D. Raphael and A. L. Macfie. Indianapolis, IN: Liberty Fund 1982.
Stueber, K. R. 2006. *Rediscovering Empathy. Agency, Folk Psychology and the Human Sciences*. Cambridge, MA: MIT Press.
Ta, V. P. and W. Ickes. 2017. Empathic Accuracy. In: H. Maibom (ed.), *The Routledge Handbook of Philosophy of Empathy*. London: Routledge.

Tappolet, C. 2000. *Emotions et valeurs*. Paris: Presses universitaires de France.
Tomasello, M. 2016. *A Natural History of Human Morality*. Cambridge, MA: Harvard University Press.
Tomasello, M. and A. Vaish. 2012. Origins of Human Cooperation and Morality. *Annual Review of Psychology*, 64, 231–55.
Underwood, B. and B. Moore. 1982. Perspective-taking and Altruism. *Psychological Bulletin*, 91, 143–73.
Vaish, A., M. Carpenter and M. Tomasello. 2009. Sympathy through Affective Perspective Taking and Its Relation to Prosocial Behaviour in Toddlers. *Developmental Psychology*, 45, 534–43.
Walton, K. 1990. *Mimesis as Make-Believe. On the Foundations of the Representational Arts*. Cambridge, MA: Harvard University Press.
Williams, B. A. O. 1981. Persons, Character and Morality. In: *Moral Luck. Philosophical Papers 1973–1980*. Cambridge: Cambridge University Press, 1–19.
Zahn-Waxler, C., M. Radke-Yarrow, E. Wagner and M. Chapman. 1992. Development of Concern for Others. *Developmental Psychology*, 28, 126–36.
Zahn-Waxler, C. and C. Van Hulle. 2012. Empathy, Guilt, Depression. When Caring for Others Becomes Costly to Children. In: B. Oakley et al. (eds.), *Pathological Altruism*. New York: Oxford University Press, 321–44.

II

Empathy, Sympathy and Concern

2 Empathy, Altruism, and Helping: Conceptual Distinctions, Empirical Relations

Dan Batson

Empathic concern produces altruistic motivation. To understand this deceptively simple *empathy-altruism hypothesis*, it is necessary to be clear about what is meant both by empathic concern and by altruistic motivation.

1. The Empathy-Altruism Hypothesis

Empathic Concern

In the empathy-altruism hypothesis, empathic concern refers to *other-oriented emotion elicited by and congruent with the perceived welfare of a person in need.* Social psychologists like myself have often called this other-oriented emotion *empathy* (e.g., Stotland 1969; Krebs 1975). To emphasize that the empathic emotion at issue is in response to another's need, I use the term *empathic concern* in the empathy-altruism hypothesis (Batson 1987, 1991, 2011).

Three points may help clarify what this emotional state involves. First, 'congruent' here involves agreement with the valence of the perceived welfare of the person for whom empathy is felt. Empathic emotion is positive when the perceived welfare of the other is positive (empathic joy – Stotland 1969; Smith, Keating, and Stotland 1989), and negative when the perceived welfare is negative (empathic concern). Empathic concern has a negative valence because it is felt for a person perceived to be in need. (By perceived need, I mean that the empathizer perceives a negative discrepancy between that person's current or impending state and the state desired for him or her along one or more dimensions of well-being – Batson 2011). The empathy-altruism hypothesis claims that only when there is a perception of need will empathic emotion produce altruistic motivation because only then is there reason to increase the other's welfare. Note that congruent here does not mean that the person feeling empathic concern feels the same emotion as the person for whom the concern is felt – or even a similar emotion. Empathic concern might, for example, involve feeling sad or sorry for someone who is upset and afraid. Or feeling compassion for the unconscious victim of a mugging, who is feeling nothing at all.

Second, empathic concern is intended as an umbrella term to cover a range of other-oriented emotions. In addition to feelings described as *empathy* and *concern*, it includes feelings reported as *sympathy, compassion, softheartedness, tenderness, pity, sorrow, sadness, upset, distress, grief,* and the like.

Third, the emotions under this umbrella are other-oriented in the sense that they involve feeling *for* the other – feeling sympathy for, compassion for, sorry for, distressed for, concerned for, and so on. (The "for" in this feeling for refers to the target of concern, not to feeling "on behalf of" or "in the place of" the other.) Although feelings described as sympathy and compassion are inherently other-oriented, we can feel sorrow, distress, or concern that is self-oriented, as when something bad happens directly to us. Both other-oriented and self-oriented versions of these emotions may be described as feeling sorry or sad, upset or distressed, concerned or grieved. This breadth of usage invites confusion. The relevant psychological distinction lies not in what emotional label is used but in whose welfare is the focus of the emotion. Is one feeling sad, distressed, concerned for the other? Or feeling this way as a result of what has befallen oneself – which may include the experience of perceiving the other in need? If the former, one is feeling empathic concern. If the latter, that individual is feeling personal sadness, distress, concern, and so on.

Some people prefer to use a different term – such as *compassion, sympathy,* or *tenderness* – to label this general class of other-oriented emotion that is a possible source of altruistic motivation. At issue for the empathy-altruism hypothesis is the other-oriented emotion, not the specific name. As long as we understand that we are talking about the same thing, use of a different label is fine.

It is, however, important to distinguish empathic concern from a number of related psychological states, each of which has also been called empathy:

- Knowing another person's internal states, including thoughts and feelings
- Adopting the posture or matching the neural response of another
- Coming to feel as another feels
- Imagining how another is thinking and feeling
- Imagining how you would think and feel in another's place
- Feeling distress at witnessing another person's suffering
- A general disposition (trait) to feel for others

Let me say a little about five of these phenomena, borrowing an example I used in previous work to make distinctions clear (see Batson 2011 for a more complete exposition).

Imagine that you meet a friend for lunch. She seems distracted, staring into space, not very talkative, a bit down. Gradually, she begins to speak, then to cry. She explains that she just learned she is losing her job because of layoffs. She says that she is not angry, but hurt – and a bit scared. You feel very sorry for her, and say so. In addition, you are reminded that there has also been talk of job cuts where you work. Seeing your friend so upset makes you feel anxious and uneasy. You also feel brief flashes of relief – "Thank God it wasn't me!"

Empathic concern as I have defined it applies to only one specific part of this episode: feeling sorry for your friend. But by other definitions, the term empathy could be applied to five other aspects.

Knowing another person's internal state, including thoughts and feelings. Knowing another's thoughts and feelings has been a focus of research on Theory of Mind in primates and humans (e. g., Premack and Woodruff 1978; Goldman 1993; Gordon 1995; Tomasello and Call 1997; Ravenscroft 1998). Sometimes, to ascertain what someone else is thinking and feeling can pose quite a challenge, especially when you have only limited clues. In our example, knowing your friend's internal state seems relatively easy. Once she explains, you may be confident that you know what is on her mind – losing her job. From what she says, and perhaps even more from how she acts, you may also think you know how she feels – hurt and scared. Of course, you could be wrong, at least about some nuances.

It might appear that accurate knowledge of the other's thoughts and feelings is a necessary condition for the other-oriented emotional response that the empathy-altruism hypothesis claims produces altruistic motivation. But it is not. Even if you are quite wrong about what your friend is thinking and feeling – not likely, given all the information – to feel sorry for her is to experience empathic concern. Empathic concern requires that we *think* we know the other's state because it is based on a perception of the other as in need. It does not, however, require that this perception be accurate. Consistent with Premack and Woodruff's original discussion of Theory of Mind, we can experience real empathic concern based on a false perception of the other's internal state. This possibility highlights a danger. Action prompted by concern based on a false perception, even altruistically motivated action, is apt to be misguided.

Coming to feel as another feels. Coming to feel the same emotion that another person feels is a common dictionary definition of empathy. And it is a definition used by some philosophers (e.g., Darwall 1998), neuroscientists (Damasio 2003; Decety and Chaminade 2003), psychologists (Englis, Vaughan, and Lanzetta 1982; Eisenberg and Strayer 1987), and primatologists (Preston and de Waal 2002; de Waal 2009). Often, those who use this definition qualify it by saying that the empathizer need not feel exactly the same emotion, only a similar one (e.g., Hoffman 2000). But what determines whether an emotion is similar enough to be considered "feeling as" is never made clear.

Key to this use of the term *empathy* is not only emotion matching but also emotion catching (Hatfield, Cacioppo, and Rapson 1994). To have evidence of matching and catching, more is required than that one person has a physiological response of roughly the same magnitude at roughly the same time as another – what Levenson and Ruef (1992) called 'shared physiology'. Rather than a match to the target's emotion, the observer's physiological response could reflect a qualitatively different emotion. Rather than being caught from the target's emotional state, it could reflect a parallel response to shared environmental cues, perhaps ones to which the target's emotional state drew attention.

In Scottish Enlightenment philosophy, coming to feel as another person feels was called 'sympathy', not empathy (Hume 1740; Smith 1759). Scientists – including psychologists – influenced by Enlightenment philosophy also typically referred to this state as sympathy (e.g., Spencer 1870; Darwin 1871; McDougall 1908; Allport 1924). In addition, feeling as another feels has been called "fellow feeling" (Hume 1740; Smith 1759), "emotional identification" (Freud 1922), "emotional contagion" (Hatfield, Cacioppo, and Rapson 1994; de Waal 2009), "emotional resonance" (Thompson 1987), "perceptually induced resonance of emotive circuits" (Panksepp 1986), and "empathic distress" (Hoffman 1981, 2000).

In one of the most frequently cited studies of the developmental origins of empathy, Sagi and Hoffman (1976) presented one- to two-day-old infants either with tape-recorded sounds of another infant crying, with sounds of a synthetic nonhuman cry, or with no sounds. Those infants presented with another infant's cry cried significantly more than those presented with a synthetic cry or with silence. Sagi and Hoffman (1976, 176) – and many others since – interpreted this difference as evidence of an inborn "rudimentary empathic distress reaction," that is, as evidence of one newborn infant catching and matching another's affective state.

But there are rather obvious alternative explanations for crying in response to another infant's cry, alternatives that have rarely been recognized in the literature. For example, such crying may be an inborn competitive response that increases the chances of getting food or comfort. Imagine that we did a similar study with baby birds in the nest. We would likely interpret the rapid spread of peeping and open-mouthed straining once one baby bird started peeping and straining as competitive, not as a rudimentary empathic reaction.

At times, coming to feel as another feels serves as a stepping stone to empathic concern. But research suggests that this step is neither necessary nor sufficient (Batson, Early, and Salvarani 1997). Returning to your friend, to feel sorry for her you need not feel hurt and afraid too. It is enough to know that she is hurt and afraid. Indeed, feeling as another feels may actually inhibit empathic concern if it leads us to become focused on our own emotional state. Sensing the nervousness of other passengers on an airplane in rough weather, I too may become nervous. If I then focus on my own nervousness, I am not likely to feel for them. Emotional contagion of this sort is quite different from the empathic concern claimed to produce altruistic motivation.

Feeling *with* is a variant on feeling *as*. At least this is true if feeling with is taken to mean something like feeling *alongside* the other – feeling sad because you know your friend is feeling sad and you wish to communicate to her that you understand her feeling, support its appropriateness, and are ready to stand by her (Bavelas et al. 1986). Some, quite naturally, call this kind of shared feeling *compassion*, which literally means "feeling with." But in English, "compassion" is most often used to mean feeling *for* – what I am calling empathic concern – without the requirement of shared feeling and social coordination just described. Recall the description of the Good Samaritan's reaction to the beaten, half-dead man who fell among thieves: "And when he saw him, he had compassion on him" (Luke 10:33). I suspect the Samaritan was feeling *for*, not *with*, this man, who, given his condition, may have been unable to feel anything.

Imagining how another is thinking and feeling. Davis (1994) called imagining how another is feeling "cognitive role taking" or "cognitive empathy." Darwall (1998) called it "proto-sympathetic empathy"; Nussbaum (2001), simply "empathy." Ruby and Decety (2004) called it both empathy and "perspective taking." Stotland (1969) spoke of it as an "imagine him" perspective. More generally, it has been called an "imagine other" perspective. This form of perspective taking can be based not only on what the other says and does but also on your knowledge of his or her situation, character, values, and desires.

Barrett-Lennard (1981) insightfully described this "empathic attentional set" as "a process of feeling into, in which Person A opens him- or herself in a deeply responsive way to Person B's feelings and experiencing but without losing awareness that B is a distinct other self" (Barrett-Lennard 1981, 92). At issue is not only the conception you form of the feelings and thoughts of the other but also how you are affected by this conception. It is a process of "responsively knowing" (ibid.), in which you are sensitive to the way the other is affected by his or her situation.

Instructions to imagine how the other is thinking and feeling have often been used to induce empathic concern in participants in laboratory experiments. Still, this imagine-other perspective should not be confused or equated with the empathic concern it evokes. There is clear evidence that they are distinct (e.g., Coke, Batson, and McDavis 1978).

Imagining how you would think and feel in another's place. Listening to your friend, you might have asked yourself how you would feel if just told you were losing your job. Imaginatively projecting yourself into another's situation is the psychological state referred to by Lipps (1903) as *"Einfühlung"'* and for which Titchener (1909) originally coined the English word *empathy*. This state has also been called "projective empathy" (Scheler 1913), "imaginative projection" (Goldman 1992), and "reenactive empathy" (Stueber 2006). Originally, empathy in this sense was used to describe an artist's act of imagining what it would be like to be some specific person or even some inanimate object – such as a gnarled, dead tree on a windswept hillside.

Adam Smith (1759) colorfully referred to the act of imagining how you would think and feel in another person's situation as "changing places in fancy." More recently, it has been called "simulation" (Goldman 1992; Darwall 1998; Nickerson 1999; Van Boven and Lowenstein 2003). Nichols (2001) called it "perspective taking." Stotland (1969) spoke of an "imagine-self" perspective to distinguish this state from the imagine-other perspective described previously.

The imagine-self and imagine-other forms of perspective taking have often been confused or treated as equivalent, despite evidence suggesting that they should not be (see Batson 2009). As noted previously, to imagine how someone in a difficult situation is thinking and feeling can stimulate empathic concern. At times, imagining how you would think and feel in that situation can too. But, in addition to stimulating empathic concern, an imagine-self perspective is likely to elicit self-oriented feelings of distress, whereas an imagine-other perspective is not (Stotland 1969; Batson et al. 1997; Lamm, Batson, and Decety 2007).

If the other's situation is unfamiliar or unclear, then imagining how you would feel in that situation may provide a useful, possibly essential, basis for understanding and appreciating his or her plight. In this way, an imagine-self perspective may provide a stepping stone to other-oriented empathic concern. But, once again, this step can be slippery. If the other differs from me, then to imagine how I would think and feel may prove misleading, especially if I do not have a good understanding of relevant self–other differences. And if the other's situation *is* familiar or clear, imagining my own reactions may actually inhibit empathic concern. I may get so wrapped up in how I would react that I lose sight of the other and his or her need (Nickerson 1999). As you listened to your friend talk about losing her job, your thoughts about how it would feel to lose your own job led you to become self-concerned, to feel anxious and uneasy, and lucky by comparison. These reactions likely dampened your empathic concern.

Feeling distress at witnessing another person's suffering. Some scholars and researchers apply the term "empathy" to any emotion evoked by witnessing another's suffering, including self-oriented feelings of distress – such as your feelings of anxiety and unease evoked by seeing how upset your friend was. To be distressed by another's suffering has been called "sympathetic pain" (McDougall 1908), "empathic distress" (Hoffman 1981), and "personal distress" (Coke et al. 1978; Batson 1987).

The importance of distinguishing this self-oriented distress from other-oriented distress (a form of empathic concern) is underscored by evidence that parents at high risk of abusing a child are the ones who more frequently report feeling distress at seeing an infant cry. Those at low risk report increased empathic concern – feelings of sympathy and compassion – rather than increased distress (Milner, Halsey, and Fultz 1995).

Summary. Each of these five phenomena is distinct from other-oriented empathic concern. The empathy-altruism hypothesis makes no claim that any of them produces altruistic motivation, except if and when it evokes empathic concern. Although each may at times promote helping behavior, insofar as I know, there is no empirical evidence that any produces altruistic motivation independent of its effect on empathic concern.

Altruistic Motivation

In the empathy-altruism hypothesis, "altruism" refers to *a motivational state with the ultimate goal of increasing another's welfare*. So defined, altruism can be juxtaposed to *egoism*: a motivational state with the ultimate goal of increasing one's own welfare. (Note that I am using the terms "altruism" and "egoism" descriptively, not normatively. Also note that we can have ultimate goals that are neither altruistic nor egoistic.) In each of these definitions, "ultimate" refers to means–end relations, not to a metaphysical first or final cause, and not to biological function. An *ultimate goal* is an end in itself. In contrast, an *instrumental goal* is a means to reach an ultimate goal. If a barrier to reaching an instrumental goal arises, alternative routes to the ultimate goal will be sought. Should the ultimate goal be reached bypassing the instrumental goal, the motivational force will disappear. If a goal is ultimate, it cannot be bypassed in this way (Lewin 1938). Both instrumental and ultimate goals should be distinguished from *unintended consequences*, results of an action – foreseen or unforeseen – that are not the goal of the action. Each ultimate goal defines a distinct goal-directed motive. Hence, altruism and egoism are distinct motives, even though they can co-occur.

Altruism and egoism have much in common. Each refers to a motivational state; each is concerned with the ultimate goal of this motivation; and, for each, the ultimate goal is to increase someone's welfare. These common features provide the context for highlighting the crucial difference. Whose welfare is the ultimate goal, another person's or one's own?

This motivational definition of altruism should be distinguished from other common uses. Let me mention only two:

Altruism as helping behavior, not motivation. Some scholars set aside the issue of motivation, simply equating altruism with costly, intentional helping behavior. This definition has been common among developmental psychologists and primatologists. If a child, without explicit inducement or instruction, opens a cabinet door for an adult who seems to be struggling (Warneken et al. 2007) – or if a chimp consoles a comrade who has just lost a fight (de Waal 2008) – this is called altruism. Such a definition has also been common among evolutionary biologists, who have defined altruism as behavior that reduces an organism's reproductive fitness (the potential to put its genes in the next generation) relative to the reproductive fitness of one or more other organisms. Using this definition, evolutionary biologists can speak of altruism across a very broad phylogenetic spectrum, ranging from social insects to humans. But as Sober and Wilson (1998) pointed out, it is important to distinguish between evolutionary altruism and psychological altruism. *Evolutionary altruism* is behavior that reduces one's reproductive fitness. *Psychological altruism* is motivation with the ultimate goal of increasing another's welfare. Evolutionary altruism is neither necessary nor sufficient to produce psychological altruism. The empathy-altruism hypothesis concerns psychological altruism.

Altruism as helping in order to gain internal rather than external rewards. Other scholars define altruism as a particular form of helping – helping in order to gain internal rather than external rewards. This use does consider the motivation for benefiting others, but it reduces altruism to a special form of egoism. By this definition, which is common among behavioral economists (see Fehr and Zehnder 2009), benefiting another as a means to benefit oneself is altruism as long as the self-benefits are internally rather than externally administered. If you help someone in need in order to gain a good feeling (e.g., a warm glow), to avoid guilt, or to reduce your distress caused by witnessing his or her suffering, then your motivation is altruistic. By the definition used in the empathy-altruism hypothesis, these ultimate goals are not altruistic. They are forms of egoism.

Back to the Hypothesis

With this explication of the terms "empathic concern" and "altruistic motivation," we can state the empathy-altruism hypothesis more precisely. The hypothesis claims that feeling other-oriented emotion elicited by and congruent with the perceived welfare of another person in need (i.e., empathic concern) produces a motivational state with the ultimate goal of increasing that person's welfare by having the empathy-inducing need removed (i.e., altruistic motivation). The hypothesis does not claim that empathic concern is the only source of altruistic motivation. Rather, it claims that empathic concern is *a* source of altruistic motivation, remaining agnostic about other sources.

It is possible to distinguish strong and weak forms of the empathy-altruism hypothesis. The strong form claims not only that empathic concern produces altruistic motivation but also that all motivation produced by empathic concern is altruistic. The weak form claims that empathic concern may produce other forms of motivation as well, including egoistic motives. To date, research on the empathy-altruism hypothesis has focused on testing the strong form. This is not because the strong form is logically or psychologically superior, but because it makes clearer predictions and so is easier to test.

To claim that empathic concern produces only altruistic motivation, as does the strong form, is not to claim that an individual who feels empathic concern is only altruistically motivated. The individual may also experience egoistic motivation arising from sources other than empathy. Indeed, perception of the other as in need, which is specified as a necessary condition for empathic concern, is likely also to produce a range of egoistic motives. To see the other as in need may arouse a desire to gain social and self-rewards for helping, as well as a desire to avoid social and self-punishments for failing to help. These egoistic motives and the altruistic motive produced by empathic concern are distinct because they have different ultimate goals, but they can co-occur. And when they do, if the goals of these motives are compatible, their magnitudes should sum.

2. Antecedents and Consequences of Empathy-Induced Altruistic Motivation

With the empathy-altruism hypothesis before us, we can consider antecedents and consequences of empathy-induced altruistic motivation. Clearly, we do not always feel much empathic concern for others in need. Under what conditions do we? Just as clearly, altruistic motivation does not always lead to action to benefit the other. When does it? What are the other possibilities? Answers to these questions provide a conceptual framework for empirical tests of whether the motivation evoked by empathic concern is altruistic, as the empathy-altruism hypothesis claims.

Two Antecedents of Empathic Concern

Think back to lunch with your friend. What caused you to feel so sorry for her? First, she had just lost her job and was hurt and scared. Second, she was a close friend; you cared about what happened to her and how she felt. More generally, in everyday life two conditions seem necessary to feel empathic concern: (a) perceiving the other as in need and (b) valuing the other's welfare.

Perceiving the other as in need. Perceiving need involves perceiving a negative discrepancy between the other's current state and what is desirable for the other on one or more dimensions of well-being. Dimensions of well-being include the absence of physical pain, negative affect, anxiety, stress, danger, and disease, as well as the presence of physical pleasure, positive affect, satisfaction, and security. The negative discrepancy at issue is for the person in need, not for the person feeling empathic concern. But the perception at issue is by the person feeling empathy, not the person in need. There are times when people perceive themselves to be in need, yet others do not. These others will not experience empathic concern – unless they consider the false perception of need itself to be a need. Alternatively, there are times when people do not perceive themselves to be in need, yet others do. These others may well feel empathic concern.

Surprisingly perhaps, perception of another as in need may be a uniquely human skill. If so, and if this perception is a necessary antecedent of empathic concern, then empathic concern and empathy-induced altruism must be uniquely human also. Consider the cognitive abilities necessary to perceive another as in need. First, one must recognize the other as an animate being who is not only qualitatively different from physical objects but also distinct from other animate beings, including oneself. Apparently, this recognition occurs in the normal child's first year of life (Hoffman 2000). It also occurs early in the normal development of nonhuman primates – and probably in the development of other higher mammals as well (Tomasello 1999).

Second, it is necessary to recognize that the other has values, goals, and feelings – components of the experience of well-being. Tomasello (1999) spoke of this ability as understanding that the other is an intentional agent, not merely an animate being. He presented evidence that it emerges in normal children at around nine to twelve months. Hoffman (2000) put the time a bit later, at around eighteen to twenty-four months. It seems, then, that somewhere in the nine- to twenty-four-month age range, most children come to recognize that they have goals, intentions, desires, and feelings. Soon thereafter – perhaps because of a uniquely human adaptation that allows them to understand other persons as beings "like me yet distinct from me" (Tomasello 1999) – they begin to recognize that others also have these attributes. With this recognition, the child sees others not simply as acting but as acting with purpose – circumventing barriers and using alternative behavioral routes to reach desired goals – and as caring about what happens to them. He or she can perceive need. Often, the child initially extends this perception too far, applying it not only to people but also to toys and machines. But experience soon hones the perception.

Some primatologists believe they see evidence of attention to the feelings, intentions, and well-being of others – and evidence of empathy and altruism – among at least some primate species other than humans (e.g., Warneken et al. 2007; de Waal 2009). Other primatologists have doubts (e.g., Silk et al. 2005; Vonk et al. 2008). At least for now, it seems wise to keep an open mind about both the ability to perceive need and the existence of empathy-induced altruism in other species.

Valuing the other's welfare. To feel empathic concern, more is required than the perception of need. One also needs to care about whether the other is in need. Apparently, in normal humans the capacity to place value on another's welfare emerges somewhere between one and three years of age (Zahn-Waxler et al. 1992; Hoffman 2000). When it fails to develop, we may speak of psychopathy or sociopathy.

One often hears lip service paid to valuing all human life or the welfare of all humanity. Most of us, however, place different value on the welfare of different others. We value the welfare of some quite highly. We value the welfare of some very little, if at all. We may even place a negative value on the welfare of some, such as a rival.

If we place *no* value on the welfare of a person perceived to be in need, then we are not likely to think about how this person is affected by the need, except perhaps as a means to control his or her behavior. The perceived need provides no basis for feeling empathic concern – or any other emotion. We understand what the other needs but do not care. This might be called a *dispassionate* or *objective orientation* to the other. At the extreme, one again thinks of psychopathy.

If we place *negative* value on a person's welfare, which we may if we dislike or are in competition with the person, then perceiving him or her in need will produce other-oriented emotions quite different from the congruent one I am calling empathic concern. We are apt to feel pleasure at the person's plight, or even the malicious glee called *schadenfreude*. In this case, although we may be well aware of the other person's desires and feelings about his or her situation, we do not adopt a congruent value assessment of events. Instead, our assessment is antithetical to this person's welfare. This might be called a *hostile orientation*.

If we *positively* value a person's welfare, then we are likely to think about how this person is affected by the events in his or her life, and to adopt a congruent value assessment of these events – that is, an assessment congruent with his or her welfare (well-being) as we see it. Positive value is placed on events that we think will bring the person pleasure, joy, satisfaction, safety, or relief; negative value is placed on events that we think will bring the person pain, sorrow, discontent, danger, or disappointment. Such valuing not only produces a lively response to events that affect this person's welfare, much as we might respond to events that affect our own welfare, but it also produces vigilance. It leads us naturally to imagine how this person thinks and feels about events – that is, to adopt an imagine-other perspective. The person's welfare becomes part of our own value structure. This might be called a *sympathetic orientation*. Other terms for positively valuing the other's welfare are caring, loving, or being close.

When one person values, cares for, loves another – for example, when a mother loves her child – there are likely to be feelings of heartache and sadness at prolonged separation, and feelings of warmth and joy at reuniting. Cognitive processes such as perceived similarity, familiarity, and attractiveness can contribute to love. But its basic character seems to be evaluative, which is reflected in affect. Like the related but more general concepts of *attitude* and *sentiment*, love involves relatively enduring value placed on the target, even though love can, of course, end. Love is often thought to be an emotion, but it seems more appropriate to think of love as a form of valuing. Threats to the welfare of a loved one can evoke a range of emotions, including empathic concern.

It is possible to value the welfare of a total stranger toward whom we have no antipathy, especially when we are induced to imagine how he or she is affected by events (Coke et al. 1978; Batson et al. 1995; Batson et al. 2007). It is also possible to value the welfare of members of other species (Batson et al. 2005). Although it is too soon to know with confidence, each of these capacities may involve generalization of parental instincts (McDougall 1908; Hrdy 2009; Batson 2010).

Specifying links to other states called empathy. How do the five other states that have been called empathy relate to these two antecedents, and to empathic concern? All but one can at times contribute to the perception of need, but only one seems to be directly related to valuing the other's welfare. To the degree that (a) feeling as the other feels, (b) imagining how the other feels, and (c) imagining how you would feel in the other's situation, each provides useful information about the other's state, it facilitates (d) knowing the other's internal state, including thoughts and feelings, which should promote perception of any need that exists.

In the natural flow of behavior, imagining how the other is thinking and feeling can be a consequence of valuing the other's welfare (Batson et al. 2007). However, in the absence of prior valuing, imagining another's thoughts and feelings (i. e., an imagine-other perspective) can be induced directly through instructions. In this case, it can serve as a proxy for valuing the other's welfare and – coupled with perception of need – can evoke empathic concern (Coke et al. 1978; Batson et al. 2007; Batson 2011). None of the other empathy-related states seems likely to stimulate valuing, except as it promotes an imagine-other perspective.

Feeling vicarious personal distress at witnessing another's distress is not likely to affect either antecedent, or to lead to empathic concern. Rather, it is a self-oriented emotion evoked by perceiving the other as in need, and is likely to produce egoistic motivation to reduce one's own distress (Batson et al. 1981).

Consequences of Empathy-Induced Altruistic Motivation

The empathy-altruism hypothesis states that empathic concern produces altruistic motivation – motivation with the ultimate goal of increasing the welfare of the person for whom empathy is felt. Given that empathic concern is evoked by perception of need, the goal of empathy-induced altruism can be specified more precisely. The goal is to remove the empathy-evoking need. Helping in a way that removes the need may seem to be the obvious behavior to reach this goal, but it is not the only possible response of a person who is altruistically motivated. Empathy-induced altruism can result in at least three possible behaviors: help, have someone else help, and provide no help. If more than one of these three options is available, the option selected will be a product not only of the altruistic motivation but also of a cost-benefit analysis prompted by the impulse to act on this motivation.

As is true of any goal-directed motive, altruism does not automatically produce behavior. It produces a desire to reach a goal. Before acting on this desire, the altruistically motivated individual weighs benefit against cost for each possible course of action. Benefits and costs included in the analysis may take many forms – tangible or intangible, immediate or long-term – and may be weighed in many ways. The analysis may be careful and slow, or impulsive and instantaneous.

The two behaviors that can remove the need for which empathy is felt (help, have another help) each offer the benefit of reaching the goal of the empathy-induced altruistic motivation. Accordingly, the magnitude of the benefit for each of these behaviors is a function of the magnitude of the altruistic motivation.

The magnitude of the cost for each is the sum of the various costs perceived to be associated with that behavior. Helping often involves cost to the self in the form of pain or risk of pain, lost time or money, and so on. Having another person provide the help does not involve these costs. Instead, it involves the cost of being unsure that the other will in fact offer help, and if so, that the help will prove effective. These costs arouse conflicting egoistic (self-interested) motives. But costs can also involve conflicting altruistic motives. Remember *Sophie's Choice* – elect the child to die or both will die (Styron 1979).

This logic can be extended to the third possible behavior – provide no help – by reversing the costs and benefits associated with helping. If no help is provided, the altruistically motivated person does not reach the goal of removing the empathy-evoking need, so this becomes a cost. At the same time, he or she does not incur the cost associated with helping, which becomes a benefit. After considering all recognized behavioral options, the one that seems to offer the greatest relative benefit (benefit minus cost) is the one most likely to be pursued.

It may seem contradictory to suggest that altruistic motivation prompts a cost-benefit analysis. After all, the goal of the analysis is to deal with the altruistic motive in a way that incurs minimal cost to self – a self-interested, egoistic goal. But the existence of this egoistic goal does not mean that the motivation to have the other's need removed is no longer altruistic. It only means that the impulse to act on this motive is likely to evoke self-interested motives as well. The presence of these egoistic motives neither negates nor contaminates the altruistic motive, although their presence complicates the relationship between the altruistic motive and behavior. A person who feels an altruistic impulse to dive into icy waters to rescue someone who is drowning may find this impulse overpowered by a self-interested fear for one's life, resulting in no action. This inaction does not mean that no motivation was present. Nor does it mean that the impulse to rescue was not altruistic.

3. Evidence of Empathy-Induced Altruistic Motivation

Given the stated definitions of altruism and egoism, helping a person in need – even at great cost to self – may be altruistically motivated, egoistically motivated, both, or neither. To know which, we must determine whether removal of the need is (a) an ultimate goal and any self-benefits are unintended consequences (altruism) or (b) an instrumental means to reach the ultimate goal of benefiting oneself (egoism). Three general classes of possible self-benefits of empathy-induced helping have been identified, producing three classes of egoistic alternatives to the empathy-altruism hypothesis: (a) aversive-arousal reduction – reducing the empathic concern caused by witnessing another in need; (b) punishment avoidance – avoiding empathy-specific material, social, and self-punishments; and (c) reward seeking – gaining empathy-specific material, social, and self-rewards. Advocates of the empathy-altruism hypothesis do not deny that relieving an empathy-inducing need is likely to enable the helper to reduce aversive arousal, avoid punishments, and gain rewards. However, they claim that these benefits to self are not the ultimate goal of empathy-induced motivation, only unintended consequences. Advocates of the egoistic alternatives disagree. They claim that one or more of the self-benefits is the ultimate goal of the motivation produced by empathic concern.

Complicating any attempt to test these alternatives, we can be mistaken about what our ultimate goals are. And we can pursue goals of which we are unaware. As a result, self-reports of what motivated our action (or inaction) cannot be trusted. Instead, behavioral experiments are needed. There are now published reports of more than thirty-five experiments designed to test the empathy-altruism hypothesis against one or more of the egoistic alternatives. Including different variations of several of the alternatives, a total of six egoistic alternative explanations have been tested. Results of these experiments have consistently patterned as predicted by the empathy-altruism hypothesis and have failed to support any of the egoistic alternatives. Batson (2011) provides a comprehensive review of the evidence relevant to each alternative, and to all combinations of the alternatives. To the best of my knowledge, there is no plausible egoistic explanation for the cumulative evidence from these experiments.

This evidence has led me to tentatively conclude that the empathy-altruism hypothesis is true – that empathic concern produces altruistic motivation. Further, the evidence indicates that this empathy-induced altruistic motivation can be surprisingly powerful. It seems Adam Smith was right in the opening lines of *The Theory of Moral Sentiments*:

> How selfish soever man may be supposed, there are evidently some principles in his nature, which interest him in the fortune of others, and render their happiness necessary to him, though he derives nothing from it except the pleasure of seeing it. Of this kind is pity or compassion, the emotion which we feel for the misery of others, when we either see it, or are made to conceive it in a very lively manner (Smith 1759, 9).

If I read him correctly, Smith did not consider these "benevolent" principles to be the source of our moral sentiments, which were the focus of his book. Again, I think he was quite right. But that is another story.

References

Allport, F. H. 1924. *Social Psychology*. Boston: Houghton Mifflin.

Barrett-Lennard, G. T. 1981. The Empathy Cycle: Refinement of a Nuclear Concept. *Journal of Counseling Psychology*, 28, 91–100.

Batson, C. D. 1987. Prosocial Motivation: Is It Ever Truly Altruistic? In: L. Berkowitz (ed.), *Advances in Experimental Social Psychology*. New York: Academic Press, vol. XX, 65–122.

  1991 *The Altruism Question: Toward a Social Psychological Answer*. Hillsdale, NJ: Erlbaum Associates.

  2009. Two Forms of Perspective Taking: Imagining How Another Feels and Imagining How You Would Feel. In: K. D. Markman, W. M. Klein, and J. A. Suhr (eds.), *The Handbook of Imagination and Mental Simulation*. New York: Psychology Press, 267–79.

  2010. The Naked Emperor: Seeking a More Plausible Genetic Basis for Psychological Altruism. *Economics and Philosophy*, 26, 149–64.

  2011. *Altruism in Humans*. New York: Oxford University Press.

Batson, C. D., Duncan, B., Ackerman, P., Buckley, T., and Birch, K. 1981. Is Empathic Emotion a Source of Altruistic Motivation? *Journal of Personality and Social Psychology*, 40, 290–302.

Batson, C. D., Early, S., and Salvarani, G. 1997. Perspective Taking: Imagining How Another Feels versus Imagining How You Would Feel. *Personality and Social Psychology Bulletin*, 23, 751–8.

Batson, C. D., Eklund, J. H., Chermok, V. L., Hoyt, J. L., and Ortiz, B. G. 2007. An Additional Antecedent of Empathic Concern: Valuing the Welfare of the Person in Need. *Journal of Personality and Social Psychology*, 93, 65–74.

Batson, C. D., Lishner, D. A., Cook, J., and Sawyer, S. 2005. Similarity and Nurturance: Two Possible Sources of Empathy for Strangers. *Basic and Applied Social Psychology*, 27, 15–25.

Batson, C. D., Turk, C. L., Shaw, L. L., and Klein, T. R. 1995. Information Function of Empathic Emotion: Learning that We Value the Other's Welfare. *Journal of Personality and Social Psychology*, 68, 300–13.

Bavelas, J. B., Black, A., Lemery, C. R., and Mullett, J. 1986. 'I Show How You Feel': Motor Mimicry as a Communicative Act. *Journal of Personality and Social Psychology*, 50, 322–9.

Coke, J. S., Batson, C. D., and McDavis, K. 1978. Empathic Mediation of Helping: A Two-Stage Model. *Journal of Personality and Social Psychology*, 36, 752–66.

Damasio, A. R. 2003. *Looking for Spinoza: Joy, Sorrow, and the Feeling Brain*. Orlando, FL: Harcourt.

Darwall, S. 1998. Empathy, Sympathy, Care. *Philosophical Studies*, 89, 261–82.

Darwin, C. 1871. *The Descent of Man and Selection in Relation to Sex*. New York: Appleton.

Davis, M. H. 1994. *Empathy: A Social Psychological Approach*. Madison, WI: Brown & Benchmark.

Decety, J. and Chaminade, T. 2003. Neural Correlates of Feeling Sympathy. *Neuropsychologia*, 41, 127–38.

de Waal, F. B. M. 2008. Putting the Altruism Back into Altruism: The Evolution of Empathy. *Annual Review of Psychology*, 59, 279–300.

 2009. *The Age of Empathy: Nature's Lessons for a Kinder Society*. New York: Harmony.

Eisenberg, N. and Strayer, J. (eds.) 1987. *Empathy and Its Development*. New York: Cambridge University Press.

Englis, B. G., Vaughan, K. B., and Lanzetta, J. T. 1982. Conditioning of Counter-Empathetic Emotional Responses. *Journal of Experimental Social Psychology*, 18, 375–91.

Fehr, E. and Zehnder, C. 2009. Altruism (Economic Perspective). In: D. Sander and K. Scherer (eds.), *The Oxford Companion to Emotion and Affective Sciences*. New York: Oxford University Press, 24–6.

Freud, S. 1922. *Group Psychology and the Analysis of the Ego*. London: International Psycho-Analytic Press.

Goldman, A. I. 1992. Empathy, Mind, and Morals. *Proceedings from the American Philosophical Association*, 66, 17–41.

 1993. Ethics and Cognitive Science. *Ethics*, 103, 337–60.

Gordon, R. M. 1995. Sympathy, Simulation, and the Impartial Spectator. *Ethics*, 105, 727–42.

Hatfield, E., Cacioppo, J. T., and Rapson, R. L. 1994. *Emotional Contagion*. New York: Cambridge University Press.

Hoffman, M. L. 1981. The Development of Empathy. In: J. P. Rushton and R. M. Sorrentino (eds.), *Altruism and Helping Behavior: Social, Personality, and Developmental Perspectives*. Hillsdale, NJ: Erlbaum, 41–63.

 2000. *Empathy and Moral Development: Implications for Caring and Justice*. New York: Cambridge University Press.

Hrdy, S. B. 2009. *Mothers and Others: The Evolutionary Origins of Mutual Understanding*. Cambridge, MA: Harvard University Press.

Hume, D. 1740. *A Treatise of Human Nature* (L. A. Selby-Bigge, ed.). Oxford: Oxford University Press 1896.

Krebs, D. L. 1975. Empathy and Altruism. *Journal of Personality and Social Psychology*, 32, 1134–46.
Lamm, C., Batson, C. D., and Decety, J. 2007. The Neural Substrate of Human Empathy: Effects of Perspective-Taking and Cognitive Appraisal. *Journal of Cognitive Neuroscience*, 19, 1–17.
Levenson, R. W. and Ruef, A. M. 1992. Empathy: A Physiological Substrate. *Journal of Personality and Social Psychology*, 63, 234–46.
Lewin, K. 1938. The Conceptual Representation and Measurement of Psychological Forces. *Contributions to Psychological Theory*, 1 (4), Whole Issue, 1–247.
Lipps, T. 1903. Einfühlung, innere Nachahmung, und Organempfindungen. *Archiv für die gesamte Psychologie*, 2, 185–204.
McDougall, W. 1908. *An Introduction to Social Psychology*. London: Methuen.
Milner, J. S., Halsey, L. B., and Fultz, J. 1995. Empathic Responsiveness and Affective Reactivity to Infant Stimuli in High- and Low-Risk for Physical Child Abuse Mothers. *Child Abuse and Neglect*, 19, 767–80.
Nichols, S. 2001. Mindreading and the Cognitive Architecture Underlying Altruistic Motivation. *Mind and Language*, 16, 425–55.
Nickerson, R. S. 1999. How We Know – and Sometimes Misjudge – What Others Know: Imputing One's Own Knowledge to Others. *Psychological Bulletin*, 125, 737–59.
Nussbaum, M. C. 2001. *Upheavals of Thought: The Intelligence of Emotions*. New York: Cambridge University Press.
Panksepp, J. 1986. The Psychobiology of Prosocial Behaviors: Separation Distress, Play, and Altruism. In: C. Zahn-Waxler, E. M. Cummings, and R. Iannotti (eds.), *Altruism and Aggression: Biological and Social Origins*. New York: Cambridge University Press, 19–57.
Premack, D. and Woodruff, G. 1978. Does the Chimpanzee Have a Theory of Mind? *Behavioral and Brain Sciences*, 1, 515–26.
Preston, S. D. and de Waal, F. B. M. 2002. Empathy: Its Ultimate and Proximate Bases. *Behavioral and Brain Sciences*, 25, 1–72.
Ravenscroft, I. 1998. What Is It Like to Be Someone Else? Simulation and Empathy. *Ratio*, XI, 170–85.
Ruby, P. and Decety, J. 2004. How Would You Feel versus How Do You Think She Would Feel? A Neuroimaging Study of Perspective Taking with Social Emotions. *Journal of Cognitive Neuroscience*, 16, 988–99.
Sagi, A. and Hoffman, M. L. 1976. Empathic Distress in the Newborn. *Developmental Psychology*, 12, 175–6.
Scheler, M. 1913. *The Nature of Sympathy* (P. Heath, trans.). Hamden, CT: Archon 1970.
Silk, J. B., Brosnan, S. F., Vonk, J., Henrich, J., Povinelli, D. J., Richardson, A. S., Lambeth, S. P., Mascaro, J. and Schapiro, S. J. 2005. Chimpanzees Are Indifferent to the Welfare of Unrelated Group Members. *Nature*, 437, 1357–9.
Smith, A. 1759. *The Theory of Moral Sentiments* (D. D. Raphael and A. L. Macfie, eds.). New York: Oxford University Press 1976.
Smith, K. D., Keating, J. P., and Stotland, E. 1989. Altruism Reconsidered: The Effect of Denying Feedback on a Victim's Status to Empathic Witnesses. *Journal of Personality and Social Psychology*, 57, 641–50.

Sober, E. and Wilson, D. S. 1998. *Unto Others: The Evolution and Psychology of Unselfish Behavior*. Cambridge, MA: Harvard University Press.

Spencer, H. 1870. *The Principles of Psychology*, 2nd edn. London: Williams & Norgate, vol. I.

Stotland, E. 1969. Exploratory Investigations of Empathy. In: L. Berkowitz (ed.), *Advances in Experimental Social Psychology*. New York: Academic Press, vol. IV, 271–313.

Stueber, K. R. 2006. *Rediscovering Empathy: Agency, Folk Psychology, and the Human Sciences*. Cambridge, MA: MIT Press.

Styron, W. 1979. *Sophie's Choice*. New York: Random House.

Thompson, R. A. 1987. Empathy and Emotional Understanding: The Early Development of Empathy. In: N. Eisenberg and J. Strayer (eds.), *Empathy and Its Development*, New York: Cambridge University Press, 119–45.

Titchener, E. B. 1909. *Lectures on the Experimental Psychology of the Thought Processes*. New York: Macmillan.

Tomasello, M. 1999. *The Cultural Origins of Human Cognition*. Cambridge, MA: Harvard University Press.

Tomasello, M. and Call, J. 1997. *Primate Cognition*. New York: Oxford University Press.

Van Boven, L. and Lowenstein, G. 2003. Social Projection of Transient Drive States. *Personality and Social Psychology Bulletin*, 29, 1159–68.

Vonk, J., Brosnan, S. F., Silk, J. B., Henrich, J., Richardson, A. S., Lambeth, S. P., Schapiro, S. J., and Povinelli, D. 2008. Chimpanzees Do Not Take Advantage of Very Low Cost Opportunities to Deliver Food to Unrelated Group Members. *Animal Behaviour*, 75, 1757–70.

Warneken, F., Hare, B., Melis, A. P., Hanus, D., and Tomasello, M. 2007. Spontaneous Altruism by Chimpanzees and Young Children. *PLoS Biology*, 5, e184.

Zahn-Waxler, C.; Radke-Yarrow, M.; Wagner, E., and Chapman, M. 1992. Development of Concern for Others. *Developmental Psychology*, 28, 126–36.

3 Self-Recognition, Empathy, and Concern for Others in Toddlers

Doris Bischof-Köhler and Norbert Bischof

1. Introduction

During the last few decades, empathy has received ever more attention in scientific debates. The term is now on everybody's lips – the call for more empathy has almost become a fashion. However, there is little agreement as to how the phenomenon should be understood and what kind of mechanism it is based on.

We approach the issue from an engineering point of view. We ask how, starting from the raw material provided by primate evolution, an information processing mechanism could be conceived that is capable of transforming sensory input into empathy-controlled behavior in such a way that the postulated modular components and the structure of their interaction are endorsed by phenomenological experience. We abstain from speculating how this mechanism may be implemented in brain anatomy since, for the time being, the question of localization (brain area X 'plays an important role in' or 'is associated with' performance Y) does not seem to lead very far as long as the causal architecture required to bring about the observable effects has not yet been clarified.

Instead of starting with a elaborate definition of empathy, we prefer to gradually narrow down this term until, eventually, we arrive at a block diagram precisely depicting the concept as we understand it. To begin with, we take the term 'empathy' to refer to a capacity that enables an observer to share affective states of another. In order to distinguish empathy from mere emotional contagion, we confine it to cases where the observer's response indicates awareness of the fact that the shared emotion belongs to the other (Bischof-Köhler 1991; 2012). On the other hand, we shall argue that the mechanism responsible for this awareness does not require a Theory of Mind (ToM).

With this position we differ from two prevailing trends in the present literature. One of them conceives of empathy as being a manifestation of a 'fundamental motive for connectedness' that forms the basis of all variants of prosocial behavior (Hoffman 1976; 2000; 2007; Davidov et al. 2013). A second trend distinguishes empathy from simpler forms of fellow feeling, such as emotional contagion, by postulating that it requires the involvement of some higher rational capacity. The competence primarily considered in this context comes close to what Flavell et al. (1981) refer to as 'level II perspective taking', the ability to imagine another person's mental state from his point of view. This competence is understood to require a Theory of Mind.

Both trends correspond in the assumption that the postulated ability develops out of less differentiated prestages, gradually becoming more and more elaborate and efficient. Consequently, it is even attributed to primates beneath the anthropoid level and to babies in their first year of life (for a survey, see Caron 2009; Sodian 2010). In both cases, we are dealing with a terminological umbrella suited to cover a variety of phenomena appearing on different phylo- and ontogenetic levels. However, such broad concepts are liable to confound mechanisms of different complexity and origin.

It is worth considering whence this thinking obtains its obvious appeal to some theorists. According to one of the arguments in favor of this view, even calling newborns already 'empathically concerned' is supposed to be 'parsimonious' and therefore particularly scientific. But this kind of parsimony is more terminological than theoretical. Empathy is defined here in a rather loose manner, allowing a host of behaviors that entail only the vaguest of social references to be included in the concept, at least as rudimentary prestages. A plethora of labels such as 'affective empathy', 'cognitive empathy', 'empathic distress', 'empathic concern', 'global empathy', and 'egocentric empathy', and nondescript classifiers like 'implicit-explicit', are used, which are meant to refer to particular nuances. However, as a matter of fact, by using the same core concept, 'empathy', such labels smooth down potentially essential distinctions and make heterogeneous issues appear as variants of ultimately one and the same issue. It can be doubted if such an approach does justice to the multifaceted nature of an organismic system that exhibits the annual rings of a long adaptive history.

Another argument in the same camp is more philosophical, or even ideological. It draws a picture of humankind as being basically peaceful and cooperative, in contrast to the Hobbesian wolf metaphor. Humans are seen as imbued with a basic disposition for sociality and affiliation, a readiness to connect with and share emotions with others, and in order to ensure that this is a dyed-in-the-wool property, it is obviously – although quite unnecessarily – felt to be crucial to demonstrate that this property exists from birth or, better yet, even before birth.

Finally, a questionable conception of development or, to be more precise, a confusion of morphological and behavioral development may be at work here. The growth of a *morphological* phenotype takes place by way of a gradual and continuous differentiation, so it is always possible to backtrack, on a seamless path, from the articulate form of an adult organism back to the primitive shape of the egg cell. The genesis of a *behavior* may in certain cases follow the same scheme, especially if it is shaped by a learning process. But a behavioral performance that owes its species-specific adaptivity primarily to a genetic blueprint doesn't, as a rule, emerge via a process of smooth differentiation out of behaviors doing the same job in a more rudimentary way.

Behavior is not an entity existing by itself, but rather the output of a *mechanism*. This mechanism has to grow into function, and it usually remains inactive as long as it is being assembled, while when mature, it delivers a ready-to-operate result that may only secondarily be refined by practicing. If, in earlier stages, a similar-looking performance can be observed, one should always be alert to the possibility that this is the work of another mechanism with a different ontogenesis. Nobody would maintain that, because both frogs and tadpoles 'breathe', gills must be vestigial lungs.

In keeping with this caveat, we prefer to use the term ToM only in cases where actions are understood as resulting from mental processes whose subjectivity is reflected upon (Perner 1991; 2009; Bischof-Köhler 2000a; Bischof and Bischof-Köhler 2007). The classical criterion is an explicit understanding of false belief. If defined in this vein, ToM is not yet available to the great apes and to children up to three years (Wellman et al. 2001). Does this consequently imply that they do not understand the mental state of others? The answer depends on what 'understanding' is supposed to mean. When infants in their first year show *social referencing* or *joint attention*, does this really mean, as some authors claim (e.g., Baron-Cohen and Swettenham 1996; Tomasello 1999), that they attribute to the other person deliberate intentions? And, are these already effects of an 'implicit' ToM?

Adaptive responses to a companion's intentional behavior, as observed in social animals far below the anthropoid level, can, after all, quite well be understood as being performed by lower-level modular subroutines that need not imply an awareness of mental phenomena in the other's subjective world at all. As the common-sense notion of an 'eye beam' suggests, a person's gaze orientation can be experienced as a centrifugal extension protruding from the head and pointing at some external target. Generally, we have to consider that the visual appearance of living creatures, frequently even of inanimate objects, quite often embodies

Self-Recognition, Empathy, and Concern

Figure 3.1.

a *dynamic orientation* prefiguring their imminent behavior (Figure 3.1). This phenomenon was studied by perceptual psychologists in the 1950s under the label of *directional dynamics* (Werner and Wapner 1954; Kaden et al. 1955). It could be shown that some perceptual objects, such as a picture of a bird in flight, the profile of a face, or even a mere triangle pointing to one side, express a 'vectorial' quality. If, for instance, a figure pointing to the left is placed in the objective median plane, it is seen relatively displaced to the left, and if the subject is required to move it so that it appears to him as straight ahead, he will have to move it to the right. Similarly, the apparent horizon (eye level) was found to shift in the opposite direction of hands pointing upward or downward. These findings were interpreted as indicating that figural dynamics exert a 'pull' on the organism in the direction of the dynamics. Obviously, no concept of the object's conscious 'intention' is required to account for such effects, which are maximal in early childhood and decrease with age, indicating that they are based on a comparably primordial and elementary mechanism.

Directional dynamics account for the dog aiming in the right direction even before its master has thrown the stick, or blue tits pecking the aluminum seals of milk bottles on seeing others do so. We have no reason to assume first signs of imitation or even ToM in such performances.

In human infants too, the mechanism of directional dynamics ought to be considered as an explanation for certain behaviors that are sometimes taken to indicate an 'implicit' ToM. For example, infants perceive a person's gaze as being goal-directed, and they expect her to reach for an object that she has previously looked at (Woodward 2003). To do so, they need not necessarily attribute any mental processes to her. Directional dynamics also becomes effective in Level I perspective taking that allows one to determine whether a person can see an object or not (Sodian 2010).

Empathy, as a matter of course, is more than a result of emotional contagion and directional dynamics. It certainly requires vicariously sharing the emotional state of somebody else; but this sharing must somehow convey an insight into the fact that it is the *other agent* who is the epicenter of the affective upheaval. On the other hand, this insight does not require level II perspective taking, nor any rational reasoning or reflection at all. It is supplied by the emotion itself, in a way that we will later elaborate. So, in order to explain empathy and distinguish it from forms of fellow feeling at earlier developmental stages, we have to understand what changes occur *within the emotional system itself*, in order that empathy can become possible.

2. Empathy Experiments

A series of investigations attempting to shed light on this field of study were carried out by the lead author starting in the 1980s (Bischof-Köhler 1988; 1991; 1994; 2012). The subjects comprised 126 boys and girls ranging in age from fifteen to twenty-four months.

There were two settings subsequently referred to as the 'teddy-bear experiment' and the 'broken spoon experiment'. In both experiments, subjects played with an adult female playmate who, after a while, pretended to have an accident. She expressed sadness by moderately sobbing for about two minutes and verbalized her predicament.

In the teddy bear experiment, the playmate brought a teddy bear along. After a while, she appeared to accidentally break its arm off. Then she lamented about her broken toy and that she was unable to continue playing. The children's responses were indicative that the situation provided incentives for an empathic response. Nevertheless, we could not exclude the possibility that their reaction was motivated merely by the wish to continue playing. This ambiguity was avoided in the broken spoon experiment with another sample of subjects. Here, the child and the playmate ate a dessert from separate plates and with separate plastic spoons. The playmate accidentally broke her spoon, pretended to be unable to continue eating, and demonstrated grief by sobbing.

It should be noted that this kind of investigation is extremely method-sensitive. We spent months conducting pilot studies before entering the main experiments. It proved necessary to familiarize the playmate with the child during an introductory play session prior to the experiment. Confronting the child with a complete stranger, like in Johnson's study (1982), yielded uninterpretable results, possibly due to a lack of readiness to identify. On the other hand, allowing the subject's own mother to undergo the mishap – a setting used by Johnson (1982), Zahn-Waxler et al. (1992) and Nichols et al. (2009) – seemed not such a good idea to us either, given how some mothers performed, and also in view of the fact that a child expects its mother to be an unviolable source of security, whose helplessness may cause undue anxiety. In both of our sessions, to be sure, the mother was present sitting in the background. She was instructed to intervene only upon her child's explicit request.

The subjects' responses turned out to be similar in both the teddy bear and the broken spoon experiments, so it seemed justified to pool the results. Four response patterns could be distinguished.

- A first group, subsequently referred to as the *helpers*, expressed concern and compassion and attempted to terminate the playmate's miserable state by means of more or less efficient interventions. They all stopped playing or eating and stayed close to the playmate for most of the grief period. Some of them attempted to repair the teddy bear, offered another stuffed toy, tried to comfort the playmate, tried to feed her with the broken spoon, or brought the broken spoon to their mother; some children urgently tried to draw their mother's attention to the playmate's accident.
- Others also stopped playing or eating, but did not intervene. They stayed near the playmate and kept their attention focused on her. Apparently they did not know what to do, or they appeared to not quite understand the situation. We called them *perplexed* children.
- A few children showed emotional *contagion*. They burst out crying and sought consolation from their mothers.
- A last group remained *indifferent*. Subjects looked momentarily startled but soon lost interest in the playmate and went on playing or eating. A few even acted in a showing-off way reminiscent of what ethologists call 'display behavior'.

Helpers were classified as empathic; perplexed children seemed more worried than empathic. The indifferent ones were classified as nonempathic. The empathy status of children displaying contagion could not be determined.

The label *helpers* may give the impression that we operationally defined empathy by prosocial interventions alone, neglecting the possibility of a mere instrumental helping (Svetlova et al. 2010) helping 'just for fun' (Warneken and Tomasello 2010, 398), or because the children wanted playing to go on. These alternative explanations can be ruled out, however, since helpers were only classified as empathic if their interventions were accompanied by an expression of concern and compassion as well, and if they focused their attention on the playmate as long as she expressed grief.[1]

The empathy status of the *perplexed* children was equivocal. Some authors prefer the label *personal distress*, coined by Batson (1987), to characterize this kind of response. However, this label would imply a motivation to withdraw from the scene whereas the perplexed subjects did not demonstrate intentions to do so. They simply looked helpless and bewildered, as if they did not understand what was going on or what one should do. They showed uneasiness in response to a situation they could not figure out. Some just seemed to wait to see what would happen next.

3. Mirror Experiments

Clearly, the subjects behaved in strikingly different ways in situations providing incentives for an empathic response. We considered several factors that could be responsible for these differences, such as the relationship to the playmate, the interest in the teddy bear, or the number of siblings. These factors, however, did not yield a recognizable relation to the readiness to respond empathically. The only correlation we definitely found was the children's ability to *recognize themselves in a mirror*.

Self-recognition was tested with the *rouge test* (Amsterdam 1972) by a different experimenter who was kept uninformed about the results of the empathy test. First, the children were exposed to a mirror. Later, a blue dot of eye shadow was inconspicuously placed on their cheek and they were brought back to the mirror again.

---

[1] It was only later, when we started investigating empathy in relation to the Ainsworth attachment classification (Ainsworth et al. 1978), that we discovered what we call 'fast helping'. This response attempts to forestall emotional involvement, thereby avoiding the distress of viewing the other one suffering. This behavior was typical for children qualifying as 'insecure-avoidant' (Type A) in the Strange Situation (see Bischof-Köhler 2000b).

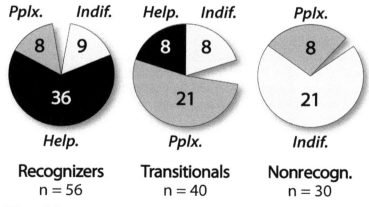

Figure 3.2.

- Children who touched the mark on their face were called *recognizers*. Some also grimaced and experimented while watching their mirror image.
- Others behaved as *nonrecognizers*. They did not take notice of the mark on their face, treated their mirror image like a playmate, and in fact sometimes searched for the other one behind the mirror.
- A third group either did or did not touch the mark, but all showed a conspicuous avoidant behavior toward their mirror image. Some of them abruptly turned away upon catching their own gaze in the mirror but were, nevertheless, a little later reattracted by the mirror only to repeat the avoidant behavior again. Others refused to look again at all. These subjects were considered to be in a *transitional* stage of self-recognition. They acted as if they already realized that the mirror image was not somebody else; however, they remained reluctant to accept that this should be nobody but themselves.

The term 'transitional' alludes to a transient period wherein nonrecognizers develop into recognizers. This, indeed, was our impression, in line with Amsterdam (1972), who also interprets mirror-avoidant behavior as a prestage of recognition. But then, since we did not perform a longitudinal study, we have no way to prove it.

Figure 3.2 shows the results concerning the relation of mirror behavior and empathy development. The three pie charts represent the types of mirror behavior – nonrecognizers, transitionals, and recognizers. The sectors denote the proportion of subjects showing indifferent, perplexed, and helping behavior in the empathy experiment. The open sectors denote children who showed contagion.

The majority of the recognizers were empathic helpers (black color). Some recognizers did not empathize, but this does not invalidate the results because self-recognition does not guarantee empathy; other factors can override the empathic response. Children in the mirror transitional stage behaved predominantly in a perplexed way (gray color) in the empathy experiment. Eight helpers avoided their mirror image and were therefore grouped among the transitionals, although six of them detected the mark on their face. Most nonrecognizers showed indifferent behavior and, most notably, not a single one of them belonged to the group of empathic helpers.

Subjects were allocated to the respective categories according to decision trees that allowed us to operationalize our intuitive classification. As in all such cases, objectivity ensures rigidity, and in a few cases classification diverged slightly from the intuitive impression, but never in a way that questioned our interpretation. Under all circumstances, a robust correlation of self-recognition and empathic helping was established, and the age distributions allow us to exclude the possibility that the correlation is simply a side-effect of two mutually independent developmental processes accidentally occurring around the same age (for statistical details, cf. Bischof-Köhler 1988; 1994).

4. Identification

Given that empathy and mirror recognition are connected, what does one have to do with the other? To begin with: Why are we able to recognize ourselves in the mirror at all? Why do chimpanzees have this ability, whereas macaques do not?

When inquiring into the biological function of a behavior, a pitfall must be avoided that has repeatedly gone unnoticed. Scholarly articles have been published, pondering the selective advantage of a given property, which straightforwardly take for granted that such an advantage must have mattered in evolution. However, not every organismic feature reified by our language has necessarily been shaped by a selection pressure of its own. Empathy is a good example to use in clarifying this issue. According to Decety and Svetlova (2012, 3), 'for empathy to have evolved it must have had major survival benefits'. But must it really? Mirror recognition is also an evolutionary achievement, yet few would argue that there was any selection premium placed directly on this aptitude. Pending evidence to the contrary, we ought to regard it as an evolutionarily neutral side-effect of some more basic cognitive mechanism that – in the primate line – evolved on the anthropoid level.

Self-Recognition, Empathy, and Concern

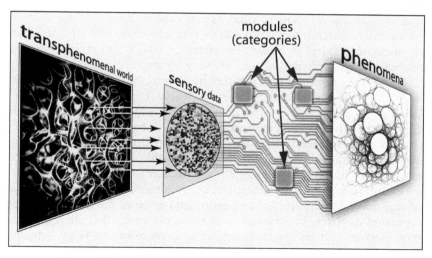

Figure 3.3.

The best candidate for such a mechanism is the ability to perceive separately given phenomena as *identical*, that is, to experience them as appearances of one and the same 'thing'.

Identity is a multifaceted term, so it seems appropriate to explain how we use it in the present chapter. We take the stance of evolutionary epistemology, elucidated in Figure 3.3. This epistemology supposes a transphenomenal reality that is not simply an unapproachable 'Ding an sich', but exerts a selection pressure on us. Therefore, the organism is driven to build a 'realistic' image of this world, realistic in the sense that acting on the basis of this cognition grants survival and reproduction. On the other hand, all information about the transphenomenal world has to pass the bottleneck of sensory perception where all meaningful relations and cross-connections dissipate in a mosaic of atomistic sensory data. From this material, the brain reconstructs the outside structure as best it can. It does so based on cognitive modules, grown during evolution, that form the brain correlates of what Kant and others have called 'categories'. Among them are, for example, the notions of figure and background; cause and effect; reality and mere appearance; and, in particular, identity. So, the term 'identity', as we use it, does not directly refer to an ontological property of transphenomenal objects, but rather to a way of processing information pointing at them. A frog, unable to recognize a fly that has temporarily been hidden by a leaf, does not yet possess this category. On the other hand, certain paradoxes in quantum theory result from our inability to refrain from applying the identity category to particles that change the location of their appearance without moving along a reconstructable trajectory. It should therefore be remembered that, when speaking of identity, we mean a neuronal module, a tool that has proven adaptive when applied to objects of everyday experience.

We have to distinguish two different identity modules appearing on different phylogenetic and ontogenetic levels (Bischof 1978). The earlier form is *diachronic identity*. It has a time-bridging characteristic. It causes percepts following each other in time to be experienced as referring to the same entity. The expectation that things continue existing even though they are not perceptible for a while, or if their appearance has changed, develops in babies already in their first few months. A second module, of particular interest in our argument, allows for *synchronic identification*. This ability unites phenomena given at the same time, but separated in space, into instances of the same entity that share a common essence, and are therefore subject to a common fate. What happens to one, affects the other. Synchronic identity must be distinguished from alikeness, with which it is frequently confounded, as in talk of 'identical twins': Both may look alike, but they are not the *same*: each of them has his own fate. In contrast, the little puppet into which the voodoo priest sticks his needles only remotely resembles the real-life victim; nevertheless, the latter is firmly expected to experience suffering as a result of the procedure – not because the puppet is felt to merely symbolize the victim, nor because a secret causal connection of both is imputed, but since both are phenomenologically experienced to share a common fate.

Synchronic identification is definitely a nontrivial cognitive achievement and requires sophisticated information processing. It would therefore be misguided to interpret newborns' joining other babies in crying (Sagi and Hoffman 1976) or infants' reflecting a happy or sad expression shown by a caregiver (Haviland and Lelwica 1987; Thompson 1987) as precursors of identification. These are plain cases of emotional contagion, and there is no good reason to interpret them as indicating that babies already perceive others as 'like me' and are thereby involved in a process of 'intersubjectivity', which enables access to the subjective world of the other (Trevarthen 1979; Stern 1985; Tomasello 1999; Meltzoff and Brooks 2001).

What, then, is synchronic identification good for? To answer this, we must proceed one step further in the search for a selection pressure. Around the middle of the second year of life, coinciding with the onset of mirror recognition, human children begin engaging in pretend play and synchronic imitation (Nielsen and Dissanayake 2004). Above all, they reveal a capacity to solve problems by *imagining* their own actions in advance (cf. Bischof-Köhler 2012). This capacity provides them, in a manner of speaking, with a mental rehearsal site on which they can test

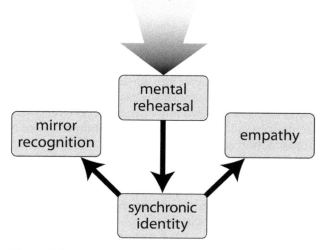

Figure 3.4.

strategies of action without risk – not unlike the flight simulator in which a trainee pilot practices steering an airplane. Here, at last, we have spotted a reasonable candidate for a capacity that provides its owner with a selective advantage over competitors that have to test every new behavioral routine by trial and error in real life.

Mental simulation of problem solving requires, additional to the perceived world, a representation of objects, processes, attributes, and relations in the form of images and verbal concepts that serve as 'material' for imagery. So we ought to distinguish between an 'encountered' and an 'imagined' mode of phenomena. Synchronic identification is indispensible in connecting both levels: it enables me to realize that a perceived object, appearing somewhere in my life-space, and its image, visualized at another place, are one and the same thing.

Once the notion of synchronic identity is available for imaginary problem solving (cf. Figure 3.4), it may well automatically yield an impression of sameness when one is confronted with one's own mirror image, so we need not search for a particular evolutionary advantage of the latter. And it remains to be shown that the same does not hold true for empathy as well. An organism equipped with a module that generates impressions of sameness in response to particular perceptual cues may necessarily cause the other one to appear 'like me'. Even though selection subsequently may, and most probably will, contribute to this effect, it would only cause a corollary reshaping, but would not occupy the pivotal position in the cascade of ultimate processes structuring the empathy system.

5. Self–Other Differentiation

Synchronic identification per se, however, may not suffice to account for empathy. For contagion to convert into empathy, the other, though being an object of identification, must nevertheless continue to be perceived as a *separate* bearer of his or her own inner experiences. Otherwise, it would be difficult to understand how the subject could remain aware of the fact that the shared emotion is actually another person's emotion.

'Self–other differentiation', as labeled by Hoffman (e.g., 2007), has become a technical term developing a life of its own in research literature. It may be questioned, though, whether this parlance is recommendable, since it does not take into account that 'self' and 'other' can be defined on widely different levels.

In order to clarify the issue, a brief epistemological interlude is necessary. The concepts 'physical' and 'mental' are ambiguous. From a behavioristic stance, 'physical' means accessible to the outside observer, whereas 'mental' refers to the contents of subjective experience. In this vein, my whole phenomenal world is 'mental'. On the other hand, this world contains, on its own part, phenomena that *appear* physical in nature – a face, a toy, my own hand, the walls of the room, the sky above, and so on – and others, such as affects, emotions, moods, and needs, that present themselves as having a mental quality. In order to prevent confusion, we shall refer to the latter, purely *phenomenological* distinction under the labels 'apparently physical' and 'apparently mental' where appropriate, in order to make them recognizable as technical terms.

It can easily be demonstrated that most apparently physical phenomena fall into two categories, viz., contoured *figures* and unbounded, atmospheric *backgrounds*. Apparently mental phenomena are less articulated, yet they are not entirely unstructured, either. Some of them, perceived as nonlocalizable, ubiquitous moods, have a tinge of background quality. Others, like the mournful character of a melody, are more figurelike – as a result, not of developing clear-cut, palpable contours of their own, but rather of being distinct in a way that allows them to attach themselves to physical objects and thus to participate in the latter's boundedness.

Among the apparently mental phenomena, *self-awareness* is of particular importance in the present context. We would like to resort, here, to the distinction between 'I' and 'Me', as it was proposed over a century ago by William James. The terminology has changed over the years, to 'explicit' versus 'implicit' self-recognition, or to the 'I' being replaced by an 'ecological self' (Neisser 1995). However, all this amounts to more of an exchange of verbal labels than to a refinement of the concepts.

'I' denotes the self as the unreflected subject of experience, the origin of one's own perspective, the omnipresent sovereign of one's own sphere of action. The crucial issue is that this form of self-sensing has background quality. Backgrounds are unbounded, albeit possibly finite. So it is with the 'I': though void of any articulate demarcation line, it reaches out as far as the phenomena comply with one's own intentions, and wanes when outside forces take over and maintain their own regime.

The essential shortcoming of sensing oneself in the 'I' mode is that such an experience alone will not suffice in order for mental imagery to become functional. Solving problems often requires that one imagine oneself in an articulate shape, at a particular place other than the place presently occupied, and executing a different activity. Hence, a representation of myself is also required in order to function as a token to be shifted around in imagery. This is the 'Me'. Its crucial difference from the 'I' is that, in order to serve as kind of an 'avatar' in the process of dreaming up a problem-solving strategy that involves one's own bodily performances, it needs to be experienced as inhabiting my body image as a mobile vessel, thus participating in the latter's figurelike delimitation. In mirror recognition, the embodied 'Me' is not only imagined, but even perceived at some spatial distance 'over there'.

In empathy, this 'Me' is mirrored in the 'You', as it were, establishing an identification that induces me to share the other person's fate. Consequently, what happens to the other is perceived as something concerning myself, as well. I respond emotionally to the other's situation as if I were in his or her place. But I remain sited on my own side of the 'social mirror', and the vicariously felt emotion or intention remains phenomenologically centered in the other.

These points should help clarify why recent claims to have demonstrated that 'self–other differentiation' occurs as early as the first year of life are missing the point. Admittedly, babies from the first months on can distinguish between their own and other babies' crying (Martin and Clark 1982; Dondi et al. 1999). They also respond differently when they watch their own body movements in a video and see the same movements executed by others (Rochat and Striano 2002). They are more thrilled by self-generated effects than by the same effects produced by others (Papousek and Papousek 1977). All this, however, only boils down to the infants' showing different responses to self-produced effects versus effects produced by others, and to the fact that an unfamiliar stimulation elicits more interest than a familiar one.

The phrasing of Hoffman's theory may lead to misunderstanding here. Davidov et al. (2013, 127) summarize it in the words 'young infants are thought to lack awareness of the self as a separate *physical* entity from others and *hence* cannot distinguish between another person's distress and their own' (italics ours). What is really at stake, however, is not the trivial ability to distinguish between one's own and another's physique or behavior, but rather, a new and essentially more elaborate way of experiencing *apparently mental phenomena*. It amounts to sensing another's distress as not swamping my own emotional condition, but as remaining centered upon and belonging to a figural 'You' that, because it has attracted the identification of 'Me', requires that 'I' tackle the obstacle.

The importance of this revision becomes apparent in light of a theoretical alternative to Hoffman's thesis proposed by Davidov et al. (2013). They contrast his postulate of a form of 'self-recognition' revealed in the mirror experiment, which they take to be 'reflective' and to require 'relatively advanced cognitive abilities', with a more basic form of 'self-knowledge', which they deem to be sufficient for empathic concern. Arguing that self-recognition is not a prerequisite for *feeling* concern, they allot empathy to a basic, 'prereflective' form of self-knowledge, present from the beginning of life, which enables the infant to distinguish between self-generated movements and being moved by someone else. In other words, they are talking about the 'I'.

And indeed, as previously mentioned, the 'I' has a way of distinguishing his own reach of action from a surrounding field that is resistant to his own intentions. In order for empathizing to occur, however, merely distinguishing between 'I' and 'non-I' is not sufficient. What is required instead is a figural, bounded 'You' to which the felt emotion can be assigned. This is why empathy is correlated with mirror recognition – not because self-recognition is a prerequisite for feeling empathy, but because it indicates that mental contents have acquired a figural status.

During the first year of life, such a status is not yet available, as self-awareness is limited to an unreflected 'I'. The 'Me' does not develop gradually and smoothly throughout infancy, it emerges in a rather rapid process around 18 months with the onset of mental imagery.

Our experimental design was not suitable for a fine-grained longitudinal study; but some unsystematic observations also suggested that a stable 'Me' is not established in one single step, but rather in a process of the type depicted in Figure 3.5. Thus, in the intermediate stages (transitional/perplexed) some irregular combinations are likely to occur, especially if the mirror and the empathy experiment are performed on different days.

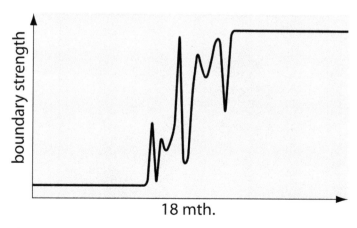

Figure 3.5.

This may contribute to the correlations visible in Figure 3.2 being not perfect, though sufficiently high.

6. A Systemic View of Empathy

A coherent theory capable of integrating the reported findings should depict the structure of the underlying causal network. We shall start with a summary of the main issues to be included in such an analysis.

The basic setting (Figure 3.6) contains a subject (*Sub*) confronted with a situation (*Sit*) that elicits an emotion. We will call this an *evaluative emotional response* (*Eval*). The releasing stimulus could be some dangerous object approaching or signs indicating a source of food, but also, particularly on the human level, situations simply indicating some structural defect that calls for repair, like, something has broken, fallen down, or been disfigured.

As a rule, the situation carries, more or less distinctly, what we earlier referred to as '*directional dynamics*', and the evaluative emotion will be elicited if the subject perceives these dynamics as oriented (*Ori*) toward himself. If they clearly point elsewhere (Figure 3.7), the situation will not evoke an emotional response in the subject. Some events, to be sure, lack clear-cut directional dynamics altogether and may then elicit some emotional arousal owing simply to the fact that, at least, they don't focus away from the subject.

Evaluative emotional responses to situations start occurring in the very first few months of life. At the same time, a second mode of eliciting emotional responses is observable: Without actually being confronted

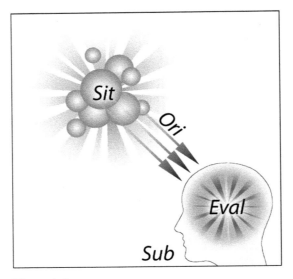

Figure 3.6.

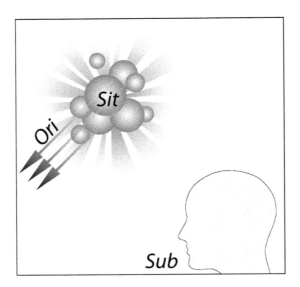

Figure 3.7.

Self-Recognition, Empathy, and Concern

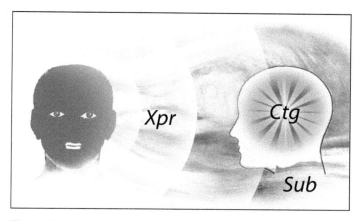

Figure 3.8.

with a situation that arouses an emotion, babies incur contagion (*Ctg*) through the *expression* (*Xpr*) of emotions in others (Figure 3.8).

Contagion is a phylogenetically old mechanism: ethologists call it *mood induction*. It has an important function in synchronizing group behavior. When a conspecific expresses a certain intention – e. g., to eat, to sleep, to fly up and away – these expressive cues will trigger the same motivation in other group members. Mood induction does not require understanding that the mood originates in the subjective state of another individual.

It should be kept in mind that even a mechanism as elementary as mood induction cannot dispense with information conveyed by directional dynamics. A group member's expression of panic will only induce me to feel fearful if it is undirected or pointing toward some outside object. If it is aimed at me (Figure 3.9), it may not elicit the same emotion but rather a *complementary* state (*Cmp*) such as a sense of triumph or an intention to appease. This is a third way of responding emotionally to an environmental scenario.

Empathy is a fourth mode. For empathy to be elicited by a companion's expression, the expressed distress must, while being sensed and responded to by the subject, remain confined inside an objectified 'You', whose boundary prevents the victim's helplessness from spilling over and paralyzing the 'I' (Figure 3.10).

Thus far, our explanation has covered only half the story. Contagion can only be induced if an emotion is expressed. However, in many cases the *situation* causing the dilemma is noticed, as well. Sometimes this situation alone suffices to release an empathic response (Radke-Yarrow et al.

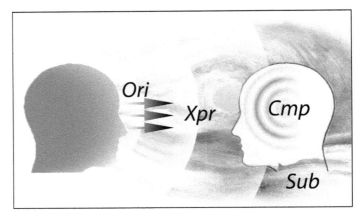

Figure 3.9.

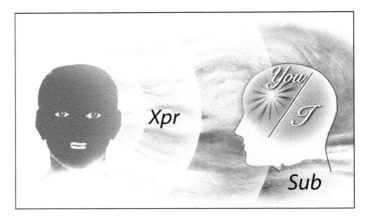

Figure 3.10.

1983). This effect can be observed beginning in the middle of the second year (Vaish et al. 2009).

In order to explain situation-induced empathy, we need to resort to *synchronic identification* (Figure 3.11). As previously indicated, a perceived situation alone will fail to induce an emotional response if its directional dynamics point to another object. As soon as synchronic identity (*Idnt*) is operational, this condition changes. Now the identification with another places my own 'Me' in the position of the other. If this occurs, the directional dynamics of the event point toward a proxy of myself, as it were, and what happens to the other is perceived as concerning me, as well.

Self-Recognition, Empathy, and Concern

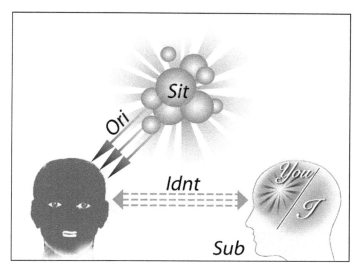

Figure 3.11.

This process qualifies as other-directed, nonetheless, because the boundary between both of us remains established, and I experience my emotional arousal as referring to 'You'.

Identification allows a person to empathize even in a situation that is novel to her, provided that this situation would concern her if she found herself in it (cf. Bischof-Köhler 2012). More importantly: only situation-mediated empathy renders cooperation possible, because expression alone does not convey sufficient information about the other's intention.

Figure 3.12 concatenates the above effects in a format explicit enough to serve as a road map for computer simulation. It should not be mistaken for a flow chart, i. e., the arrows are not to be read as prescribing temporal succeeding steps of a process, but rather as indicating the time-transcending causal structure of the system. The black lines stand for processes determining each other in the direction of the arrowheads. At the railroad-junction icons the input arrow has two possible effects depending on the value of the moderator variable entering the icon via a black square.

The two modules picked out by hexagonal shapes constitute the core of the system. One, the *identity module*, enables perceptual or imaginary items that are spatially separate (or otherwise distinguishable) to be experienced as representing one and the same entity. The other, called the *boundary module* for lack of a better term, imparts a figural status to apparently-mental phenomena (thus allowing moods to turn into

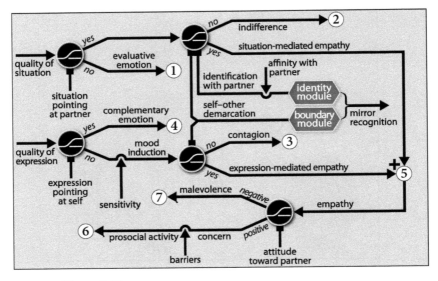

Figure 3.12.

emotions, self-awareness to adopt a reified 'Me' status, or an inarticulate 'non-I' to become an objectified 'You').

These modules are hypothesized to develop according to a genetic blueprint during a maturational shift around the middle of the second year. Their emergence is indicated by the appearance of *mirror recognition*. Although there is no reason to doubt that we have to deal with two separate modules, they appear to become active at the same time. However, in some children the identity module may be a little bit ahead of the boundary module. This could explain why, paradoxically, we had six cases of contagion among transitionals and recognizers, but only one in non-recognizers: This effect is to be expected in children who already identify with the playmate and therefore, in addition to being exposed to her expression, become susceptible to her situation, but cannot yet establish a solid boundary.

In what follows, the diagram will be explained in the order of the encircled numbers at the end points of the causal chains to be distinguished.

1. If an emotionally relevant situation is empty of directional dynamics that are explicitly focused on somebody else, the subject is likely to refer it to himself and respond with an evaluative emotional response.
2. Otherwise, the outcome depends upon the identity and boundary modules. As long as these are not yet operative, the situation

will not be empathically responded to. It may exert what Gestalt psychologists call a 'Prägnanzdruck', an impression of a situational defect calling for repair, but this response is not meant to pacify another person, therefore the label 'instrumental helping' (Svetlova et al. 2010) would be misleading in this connection.

3. If a partner's expression is perceivable and this expression is not explicitly directed toward the subject, mood induction can ensue and the subject will be prone to emotional contagion, provided again that the identity and the boundary modules have not yet become operational. As previously reported, contagion did not occur all that frequently in our experiments. The reason may be that the playmate's feigned sobbing was not pronounced enough. Moreover, certain less conspicuous forms of looking concerned may actually be rudiments of contagion. However, we must also consider the possibility that the children were not equally sensitive to expressive cues, so the model allows for *sensitivity* as a moderator variable here.

4. If the expression is directed toward the subject, this may be responded to with a complementary emotion, instead. One might question whether this variant already occurs in infancy or not, but then, an infant smiling in response to the friendly face of its caregiver, hardly qualifies as a case of *emotional* contagion, even though the two *expressions* mirror each other, since the infant's mood does not carry a tinge of care-giving but, understood literally, of care-taking.

5. Thus far, we have considered only the situation prior to the onset of mental imagery around the middle of the second year, i. e., prior to the point at which the identity and the boundary modules allow a figural 'Me' to appear. With these modules active, two new effects become detectable, namely, situation-mediated and expression-mediated empathy. *Situation-mediated empathy* occurs when an emotionally relevant situation points at a partner with whom the subject identifies from whom he is at the same time separated by the boundary module. Of course, identification will be modified by the degree of *affinity* felt toward this particular person. This moderator variable, along with others, may account for cases of disinterest in the fate of victims belonging to outgroups. *Expression-mediated empathy* occurs if the boundary module imparts the awareness that an emotion incurred by the other belongs to the other and calls for a response changing his, rather than one's own, state.

6. Situation- and expression-mediated empathy, singly or combined, prompt under favorable circumstances some activity relieving the

partner's predicament. For this to occur, however, empathy must turn into *concern*, and concern requires an *attitude* in favor of the victim. Compassion, sympathy, and cooperation can result if this attitude is *positive*. Even then, prosocial activities may be suppressed if the empathizer encounters *barriers* he or she is unable to overcome. Small children just may not know what to do. Even adult bystanders are known to balk at intervening for fear of being suspected of showing off (Staub 1986). Generally, prosocial intervention is costly, and the costs may be considered too high. Some of our subjects did not realize that there was a substitute spoon lying unused on the table and were confronted with the insurmountable obstacle of giving away their own spoon and being unable to continue eating. A charming example was provided by one little boy who, when viewing the playmate's grief, froze with the spoon in his hand hovering in mid-air. Ultimately, when his mother drew his attention to the third spoon, he noticeably relaxed, handed his *own* spoon to the partner and continued eating with the substitute spoon.

7. Finally, if the observer is in some way opposed to the victim, empathy can even be the basis of *malevolent* responses. This aspect is neglected in most of the literature, as it runs counter to the current vogue, which regards empathy as the root of human morality. In fact, if the observer carries a grudge against the person in need, the miserable state of the other may be empathically shared, yet, at the same time, enjoyed – such as in the case of *malicious gloating*. Immoral consequences of empathy occur when it is combined with aggression. Aggression in animals below the great apes and in small children is, as it were, innocent because the aggressors have no awareness of how the victim feels. This innocence was lost, when, in the course of phylogenesis, empathy emerged, enabling, for instance, chimpanzees to torture their victims while killing them (Goodall 1986). And human children, as well, once they are able to empathize, may start committing acts that are obviously intended to hurt other people and they may continue to do so, even if their victims complain (Zahn-Waxler et al. 1979). In sadism, empathic participation in the pain of the suffering victim is the very aim of the experience.

Probably the most important determinant influencing the motivational consequences of empathy is *familiarity*. Its lack can have two effects: unfamiliarity may reduce the *affinity* toward the other and, consequently, the readiness to identify with him or her, or it can foster prejudices and, thus, build up a negative *attitude*.

Finally, one other factor that is likely to have an effect on empathy is *educational style*. Inductive education ('Don't do it because it will hurt the other!' as opposed to plain 'Cut it out because I tell you so!') fosters the readiness to empathize (Zahn-Waxler et al. 1979). In terms of our model, this is presumably mediated by a strengthening of both the readiness to *identify* with the victim and the *sensitivity* for his expressive signals. It should be noted in parentheses that this way of bringing up children ought not be overdone, as it may foster excessive feelings of guilt even for damage not caused by oneself.

So much for an outline of the model. It provides a nomological net useful for avoiding terminological pigeonholes that carry misleading connotations. In particular, the model should help clarify some issues raised by Eisenberg et al. (1991). The authors distinguish between three forms of emotional response induced by another's (negative) expression or situation: *sympathy*, defined as involving feelings of concern for the other, *personal distress* taken to comprise self-oriented concern, and *empathy* as sharing the other's emotional state without self- or other-orientation.

'Personal distress' is the problem child in this concept family. It is introduced as denoting cases where a person, without really caring for the other, alleviates the other's condition solely to put an end to all that annoying fuss. This strategy is assumed to involve advanced reasoning and, therefore, to be confined to an older age. On the other hand, personal distress is said to be the typical response of very young children, as well, who are still 'confused about the boundaries of one's own and the other's distress'. Here, personal distress would clearly qualify as *emotional contagion*. But then again, the latter is felt to belong – as a precursor, or maybe a border-case – to the category of 'empathy'.

We question the usefulness of this terminology. One can classify items according to their outside appearances and file, e. g., herrings and whales under the heading of 'fish'. Or one can develop a taxonomy based on a causal analysis. If one starts with the former hoping to arrive at the latter, one is bound to end up with contradictory propositions amounting to a 'chicken and the egg dilemma'. There is no such dilemma if we start, instead, from a systemic analysis like the one depicted in Figure 3.12: What is meant by 'sympathy' is easily identifiable with 'concern' leading to point ⑥, 'personal distress' has to be split into emotional contagion (③) on one hand, and some higher-level strategy, on the other, which requires meta-cognition and is not covered by the model. What the authors mean by the claim that 'empathy' is neither self- nor other-oriented poses an enigma; such a concept fits, at best, into the position of 'mood-induction' in Figure 3.12, but we doubt if this is what the authors really have in mind.

7. Conclusion

In the present paper, we have argued against interpreting empathy on either too high or too low a level of complexity. Too high would mean that empathy requires a Theory of Mind, too low that empathy is only a slightly more advanced developmental stage of emotional contagion.

Empathy involves some form of insight, but this insight lies in the quality of the emotion *per se*. Empathizing does not require pondering what I would feel if I were in the other's place. The insight into another's emotional state being at stake is part and parcel of the empathic experience itself. An empathically shared emotion is experienced as belonging to the other from the outset. Thus, it is a qualitatively new emotion, transporting a novel insight not amenable to someone who simply absorbs another's feeling by contagion.

It may have come to the reader's notice that we have refrained from adopting the habit of opposing 'affective' and 'cognitive' processes, as if these terms were self-explanatory. As a matter of fact, this juxtaposition, popular as it may be, conceals the fact that emotions, of necessity, have a cognitive semantics of their own. If I sense fear upon suddenly discovering, say, a snake, doesn't this experience convey a nonreflective apprehension that could be verbalized as 'This beast is dangerous'? If so, does not the emotion, in and of itself, have a cognitive dimension? *Every organismic process triggered by an environmental event and having the biological function of mediating an adaptive response to this event is a cognition.* We are aware that this statement may sound unfamiliar to non-biologists. However, even a plain sensory signal such as, e. g., the message of a baroreceptor informing the brain-stem about blood pressure, conveys information – as opposed to the mechanical processes taking place in the inanimate world following the laws of physics. This is the rationale of Konrad Lorenz's dictum that 'life, as a whole, is a knowledge-acquiring process'. This goes for emotions as well. What can be contrasted with 'emotional' or 'affective', then, cannot be 'cognitive'; it must be a special, more sophisticated *subclass* of cognition – most plausibly 'rational'. There are, indeed, reasons to assume that emotions fulfilled the functions of cognition in phylogenetic times when rational thinking and planning was yet to be invented. In this vein, empathy could be characterized as prerational or, to use a term coined by Brunswik (1955), 'ratiomorphic' cognition. This clarification alone could probably help to dissolve most facets of the 'chicken and the egg dilemma' discussed by Eisenberg et al. (1991).

References

Ainsworth, M. D. S.; Blehar, M.; Waters, E. and Wall, S. 1978. *Patterns of Attachment*. Hillsdale, NJ: Lawrence Erlbaum.
Amsterdam, B. K. 1972. Mirror Self-image Reactions before Age Two. *Developmental Psychobiology*, 1, 297–305.
Baron-Cohen, S. and Swettenham, J. 1996. The Relationship between SAM and ToM: Two Hypothesis. In: P. Carruthers and P. K. Smith (eds.), *Theories of Theory of Mind*. Cambridge University Press, 158–68.
Batson, C. D. 1987. Prosocial Motivation: Is it ever truly Altruistic? In: L. Berkowitz (ed.), *Advances in Experimental Social Psychology*. New York, NY: Academic Press, 65–122.
Bischof, N. 1978. On the Phylogeny of Human Morality. In: G. Stent (ed.), *Morality as a Biological Phenomenon*. Berkeley, CA: University of California Press, 48–66.
Bischof, N. and Bischof-Köhler, D. 2007. Is Mental Time Travel a Frame-of-Reference Issue? *Behavioral and Brain Sciences*, 30, 316–17.
Bischof-Köhler, D. 1988. Über den Zusammenhang von Empathie und der Fähigkeit, sich im Spiegel zu erkennen [On the Connection between Empathy and the Ability to Recognize Oneself in the Mirror]. *Schweiz. Zeitschrift für Psychologie*, 4, 147–59.
1991. The Development of Empathy in Infants. In: M. E. Lamb and H. Keller (eds.), *Infant Development: Perspectives from German-speaking Countries*. Hillsdale, NJ: Lawrence Erlbaum, 245–73.
1994. Selbstobjektivierung und fremdbezogene Emotionen. Identifikation des eigenen Spiegelbildes, Empathie und prosoziales Verhalten im 2. Lebensjahr [Self-objectification and Other-oriented Emotions. Mirror-recognition, Empathy and Prosocial Behavior in the Second Year]. *Zeitschrift für Psychologie*, 202, 349–77.
2000a. *Kinder auf Zeitreise. Theory of Mind, Zeitverständnis und Handlungsorganisation [Time Travel in Children. Theory of Mind, Time Comprehension and Organization of Actions]*. Bern, Switzerland: Huber.
2000b. Empathie, prosoziales Verhalten und Bindungsqualität bei Zweijährigen [Empathy, Prosocial Behavior and Security of Attachment in Two Years Olds]. *Psychologie in Erziehung und Unterricht*, 47, 142–58.
2012. Empathy and Self-recognition in Phylogenetic and Ontogenetic Perspective. *Emotion Review*, 4, 40–8.
Brunswik, E. 1955. 'Ratiomorphic' Models of Perception and Thinking. *Acta Psychologica*, 11, 108–9.
Caron, A. J. 2009. Comprehension of the Representational Mind in Infancy. *Developmental Review*, 29, 69–95.
Davidov, M.; Zahn-Waxler, C.; Roth-Hanania, R. and Knafo, A. 2013. Concern for Others in the first Year of Life: Theory, Evidence, and Avenues for Research. *Child Development Perspectives*, 7, 126–31.
Decety, J. and Svetlova, M. 2012. Putting together Phylogenetic and Ontogenetic Perspectives on Empathy. *Developmental Cognitive Neuroscience*, 2, 1–24.

Dondi, M.; Simion, F. and Caltran, G. 1999. Can Newborns discriminate between their own Cry and the Cry of another Newborn Infant? *Developmental Psychology*, 35, 418–26.

Eisenberg, N.; Shea, C.L.; Carlo, G and Knight, G.P. 1991. Empathy-related Responding and Cognition: A 'Chicken and the Egg' Dilemma. In: W. M. Kurtines (ed.), *Advances in Moral Development*. New York: Wiley, vol. I, 63–83.

Flavell, J. H.; Everett, B. A.; Croft, K. and Flavell, E. R. 1981. Young Children's Knowledge about Visual Perception. Further Evidence for the Level 1-Level 2 Distinction. *Developmental Psychology*, 17, 99–103.

Goodall, J. 1986. *The Chimpanzees of Gombe*. Cambridge, MA: Harvard University Press.

Haviland, J. M. and Lelwica, M. 1987. The Induced Affect Response: Ten-week old Infants' Responses to three Emotion Expressions. *Developmental Psychology*, 23, 97–104.

Hoffman, M. L. 1976. Empathy, Roletaking, Guilt and the Development of Altruistic Motives. In: T. Lickona (ed.), *Moral Development and Behavior*. New York, NY: Holt, Rinehart & Winston, 124–43.

2000. *Empathy and Moral Development*. Cambridge: University Press.

2007. The Origins of Empathic Morality in Toddlerhood. In: Celia A. Brownell and Claire B. Kopp (eds.), *Socioemotional Development in the Toddler Years: Transitions and Transformations*. New York: Guilford Press, 132–48.

Johnson, D. B. 1982. Altruistic Behavior and the Development of the Self in Infants. *Merrill-Palmer Quarterly*, 28, 379–88.

Kaden, S.E.; Wapner, S. and Werner, H. 1955. Studies in Physiognomic Perception II: Effect of Directional Dynamics of Pictured Objects and of Words on the Position of the Apparent Horizon. *Journal of Psychology*, 39, 61–70.

Martin, G. B. and Clark, R. D. 1982. Distress Crying in Neonates: Species and Peer Specificity. *Developmental Psychology*, 18, 3–9.

Meltzoff, A. N. and Brooks, R. 2001. 'Like me' as a Building Block for Understanding other Minds: Bodily Acts, Attention and Intention. In: B. F. Malle, L. J. Moses and D. A. Baldwin (eds.), *Intentions and intentionality. Foundations of Social Cognition*. Cambridge, MA: MIT Press, 171–91.

Neisser, U. 1995. Criteria for an Ecological Self. In: P. Rochat (ed.), *The self in infancy: Theory and Research*. Amsterdam, Elsevier, 17–34.

Nichols, S.R.; Svetlova, M. and Brownell, C.A. 2009. The Role of Social Understanding and Empathic Disposition in Young Children's Responsiveness to Distress in Parents and Peers. *Cognition, Brain, Behavior*, 13, 449–78.

Nielsen, M. and Dissanayake, C. 2004. Pretend Play, Mirror Self-recognition and Imitation: A Longitudinal Investigation through the Second Year. *Infant Behavior and Development*, 27, 342–65.

Papousek, H. and Papousek, M. 1977. Mothering and the Cognitive Head-start: Psychobiological Considerations. In: H. R. Schaffer (ed.), *Studies in mother-infant interaction*. New York, NY: Academic Press, 63–85.

Perner, J. 1991. *Understanding the Representational Mind*. Cambridge, MA: MIT Press.

2009. Who took the Cog out of Cognitive Science? Mentalism in an Era of Anti-cognitivism. In: P. A. Frensch and R. Schwarzer (eds.), *Perception,*

Attention, and Action: International Perspectives of Psychological Science. Hove, UK: Psychology Press, vol. I, 141–261.

Radke-Yarrow, M.; Zahn-Waxler, C. and Chapman, M. 1983. Children's Prosocial Disposition and Behavior. In: P.H. Mussen (ed.), *Handbook of Child Psychology.* New York, Wiley, vol. IV, 469–545.

Rochat, P. and Striano, T. 2002. Who's in the Mirror? Self–other Discrimination in Specular Images by Four- and Nine-month-old Infants. *Child Development,* 73, 35–46.

Sagi, A. and Hoffman, M. L. 1976. Empathic Distress in the Newborn. *Developmental Psychology,* 12, 175–6.

Sodian, B. 2010. Theory of Mind in Infancy. *Child Development Perspectives,* 3, 267–71.

Staub, E. A. 1986. Conception of the Determinants and Development of Altruism and Aggression: Motives, the Self, and the Environment. In: C. Zahn-Waxler, M. E. Cummings and R. Iannotti (eds.), *Altruism and Aggression.* Cambridge University Press, 135–64.

Stern, D. N. 1985. *The Interpersonal World of the Infant.* New York, NY: Basic Book.

Svetlova, M.; Nichols, S. R. and Brownell, C. A. 2010. Toddlers' Prosocial Behavior: from Instrumental to Empathic to Altruistic Helping. *Child Development,* 81, 1814–27.

Thompson, R. A. 1987. Empathy and Emotional Understanding: The Early Development of Empathy. In: N. Eisenberg and J. Strayer (eds.), *Empathy and its Development.* Cambridge University Press, 119–45.

Tomasello, M. 1999. Having Intentions, Understanding Intentions, and Understanding Communicative Intentions. In: P. D. Zelazo, J. W. Astington and D. R. Olson (eds.), *Developing Theories of Intention.* Mahwah, NJ: Lawrence Erlbaum, 43–61.

Trevarthen, C. 1979. Communication and Cooperation in Early Infancy: A Description of Primary Intersubjectivity. In: M. Bullowa (ed.), *Before Speech: The Beginning of Human Communication.* Cambridge University Press, 321–47.

Vaish, A.; Carpenter, M. and Tomasello, M. 2009. Sympathy through Affective Perspective-taking and its Relation to Prosocial Behavior in Toddlers. *Developmental Psychology,* 45, 534–43.

Warneken, F. and Tomasello, M. 2010. Varieties of Altruism in Children and Chimpanzees. *Trends in Cognitive Science,* 13, 397–402.

Wellman, H. M.; Cross, D. and Watson, J. 2001. Meta-analysis of Theory of Mind Development: The Truth about False Belief. *Child Development,* 72, 655–84.

Werner, H. and Wapner, S. 1954. Studies in Physiognomic Perception: I. Effect of Configurational Dynamics and Meaning-induced Sets on the Position of the Apparent Median Plane. *The Journal of Psychology,* 38, 51–65.

Woodward, A.L. 2003. Infants' Developing Understanding of the Link between Looker and Object. *Developmental Science,* 6, 297–311.

Zahn-Waxler, C.; Radke-Yarrow, M. and Kind, R. A. 1979. Child Rearing and Children's Prosocial Initiations toward Victims of Distress. *Child Development,* 50, 319–30.

Zahn-Waxler, C.; Radke-Yarrow, M.; Wagner, E. and Chapman, M. 1992. Development of Concern for Others. *Developmental Psychology,* 28, 126–36.

III

Understanding Empathy

4 Self-Simulation and Empathy

Heidi L. Maibom

Many things make us empathize with others. But if our sensibilities are sluggish, one method is often appealed to: taking the other's perspective. As Hermia says to her father in *A Midsummer Night's Dream*, "I would my father look'd but with my eyes" (Shakespeare 1600/1993, Act I, Scene I). Her thought is that if her father took her perspective, he would be moved by her plight and would not insist on her marrying a man she does not love. Parents, too, induce empathy or sympathy by asking their children to imagine how they would feel if someone did to them what they just did to another. Philosophers have also argued that taking another's perspective has special powers to produce empathic affect for another (Maibom 2007), or that it "is the standard way by which vicarious or resonant emotions are generated" (Goldman 1995, 198). All this seems to be confirmed by the extensive social psychology research on empathy and sympathy[1] (Eisenberg and Fabes 1990; Batson 1991; 2011; Davis 1994; Hoffman 2000). Why is that?

It seems plausible that there is something about the subjective, first-personal engagement with the other in perspective taking that is particularly fruitful when it comes to production of affective responses. There is something about conceiving of the situation happening *to me* that helps produce empathy. What might this be? Well, when we imagine being in the situation the other person is in, the emotions follow readily. By imagining being in the situation, we come to feel what we would feel were we *actually* in the situation. This account is not only plausible and does justice to common sense, but has also been defended in one form of other by a variety of philosophers (Goldman 1995; Maibom 2007).

---

[1] By 'empathy', I mean an emotion consonant with the emotion that one takes the other person to be experiencing, and that one experiences because they are experiencing it, as it were for their sake. By 'sympathy', I mean a feeling of concern for the well-being of another person, where this feeling need not be consonant with the emotion that that person is experiencing. Perspective taking is sometimes also called empathy, specifically cognitive empathy. To avoid confusing cognitive empathy with affective empathy, I call the former 'perspective taking' and the latter 'empathy'.

The trouble with it is that it seems to be false. Data from psychology on people's failure to forecast their own reactions to counterfactual events point to forecasting not being so much a matter of reenacting as of figuring out what it would be *reasonable* for oneself and, by extension, the other person to feel. This leaves it a bit mysterious why perspective taking seems to have especially felicitous results for empathy because now the subjective element appears to have largely dropped out. Instead we have a normative calculation of what a reasonable reaction would be.

Once I have set up the details of this problem, I set to work on offering a solution according to which what does most of the work in perspective taking producing empathy is the change of description of the situation, action, or event that such an act forces on the individual. The empathy is in the details, as it were. Because taking another's perspective typically requires us imagining all the individual events and interactions that make up the overall situation she is in, her plight is made more vivid, and the impact is more easily recognizable. It is, therefore, not the subjective element of perspective taking that gives it its power to induce affect, but the fact that it forces us to think of the other person's situation in a more detailed way. Put differently: it is not the fact that *you* know that this is how you would feel because this is what your imaginative exercise shows, but the fact that you can see how *anyone* in that particular situation would plausibly feel thus-and-so. I give several examples of when we use perspective taking that highlight this feature. Lastly, I take a careful look at the psychology literature on perspective taking and empathy and show that it is compatible with my proposal.

1. The Compelling View: Subjective Engagement with the Other

It is compelling to think that when we take another's perspective, we imagine that we are in her position, and in virtue of so imagining, we evoke in ourselves the kinds of thoughts and emotions that *we* would have were we actually in that situation. Of course, we only try out such thoughts and emotions. We do not adopt the beliefs we try on. The reason has to do either with the particular nature of belief in perspective taking – it is not real belief, but pretend belief or a supposition – or with the fact that when we *imagine* things we create a small, contained cognitive-emotional environment that is relatively quarantined from our larger cognitive system. But if this is true of beliefs, it does not appear to be so for emotions. For when we imagine being in a distressing situation, often we actually become distressed. Typically, we do not become *as* distressed as we would were we actually in the situation. Nonetheless, that act of imagination evokes in us emotions that have the same qualitative feel and that are associated with the same physiological and brain changes as emotions that are not induced by the imagination (e.g., Lamm, Batson, and Decety 2007). Furthermore, such affect is powerful enough to have some of the same motivational effects that the emotion felt in response to the *actual* situation has. This all happens, the story goes, because the emotion – the distress, for instance – remains after the act of imagination and is, at least partially, transformed into distress *for* the person whose situation we have imagined being in. Ordinary distress – or "personal" distress, as they say in the psychology literature – has been transformed into empathic distress (Maibom 2007).

The mechanism by which this emotional transformation might take place has been described by Antonio Damasio (1994), who famously argues that the existence and use of somatic markers are an essential part of decision-making. The idea is roughly this. With experience, our representations of the world become associated with affect, positive or negative. When a representation is marked with negative affect, we are disposed to not engage in actions that bring about the situation represented. Conversely, if a representation is marked with positive affect, we are disposed to bring about the represented situation *ceteris paribus*. Damasio uses evidence from people with damage to their ventromedial prefrontal cortex as evidence for his theory. These patients have emotional impairments, but no real reasoning deficits on standard psychological tasks. Yet, they show a peculiar inability to act in their own best interest.[2] It may not just be the ability to feel correctly valenced emotions that is essential to good decision-making. There is also reason to think that being able to have the adequate specific emotional response to a situation is required. Relying on clinical data again, Damasio (1999) describes a patient with extensive calcification of the amygdala, who comprehends intellectually what fear is and what it does, but who does not appear to experience it. She shows little fear in social situations, cannot recognize fear on others' faces, and cannot even represent it on paper though she draws well. The

---

[2] Damasio uses performance on the Iowa Gambling Task as evidence for his theory. When different decks are associated with different probabilities of winning and losing, people learn to choose from the decks that accumulatively lead to higher gains and fewer losses. At the same time, the decision not to choose a card from a risky deck is preceded by a spike in skin conductance. It seems that affective responses of the body have come to be associated with good decision-making. In fact, Damasio suggests that reasoning at the conscious level is not sufficient in these types of situations. The affective response is *necessary* for good decision-making, perhaps in part because the connection between particular representations and affective responses is often not conscious (Damasio 1999). This is particularly clear in people with focal brain damage. People with damage to their orbitofrontal cortex do not perform appropriately on the Iowa Gambling Task (Bechara et al. 1994) *and* fail to have the appropriate skin conductance response (Bechara et al. 1996).

amygdala is implicated in, and likely necessary for, the ability to experience fear and for fear conditioning. Her bad decisions in social situations are, Damasio argues, a result of her deficient fear responses: what others regard as social threats, she cannot see as such.

We are now in a position to explain what is special about perspective taking, it seems. When asked to imagine being in someone else's position, we conjure up somatically marked representations of that situation from the perspective of someone who is in it. For instance, I imagine having lost my parents in a car crash, and I am suffused with sadness. But when I return to my own perspective, my sadness does not just dissipate. Affect tends to linger, particularly where there are not very good reasons to feel differently about the situation. Recognizing that I am not actually in your situation is not a reason not to feel sad; in particular, it is not a reason not to feel sad *for you*. I am aware that I became sad by imagining being in another's situation, and I now see at least part of my sadness as sadness *for the other*. In short, my sadness is *empathic* (Maibom 2007).

One more thing is needed for this line of thinking to lead to the conclusion that perspective taking has special powers to induce empathy. After all, simply *knowing* that someone is in a difficult situation can induce empathy *without* any engagement of the imagination or of perspective taking. Therefore, the thought must be that there is something about the act of taking another's perspective *itself* that induces the deeper understanding and the emotional empathy that are typically associated with perspective taking. What might that be? One reason is hinted at by Goldman when he says that perspective takers need not "know the nomological properties that govern his decision-making system (or his other psychological mechanisms). It only requires the predictor to *possess* a decision-making system and to be capable of feeding it appropriate inputs and interpreting its outputs" (Goldman 1995, 190). If we do not *know* how one might react to something, we can try it out in the imagination, and because we have knowledge locked inside our decision-making system about our reactions that we need not otherwise have access to, our imagined reactions contain the answer. Or, at any rate, they will give us a very good shot at the answer. In other words, we may access knowledge via perspective taking that we could not otherwise access.

Others may think that the imagined lived experience in the imaginarium of the body of the perspective taker is of central importance for us to "know what it's like." When we enact another's situation with ourselves as protagonists, we deploy distinctively first-personal resources that make this form of relating to others more intimate and more apt to induce other-directed emotions. The point about perspective taking as enactment is that it engages resources that are not accessible to us via more discursive, conceptual, or abstract thought about the subject matter. Our knowledge may be implicit and embodied and can be triggered automatically by the right input. Moreover, we may enact part of the phenomenology of the other, which gives us additional understanding. When we enact emotion, say elation, we "conjure up a state that feels, phenomenologically, rather like a trace or tincture of elation" (Goldman 2006, 47).

The preceding explains why perspective taking would be more effective in eliciting empathy than other methods: personal or subjective involvement with the other person's point of view. Of course, this presupposes that we are capable of self-inducing emotional responses by imagining being in situations that we are not currently in, responses that match or parallel the emotional response we would have were we *actually* in that situation, or one very much like it. The trouble is that there is a wealth of evidence suggesting that we face remarkable difficulties in forecasting our own reactions to situations by means of the imagination. In particular, it seems that we are often, even usually, unable to predict at the right level of detail how we will feel, think, or want, and what we would do under circumstances different from the ones that we are in. And what is more, the *kinds* of errors that we make indicate that when we imagine ourselves in counterfactual situations, we do not enact in any interesting sense. There does not appear to be any involvement of what we may call distinctively first-personal resources, as opposed to the application of general-use conceptual knowledge and constraints on rational action. Perspective taking in the nonperceptual sense does not seem to involve a distinctively subjective perspective on the situation, but seems rather to deploy general normative resources for deciding appropriate action or reaction. Let us have a look at the evidence.

2. Failure to Forecast

Here is a summary of some of these failures to forecast our reactions correctly. We fail to anticipate the effects that owning an object has on our evaluation of its value (Kahneman, Knetsch, and Thaler 1991; Van Boven, Dunning, and Loewenstein 2000); the ways literary passages affect our emotions or noise affects our appreciation of a movie (Nisbett and Wilson 1977); our willingness to endure electric shock (ibid.) or to shock other people when asked by an experimenter to do so (Milgram 1963; 1974); our likelihood of helping a person in need when others are present (Latané and Darley 1970; Hart and Miethe 2008); our tendency to steal for nonmonetary gain (Mazar and Ariely 2006; Amir, Ariely, and Mazar 2008) or to cheat on tests (Teper, Inzlit, and Page-Gould 2011);

the lengths we are willing to go to not to be impolite or be embarrassed (Biderman 1960; Van Boven et al. 2012); how we will react to sexual harassment or interrogation (Biderman 1960; Woodzicka and LaFrance 2001); and how much we will change in the future (Quoidbach, Gilbert, and Wilson 2013).

Affective forecasting is often a particular problem. Take visceral affect, for instance. On the one hand, we are bad at abstracting away from visceral reactions we currently experience so that our perspective taking is not affected by it. On the other, we are largely unable to re-create the phenomenological qualities associated with such reactions (Morley 1993; Loewenstein 1996; Gilbert, Gill, and Wilson 2002; Van Boven and Loewenstein 2003). Hunger affects how we think and what we are likely to do in ways that we do not foresee when we are not hungry (Read and van Leeuwen 1998; Gilbert, Gill, and Wilson 2002). When we are hungry, we predict that we will eat more unhealthy snacks than we do when we are not hungry (Read and van Leeuwen 1998). This is true despite the fact that most of us have experienced being hungry and consuming excess unhealthy snacks under such circumstances. Merely imagining being hungry, when we are not, does not engage our affective or visceral machinery in the same way as *actually* being hungry does (even in heavily constrained circumstances). Similarly, if one is thirsty at the time one imagines being in a certain situation, one values drinking more (than eating, say) in that situation than one would were one not thirsty at the time of imagining the situation (Van Boven and Loewenstein 2003).

The literature on pain suggests similar difficulties forecasting reactions. It is often thought that we use our memories of affective experiences when imagining experiencing affect. Such memories, however, are not very accurate. Pain is typically remembered as being worse than it was (Gilbert and Wilson 2000). Women tend to remember labor as being worse than they reported it being during labor (Terry and Gijsbers 2000), and people who donate blood remember the experience as worse than they said it was at the time (Breckler 1994). In general, people are not particularly good at remembering the quality of their pain (Beese and Morley 1993; Terry and Gijsbers 2000). Given people's tendency to magnify their previous pain, it is rather curious that they, at the same time, seem to underestimate the effects such pain had, or will have, on their behavior. Going back to childbirth, many women choose not to have anesthesia to ease the pain of labor when asked one month before labor and during the early stages of it. However, a sizable number of those women reverse their decision once they have gone into full labor. This is true of first-timers, as well as women who have given birth before (Christensen-Szalanski 1984). It is a testament to human optimism that women tend to magnify both the pain of labor and their ability to endure it without a little help from modern medicine. Similarly, alcoholics (Osiatynski 1992) and drug addicts (Gardner and Lowinson 1993) radically underestimate the effects of having a drink or taking a bit of the drug while overestimating their ability to resist future abuse.

Students predict enjoying spring break more than they actually do (Witrz et al. 2003). And people diagnosed with HIV are less distressed by it than they thought they would be (Sieff, Dawes, and Loewenstein 1999). People tend to overestimate how strongly and for how long they experience positive or negative affect, including guilt or regret (Wilson and Gilbert 2005). Similarly, they underestimate the effects of embarrassment on how they would act in different circumstances (Van Boven et al. 2012). The downstream effects of such failures of affective forecasting are significant. For example, holidays are typically expected to be, and remembered as, more enjoyable than they actually are, and it is how people remember the experience that affects their decision to repeat it (Wirtz et al. 2003).

Is this surprising? Should we not expect some minor differences between what we forecast and what we are actually likely to do, feel, and think? Well, subjects themselves are often surprised when confronted with the evidence. Take the Milgram experiment. Even people who know of the effect *still* predict that neither they, nor their family members, nor their friends will continue to shock the subject (Bierbrauer 1979). Sadly, we are quick to see biases in others, but slow to see them in ourselves (Epley 2014). To make this phenomenon more vivid, estimate the amount of time it will take you to buy your Christmas presents or write a paper, for instance. Give the best-case and the worst-case scenarios. If you are like most, you will get it wrong. You will complete your project later than your most pessimistic estimate (Epley 2014). The so-called planning fallacy is common, and yet surprising to us even though we fail to meet our own deadlines or estimates all the time (Buehler, Griffin, and Ross 1995). How we fail to notice this is a fascinating question. Perhaps we overestimate how likely we thought something that actually happened was (Fischhoff 1975), another common fallacy, or we simply forget or ignore our mistaken prognoses. Whatever the explanation, we clearly fail to forecast our actions or reactions correctly in situations that we are commonly in, yet we persevere in making such mistakes, either because we don't notice our mistakes or because we are very sure in our own predictive ability. We are more wrong about our ability to predict things about ourselves than we think we are.

The range of situations where our forecasts are wrong or surprisingly inaccurate suggests that we are dealing with a more principled and pervasive difficulty than simply a handful of biases. When we imagine being in a situation, even a situation that we have been in before, we do not seem to provoke the kind of emotional reaction we would have were we actually in the situation. This makes sense if we consider that when we imagine being in a scary situation, for instance, we feel scared, but not as much as we would were we actually in that scary situation. But interestingly, this type of emotion-attenuation error is *not* the one that we commit in the cases just enumerated. When a woman imagines labor, she imagines it to be *worse* than she reports during labor, *even if it is her second birth*. If such a reaction were based on her experiencing pain as a result of imagining being in labor, relying on her personal experience, we would expect the opposite pattern. Of course, pain is a rather extreme example. Pain may be unusual insofar as imagining being in a painful situation will not bring about any sensation of being in pain. At best, we will have some generic unpleasant sensation. But it is not only pain that we have problems evoking via the imagination. Think of this example from sexual harassment research. Julie Woodzicka and Marianne LaFrance (2001) told women to imagine being interviewed for a job where the male interviewer asks them questions about their dating status and the importance to them of their being sexually attractive. Most women predict that they will experience mostly anger and will confront the interviewer. However, when being interviewed by a male interviewer who *in fact* asks them whether they are dating and whether it is important to them that they are sexually attractive (in an experimental setup), most women report feeling afraid, nobody reports anger, and not a single woman confronts the interviewer. The most extreme protest was politely asking the interviewer to repeat the offensive questions. When he did, their small protest stopped. Here, what is imagined is a different emotion altogether than the one that is *actually* experienced in the situation. This is not what we would expect if the power of the imagination were what we have been led to believe.

Now, it may be argued that I am setting the bar too high. We cannot expect people to be able to imaginatively re-create what they have not experienced. Alvin Goldman (1995), for instance, considers sexual harassment and argues that it is likely that men are unable to properly use their imagination to get to understand what it's like or what they would do were they, themselves, sexually harassed. This is due to the fact that men simply have not had the requisite experience, he says. Lack of experience is not the problem in the Woodzicka and LeFrance study, however. For the people who fail to forecast their own reactions are *women*. A large proportion of women have been sexually harassed in one form or another, and all have been exposed to sexist behavior. These experiences ought to facilitate imagining their reaction in the experimental situation more successfully, and yet they do not appear to do so. This, incidentally, is true of most of the preceding examples. Given people's rather intimate experience with the phenomenon in question (hunger, say), they ought to do better. At any rate, on a view of the imagination as being a relatively powerful tool for reenactment of our psychological reactions to things, the fact that people do not do better is a problem. If we do not *re-create* the cognitive and affective reactions that we would have in the actual situation when we merely *imagine* being in that situation, what is it that we do? Read on to see my suggestion.

3. Forecasting

When we look at mistakes that we tend to make, we can discern a *pattern*. We tend to think our reactions are more reasonable, given the description of the situation, than they actually turn out to be. What do you do when someone is in need? You help them if doing so is not too demanding. Does it matter whether other people around you do not help? Of course not. And so we forecast that we will help. What do you do when you are sexually harassed? You protest. And so we forecast that we will protest. A sort of regulative ideal of rationality seems to govern our perspective taking. 'Rationality' here should, of course, be understood quite broadly to include what is reasonable or sensible (see also Heal 1986). The idea that such an ideal governs mental state ascription is hardly new (Dennett 1987; Davidson 2001), but that it should govern perspective taking too is, perhaps, surprising (though see Heal 1986; 1998; Davies and Stone 1998). On this picture, the first step of perspective taking – where we imagine how *we* would think, feel, and so on – is a form of counterfactual reasoning that is regulated by the overall aim of *making good decisions*. Hence the regulative ideal of (practical) rationality. As a result, we are in the habit of producing ideal or normatively correct reactions to imagined situations. In other words, what typically happens when we are asked to imagine what we *would* do, think, feel, and so on, is that we imagine what we *should* do, think, feel, and so on.

Subsuming beliefs and desires under a regulative ideal of rationality is fine, it might be thought, but how do emotions fit? We have arrived at the thorny question of the extent to which emotions are rational. Since that debate is alive and well and some of us are far from impressed with the so-called rationality of emotions, the move to institute a regulative ideal on emotion ascription seems unfortunate. However, there are really two distinct issues. Emotions may not, as a matter of fact, be particularly rational. Nonetheless, it is indisputable that we often think of emotional reactions as at least being reasonable or unreasonable. Therefore, when asked to imagine what we would feel under certain circumstances, it is quite plausible that we are guided by considerations of what emotions it *would be reasonable* or *it would make sense* to have. As we saw, we are often wrong about the nature of our affective reactions to an event, or about how strongly we will feel an emotion or for how long. At times we are wrong, but not that wrong. Nevertheless, the sexual harassment study suggests that we are sometimes *completely wrong* about how we will feel. Women feel afraid, but predict they will feel angry. What is going on in this case? I see two options. First, women might already get a bit angry reading about the scenario and, since there is good evidence that what we feel when we forecast affects our forecasting in terms of those emotions, they project that feeling on to their counterfactual selves. Second, they may think that this situation calls for anger, or that feeling anger would be appropriate. The interviewer is, after all, acting offensively. I doubt that the situation is one of simple projection, as the first option suggests. We don't project any old emotion that we have into the situation we imagine being in. For instance, I don't imagine being angry if a friend invites me out for dinner, just because I'm angry when I imagine how I would react. The emotion that I am experiencing at the time of imagining has to be at least consonant with an emotion that it would be appropriate or it would make sense to feel in the imagined situation. Of course, if I am angry and irritated, it is quite likely that I will be less enthused by my friend's invitation than I might otherwise be. But that does not change the fact discordant moods or emotions are rarely projected onto an imagined scenario where such reactions would not make sense.

It would appear, then, that when forecasting emotional reactions, we err in the direction of *reasonable* or *sensible* reactions to situations. This makes sense of our tendencies *not* to foresee: that we value an object that we own more than an almost indistinguishable object that we do not own, that we are often quite willing to endure electric shocks and inflict them on others if asked by a experimenter, that we are unlikely to help a person in need if we are with others who do not help, that we are more likely to steal for nonmonetary gain, that we tend not to confront a sexual harasser, that we have a deep-seated desire to be cooperative even when interrogated by an enemy, that we will feel like eating more unhealthy snacks in the future if we are hungry, that one drink often leads to another, that holidays are not as fun as we expect or remember them to be, that we don't feel as guilty as we think we would or for as long, and that we think we will be more devastated by news that we have an untreatable deadly disease. These reactions

Self-Simulation and Empathy

are counterintuitive. Our mistaken forecasts, however, are not. What should you do if sexually harassed? Confront the harasser. Hence I imagine confronting the harasser, or at least being angry, in response to imagining being harassed. And clearly we should not cooperate with the enemy, even if they seem to be very nice people. It is therefore hard to imagine such a situation. These forecasting errors reflect a discrepancy between reactions that we decide are appropriate when we are not in the situation and the reactions we actually have when we are in the situation.

If we look at the other types of errors found, we find more support for the normative idea. Why would people think they would feel more guilt and remorse and for longer than they do (Wilson and Gilbert 2005)? Here people imagine feeling an appropriate emotion, but exaggerate its importance. Evidently, this type of error should deter someone from acting in ways that she deems to be wrong or nonoptimal. What she fails to consider is that her ability to cope with her guilt or regret is better than she thought (think of Woody Allen's *Crimes and Misdemeanors*). But there is clearly a sense in which this coping response is not quite reasonable. If I imagine feeling guilt or remorse upon having performed an action, there may be ways to make myself feel better, but it seems that guilt and remorse would still be reasonable to feel for a while since the objective situation hasn't changed. Whether or not I find a way not to think about it, create an inventive justification for what I did, and so on, the relevant action is surely still wrong or culpable. The situation with guilt and regret also throws light on the normativity of imagination. It has been shown that people's overall happiness is less affected by undesirable events – for example, crippling accidents, being denied tenure, being told one has a deadly disease, being assigned a bad dorm room – than people think (Wilson and Gilbert 2005). However, it would not be rational to consider this at the time of acting, since that might very well lead to suboptimal choices. In other words, it is useful for you now to imagine negative events to have a greater impact on your well-being than they might have, due to your ability to cope, since that will increase your motivation to avoid them. Once you have been disabled, however, you do well to deal with the situation as best you can. Nevertheless, for now you ought to behave prudently so as *not* to be injured in the first place. In other words, it may be that affective forecasting has magnitude errors built into it that are part and parcel of our decision-making system or systems. One last thing: it follows from what I have argued that we only make forecasting errors when our reactions differ from our conception of what the reasonable or sensible reaction under those circumstances would be.

4. Perspective Taking and Empathy

If what I have said is right, it is hard to see how perspective taking would increase our tendency to empathize with others. Why wouldn't we just think about what the reasonable thing for someone to do would be, and go from there? Thinking first of what we, ourselves, would do seems like an unnecessary complication! Secondly, it also seems that perspective taking doesn't have anything to offer with respect to empathy compared to other, more straightforward, approaches. Common sense, however, suggests that it does, and there is much evidence that links perspective taking and empathy too.

On the first point, I stand guilty as charged. On the account that I'll be presenting, there is nothing special about taking a first-person stance vis-à-vis what perspective taking yields. Subjectivity is neither here nor there. The usefulness of imagining that *one, oneself,* is experiencing what the other is experiencing lies not in the personal element (as in "it's me, not her"), but in what is imagined. What I have in mind here won't really be clear until we think more about what we actually do when we take another's perspective. So far, we have simply discussed the peculiar personal element that is involved in us first working out what *we* would think, feel, and so on, in order to figure out what the other person thinks, feels, and such.

When we imagine a being in a certain situation, we typically have to fill in details of an otherwise denuded description. For instance, ask me to imagine having been broken up with. Well, somebody must have broken up with me, someone I really cared about, the relationship must have lasted for a certain amount of time, and so on. Being inspired, as it were, to fill in details is something we might be if we are merely asked to consider someone's situation in detail too. Psychologists tend to call this type of perspective taking 'imagine-other perspective taking'. It is a good exercise to think about the typical cases when we take another's perspective to see what I have in mind. Here are three paradigm cases: (i) socialization, (ii) explanation (or "getting it"), and (iii) dislodging someone from his egocentric perspective on the situation.

Let us think briefly about socialization first. Parents use perspective-taking instructions with their children to encourage them to be considerate toward others. "How would you feel if someone took your toy and wouldn't give it back to you?" would be an example. This would be a response to the child not thinking much about the other child, but being largely focused on playing with the new toy. According to Martin Hoffman (2000), inducing empathic concern in children has powerful downstream effects for their socialization. This form of taking another's perspective does seem to serve two functions. On the one hand, it interrupts the child's ongoing behavior and thinking, and on the other it focuses the child's attention on different aspects of his action. By making him think about his action in a different light, the child is ultimately induced to feel bad about his action (guilt). This type of socialization is an important moral tool as it teaches the child to conceive of actions in ways that she would not otherwise do. And it also imparts the more general lesson that an action has many descriptions, and to access the relevant ones might require some work. This aspect of socialization is crucial for moral development also (cf. Maibom 2014). It should be noted, however, that in this scenario perspective taking plays the sole role of focusing the child's attention on another aspect of the situation. But that is only one way in which the desired result can be reached. One could also have asked the child simply to think about how the other child feels in her situation (psychologists would call this 'imagine-other').

Perspective taking can also be a way to reach an understanding of a reaction that seems, on the face of it, to make little sense. Typically strange reactions make us focus on the individual and his or her situation, and the perspective taking here is an extra step taken to reach an understanding that is not forthcoming from such focusing. Perspective taking in such situations often involves decomposing the situation the person is in, or the event that has occurred, into the many small events that led up to or constituted the greater event. Why might a housewife be depressed and bored? She has a big house, a nice garden, a loving husband, and a fair amount of free time (let's suppose). Let us imagine her day as if we were living it. You wake up in the morning with nothing to do but to watch your mate leave for work after which you are trapped in an empty house in a forlorn suburb having to busy yourself with household chores. How exciting is doing laundry? How stimulating is supermarket shopping? Did you have dreams of a career of your own, of doing something more meaningful? Literature and motion pictures often do a wonderful job at bringing to life the details of other existences. Those are details that, in one way or other, we must have been aware were there, but that we would not normally consider. This may also account for why literature is thought to have such a great effect on people's tendency to empathize with others. Harriet Beecher Stowe's *Uncle Tom's Cabin* is often credited with turning many people against slavery through its detailed portrayal of Uncle Tom's life. Fictional portrayals of other people fill in the many fine details that make up a person's life in a way that most of us are too unimaginative or too lazy to imagine. And so although we grasp intellectually that slavery is a bad thing, seeing how an actual slave lives and what happens to him or her is another thing altogether, and one that is more likely to induce empathic affect.

Third, we often induce others or ourselves to take the perspective of someone with whom we are in conflict. We may be angry with the person for one reason or another – they stood us up, said something inconsiderate, or spilled coffee on one of our first editions – and we understand their action in terms of our own projects, concerns, and well-being. What perspective taking ideally does in cases such as these is dislodge us from our own egocentric construal of the situation. It allows us to reach a more objective assessment of it by counterbalancing our own egocentric construal with the construal of another person, perhaps equally egocentric. Seeing another person's action from the perspective of her projects and concerns won't invariably change our assessment of it, of course. But often we see that what was understood as a deliberate attempt to insult us was merely a slip of the tongue, that failure to keep our appointment is a result of overwork and stress not of disregard for us, or that the spillage tragedy was an accident, and so on. Ancient anger manuals – such as Seneca's (1995) *De Ira* – are wonderful treatises encouraging us to reconceptualize actions that we are inclined to see as offensive or insulting as something different altogether. Although anger management might be one of the prime instances of this use of perspective taking, I suspect that the general aim here is to use perspective change as a counterbalance to the view of the world that (strong) emotional reactions present us with. There is near consensus among emotion researchers that an assessment or evaluation of the world in terms of our well-being, plans, or projects, however cognitively inchoate, is part of the emotional experience. Emotions represent, you might say, the relevance *to us* of some aspect(s) of the world. Perspective taking is therefore perfectly poised to counterbalance such a biased view of the world.

This is not meant to be an exhaustive list, of course, nor is the idea that the project of socializing someone is fundamentally different from dislodging her from her own perspective. Looking to the practice of perspective taking, however, may help us solve problems that our more theoretical reflections raise. If the preceding uses are representative of the practice of perspective taking, then enactment is neither here nor there. Perspective taking dislodges you from your particular favored assessment or evaluation of the situation by alerting you to the fact that your view of the situation is one of many possible ones. This other way of thinking about the situation may be reached by imaginatively projecting yourself into the other's situation. The key, however, is reconceptualization or redescription, not subjective engagement with the other's situation. Such reconceptualization is often accomplished by falling to a lower level of description or, if you like, considering the many *details* that make up the situation that you are considering. Once the situation is conceptualized in another way, namely in a way where the other person figures centrally, empathy may be induced where formerly it was not.

The idea is not that where abstract characterizations fail to inspire enactment, detailed descriptions do. I am not claiming that we reenact even in the detailed imagined situations I have just described. But what perspective taking does is give us details that often help us make better sense of how people think or feel about something, or why they decide to act as they do. The process is still the same: we are really calculating a sensible response from the details that we are provided with. Often abstract characterizations of a situation are hard to relate to because of the level of abstraction, sometimes they distort given the interest of the speaker, and so on. If these details leave us as cold as the abstract description of the situation does, there is nothing more perspective taking can accomplish. For, after all, if something else is to do the job it must be the fact that *you* are the one in that situation. But only an egoist requires this kind of prompting. And although this type of instruction appears to make psychopaths empathize with pictures of people in pain, it is not required for ordinary people. Moreover, when psychopaths imagine the *other* in pain, he ceases to empathize (Decety et al. 2013). What I'm trying to get across here is that personal involvement is not normally needed for empathy. And when it is, it is not well correlated with empathy *for others*. But it is not easy to see what else, other than this personal involvement or the details provided, could account for perspective taking's special link to empathy. And so, detailed engagement with the subject in her situation is a good starter for explaining why perspective taking is so good at evoking empathy.

It would be fair to object that the many experiments in social psychology that show distinctive yields of perspective taking when it comes to empathizing or sympathizing with a subject in need suggest that I have missed something. There is something distinctive about taking another's perspective compared to simply thinking about the situation, however detailed. It is evidenced in the greater amount of empathy and willingness to help those in need that perspective taking induces, among other things (Batson 1991; 2011). This is, of course, true. But it is less true than one might think. Most experiments on perspective taking induce empathy using the following design. You are asked to imagine either what you would feel if you were in the other person's situation, the so-called imagine-self experimental condition; to imagine what the other person feels in his or her situation, the so-called imagine-other (or imagine-target) condition; or to objectively assess the person in their situation and *not* get caught up in what they are feeling, the so-called objective condition. Typically, the experimental subject is given these instructions just prior to watching or listening to an interview with the target person. In this interview, the target describes the very difficult situation that she is in. It is tempting to think that subjects in the perspective-taking conditions (imagine-self and imagine-other) are asked to do something they would not ordinarily do. But more likely the opposite is true. The objective experimental condition is not simply a control condition. It explicitly asks the subject to *avoid* focusing on what the other person is feeling. Since other people's feelings are salient features that we tend to pay attention to, chances are that in the objective condition subjects *suppress* their natural tendency to think of what the other person is thinking or feeling, which would have led many of them to empathize with her. This interpretation of the objective condition is supported by subjects' self-reports. Most reported that the objective condition was the hardest to adopt (Myers, Laurent, and Hodges 2014; Negd, Mallan, and Lipp 2011).

Does this mean that people naturally take others' perspectives? Unfortunately, most of the literature on empathy deploys experimental conditions that do not fit our way of thinking of perspective taking. Recall that you imagine yourself in the others' situation, not simply as yourself, but as yourself suitably changed so as to be prognostic of the other person's reactions. You might imagine that you believe certain things you do not believe, want certain things, and so on, while at the same time quarantining some of your own beliefs, desires, and feelings. The aim of the exercise is, after all, not just a fanciful play of the imagination, but to gain some form of intimate insight into the situation of another person. But the two so-called perspective-taking conditions that social psychologists use instruct subjects either to focus on the other person and what he is feeling or to project themselves wholesale into the other's situation and see how *they themselves* would be feeling in that situation. The so-called imagine-other perspective taking requires no change of perspective and may not use imagination much at all. All that is required to complete the exercise is to reflect on the other person and his or her situation. Some evidence suggests that imagine-other is what we naturally do when we are not instructed to do something else (Davis et al. 2004). However, it may be more accurate to say that imagine-other is what we do when we are presented with a generally likeable subject in need; we tend to take an objective perspective on people we disapprove of, such as criminals, people we already dislike, or people who are not perceived to be in great need (cf. Batson et al. 2007; Chambers and Davis 2012).

Imagine-self perspective taking comes closest to substantive perspective taking and to what simulation theorists claim that we do: imagine that *we* are in another's situation to see how we would think, feel, act, and so on. The psychology experiments do not ask for any adjustments in this act of perspective taking, but imagine-self at least requires such a perspective change, and this seems essential to the act of imagining being in another's situation. So this is what comes closest to the case we are interested in. Taking an imagine-self perspective tends to make the person think more about herself (Davis et al. 2004), to feel more personal distress (Batson et al. 1997), and to think that she is more similar to the subject whom she imagines being (Myers, Laurent, and Hodges 2014) than had she taken an imagine-other perspective. It also leads to higher arousal (Stotland 1969). Imagine-self and imagine-other perspective taking generally lead to about the same amount of sympathy for the person in need. And both produce distress for the other and for the self, imagine-self perspective taking more so than imagine-other perspective taking (Batson et al. 1997). Where imagine-self perspective taking really stands out compared to imagine-other is that it is often associated with helping another in need *less* than people who have been induced to think of the other's feelings. Daniel Batson (1991; 2011) argues that this is because imagine-other perspective taking induces *altruistic* motivation to help those in need, whereas imagine-self perspective taking induces *egoistic* motivation to help – egoistic because the object is to rid the subject of the negative affect she experienced when contemplating the others' plight or being presented with her suffering. Jacquie Vorauer has found that under certain circumstances asking a person to imagine that she is the person she is about to interact with has negative consequences because the person tends to focus on how she is perceived by the other (Vorauer, Martens, and Sasaki 2009; Vorauer and Quesnel 2013; Vorauer and Sucharyna 2013; Vorauer and Sasaki 2014).

Despite these differences between ways of thinking about others, what stands out is how many experiments show that there is either very little or no emotional, cognitive, or behavioral difference between taking an imagine-other and taking an imagine-self perspective. This militates against the idea that imagining being in someone else's position deploys fundamentally different resources than thinking about what someone feels given the situation that he is in. Instead, it suggests is that there is not much of a difference between imagining oneself in someone's situation and thinking about that person in his situation. This is certainly true when it comes to the *experience* of empathy. Batson and colleagues (1997) actually found *no* significant difference between the amount of sympathy and empathic distress felt for someone in need in imagine-self and imagine-other perspective taking. The main difference was that people who had been asked to project themselves into the other's distressing situation were more distressed – *directly or for themselves* – than people who had been asked to focus on the plight of the other. And that, in turn, leads to what Batson calls a motivation to escape the distressing situation if escape is relatively easy. Note, however, that if escape is difficult, or the cost of helping high, personally distressed people are *more* likely to help the person in need (Batson et al. 1981; 1983). This difference in self-orientation is readily explained by the self-focus that imagine-self perspective-taking instructions induce. It would therefore seem that looking at what is *common* to imagine-self and imagine-other is the best way to find out what is especially effective in inducing empathy.

What is distinctive about almost all perspective-taking inductions is that they are attached to a more detailed story, for instance an audio or videotaped interview with a person in need (e.g., Batson's Katie Banks scenario, Batson et al. 1997). Alternatively, subjects are asked to write out a somewhat detailed account of a day in that person's life (e.g., Galinsky and Moskowitz 2000). All these exercises provide details of the person's situation instead of a more abstract overview of it. One of the better-known scenarios is that of Katie Banks, who has recently lost both her parents in a car crash. She is now the sole provider of her siblings and is struggling to do that while finishing college. We can all understand what a difficult situation Katie is in given this relatively abstract characterization, but the interview with her gives details of her struggling that are more vivid and touching. Katie says that she has little money for food and transportation and does not have a car, but the distance to the laundromat and the supermarket are too great for her to walk. She must get sitters for her siblings in order to attend classes. And so on.

The types of scenarios used for empathy studies, then, all typically involve a level of description where there is not an abstract characterization of the person's situation, but a drop to a level of description that involves details of the person's life. They exemplify what the situation involves, as a matter of fact. And that may be much easier to relate to. These descriptions help people become aware of how a person's life is affected by a loss – in everyday activities – instead of their merely associating some abstract emotional term, 'grief', for instance, with another somewhat abstract term, 'loss'. My point is not, of course, that knowing that someone has lost a loved one is not sufficient to move us. The idea is just that descriptions that provide more detail of what is involved in such a loss make the loss more vivid and, as a consequence, compels us to feel empathy and sympathy for the individual, who has sustained it, to a larger extent. Conversely, it is easier to emotionally detach from a person's situation when it is described in relatively abstract terms, than when we are given the details of how it affects their lives.

If this is right, then we do not need to assume that imagining being in someone else's position has to involve something more than imagining a person's life in more detail; we do not need a personal or subjective element. In particular, it need not involve an engagement of perhaps largely unconscious bodily resources in such a way that the process may properly be called an enactment of what is imagined. The power of the imagination, when it comes to inducing empathy, seems to lie in bringing life to abstract states of affairs by infusing them with detail and color.

5. Conclusion

I have presented the outlines of an account of perspective taking according to which its most distinguishing feature is the way it helps us reconceptualize situations. I have mostly focused on the way that taking another's perspective forces us to fill in details that a cursory assessment of her situation does not. Sometimes those details lead us to recognize that the situation or action is better described, at a more abstract level, in terms different from the ones we started out with. This whole process is regulated by a sort of ideal of reasonableness, which is reflected in the way we forecast our own reactions (made most clear in our mistaken forecasts). What is notably absent from this picture is the idea that there is a substantive first-personal or subjective element to perspective taking that is its *sine non qua*. It is not the fact that I imagine that *I* am in your situation that moves me; it is knowledge of what your situation involves that does so. I cannot, of course, exclude that there is *anything* distinctively subjective about perspective taking that makes it a special kind of activity. But I believe that, for now, I have provided good reasons for us to think that subjectivity is a bit of a red herring when it comes to understanding the distinctive contribution of perspective taking to empathizing with others.

Bibliography

Amir, O.; Ariely, D. and Mazar, N. 2008. The Dishonesty of Honest People: A Theory of Self-Concept Maintenance. *Journal of Marketing Research*, 45, 633–4.

Batson. C. D. 1991. *The Altruism Question: Toward a Social-Psychological Answer*. Hove, UK: Lawrence Erlbaum Ass.

2011. *Altruism in Humans*. New York: Oxford University Press.

Batson, C. D.; Duncan, B. D.; Ackerman, P.; Buckley, T. and Birch, K. 1981. Is Empathic Emotion a Source of Altruistic Motivation? *Journal of Personality and Social Psychology*, 40, 290–302.

Batson, C. D.; Early, S., and Salvarini, G. 1997. Perspective Taking: Imagining How Another Feels versus Imagining How You Would Feel. *Personality and Social Psychology Bulletin*, 23, 751–8.

Batson, C. D.; Eklund, J. H.; Chermok, V. L.; Hoyt, J. L. and Ortiz, B. G. 2007. An Additional Antecedent of Empathic Concern: Valuing the Welfare of the Person in Need. *Journal of Personality and Social Psychology*, 93, 65–74.

Batson, C. D.; O'Quinn, K.; Fultz, J.; Vanderpas, M. and Isen, A. M. 1983. Influence of Self-Reported Distress and Empathy on Egoistic Versus Altruistic Motivation to Help. *Journal of Personality and Social Psychology*, 45, 706–18.

Bechara, A.; Damasio, A. R.; Damasio, H. and Anderson, S. W. 1994. Insensitivity to Future Consequences Following Damage to Human Prefrontal Cortex. *Cognition*, 50, 7–15.

Bechara, A.; Tranel, D.; Damasio, H. and Damasio, A. R. 1996. Failure to Respond Autonomically to Anticipated Future Outcomes Following Damage to Prefrontal Cortex. *Cerebral Cortex*, 6, 215–25.

Beese, A. and Morley, S. 1993. Memory for Acute Pain Experience Is Specifically Inaccurate but Generally Reliable. *Pain*, 53, 183–9.

Biderman, A. 1960. Social-Psychological Needs and Involuntary Behavior as Illustrated by Compliance in Interrogation. *Sociometry*, 23, 120–47.

Bierbrauer, G. 1979. Why Did He Do It? Attribution of Obedience and the Phenomenon of Dispositional Bias. *European Journal of Social Psychology*, 9, 67–84.

Bisiach, E. and Luzzatti, C. 1978. Unilateral Neglect of Representational Space. *Cortex*, 14, 129–33.

Breckler, S. 1994. Memory for the Experience of Donating Blood: Just How Bad Was It? *Basic and Applied Social Psychology*, 15, 467–88.

Buehler, R.; Griffin, D. and Ross, M. 1995. Exploring the "Planning Fallacy": Why People Underestimate Their Task Completion Times. *Journal of Personality and Social Psychology*, 67, 366–81.

Chambers, J. R. and Davis, M. H. 2012. The Role of the Self in Perspective Taking and Empathy: Ease of Self-Simulation as a Heuristic for Inferring Empathic Feelings. *Social Cognition*, 30, 153–80.

Christensen-Szalanski, J. 1984. Discount Functions and the Measurement of Patients' Values: Women's Decisions during Childbirth. *Medical Decision Making*, 44, 47–58.

Damasio, A. 1994. *Descartes' Error: Emotion, Reason, and the Human Brain*. New York: Grosset/Putnam.

1999. *The Feeling of What Happens*. London: William Heineman.

Davidson, D. 2001. *Essays on Actions and Events*. Oxford: Clarendon Press.

Davies, M. and Stone, T. 1998. Folk Psychology and Mental Simulation. In: A. O'Hear (ed.), *Current Issues in Philosophy of Mind: Royal Institute of Philosophy Supplement: 43*. Cambridge: Cambridge University Press, 53–82.

Davis, M. H. 1994. *Empathy: A Social Psychological Approach*. Boulder, CO: Westview Press.

Davis, M. H.; Soderlund, T.; Cole, J.; Gadol, E.; Kute, M.; Myers, M. and Weihing, J. 2004. Cognitions Associated with Attempts to Empathize: How

Do We Imagine the Perspective of Another? *Personality and Social Psychology Bulletin,* 30, 1625–35.

Decety, J.; Chen, C.; Harenski, C. L. and Kiehl, K. A. 2013. An fMRI Study of Affective Perspective Taking in Individuals with Psychopathy: Imagining Another in Pain Does Not Evoke Empathy. *Frontiers of Human Neuroscience,* 7, 489.

Dennett, D. C. 1987. *The Intentional Stance.* Cambridge, MA: MIT Press.

Eisenberg, N. and Fabes, R. A. 1990. Empathy: Conceptualization, Measurement, and Relation to Prosocial Behavior. *Motivation and Emotion,* 14, 131–49.

Epley, N. 2014. *Mindwise: How We Understand What Others Think, Believe, Feel, and Want.* New York: Alfred A. Knopf.

Fischhoff, B. 1975. Hindsight ≠ Foresight: The Effect of Outcome Knowledge on Judgment under Uncertainty. *Journal of Experimental Psychology: Human Perception and Performance,* 1, 288–99.

Galinsky, A. D. and Moskowitz, G. B. 2000. Perspective-Taking: Decreasing Stereotype Expression, Stereotype Accessibility, and In-Group Favoritism. *Journal of Personality and Social Psychology,* 78, 708–24.

Galper, R. E. 1976. Turning Observers into Actors: Differential Causal Attributions as a Function of Empathy. *Journal of Research in Personality,* 10, 328–35.

Gardner, E. and Lowinson, J. 1993. Drug Craving and Positive/Negative Hedonic Brain Substrates Activated by Addictive Drugs. *Seminars in the Neurosciences,* 5, 359–68.

Gilbert, D. and Wilson, T. 2000. Miswanting: Some Problems in the Forecasting of Future Affective States. In: J. Forgas (ed.), *Feeling and Thinking: The Role of Affect in Social Cognition.* New York: Cambridge University Press, 178–98.

Gilbert, D.; Gill, M. and Wilson, T. 2002. The Future Is Now: Temporal Correction in Affective Forecasting. *Organizational Behavior and Human Decision Processes,* 88, 430–44.

Goldman, A. 1995. Empathy, Mind, and Morals. In: M. Davies and T. Stone (eds.), *Mental Simulation. Evaluations and Applications.* Oxford: Blackwell, 185–208.

2006. *Simulating Minds: The Philosophy, Psychology, and Neuroscience of Mindreading.* New York: Oxford University Press.

Hart, T. C. and Miethe, T. D. 2008. Exploring Bystander Presence and Intervention in Non-Fatal Violent Victimization: When Does Helping Really Help? *Violence and Victims,* 23, 637–51.

Hatfield, E.; Cacioppo, J. T., and Rapson, R. L. 1994. *Emotional Contagion.* New York: Cambridge University Press.

Heal, J. 1986. Replication and Functionalism. In: J. Butterfield: (ed.), *Language, Mind and Logic.* Cambridge: Cambridge University Press, 135–50.

1998. Understanding Other Minds from the Inside. In: A. O'Hear (ed.), *Current Issues in Philosophy of Mind: Royal Institute of Philosophy Supplement: 43.* Cambridge: Cambridge University Press, 83–99.

Hoffman, M. 2000. *Empathy and Moral Development.* Cambridge: Cambridge University Press.

Kahneman, D.; Knetsch, J. L. and Thaler, R. H. 1991. Anomalies: The Endowment Effect, Loss Aversion, and Status quo Bias. *Journal of Economic Perspectives*, 5, 193–206.

Kind, A. Forthcoming. How Imagination Leads to Knowledge. In: F. Dorsch and F. Macpherson: (eds.), *Perceptual Memory and Perceptual Imagination*. Oxford University Press.

Kosslyn, S. M.; Thompson, W. L. and Ganis, G. 2006. *The Case for Mental Imagery*. Oxford: Oxford University Press.

Lamm, C.; Batson, C. D. and Decety, J. 2007. The Neural Substrate of Human Empathy: Effects of Perspective-Taking and Cognitive Appraisals. *Journal of Cognitive Neuroscience*, 19, 42–58.

Latané, B. and Darley, J. 1970. *The Unresponsive Bystander: Why Doesn't He Help?* New York: Century Appleton-Crofts.

Loewenstein, G. 1996. Out of Control: Visceral Influences on Behavior. *Organizational Behavior and Human Decision Processes*, 65, 272–92.

Maibom, H. L. 2007. The Presence of Others. *Philosophical Studies*, 132, 161–90.

—— 2014. Knowing What We Are Doing. In: J. D'Arms and D. Jacobson (eds.), *Moral Psychology and Human Agency: Philosophical Essay on the Science of Ethics*. New York: Oxford University Press, 108–22.

—— Forthcoming. Knowing Me, Knowing You: Failure to Forecast and the Empathic Imagination. In: A. Kind and P. Kung (eds.), *Knowledge through Imagination*. New York: Oxford University Press.

Malle, B. F. 2006. The Actor-Observer Asymmetry in Attribution: A (Surprising) Meta-Analysis. *Psychological Bulletin*, 132, 895–919.

Mazar, N. and Ariely, D. 2006 Dishonesty in Everyday Life and Its Policy Implications. *Journal of Public Policy and Marketing*, 25, 117–26.

Michelon, P. and Zachs, J. M. 2006. Two Kinds of Visual Perspective Taking. *Perception and Psychophysics*, 68, 327–37.

Milgram, S. 1963. Behavioral Study of Obedience. *Journal of Abnormal Social Psychology*, 67, 371–8.

—— 1974. *Obedience to Authority*. New York: Harper Collins.

Morley, S. 1993. Vivid Memory for "Everyday" Pains. *Pain*, 55, 55–62.

Myers, M. W.; Laurent, S. M. and Hodges, S. D. 2014. Perspective Taking Instructions and Self–Other Overlap: Different Motives for Helping. *Motivation and Emotion*, 38, 224–34.

Negd, M.; Mallan, K. M., and Lipp, O. V. 2011. The Role of Anxiety and Perspective-Taking Strategy on Affective Empathic Responses. *Behaviour Research and Therapy*, 49, 852–7.

Nisbett, R. E.; Caputo, C.; Legant, P. and Mareck, J. 1973. Behavior as Seen by the Actor and as Seen by the Observer, *Journal of Personality and Social Psychology*, 27, 154–64.

Nisbett, R. and Wilson, T. 1977. Telling More than We Can Know: Verbal Reports on Mental Processes. *Psychological Review*, 84, 231–59.

Osiatynski, W. 1992. *Choroba Kontroli [The Disease of Control]*. Warsaw: Instytut Psychiatrii i Neuorologii.

Quoidbach, J.; Gilbert, D. and Wilson, T. 2013. The End of History Illusion. *Science*, 339, 96–8.

Read, D. and van Leeuwen, B. 1998. Predicting Hunger: The Effects of Appetite and Delay on Choice. *Organization Behavior and Human Decision Processes*, 76, 189–205.

Seneca, L. A. 1995. On Anger. In: *Seneca: Moral and Political Essays* (J. M. Cooper and J. F. Procopé, ed. and transl.). Cambridge: Cambridge University Press.

Shakespeare, W. 1600/1993. *A Midsummer Night's Dream.* shakespeare.mit.edu/midsummer/full.html (accessed July 2016).

Sieff, E.; Dawes, R. and Loewenstein, G. 1999. Anticipated versus Actual Reaction to HIV Test Results. *American Journal of Psychology*, 112, 297–311.

Singer, T. and Lamm, C. 2009. The Social Neuroscience of Empathy. *The Year in Cognitive Neuroscience: Annals of the New York Academy of Sciences*, 1156, 81–96.

Sober, E. and Wilson, D. S. 1998. *Unto Others.* Cambridge, MA: Harvard University Press.

Stotland, E. 1969. *Exploratory Investigations of Empathy.* In: L. Berkowitz (ed.), *Advances in Experimental Social Psychology*, 4, 271–314.

Teper, R.; Inzlit, M. and Page-Gould, E. 2011. Are We More Moral than We Think? Exploring the Role of Affect in Moral Behavior and Moral Forecasting. *Psychological Science*, 22, 553–8.

Terry, R. and Gijsbers, K. 2000. Memory for the Quantitative and Qualitative Aspects of Labour Pain: A Preliminary Study. *Journal of Reproductive and Infant Psychology*, 18, 143–52.

Van Boven, L. and Loewenstein, G. 2003. Social Projection of Transient Drive States. *Personality and Social Psychology Bulletin*, 29, 1159–68.

Van Boven, L.; Dunning, D. and Loewenstein, G. 2000. Egocentric Empathy Gaps between Owners and Buyers: Misperceptions of the Endowment Effect. *Journal of Personality and Social Psychology*, 79, 66–76.

Van Boven, L.; Kane, J., and McGraw. A. P. 2009. Temporally Asymmetric Constraints on Mental Simulation: Retrospection Is More Constrained than Prospection. In: K. D. Markman, W. M. P. Klein and J. A. Suhr (eds.), *Handbook of Imagination and Mental Simulation.* New York: Psychology Press, 131–47.

Van Boven, L.; Loewenstein, G.; Welch, E. and Dunning, D. 2012. The Illusion of Courage in Self-Predictions: Mispredicting One's Own Behavior in Embarrassing Situations. *Journal of Behavioral Decision Making*, 25, 1–12.

Vorauer, J. D.; Martens, V. and Sasaki, S. J. 2009. When Trying to Understand Detracts from Trying to Behave: Effects of Perspective Taking in Intergroup Interactions. *Journal of Personality and Social Psychology*, 96, 811–27.

Vorauer, J. D. and Quesnel, M. 2013. You Don't Really Love Me, Do You? Negative Effects of Imagine-Other Perspective-Taking on Lower Self-Esteem Individual's Relation Wellbeing. *Personality and Social Psychology Bulletin*, 39, 1428–40.

Vorauer, J. D. and Sasaki, S. J. 2014. Distinct Effects of Imagine-Other versus Imagine-Self Perspective Taking on Prejudice Reduction. *Social Cognition*, 32, 130–47.

Vorauer, J. D. and Sucharyna, T. A. 2013. Potential Negative Effects of Perspective Taking Efforts in the Context of Close Relationships: Increased

Bias and Reduced Satisfaction. *Journal of Personality and Social Psychology*, 104, 70–86.

Wilson, T. and Gilbert, D. 2005. Knowing What to Want. *Current Directions in Psychological Science*, 14, 131–4.

Wilson, T.; Wheatley, T.; Meyers, J.; Gilbert, D. and Axsom, D. 2000. Focalism: A Source of Durability Bias in Affective Forecasting. *Journal of Personality and Social Psychology*, 78, 821–36.

Wirtz, D.; Kruger, J.; Napa Scollon, C. K. and Diener, E. 2003. What to Do on Spring Break? The Role of Predicted, Online, and Remembered Experience in Future Choice. *Psychological Science*, 14, 520–4.

Woodzicka, J. and LaFrance, M. 2001. Real versus Imagined Gender Harassment. *Journal of Social Issues*, 57, 15–30.

5 Empathy as an Instinct

Michael Slote

There has been an enormous amount of interest in empathy over the past decade or so, and not just among academics and researchers, but for the general public as well. Frans de Waal has even titled one of his books *The Age of Empathy*, and that seems far from inappropriate for a book on empathy (de Waal 2009). (To be honest, I had hoped to use that title myself before I found that de Waal had beat me to it.)

But however much interest there has been in empathy in academic circles and among practicing psychologists, I think some of the most important conceptual and empirical facts about empathy have not previously come to light. And the present chapter will try to make the case for this conclusion by actually bringing out aspects of empathy that have so far not been paid proper attention (except, in one instance and only in passing, by David Hume). But before I try to establish these conclusions and bring the new aspects of empathy to light, I think I should make some distinctions that are fairly widely known but represent the background to what I shall be arguing for here.

1

To begin with, there is the distinction between empathy and sympathy, which, partly thanks to Bill Clinton, has become a fairly familiar and largely settled matter. When Clinton said, "I feel your pain," he was implicitly referring to what we now tend to think of as empathy; and sympathy, by contrast, is not so much a matter of feeling someone's pain as of feeling bad or regretful *about* the pain someone is feeling. Now most psychologists and many philosophers will tell you that there is some kind of empirical connection between empathy and sympathy. Martin Hoffman, I, and others have subscribed to the view that empathy helps to power and sustain sympathy and sympathetic concern for others and to its presumable implication that helping to increase or strengthen a child's empathy makes the child more capable of sympathetic concern for or altruism toward others (Hoffman 2000; Slote 2010). But we have assumed that the connection between empathy and sympathy is an empirical matter, one that psychological research seems on the whole to support, and I now believe that this connection isn't in fact empirical. However, I don't propose to consider this issue further till after I have discussed the aspect of empathy that will be the main focus of this chapter: its function, arguably, as a human instinct.

But this main theme of the present chapter also requires some stage setting. We have to remember, to begin with, that most researchers and philosophers conceive there to be two kinds of empathy (at least). One kind involves deliberately putting oneself into the head (or shoes) of another person and is called "projective empathy" ("simulation" is another term for this kind of empathy). But there is also the kind of empathy Hume spoke of when he said that the feelings or attitudes of one person can infuse themselves into another or spread by contagion from one person to another. Hume didn't have the term "empathy" and spoke of sympathy in this connection, but nowadays the phenomenon Hume described is spoken of as a kind of empathy that differs from projective empathy because it involves the spread of emotion. This different, Humean kind of empathy is sometimes referred to as "emotional empathy," "associative empathy," or "receptive empathy"; and the receptivity involved here clearly distinguishes this kind of empathy from the projective type. In projection, we (in masculine fashion?) put ourselves into the shoes or mind of another. In emotional/associative/receptive empathy, we (in a traditionally feminine way?) receive or are invaded/flooded by the emotions or attitudes of another (it is generally recognized that this often may require the empathizer to already have certain relevant concepts and cognitive abilities). So there seems to be something more passive or closer to passive about emotional empathy, and this relates to another property commonly ascribed to receptive or emotional empathy: namely, that it occurs in or to someone without that person's intending for it to occur or trying to make it occur and, indeed, without the empathizer often being consciously aware of the empathic process going on within them. Receptive empathy is typically seen not as a psychological result or feeling, but as a psychological mechanism or process for creating feelings that isn't deliberate, and although I too have regarded such empathy in that light, I think and shall argue here that this is a mistake.

Projective empathy needn't involve emotional involvement, and that is why psychopaths are typically thought to be quite capable of projective empathy: they are quite good at getting into the heads of their intended victims in a cold and unemotional way. Receptive empathy does involve emotional involvement, and that is a contrast I don't want to question. But the idea that the mechanism of receptive/emotional empathy typically occurs without any volition or desire to that effect being present in the empathizer now seems to me to be incorrect. Projective empathy may be deliberate and intentional, but something like this is also true, I believe, of emotional empathy, and so if I am not mistaken, the two basic kinds of empathy are more closely related than I and others have realized. I want to argue that empathy of the emotional kind is or involves an instinct for empathizing, but in order to make the case for this conclusion I think I need to generalize our discussion by showing that empathy is just one of many *nonegoistic* instincts or basic desires/dispositions/penchants that human beings are subject to (or blessed with).

2

In order to accomplish all this, I need to bring in the work of psychologist Abraham Maslow. In *Motivation and Personality* and other works, Maslow argued for a hierarchy of instincts or basic motives operating in human life, and though I don't want to rely on his idea of a hierarchy (even some of his followers have questioned this), I do think Maslow pointed to some human instincts that others hadn't (in print) previously identified (Maslow 1954). Maslow held that the need/desire for love, the need/desire to belong, and the need/desire for the esteem or approval of others were basic to human psychology, not reducible, that is, to more basic tissue needs. There doesn't seem to be anything selfish or egoistic about these motives because they place an enormous intrinsic importance on other people. The person, for example, who seeks or needs the approval of others typically doesn't do so (merely) in order to make more money and so on; we simply don't like being disapproved of or disesteemed, and this means that other people are intrinsically important to us in a way that seems incompatible with a purely egoistic and self-centered psychology.

Now Maslow also spoke of a basic need for self-actualization, but I am not going to discuss this need here because I find Maslow's discussion of it hard to follow and less than convincing. But I do want to add some further instincts to Maslow's list, and this will help us toward the idea that empathy is an instinct. First, human beings seem to have a basic need or desire for proximity with other human beings (the various institutions and practices of social media don't, I think, call this assumption into question). And this is an instinct we share with other animals, as with the flocking behavior of sheep, birds, and such. Human contact is something we don't want/wish to be deprived of for too long, and this seems to be something that runs rather deep in us.

But we also, I believe, have an instinct or deep desire for imitating others. Very young children are always imitating those around them, and of course one can see how such an instinct would be evolutionarily useful to humans as a species. And there are instincts of imitation in other animals, even in reptiles, that help show how basic this phenomenon is in ourselves. In so-called lower animals, imitation is largely a matter of replicating behavior, but in us humans and certain other species, there can also be imitation of the mental states of others, and I believe receptive/emotional empathy is one form of such psychological imitation. In other words, just as I believe that a drive or impetus toward the imitation of behavior can have its evolutionary uses, I think a drive toward mental imitation can also be useful, and our capacity and tendency to take in the feelings, attitudes, and such of others is therefore, I think, just one instance of the usefulness of imitation in animal life. It represents an evolutionary advance over the ability to imitate sheer behavior or bodily motions (or directions of motion), and I shall say more about how and why such an advance might have occurred a bit later in this chapter. But for now I think I need to focus on how such a view of emotional empathy contrasts with, but is superior to, the received notion that such empathy isn't willed or sought after and is basically passive.

First, a conceptual point. Passivity isn't the same thing as receptivity, and to say, as so many have, that emotional/associative empathy shows us as receptive is absolutely not to say that it shows us as passive. The very term "receptive" connotes a certain disposition toward or penchant for receiving that passivity rules out altogether, so the fact that we have naturally characterized emotional empathy as receptive actually points toward the idea of an instinct or penchant for such empathy. To see empathy (and I mean emotional empathy) as involving receptivity is to see it as more like listening than like hearing, and listening involves an eagerness or desire for hearing, not just the capacity or tendency to hear. But this characteristically more active or motivated side of empathy has been ignored in the psychological literature on empathy, and the earlier history of discussions of empathy also shows an almost total failure to reckon with the "listening side" of empathy.

Thus Confucius in the *Analects* (XII.19.) was the first thinker we have any record of describing what we would nowadays call a process or processes of empathy (he didn't have the term, of course). He described the influence a ruler's virtue would have on his subjects' virtue via the metaphor of grass bending as the wind blows through it, and this suggests that the subjects' intake and eventual exemplification of virtue is pretty much entirely a passive matter. And we get a similar implication from Hume's descriptions of what he called sympathy and we would call empathy as involving an infusion of one person's feeling into another person and/or the contagion of feeling from one person to another. However, Hume, almost inconsistently with these just-mentioned characterizations, had another way of describing emotional empathy that fits in better, much better, with the idea of empathy as a nonpassive but receptive instinct. In the famous "Of the Love of Fame" section of the *Treatise of Human Nature*, he says that we tend to *embrace* the sentiments and opinions of others, and this is certainly an active-sounding verb that suggests, and more than suggests, that humans are motivated and even eager to take in the feelings, attitudes, and sentiments of others.

3

So I propose that we think of emotional empathy as involving a receptivity that has a motivational aspect, that is based in a certain penchant for or instinct of psychological imitation that is a more advanced form of the instinctual behavioral imitation we find through large portions of the animal kingdom. (An animal needn't be aware of or self-conscious about having or acting on such a penchant or instinct.) But I would like to say more about possible evolutionary origins. The case for seeing empathy as an instinct partly depends on conceptual points but can also be strengthened by situating empathy within a wider range of similar instincts and by describing how some of those instincts could have evolved out of others. And let me propose that emotional empathy can sensibly be seen as evolutionarily developing out of two other instincts or basic desires we spoke of earlier: the desire/need for proximity to conspecifics and the desire/need to imitate conspecifics.

As Hume noted in the *Treatise* and recent psychology tends to assume, empathy is easier when the "target" of empathy is close by. So the evolution of empathy may well depend on the previous emergence of an instinct or basic desire for proximity to conspecifics. But imitation too depends for the most part on the proximity required for observing or perceiving what another creature is doing, so I propose that the evolution of empathy can be seen as a two-stage or two-tier process. A desire for proximity or flocking has to have evolutionary advantages for certain groups and then provide the launching pad for a form of instinct that seems to depend on proximity, namely, imitation, and, of course, imitation must afford evolutionary advantages too. But, then, given what has been said in the preceding, empathy can be seen as a "higher" form of imitation that affords the creatures capable of such mental imitation an evolutionary advantage over and above the advantage of being able and disposed to imitate behavior.

Now the tendency toward group flocking and the drive toward proximity seem to have emerged fairly early on in the evolution of vertebrates. Fish school together, but some species of reptiles also seek proximity with one another: both crocodiles and marine iguanas tend to sun themselves together in groups. The idea that living in groups affords evolutionary advantages is hardly a new one, and I don't propose to offer or discuss any arguments to that effect here. And in a certain sense, living or spending time together in groups, schools, or flocks already represents a form of imitation. But if this is imitation, it isn't yet an imitation of anything other than behavior, and it seems fairly clear that there are creatures capable of imitation that aren't capable of empathy. There is imitation in reptiles apart from the sunning behavior, as when the red-footed tortoise learns a task more easily after it has observed a conspecific master that task (Wilkinson et al. 2010). But it is generally held that empathy occurs only in mammalian and perhaps avian species. So empathy emerges later in evolutionary terms than imitation in general does, but it seems clear that both imitative behavior and imitative empathy afford evolutionary advantages.

A creature that can imitate a conspecific can quickly learn from that conspecific what would have taken a long process of effortful trial and error for it to learn on its own. And if the skills or useful habits of a group can transmit themselves via imitation throughout a group and to the younger members of the group in particular, the group will likely thrive better, and it will allow its members to thrive better as well. (I realize this is an appeal to "group selection," but such an appeal is not essential to my argument.) And similar points apply to empathy, to the penchant or drive toward mental imitation. If it is an advantage to be able to replicate the useful habits of one's parents or elders, wouldn't it also be useful, to individuals (and to the groups composed of such individuals), to be able to empathically imbibe what older members of the group have learned from experience (e.g., about dangers or opportunities), that is, imbibe their informed attitudes and cognitive preferences? So I think we at this point have a picture of how three of the basic desires or instincts spoken of in the preceding may relate to one another in evolutionary terms. The desire for proximity and a desire to imitate are both useful, and imitation can more readily occur in conditions of proximity to conspecifics. Similarly, the desire/instinct for imitation and the desire/instinct for empathically taking in others' psychological states are both useful in evolutionary terms, and empathy as an instinct of psychological imitation can more readily occur or emerge when and where conspecifics seek out each other's company and are capable of the simpler tasks involved in imitating behavior.

4

But I have been ignoring the role that sympathy and its development may play in the phylogenetic development of empathy. Many have argued that sympathy has adaptive advantages both for individuals and for the groups that include such individuals, and, again, I don't propose to discuss or further support those arguments here. But there is also reason to believe that genuine sympathy and genuine altruism depend on the development or presence of emotional empathy. Projective empathy doesn't seem sufficient for altruism because psychopaths are capable of that kind of empathy, yet incapable of genuine sympathy or caring. And what they are lacking in seems precisely to be the capacity for emotional involvement and empathy with others.

In that case, emotional empathy may have emerged in the human species at least partly because of its necessary role in the evolutionarily advantageous development of human altruism (and morality to the extent it depends on altruism). But that is a point in or of evolutionary psychology, and, reversing engines if I may, I think it is also true that empathy plays a crucial ontogenetic role in the launching of individual altruism.

Let us assume that mothers and many fathers tend to have (instincts of) sympathy and concern for their offspring. Maternal instinct can be found in many reptiles (certain rattle snakes and crocodiles), and there is no need here to chart or attempt to chart the evolutionary processes whereby that instinct was shaped into the kind of solicitude for offspring that is so distinctive of mammalian species (involving, as it does, both close physical proximity and breastfeeding). But I want to consider now how children (ontogenetically) develop sympathetic concern for or altruism toward others, and I think this to at least some extent involves both the presence of (childbirth-triggered) maternal instinct and an inborn capacity/disposition for empathy on the part of the child. We know that newborn babies in the hospital tend to start crying when other babies start crying, and this seems to be a kind of primitive empathic response (Hoffman 2000). But when a child has a clearer sense of its own identity as different from other people around him (this can be in the second year of life), a capacity for genuine empathy exists or starts to exist, and for reasons I shall be more specific about in the following, empathy with others automatically supports sympathy and altruism toward others. This works from the original point of view of the child, but also occurs when the child empathically takes in and models his or her parents' sympathy for or caring attitudes toward third parties. But, in addition to these well-known ways in which empathy can lead to greater sympathy in children and the adults they eventually become, I think that childhood or even infant empathy operates on (or responds to) maternal or parental love in a way that constitutes or results in a strengthened capacity and disposition for sympathy and concern for others. And this may be the ontogenetically earliest way in which empathy gears us toward sympathy and altruism. Let me explain how this may be possible.

If the infant or young child has a capacity for empathy, then they can and presumably will empathically take in their mother's solicitude for them, their mother's love. Something similar may happen with fathers and their children, but the sheer proximity that breastfeeding requires would clearly facilitate the empathic transmission of feelings felt toward the child. Now think what the child must take in if they are taking in their mother's sympathetic solicitude toward them. The mother feels love *for her child*, and presumably the child takes this in as love directed toward herself. The resultant state will to that extent be or involve a sense of self-love or even self-esteem (the loving parent thinks his or her child is *wonderful*). But it will involve more. For what the mother feels toward her child is also *sympathy*. She is in a state that can be characterized as sympathetic, and if the child imbibes the mother's sympathy as sympathy (as the sympathetic state, felt toward another, that it is), then they will start feeling a kind of sympathy too. The mother's sympathy may be directed toward the child, but the fact that it is directed toward someone other than the mother, that it is other-directed, is also part of its intentionality. I think that the child can take this intentionality in through their capacity for empathy and that when the child does so, he or she too becomes sympathetic in an other-directed way.

Now the sympathy a child who feels loved feels will in its primary exemplification be focused back on his mother (as a kind of primal gratitude), but sympathy and love (like other emotions) have a tendency to spread from their original targets to other objects. So one way in which sympathy and altruism can develop is through the child's empathic identification with the sympathy his or her mother (or father) feels toward the child. But, of course, as I have just indicated, the sheer capacity for empathy can help us develop sympathy and altruism somewhat independently of how we are relating to our parents. And it is time for me to say more about how this can and does happen. I earlier mentioned the prevalent assumption that the connection between empathy and sympathy/altruism is an empirical (and contingent) one and mentioned that I was now convinced that the connection is actually conceptual. It is time now for me to try to convince you of this new way of seeing things.

Empathy can take in the positive or negative quality of someone else's feelings or attitudes, but it can and does also take in the intentionality of the other's mental state. The father who is bitten by his daughter's enthusiasm for stamp collecting doesn't just feel some unfocused state of (positive) enthusiasm. He feels or comes to feel enthusiasm for stamp collecting. And by the same token, when we take in, by a kind of empathic osmosis, our parents' attitude toward Martin Luther, the attitude we come to have has an intentional object, the same object (at least in normal cases) that our parents' attitude has. But then consider what typically happens when I feel your pain, when I feel your distress at the pain you are experiencing. Your distress is focused on the pain(ful sensation) you feel, and on conceptual grounds distress at the existence of something involves a motivation to get rid of it. So if I take in your pain distress, and it is directed at the same intentional object to which your pain distress is directed, then I am distressed at your pain (not at any potential or actual pain of my own), and on the same conceptual grounds just mentioned, this means that I have some motivation to help get rid of your pain. And the sheer desire to help another get rid of their pain seems to be altruistic and to involve what (again on conceptual grounds) would have to be characterized as sympathy and sympathetic concern for them or for their plight. So empathy in such cases necessarily involves sympathetic concern, and this connection between empathy and sympathy or altruism is thus not an empirical one.

Kant tells us that all knowledge begins with experience but isn't all based on experience, and the knowledge or belief that empathy is correlated with sympathy may be acquired in empirical ways. But once we think about the concepts involved, we can see that the connection is tighter than we may initially have imagined. And this means too that what was said in evolutionary psychological terms about the emergence of empathy in relation to sympathy has to be conceived in a certain way. When emotional/receptive empathy evolves, it brings cognitive benefits that I spoke of in the preceding. But when it evolves, it also, *ipso facto*, and without any other or further evolutionary developments, brings with it any benefits that sympathetic concern for others may bring to individuals and their societies. So if, as so many have assumed, there is an evolutionary advantage to having sympathy for others, that is an advantage that the emergence of emotional empathy affords us all on its own.

References

De Waal, F. B. M. 2009. *The Age of Empathy*. New York: Random House.
Hoffman, M. 2000. *Empathy and Moral Development: Implications for Caring and Justice*. Cambridge: Cambridge University Press.
Maslow, A. H. 1954. *Motivation and Personality*. New York: Harper and Row.
Slote, M. 2010. *Moral Sentimentalism*. New York: Oxford University Press.
Wilkinson, A.; Kuenstner, K.; Mueller, J. and Huber, L. 2010. Social Learning in a Non-Social Reptile (Geochelone carbonaria). *Biology Letters*, 6, 614–16.

6 A Moral Account of Empathy and Fellow Feeling

Lawrence Blum

It seems clear that in psychology and philosophy there is no single plausible conception of "empathy," either historically or if we confine ourselves to the present (Batson 2011; Coplan 2011). What I aim to do in this chapter is to present a conception of empathy that treats it more explicitly as a moral phenomenon than do many other current views. This moral conception is linked with its verbal form "empathize," so that "to empathize with" roughly means "to have empathy with or for," in the moral sense I shall be developing. Another way to put the point is to say that I see empathy as a species of "fellow feeling," of which other forms are compassion, concern, sympathy, care, and commiseration. All are affective phenomena that take an intentional object, the other person with respect to her well-being, and are generally seen as morally worthy phenomena.

I will begin with a discussion of the great philosopher of fellow feeling, Max Scheler. A consideration of Scheler will help to keep the moral character of fellow feeling, and empathy specifically, in focus. At the same time, Scheler's conception fails to give a full and accurate account of the moral character of fellow feeling and specifically of empathy.

I argue that this character has three components: (1) motivating helping behavior, (2) a disposition to help (even when one is unable to help in the given situation), and (3) a recognition or acknowledgment of the other as someone whose well-being is valuable. The latter value is a species of a larger category that includes other types of recognition or acknowledgment, for example, of accomplishments or standing as an equal citizen, not directly focused on the other's well-being.

I reject the view that all beneficent motivation is grounded in fellow feeling (and specifically in empathy) by discussing various other motivations that can produce beneficent behavior (grounded in duty, moral perception, religion, or a desire to help the other). I also argue that many currently influential accounts of empathy (Darwall, Prinz, Eisenberg, Hoffman) fail to capture these three features, either because they do not aspire to be moral accounts at all, or do so but fail to give the full picture.

I especially reject the view that empathy means having the same feeling state as the other. I then examine the assumption made by most accounts of empathy (including Scheler's of fellow feeling generally) that its object is a feeling state of the other. I argue, drawing on Hoffman, that its object is rather the situation of the other with respect to his well-being.

Finally, I tentatively explore the difference between different forms of fellow feeling, in particular rejecting the popular view that empathy differs from sympathy in requiring the same feeling in the subject and object, while the latter involves a concern that does not require this alignment.

1. Max Scheler

Max Scheler was a German philosopher influenced by the phenomenological tradition. His *The Nature of Sympathy (Wesen und Formen der Sympathie)*, first published in 1913 with a fifth and final edition in 1948, is essential to any exploration of fellow feeling (Scheler 1948). This work has been less influential in Anglo-American moral psychology concerning fellow feeling than it deserves to be. Scheler has some continuity with Schopenhauer, another philosopher whose work on compassion and morality is insufficiently attended to today. One way to characterize the difference between the Schopenhauerian/Schelerian tradition and that which is currently dominant is that Anglo-American philosophers today have followed Adam Smith and especially David Hume in considering fellow feeling – especially sympathy but also empathy – primarily in relation to *moral judgment*. Their view has been called "(moral) sentimentalism." By contrast, Schopenhauer and Scheler are interested in the connection between fellow feeling and moral motivation, or moral character more generally, not so much with moral judgment.[1] In a sense, Schopenhauer and Scheler are in this way closer to the work of social psychologists such as Eisenberg, Hoffman, and Batson, who locate the primary moral significance of empathy in its relation to "prosocial" motivation (Eisenberg and Miller 1987; Hoffman 2000; Batson 2011).

Scheler sharply differentiates fellow feeling from three other phenomena involving the emotional states of others. One is apprehending the emotional state of others. He thinks that apprehension is a prelude to and a necessary condition for fellow feeling. One first understands that

[1] Smith and Hume are interested in motivational matters also, but this aspect of their thought has played less of a role in debates within contemporary Anglo-American neosentimentalism. For an explicit critique of neosentimentalism (in the form it takes in Shaun Nichols's influential work), in favor of the Schopenhauerian and Schelerian tradition, see Blum 2011.

the other is in state X and then either does or does not come to have fellow feeling for the other with respect to state X. Scheler points out that the cruel person lacks fellow feeling but has an acute understanding and sensing of the quality of the other's experience, and this understanding indeed contributes to his cruelty as he savors the other's suffering (Scheler 1948, 13). As far as I can tell, Scheler nowhere presents a formal and comprehensive definition of fellow feeling, but he seems to see it as a feeling for the other in light of a prior understanding of her state of mind as related to her well-being.

Scheler often uses *commiseration (Mitleid)* as his central example of fellow feeling, although as he develops his view it seems clear that commiseration is only one type of fellow feeling among others. He uses it to illustrate a contrast with other processes and states of mind that others have seen as constituting fellow feeling. Scheler says that to commiserate is to be sorry *at another's sorrow as being his*, not one's own. This treating the other person as commiseration's intentional object is part of Scheler's way of distinguishing fellow feeling from any view that locates it in the mere feeling state of the agent, no matter how alike that state is to the feeling state of the other.

Scheler sharply distinguishes fellow feeling from a second phenomenon, that he calls "emotional infection," an idea that has been taken over in contemporary philosophy and psychology, where it is generally called "emotional contagion." Emotional infection is a transference of a state of feeling in another to the agent, as when the agent comes to a party and imbibes the affective, festive atmosphere of the party. Emotional infection by itself involves no knowledge on the part of the agent that the other is in this particular feeling state. The feeling state is just transferred (but not in the sense that it leaves the other, only that it jumps from the other to the agent). There is no feeling *for* the other but only a feeling in oneself that is the same as that in the other. This is why it is entirely different from fellow feeling.

Scheler also sharply distinguishes fellow feeling from what he calls "comparison," in which the agent imagines what he would feel if what the victim is going through happened to him. Scheler says this is not fellow feeling, partly because the other may well experience the same happenings quite differently from the agent: "Had it happened to me, with my character and temperament, it would not have been so bad; but being the sort of person he is, it is a serious matter for him" (Scheler 1948, 39).[2] It is also not fellow feeling because it does not take the other as its

---

[2] While I agree with Scheler that imagining oneself in the other's situation is not the same as imagining what the other himself feels, something that tends to get lost in Scheler's account is that imagining oneself into someone else's situation *can* be a tool for gaining an

intentional object, even though it involves envisioning the mental state of the other by imagining what one would feel in his place.

Scheler has some quite insightful things to say about other mental processes that contemporary philosophers and psychologists are not likely to see as examples of fellow feeling, but that Scheler sees as defective forms of it. In this way, he helps to bring out the distinctive character, and moral character, of (nondefective) fellow feeling. For example, he mentions someone who upon hearing of the distressed condition of another is put in a state of distress himself, abandoning (not necessarily intentionally) any reference to the other's state, except perhaps its recognition as what has caused his own distress. There remains no intentional focus on the distressed state of the other. Scheler emphasizes that such "personal distress," as psychologists (following Batson) tend to call it, can crowd out genuine fellow feeling for the other, and that the distress of others can lead to *either* reaction – fellow feeling or personal distress.

A different example of a distortion of fellow feeling, one drawing implicitly on psychoanalytical insights, is when the agent is so caught up in the moods, feelings, and experiences of the other that she no longer seems to lead a life of her own. This person lacks the clear sense of the differentiation between herself and the other that Scheler regards as a prerequisite of genuine fellow feeling. Again, one must feel the state of sorrow, hurt, depression, humiliation, and the like as something the other is going through, not oneself, in order for genuine fellow feeling to be present. This differentiation between self and other is generally emphasized by contemporary philosophers and psychologists as a requirement of empathy (Decety and Lamm 2009; Coplan 2011). But they tend to see the differentiation as a purely cognitive recognition – I recognize cognitively that you are a different person than I. While Scheler is not denying the cognitive aspect, his example of the person who lives as if she is living through the experiences of others shows that adequately distinguishing self and other is not purely cognitive, but also involves very complex emotional, attitudinal, and behavioral dispositions, not all of them conscious – the awareness and feeling of being oneself, of leading one's own life, of being "separate" from others (Scheler 1948, 44).

An excellent example of the sort of self/other confusion Scheler is pointing to is given by Anna Freud in *Ego and the Mechanisms of Defense*

---

understanding of what the other is going through (cf. Batson this volume). But in order for it to do so, that process has to be guided by a recognition that the other may feel differently from what oneself would feel. Such a recognition might, for example, encourage one to think about differences in personality and valuings between you and the other, differences that might affect differences in response to the given situation between oneself and the other.

(Freud 1936). Freud describes a patient of hers, a governess, who presents herself as having almost no wants and desires of her own, no personal projects to which she is strongly attached. Yet she is very persistent in promoting the desires and projects of others, either friends of hers, the children she is caring for, or men to whom she becomes attached. The governess exemplifies a kind of losing of self in the other that Scheler is pointing to. This challenge of self/other differentiation has also been emphasized by feminist psychologists and philosophers, such as Carol Gilligan and Marilyn Friedman, who see in it a peril to women in a male-dominated society – a pressure to give up their own wants in favor of others, especially men (Gilligan 1982; Friedman 1993).

Scheler sees this lived differentiation between self and other as a prerequisite for a key feature in the moral character of fellow feeling: "True fellow feeling is a genuine out-reaching and entry into the other person and his individual situation, a true and authentic transcendence of one's self" (Scheler 1948, 46). One must have a clear, lived sense of oneself as distinct from the other in order to engage in this transcendence of self.

2. Fellow Feeling and Commitment to/Responsiveness to Others' Well-Being

In getting clear on the moral character of fellow feeling, it is worth reminding ourselves that fellow feeling is not the only nonegoistic or moral motive that prompts us to help others. Although neither philosophers nor psychologists are generally tempted by the view that all moral motivation to help others is grounded in fellow feeling, it is still valuable to situate that motivation within this larger field. (I will call these "beneficent" motives – nonegoistic, moral motives that prompt furthering the good of others.)

Some beneficent motives may be of a Kantian nature – promoting others' well-being because of seeing oneself as having a duty of beneficence. The agent could do so because she is convinced of the Kantian view that we should always act out of rational, universalizable principles, and she sees the furthering of the welfare of others as such a principle. But she could also just regard herself as under a duty of beneficence without thinking about this in a Kantian/rational principle way.[3]

People can also act beneficently because they think God has commanded them to do so. I would regard this as a genuinely beneficent

---

[3] This more intuitionist conception of duty is actually in accord with one part of Kant's thinking, in that he thought the ordinary unreflective moral conscience involves believing we have certain duties, including that of beneficence, prior to recognizing explicitly that this is a universal, rational principle.

motive unless the person is really motivated by a reward he thinks is implicitly promised him by God, or by God's punishment if he failed to obey the commandments. It is perfectly coherent to be motivated by God's commands without having either of these egoistic motives.

Iris Murdoch suggests yet another way we can be motivated to help others without the intermediation of fellow feeling (Murdoch 1970b). She thinks we sometimes just see another person's need, and act out of this immediate perception of moral reality, as she puts it. She illustrates this in her novel *A Fairly Honorable Defeat*, where one character, Tallis, a white man, sees a black man threatened by some white thugs in a pub and immediately acts to help (Murdoch 1970a). Murdoch does not portray Tallis as acting out of duty, or out of a general rational principle. And, while someone else in the same situation could help the black man from such a motive, I think Murdoch is certainly right that we often act in an immediate way in response to a perceived need, without the intervention of fellow feeling (or of principle), although the immediacy does not by itself preclude fellow feeling. Murdoch's idea of "attention," which she draws from Simone Weil, helps her to articulate how this particular form of altruistic motivation operates.

Finally, we are often motivated to help others achieve their goals, but not by a plight that would elicit fellow feeling such as compassion or empathy. Suppose a colleague is writing a philosophy article and asks for my feedback on the article because she values my expertise in the area of the article. I might help her because I would like to help a colleague, or because she needs help, but not because her plight is distressful or concerning in a way that would elicit fellow feeling. Vaish and Warneken (2011) show that very young children, fourteen to eighteen months of age, can discern the intentions and goals of others and help others based on that discernment. For example, children who see someone try to hang clothes on a clothes line but drop a clothespin in doing so will often retrieve the clothespin and hand it to the person. Indeed, we quite frequently help people simply because they wish to attain some goal. As long as we regard the goal as worthy of attainment, we are capable of being motivated by recognition of their desire to attain it, and we need not have any fellow feeling toward the other in doing so.[4] Thus I think we should take seriously the Swedish early childhood developmentalist Eva Johansson's claim that it is doubtful whether empathy is

---

[4] I have argued elsewhere that the ability to be motivated by the plight of others to help them might require an emotion-based capacity that includes fellow feeling, even if it does not require an affective occurrence on each occasion of being so moved to action (Blum 2011, 186).

the most important basis of children's commitment to others' well-being (Johansson 2008). And this supports the view that helping behavior in adults need not be motivated by fellow feeling.

Thus fellow feeling is only one among a number of morally valuable motives that can prompt us to help others.

3. Fellow Feeling and Recognitional Attitudes

But the moral significance of fellow feeling does not reside solely in its conative status as motivating helping. We can see this by comparing fellow feeling with a group of attitudes that includes respect, recognition, acknowledgment, affirmation, and appreciation. I will (admittedly somewhat arbitrarily) refer to these as "recognitional" attitudes. Fellow feeling (and the different sentiments and emotions that constitute it) is engaged with the other's well-being. Fellow feeling responds to the other's situation of negative or positive well-being. Some species of fellow feeling, for example, compassion and concern, are confined to the other's (perceived) negative welfare. Others, such as empathy, may be directed to the other in light of her positive welfare; I can empathize with my friend's triumph or good fortune.

Recognitional attitudes are not engaged with welfare in this way. Some of them concern a particular status that we wish to be recognized or affirmed. For example, we wish our status as citizens of a polity shared with others to be recognized by those others and we wish it recognized that in this respect we are the equals of others. We can also desire that our human status be respected, recognized, or affirmed, and this recognition can sometimes be demanded of others. Sometimes, by contrast, the status that is appropriately recognized or affirmed is one we have attained through effort or the display of some excellence – for example, that we have completed a PhD or that we are a master carpenter. Or we can wish a particular identity component that is important to us, though not attained, or even always voluntarily adopted – racial, ethnic, gender, religious, sexual orientation, national, and so forth – to be acknowledged, recognized, or affirmed.

I will not attempt to characterize the differences among the items I have listed in the recognitional category, nor, as I said, their overall character. It is worth mentioning that in the recent Anglo-American tradition most attention among this group seems to have been paid to *respect*. This may have something to do with the impact of Kantianism in moral philosophy within this tradition. In contrast, *recognition* has been, more recently, the centerpiece of Axel Honneth's work in the Frankfurt School Critical Theory tradition.

Recognitional attitudes are moral attitudes, even though they are not focused on the other's welfare. We wish to be respected, (appropriately) appreciated, acknowledged, affirmed, and so forth, and sometimes think we can demand that others exhibit these attitudes toward us or appropriate others. It can be morally deficient to be unable or unwilling to respect or appreciate those who deserve or warrant it.

That recognitional attitudes have a moral character, though not one derived from a focus on the other's well-being, can help us understand the value of fellow feeling itself. Note that while all forms of fellow feeling are engaged with well-being, they are not all equally engaged with the *promotion* of well-being. That is, to use the language of psychology on this matter, they are not all concerned with prompting or motivating prosocial or helping behavior. Take *commiseration*, for example, Scheler's most common example of fellow feeling. Merriam-Webster defines this as "to feel or express sympathy for" (Merriam-Webster Online). My linguistic intuitions about this word are slightly different. I think commiseration requires expressing to someone that you understand that she is going through something negative and that you affirm her negative take on whatever it is. So the point and value of commiseration lie in the affirmation of the other's view and the sense that she is being understood by you. But commiseration does not seem to me to imply that the subject is undertaking to or is disposed to *help* the other person. This may be a limitation to the value of commiseration; but at the same time, it seems to me to possess a distinctive value in both the affirmation of the other's experience and of her take on her own situation, and also in her being understood by another person whom she cares understands her.

Commiseration seems to contrast with compassion, another instance of fellow feeling, in respect of the character of its value. Compassion seems to require at least some degree of concern for the negative state of the other that would motivate one to help if one could, and to look for ways to do so. Some of the value of compassion to its object lies in this conative aspect – motivating helping behavior – that is absent in commiseration.

At the same time, I do not think the value of compassion lies solely in its conativity. If I am in a bad way and an appropriate person shows compassion for me, I may well value this and be glad for her compassion even if there is no way that she can help me. One might reply that the value in question could be the value of the disposition to help, and I might value that over and above the actual help, and also in the absence of the help. But there are two different ways we could value the disposition to help. If I am in an ongoing relationship with the other and she has such a disposition toward me, I could be reassured that she will come to my aid in the future even if she cannot do so in present circumstances. I may value the assurance or intention of future help. However, this cannot be the form of valuing of the disposition to help when one is *not* in such a relationship and is unlikely to encounter the person again. In that case, valuing the disposition to help does not seem to me very different from valuing the mere fact of the other's concern that expresses itself in that disposition.

The value of compassion independent of help is well expressed in two articles written in a Polish journal in the 1980s about whether Christian Poles should have done more to shield Jews from the genocide the Nazis were perpetrating against Jews on Polish soil. Jerzy Turowicz, the editor of the journal, says that anti-Semitism kept Poles from having sympathy or compassion for the Jews. He does not think Poles could have done much to stop the killing of the Jews; but he thinks that anti-Semitism made them indifferent to the Jews' fate (Turowicz 1990). Ewa Berberyusz expresses this point well in another article in the journal: "If more of us had turned out to be more Christian, it would have made no difference to the statistics of the extermination, but maybe it would not have been such a lonely death?" (Berberyusz 1990). If these writers are correct to think that Jews who were going to die anyway would still prefer being cared about by their Polish fellow citizens to not being so, then the value of fellow feeling transcends the help it may motivate.

Bernard Williams made a version of this point in his influential 1965 paper *Morality and the Emotions* (Williams 1973). Williams asks us to envision someone helping us out of duty as contrasted with doing the same act out of concern for our welfare. We do not value only the help, but also what motivates it. Williams expresses this by saying we often prefer "the human gesture" to action founded on principle or conscientiousness.

If this line of thought is sound, then fellow feeling is less different from recognition, affirmation, and so on, than it initially appeared to be. For now, it seems that although fellow feeling engages with others' well-being in a way that recognitional attitudes do not, it is also true that part of the way we value fellow feeling is at least somewhat akin to the way we value recognition and affirmation. In the case of commiseration, there is something like an affirmation of the other. In the case of empathy, sympathy, and compassion, there is a concern for the other that also involves a kind of affirmation. These are valued by us (insofar as we are their objects) in their own right, independent of their conativity in motivating behavior that benefits us or redounds to our good in some way.[5] So fellow feeling

---

[5] Baron-Cohen expresses this point as follows: "Empathy makes the other person feel valued, enabling them to feel that their thoughts and feelings have been heard, acknowledged, and respected" (Baron-Cohen 2011, 20).

as a type of emotion or attitude is valuable not only in *motivating* action but as *being expressed in* action.

To pull the threads together, it seems that we value fellow feeling for three different reasons: (1) It motivates beneficent action (this is the aspect most emphasized in social psychological work on empathy and fellow feeling); (2) it involves a disposition to engage in beneficent action; and (3) it has an affirmational or recognitional element that it shares with what I have called the recognitional attitudes, and which in itself does not involve the intentional promotion of others' welfare. This last element has not been highlighted in the common focus on the conative dimension of fellow feeling.[6]

4. Common Conceptions of Empathy in Light of this Moral Analysis

In light of this discussion of the moral value of fellow feeling, I want to look at some currently common conceptions of what empathy consists in. Of the different forms of fellow feeling, empathy seems to have garnered the most attention, especially recently, from psychologists and, though to a somewhat lesser extent, from philosophers.

I mentioned earlier that there seem to be genuinely distinct views of empathy out there, so I do not offer this discussion in the spirit of using my previous moral analysis to provide the "correct" view of empathy. The point is rather to look at these current analyses from a moral value point of view and see how they stack up from that particular vantage point.

1. *Empathy as having the same feeling as the other/"sharing" a feeling* (Darwall 2002, 54; 2011, 8; Slote 2007, 13). This is perhaps the most common conception of empathy in the contemporary scene in both philosophy and psychology. But it will not pass muster by the morality of fellow feeling test. On the "same feeling" view, if the target is in a state of anger or depression, then the subject is also in that feeling state. But why would the target value the subject's being angry or depressed? The latter's anger, or depression, might have absolutely nothing to do with the target's being in that state. It is not directed toward the target's well-being, does not involve a

---

[6] One could challenge my distinguishing fellow feeling from recognitional attitudes by saying that if the recognitional attitudes contribute to the other's good – if we desire to be the (appropriate) object of affirmation, respect, and so on – then both sorts of attitude promote human good or welfare and the distinction between them disappears. But a distinction would still remain between attitudes that are directly engaged with the promotion of the other's welfare, and those that are engaged with other aspects of the other's character, identity, status, or situation and do not aim to promote the other's welfare.

motivation to help the target, nor is it an affirmation or recognition of him.

A minor variant of this account is that the subject's anger or depression is *caused by* the target's anger or depression. The causality connects the two parties' feeling states. But it does not do so in a way that captures the appropriate valuing relationship. If the target's depression causes the subject to be depressed, this does not involve any concern on the subject's part for the target, nor a directedness of her feeling state toward him. So he has no reason to place value on the fact that her state of mind is the same as his.

It matters what the depression is about. If the subject is depressed about her life and the target is depressed about his, this is not yet (moral) empathy, though it could lead to it by her using her depression as a way to focus attention on the target and appreciate what he is going through. Only then would it constitute fellow feeling in the moral sense.

On the other side, the subject can have empathy without having the same feeling state as the target, and typically does. If my friend is disappointed, I can empathize with her without being disappointed myself – without being in a state of disappointment. Or if the target is humiliated, the subject's empathy for him does not consist in her being or feeling humiliated. So having the same feeling is neither necessary nor sufficient for fellow feeling or empathy in particular.

2. *Empathy is feeling an emotion we take the other to have* (Prinz 2011). This view is the same as the previous but with an epistemic qualifier. If the subject takes the target to be depressed and the subject is depressed, that does not mean her depression has anything to do with a concern for him or as affirming of him. Her taking him to be depressed and her being depressed herself could be two unrelated things. If they are causally related, this essentially collapses into the variant of discussed in the preceding (1).

I think the fact that (moral) empathy does not require the same feeling on the subject's and target's part is partly masked in the psychological literature by its focus on *distress* as the state of mind taken as paradigmatic of the target's state of mind. More than anger, depression, disappointment, or humiliation, distress in the target tends to cause some sort of distress in the subject. Such distress would still not constitute empathy in the moral sense, but might help explain some of the attraction of the "same feeling" view.

3. *Empathy is an affective response stemming from apprehension or comprehension of the other's emotional state or condition and is similar to what*

A Moral Account of Empathy and Fellow Feeling

the other is feeling or could be expected to feel (Eisenberg and Miller 1987, 671). Unlike the previous two accounts, Eisenberg's definition captures Scheler's point that apprehending the other's state of mind is distinct from the emotional response to it constituting fellow feeling proper. But the "similar feeling" still does not get us to moral empathy. If the target's depression causes the subject to be depressed or (a different but similar feeling) deeply despondent about her own situation, that is not empathy for him on her part. Eisenberg is more clear-headed than other authors about the implication of her view. She says explicitly that empathy on her definition is not other-directed – though she says it often gives rise to sympathy, which she does take to be other-directed (Eisenberg and Miller 1987). But this view severs empathy from empathizing and having empathy for, and makes it not a species of fellow feeling in the moral sense proposed here.

4. *Empathy is a feeling more congruent with the other's situation than one's own* (Hoffman 2000). The "congruent with" language is used by psychologists, but has been picked up by some philosophers. It seems to mean "appropriate to," and I will use it that way.[7] This account captures the focus on the other, but mischaracterizes it. Suppose you are going through a very traumatic divorce. I on the other hand am in a stable and loving relationship; but suppose that despite this, I am in a state of distress. That distress is more congruent with your situation than mine, since yours is more genuinely distressful. But it is not empathy for you. It does not have the quality of being directed toward you in light of your situation. It just happens to be a feeling that is more appropriate to your situation than to mine. You have no reason to value my having a feeling that is appropriate to your situation in the absence of that feeling's expressing a concern on my part toward you or affirming you through a recognition of your situation.

5. Suppose we tweak the previous two definitions and say that *empathy is my having a feeling that it would be appropriate for you to have, given your situation, and I have it on your behalf*. For example, suppose you are having a traumatic divorce and I am depressed on your behalf; or you have been grievously wronged by a colleague and I am outraged at the colleague on your behalf. Would this be empathizing, that is, moral empathy as fellow feeling?

---

[7] But Batson uses "congruence" to mean simply that the valence of the emotion is either positive or negative depending on whether the other's state of mind or situation is positive or negative (Batson 2009; see also Batson this volume).

It seems to me not. My feeling or emotion is directed toward an object in your world; but empathy has to be directed toward you – toward the other person. In this account, my depression and outrage are not directed at you, and so they are not empathy as fellow feeling.

Perhaps empathy for X can *lead* to "on the other's behalf" emotions or attitudes such as those discussed previously; and, in contrast to 1 through 4, "on the other's behalf" emotions may have a moral character in being responsive to the other's situation. I do have a reason to value your having a reaction on my behalf that I do not have in the case merely of either "same emotion" or "appropriate emotion." On the other's behalf does involve a concern for the other, and again such concern could be an outgrowth of genuine empathy. But it is not itself fellow feeling. It is not directed toward the target in the way that fellow feeling is.

> 6. *Empathy as imaginative entering into another's situation* (Darwall 2011). I have acknowledged that empathy must involve a grasp of another's situation; but it does not follow that imaginative projection[8] is required for this.[9] We sometimes have an immediate grasp of another's expressed reaction to her situation just by perceiving it, as Scheler, for example, emphasizes (Scheler 1948, ch. III). We can often see immediately that someone is angry, outraged, despondent, regretful, or depressed about something in their life situation without having to engage in the mental act of imagining ourselves into their situation.

Finally, the imaginative projection account cannot do the moral work the moral conception of fellow feeling requires. It does not by itself involve a concern for the welfare of the target. One could project oneself into the target's situation for a number of different reasons other than to have a better grasp of his situation motivated by concern for him. We do not have reason to value the other's imaginative projection just by itself, but only if it involves the concern for our welfare with the attendant affirmation of us involved in the moral account of fellow feeling.

---

[8] It could be argued that not every instance of fellow feeling needs to be accompanied by a projective imagination *token*, but that the general capacity for projective imagination may be necessary to develop fellow feelings.

[9] In our earlier discussion of Scheler, we saw that there are two distinct ways of construing this imaginative "entering into." One is imagining what oneself would feel in that situation (perhaps going on to infer that this is what the other would himself feel), the other imagining what it would be like for that person, in his differences from oneself, to experience that situation. I am suggesting, following Scheler, that neither of these processes is required for the understanding of the other essential to empathy.

5. What Is the Intentional Object of Fellow Feeling: State of Mind, Objective Situation

In most but not all of these accounts, empathy and fellow feeling more generally take as their focus the other's state of mind. It is the simulation of, or having the same state of mind as, the other that is taken to constitute empathy. Scheler's own theory shares this feature with these accounts; the other's feeling is what the subject's fellow feeling takes as its intentional object. Indeed, the word "fellow feeling" could be taken to carry this implication – that the subject has a feeling that is connected with a feeling of the target.

However, some phenomena called "empathy" in ordinary speech, and certainly other examples of fellow feeling such as compassion, sympathy, and concern, do not confine their intentional objects to the other's state of mind. Consider the following three examples:

1. Presidential candidate Barack Obama speaking about how he would decide whom to nominate for the Supreme Court: "We need somebody who's got . . . the empathy to recognize what it's like to be poor or African-American or gay or disabled or old" (Coplan 2011, 3).
2. Mamphela Ramphele, a South African political commentator, speaking about the then-current (2008) atmosphere in South Africa: "It is difficult to see how we can continue to claim to be informed by the spirit of *ubuntu* [humanity or human kindness] when there is so little empathy with those who are most vulnerable" (Ramphele 2008, 68).
3. Ramphele speaking about the then-president of South Africa: "A country that is losing 1000 people a day from HIV/AIDS-related causes needs an explanation from its president. Even if he had no personal relationships with those affected one would expect our leader to seek to publicly show his empathy for those affected" (Ramphele 2008, 240).

In all three of these familiar uses of "empathy," the object of empathy is not a particular state of mind of the target but the target's specific negative life situation (e.g., having HIV/AIDS, or a more general life situation involving vulnerability to something negative [as being a member of a particular vulnerable group, as in Obama's remark]). These familiar uses are in line with the moral notion of empathy, as they have as the focus of empathy the welfare of the target, something concerning her welfare, or her with regard to her welfare. Both Obama and Ramphele use empathy to imply an understanding and appreciation of, and some degree of concern for, certain groups of persons suffering from, or vulnerable to, loss of well-being. Both clearly see empathy as a type of moral attitude or emotion, one whose absence betokens moral deficiency of some kind and whose presence is seen as a moral positive.

This point of view, or something close to it, is present in some of the psychological literature on empathy. Martin Hoffman, a leading empathy scholar, particularly emphasizes the way that as children get older they are able to differentiate a person's feelings of the moment from their more general life situation. They recognize that sometimes the overall life situation can be out of line with the target's current state of mind, and that the former is the more appropriate object of empathy. He gives two examples – one of someone with a terminal illness who does not yet know this, another of a child who is too young to understand the significance of his mother having died (Hoffman 2000, 81ff.). In both cases, he envisions an adult having empathy for the target, but focused on their situation in light of their well-being, rather than their current state of mind.

Hoffman calls the object of empathy in these cases the "objective situation." That is accurate but does not explicitly enough bring out that it is the objective situation understood in relation to the target's well-being, as Hoffman implicitly recognizes. And it is plausible to think that at least in some cases when the other's state of mind is the object of empathy, it is that state of mind as it bears on or indicates their well-being – as when the other is sad, anxious, worried, distressed. Indeed, these types of states of mind are generally the ones cited by theorists of empathy. It is rare to say that I empathize with Joan with respect to her contemplating the sunset, or thinking about the tasks ahead of her today. I do not take the view that it is inappropriate or incoherent to use empathy in such ways, because I acknowledge different meanings and usages of "empathy." My argument is only that we can recognize a morally informed use of empathy, illustrated by the quotes from Obama and Ramphele. In that usage, the formal object of empathy is the other's well-being, or her situation in light of her well-being. In this usage, when the other's state of mind is the object of empathy, it is that state of mind as bearing on or indicating the target's well-being.

To pull together the threads of this discussion, fellow feeling in the moral understanding involves the subject's affectively engaging with and responding to the situation of the target with respect to her well-being. As mentioned, Scheler puts it this way: "[F]ellow-feeling ... is a genuine outreaching and entry into the other person and his individual situation, a true and authentic *transcendence* of one's self" (Scheler 1948, 46; emphasis in original).[10] The concern with the other's welfare,

---

[10] The philosopher Arne Johan Vetlesen states the outreaching aspect of empathy thus: "[Empathy] is reaching out toward the other's situation" (Vetlesen 1993, 204). Vetlesen's book contains a rich discussion of the moral conception of empathy.

whether able to be acted upon in the current situation or not, provides the source of fellow feeling's moral value. We value the help the fellow feeling prompts (when it does), the disposition to help involved in its presence, and the affirmation of the significance of ourselves and our welfare over and above (though connected with) these two other features.

6. Barriers to the Understanding of the Other Required by Fellow Feeling

As Scheler emphasizes, the self-transcending dimension of fellow feeling requires a clear sense of the otherness of the other, her distinctness and difference from the self. This in turn requires that the subject recognize how the significance of the other's situation is not always easy to discern. Iris Murdoch emphasizes this point and discusses it in an acute manner. She mentions several distinct sorts of barriers and obstacles to person A's seeing person B's situation clearly. Although the previously surveyed views of empathy are not inconsistent with this insight, they generally pay scant attention to this moral challenge. One way that challenge is recognized in some of this literature is in the idea of "egoistic mind-reading" or "self-oriented perspective-taking," which means imagining myself in the other's situation as a way of understanding her in that situation (Nichols 2004; Coplan 2011). But that cognitive fault does not capture Scheler's examples of people who may well consciously make the distinction between seeing the other through imagining oneself in her situation versus imagining *her* in her situation, but who at a deeper and less conscious level are not living out their own lives sufficiently distinct from that other. My earlier example of Anna Freud's governess illustrates this. On Scheler's view, such a person lacks the lived sense of distinctness required for the full moral value of fellow feeling. She cannot truly affirm and have concern for the other because she still lives through the other, and that includes an inability to have true fellow feeling.

Murdoch's Freudianlike insights, expressed both in her philosophical writings and her novels, illuminate self-oriented perspective taking. She emphasizes myriad forms of our own fantasies and personal investments in false ways of seeing others. But the philosophical literature employing this formulation makes it seem too easy to avoid this cognitive and moral distortion – as if it were sufficient simply to engage in an attempt to know the other under the description (drawn from Coplan) "other-oriented perspective-taking." Murdoch shows how complicated it is to rid ourselves of these distortions in our views of particular other persons, and how much moral work it takes to do so.[11]

7. Difference between Different Forms of Fellow Feeling

I have attempted to provide a morally based account of fellow feeling. With the partial exception of empathy and commiseration, I have not said much about what distinguishes the different forms of fellow feeling from one another. Some brief remarks on this are in order, partly to further highlight the differences between the reigning conceptions of empathy and my morally based one. A fair amount of attention has been given to the difference between sympathy and empathy by both psychologists and philosophers (Wispé 1986; Eisenberg and Miller 1987; Darwall 2011). A common view is that empathy is having the same feeling as another, whereas sympathy is a feeling of concern for the other but without a corresponding or congruent feeling. On my view, this cannot be what distinguishes the two because empathy does not require having the same feeling as the other.

But in addition, sympathy cannot be identified with all forms of concern, as this view implies without quite saying it explicitly. Keep in mind the earlier argument that many forms of engagement with others' well-being are not forms of fellow feeling at all. The responsiveness to the other involved in many types of altruistically motivated helping are not driven by fellow feeling but by moral principle, duty, or only by a concern or desire that the other achieve her ends. Remember the Vaish/Warneken experiments on young children mentioned earlier, where the child picks up an item dropped by an adult and gives it to her. Sometimes the end desired by the other is simply too minimal for the sense of being moved by the other's plight that is involved in all fellow feeling. For example, if someone asks me how to get to the nearest bus stop, and I am prompted to help him, it does not seem proper to say this is driven by sympathy for him, and at least to my English language intuitions neither is it appropriate to say that I have concern for him. Perhaps if he conveys that he is distressed because he has been wandering around for a while without

---

[11] In Blum 2012, I argue that Murdoch gives short shrift to social obstacles (as opposed to psychological ones) to seeing others clearly. If this argument is correct, then the moral challenge Murdoch poses is even more difficult to meet than she recognizes.

However, Scheler, despite his recognition on the emotional complexity of being separate from the other, is not as attuned as is Murdoch to obstacles in the way of understanding the other. He emphasizes that the possibility of understanding the other's experience does not require having had a similar experience oneself (Scheler 1948, 47). But he does not give any guidance about how one goes about meeting the challenge of achieving understanding in such circumstances.

finding the bus stop, or is in a great hurry, concern or sympathy might be a possible and natural response to his plight. But the mere recognition that the passerby desires to be steered to a bus stop would not characteristically, or even fully intelligibly, elicit sympathy or concern.

At the other end of the spectrum, sometimes the plight of the other is so dire that to say that one has sympathy for her, or sympathizes with her, is too weak a form of engagement with her well-being. Consider an example from Primo Levi's Auschwitz memoir, *If This Is A Man*. It is 1945. The Germans have fled the camp in advance of the Soviet forces. In the infirmary remain sick patients, all in danger of perishing of various illnesses. Lakmaker, a very sick prisoner on a top bunk, falls to the floor, attempting unsuccessfully to get to the latrine. He is fevered, and speaks no language in common with anyone else on the ward. He is wallowing in his own waste, and there is reason to worry that his condition will exacerbate the fragile health of the other inmates. One prisoner, Charles, rises to the occasion, cleans Lakmaker's straw mattress, lifts Lakmaker back on it "with the tenderness of a mother," as Levi puts it, and cleans Lakmaker as well as he can with straw taken from the mattress (Levi 1947, 167).

Charles has certainly acted out of concern for Lakmaker. But does he have *sympathy* for Lakmaker? My linguistic intuitions say that sympathy is too weak a sentiment to express the extraordinary depth of care, concern, and attunement to Lakmaker's humanity that Charles's actions express. Levi reports this incident with amazement that in the midst of what he so movingly describes as the dehumanized condition to which most of the prisoners have been subjected and descended, himself very much included, Charles has summoned a degree of humanity in himself that is responsive to the humanity in Lakmaker. Sympathy does not seem the right vocabulary in which to express this responsiveness.[12]

One lesson here is that "concern" and "care" cover a somewhat different or at least more extensive spectrum of forms of engagement with the well-being of others than does "sympathy," and possibly "empathy" as well. It might be part of the point of our having these distinct terms to mark distinctions within this territory. Another difference might be the degree of conativity to help the other. In this respect, sympathy seems to me weaker than concern and care. "Caring about"' seems to me to carry

---

[12] Notice that the extraordinariness of Charles's actions does not lie in the degree of self-sacrifice or cost to him of caring for Lakmaker, a common criterion of exceptional moral worth. It is the depth of his concern and humanity, and his ability to see the humanity in a dehumanized other that better captures this extraordinariness. His actions do not really involve self-sacrifice or cost to him. Levi does not portray him as more endangered by helping Lakmaker, for example, than the other members of the ward.

a stronger motivational sense than "have sympathy for." "Empathy" seems to me even weaker from a conative point of view. It is not as weak as "commiseration," which seems to carry no implication of conativity at all, as argued earlier.[13] In the quotes regarding empathy from Obama and Ramphele, there is an implication that if the political leaders in question have empathy for the groups mentioned, this will motivate them to do something for those persons – but not (to my linguistic intuitions) as much as would be implied by *concern* or *care*. What empathy seems to me to offer the other is a more acute envisioning of her situation than is implied in sympathy, and (therefore?) a stronger affective reaction to that situation. In that sense, empathy carries a stronger acknowledgment of the other than does sympathy, though perhaps a weaker motivation to help.

These remarks are meant to be suggestive only. I am not placing substantial stock in my intuitions. Their point is to show that if one looks at instances or examples of fellow feeling from the vantage point of the proposed moral analysis, one sees a range of different values and distinctions in that terrain captured by the differences among the forms of fellow feeling.

My argument in this chapter has not been to reject reigning views of "empathy" as being inaccurate accounts. Rather, I have asked what an account of empathy might look like if we see it as a species of fellow feeling, like compassion, sympathy, care, and commiseration, and in that respect a moral phenomenon. I have tried to show that the reigning accounts fail to capture the moral value of empathy in that particular sense, which is compatible with someone saying that this does not constitute a criticism of these accounts if they are aimed at a nonmoral version of empathy. In addition, I have tried to bring out the moral character of fellow feeling, drawing partly on Scheler's idea of self-transcendence that requires a lived sense of distinctness between subject and target, but going beyond Scheler's (not entirely consistent) focus on the object of fellow feeling as the target's state of mind. Empathy is a more morally worthy phenomenon if its target is the other's situation with respect to his well-being than if it is merely his state of mind, which could be quite misaligned with his welfare.

---

[13] Eisenberg and others have investigated empirically the relation between empathy and helping behavior. I agree that there is room for such investigation, but my argument here does claim a conceptual relation between empathy and helping, though a weak one. If A claims empathy for B and is in a situation in which she could help with extremely minimal or no cost to herself, yet fails to do so, I am claiming that what she claims to feel is not in fact empathy (Eisenberg 1987).

Bibliography

Baron-Cohen, S. 2011. *The Science of Evil: On Empathy and the Origins of Cruelty.* New York: Basic Books.

Batson, C. D. 2009. These Things Called Empathy: Eight Related but Distinct Phenomena. In: J. Decety and W. Ickes (eds.), *The Social Neuroscience of Empathy.* Cambridge, MA: MIT Press, 3–15.

2011 *Altruism in Humans.* New York: Oxford University Press.

Blum, L. 2011. Empathy and Moral Psychology: A Critique of Shaun Nichols's Neo-Sentimentalism. In: C. Bagnoli (ed.), *Morality and the Emotions.* New York: Oxford University Press, 170–93.

2012. Visual Metaphors in Iris Murdoch's Moral Philosophy. In: Justin Broackes (ed.), *Iris Murdoch, Philosopher.* Oxford: Oxford University Press, 303–19.

Berberyusz, E. 1990. Guilt by Neglect. In: A. Polonsky (ed.), *My Brother's Keeper? Recent Polish Debates on the Holocaust.* London: Routledge, 69–71.

Coplan, A. 2011. Understanding Empathy: Its Features and Effects. In: A. Coplan and P. Goldie (eds.), *Empathy: Philosophical and Psychological Perspectives.* New York: Oxford University Press, 2–18.

Darwall, S. 2002. *Welfare and Rational Care.* Princeton, NJ: Princeton University Press.

2011 Being With. *Southern Journal of Philosophy,* 49 (Spindel suppl.), 4–24.

Decety, J. and Lamm, C. 2009. Empathy versus Personal Distress: Recent Evidence from Social Neuroscience. In: J. Decety and W. Ickes (eds.), *The Social Neuroscience of Empathy.* Cambridge, MA: MIT Press, 199–213.

Eisenberg, N. and Miller, P. 1987. The Relation of Empathy to Prosocial and Related Behaviors. *Psychological Bulletin,* 101 (1), 91–119.

Freud, A. 1936. *Ego and the Mechanisms of Defense.* Madison, CT: International Universities Press.

Friedman, M. 1993. *What Are Friends For? Feminist Perspectives on Personal Relationships and Moral Theory.* Ithaca, NY: Cornell University Press.

Gilligan, C. 1982. *In a Different Voice.* Cambridge, MA: Harvard University Press.

Hoffman, M. 2000. *Empathy and Moral Development: Implications for Caring and Justice.* New York: Cambridge University Press.

Johansson, E. 2008. Empathy or Intersubjectivity? Understanding the Origins of Morality in Young Children. *Studies in Philosophy of Education,* 27, 33–47.

Levi, P. 1947. *If This Is a Man. Survival in Auschwitz.* Transl. by G. Einaudi of *Se questo è u uomo.* New York: Touchstone 1993.

Merriam-Webster. *Commiserate.* www.merriam-webster.com/dictionary/commiserate (accessed July 2016).

Murdoch, I. 1970a. *A Fairly Honorable Defeat.* London: Penguin.

1970b. *The Sovereignty of Good.* New York: Schocken.

Nichols, S. 2004. *Sentimental Rules: On the Natural Foundation of Moral Judgment.* New York: Oxford University Press.

Prinz, J. 2011. Against Empathy. *Southern Journal of Philosophy,* 49 (Spindel suppl.), 214–33.

Ramphele, M. 2008. *Laying Ghosts to Rest: Dilemmas of the Transformation in South Africa.* Cape Town, ZA: Tafelberg.

Scheler, M. 1923. *The Nature of Sympathy*, 5th edition. Transl. by P. Heath. London: Routledge and Kegan Paul 1954.

Slote, M. 2007. *The Ethics of Care and Empathy.* New York: Routledge.

Turowicz, J. 1990. Polish Reasons and Jewish Reasons. In: A. Polonsky (ed.), *My Brother's Keeper? Recent Polish Debates on the Holocaust.* London: Routledge, 134–43.

Vaish, A. and Warneken, F. 2011. Social-Cognitive Contributors to Young Children's Empathic and Prosocial Behavior. In: J. Decety (ed.), *Empathy: From Bench to Bedside.* Cambridge, MA: MIT Press, 131–46.

Vetlesen, A. J. 1993. *Perception, Empathy, and Judgment: An Inquiry into the Preconditions of Moral Performance.* State College, PA: Penn State University Press.

Williams, B. A. O. 1973. Morality and the Emotions. *In Problems of the Self.* Cambridge, UK: Cambridge University Press, 207-29.

Wispé, L. 1986. The Distinction between Sympathy and Empathy: To Call Forth a Concept, a Word Is Needed. *Journal of Personality and Social Psychology*, 50 (2), 314–21.

IV

Fellow Feeling and the Development of Prosociality

7 Empathy-Related Responding and Its Relations to Positive Development

Nancy Eisenberg

Empathy and related vicarious emotions such as sympathy frequently have been viewed as morally relevant emotions. Indeed, for centuries, a subgroup of philosophers (e.g., Hume 1777; Blum 1980) and, more recently, numerous psychologists (e.g., Eisenberg 1986; Hoffman 1987) have argued that empathy and/or related emotional reactions motivate positive behaviors such as caring and altruism. This perspective differs from the alternative view that morality is primarily due to sociocognitive development or cognitively based values (e.g., Kohlberg 1981), but it is a perspective that has received greater acceptance in psychology in recent decades.

It is natural that individuals who tend to vicariously experience another's negative emotions and/or feel concern for another person would be relatively likely to try to assist a distressed, sad, or needy individual. However, in a meta-analytic review, Underwood and Moore (1982) found no statistical relation between empathy and prosocial behaviors such as helping or sharing. Since the publication of that paper, psychologists have spent considerable effort examining the relations of empathy-related responding to morality. In this chapter, I argue that empathy-related reactions can play a crucial role in moral development, but that not all aspects of vicarious emotional responding relate to moral outcomes (including prosocial behavior) to the same degree or even in the same direction. Thus, it is critical to make conceptual distinctions among empathy-related reactions. In addition, I briefly summarize theory and research on the relation of individual differences in children's self-regulation to empathy-related responding and the potential role of socialization in individual differences in empathy-related responding.

1. Limitations of the Early Research on Empathy-Related Responding

Much of the data included in the Underwood and Moore's (1982) meta-analysis was from research in which children's empathy was assessed with story-picture methods, which was arguably the best existing measure of children's empathy prior to 1980. Unfortunately, subsequent research suggests that there were methodological limitations of this measure of empathy. This procedure typically involved an adult reading a child a series of short stories (e.g., several sentences), each involving a situation expected to elicit an emotion in the story protagonist, and then asking the child how the story protagonist felt (a measure of cognitive perspective taking) and how the story made the child feel (the index of empathy). Because the stories were so brief and typically were illustrated with, at best, only a few line drawings, they probably were not very evocative. Moreover, in the most common procedure (Feshbach and Feshbach, 1969), children were read a number of stories (e.g., eight) in a succession, which resulted in presenting vignettes that switched quickly between from one emotion to another (e.g., anger, fear, sadness, or happiness). Children's responses on this type of measure seemed to be affected by self-presentational issues and/or how much they wanted to please the experimenter (see Eisenberg and Lennon 1983; Lennon, Eisenberg, and Carroll 1983; Eisenberg and Miller 1987). Because picture-stories of this sort were common in the Underwood and Moore meta-analysis, it is not surprising that they did not finding a relation between empathy and prosocial behavior.

Furthermore, in research prior to 1982 (and often thereafter), there often was a lack of conceptual differentiation in regard to the construct of empathy. Based on the pioneering work of Batson (1991), who differentiated between empathy (what we call sympathy in this chapter) and personal distress, Eisenberg and colleagues (e.g., Eisenberg, Shea et al. 1991) discussed multiple types of empathy-related responding, including empathy, sympathy, and personal distress. I define *empathy* as an affective response that stems from the apprehension or comprehension of another's emotional state or condition, and is similar to what another person (or animal) is feeling or would be expected to feel. It involves at least a rudimentary level of self–other distinction (whereas emotional contagion may not). Sympathy often may stem from empathy (although it can also occur due to cognitive perspective taking or accessing relevant information about another's feels or situation from memory); we define it as an emotional response stemming from the apprehension or comprehension of another's emotional state or condition, which is not the same as the other's state or condition but consists of feelings of sorrow or concern for the other. Finally, personal distress is defined as a self-focused, aversive affective reaction to the apprehension of another's emotional state, e.g., as discomfort, anxiety, or distress in reaction to another's actual or assumed emotional state (including distress and other negative emotions;

Batson 1991; Eisenberg, Fabes, and Spinrad 2006). We have argued that personal distress might often stem from empathic overarousal, which is experienced as aversive (e.g., Eisenberg, Fabes et al. 1996).

The distinction between sympathy and personal distress is important because sympathy and personal distress are believed to relate differently to altruism. Specifically, sympathy is believed to motivate altruism, the type of prosocial behavior (i.e., voluntary behaviors intended to benefit another) motivated by other-oriented or moral concerns or emotion rather than concrete rewards, social rewards, or the desire to reduce one's own aversive affective state (Batson 1991; Eisenberg, Fabes, and Spinrad 2006). In contrast, personal distress, because it is experienced as aversive, is believed to lead to the egoistic motivation to make oneself feel better and, thus, typically leads to escape and avoidance of needy individuals, if it is easy to do so (Batson 1991). Finally, if empathy does not simply dissipate, it could lead to either sympathy or personal distress (although likely more to the former than the latter unless the situation is highly evocative). Thus, I would argue that empathy is less consistently related to other-oriented prosocial behavior than is sympathy.

2. Does Empathy-Related Responding Relate to Prosocial Behavior?

The empirical data provide support for differentiating sympathy from personal distress. Batson (1991), in a series of experimental studies, found that situationally induced sympathy was positively related to adults' prosocial behavior or their intention to act in a prosocial manner, whereas personal distress tended to be negatively related or unrelated to prosocial behavior. However, the methods he used were not optimal for use with children, and Batson was not very interested in individual differences in empathy-related responding. Thus, we began a series of studies to develop physiological, facial, and self-report measures of empathy-related responding to assess children's sympathy and personal distress and individual differences in their relations to prosocial behavior.

Our first task was to validate our measures of empathy-related responding. In a series of studies, we exposed children to empathy-inducing film clips or asked them talk about situations in the past that elicited sympathy and personal distress. We found that, in general, children and adults exhibited facial concerned attention (or empathic sadness) in sympathy-inducing contexts and, to a lesser degree, facial distress in situations expected to evoke personal distress (the latter more so for children than adults). Consistent with the notion that personal distress is aversive and involves high arousal, heart rate (HR) acceleration and skin conductance (SC) tended to be higher in the vicarious distress condition than in the sympathy (or baseline) condition. Self-reports of emotion (e.g., concern, distress) experienced when viewing the tape clips or talking tended to be somewhat consistent with the emotional context, even for younger children, albeit less so (Eisenberg, Fabes et al. 1988; Eisenberg, Schaller et al. 1988; Eisenberg and Fabes 1990; Eisenberg, Fabes et al. 1991a; 1991b; Eisenberg, Fabes, and Spinrad 2006). Thus, our measures appeared to have some validity.

In additional studies, we used the aforementioned facial, physiological, and self-report measures to assess both individual differences in responses to empathy-inducing stimuli (e.g., films) and whether these individual differences predicted helping of, or sharing with, children in the film or other children with similar problems. (Sometimes adult targets were used in studies with adult participants.) Across studies, individual differences on the markers of sympathy tended to predict greater helping or sharing, whereas individual differences in regard to markers of personal distress predicted less prosocial behavior or were unrelated to prosocial behavior. For example, prosocial behaviors or intention were predicted by lower SC, greater heart rate deceleration (during short evocation sections of films), more facial concerned attention or sadness while watching the films, lower facial distress during the films (more for children than adults), and self-reported sadness/sympathy or low happiness (more so for older children and adults than young children; e.g., Eisenberg, Fabes et al. 1989; 1990; 1991a; see Eisenberg and Fabes 1990; Eisenberg, Fabes, and Spinrad 2006).

Findings similar to ours in regard to the relations of sympathy and personal distress to other-oriented prosocial responding have been found in other laboratories studying children, in addition to the work by Batson (1991) with adults (although findings on heart rate tend to vary with when and how it is assessed). For example, Knafo et al. (2008) found that very young children's sympathetic reactions to their mother or stranger in an evocative context were positively related to their prosocial behavior toward their mothers at fourteen, twenty, twenty-four, and thirty months of age and, toward strangers by age thirty-six months (also see Vaish, Carpenter, and Tomasello 2009). In contrast, young children's self-distress was unrelated to their prosocial behavior (Zahn-Waxler, Robinson, and Emde 1992). A similar differential pattern of relations was found for preschoolers in four cultures (Germany, Israel, Indonesia, and Malaysia) (Trommsdorff, Friedlmeier, and Mayer 2007), although in this study, self-focused distress was negatively related to prosocial behavior.

Prosocial behavior, measured in diverse ways, has been positively associated not only with sympathy in a given context, but also with self-reported or other-reported measures of dispositional (i.e., trait-like) sympathy (see Eisenberg, Fabes, and Spinrad 2006, and Eisenberg, Spinrad, and Knafo-Noam 2015, for reviews). Moreover, early individual differences in prosocial behaviors that appear to be motivated by empathy-related concerns have predicted the development of a prosocial personality – that is, stable individual differences in prosocial behavior. Eisenberg-Berg and Hand (1979) observed naturally occurring prosocial behaviors in four-to-five-year-olds' preschool classrooms. Naturally occurring observed prosocial behaviors were coded as spontaneous (occurred without a verbal or nonverbal request) versus compliant (i.e., occurred in response to a verbal or nonverbal request), and also as sharing (giving up an object or space; such behavior typically involves a cost) or helping (low-cost acts of assistance, such as passing crayons the child was not using). Children who engaged relatively frequently in spontaneous sharing – costly prosocial behavior that spontaneously emitted – were more likely than their peers to make reference to others' needs in their moral reasoning about prosocial moral dilemmas; moral reasoning was not related to other modes of prosocial behavior (i.e., spontaneous helping, compliant sharing, or compliant helping). In contrast, children who engaged in relatively frequent compliant prosocial behavior were nonassertive and prone to personal distress (e.g., Eisenberg, Cameron et al. 1981; Eisenberg, McCreath, and Ahn 1988; Eisenberg, Fabes et al. 1990).

The prosocial tendencies of the children in the aforementioned study were subsequently assessed every two years from nine to ten years to thirty-one to thirty-two years. Eisenberg and colleagues obtained behavioral measures of prosocial behavior (e.g., donating part of the child's prize/payment [a higher-cost prosocial behavior] or helping pick up dropped pencils [a lower-cost prosocial behavior]), as well as self-reports and mothers' reports of prosocial behavior in adolescence; self-reports of sympathy/empathy in late childhood to adulthood; and self- and friend-reported prosocial dispositions in adulthood. Spontaneous sharing behavior in preschool frequently predicted these prosocial measures in late childhood, adolescence, and early adulthood (Eisenberg, Guthrie et al. 1999; 2002; Eisenberg, Hofer et al. 2014). Specifically, preschool spontaneous sharing, but usually not other modes of early prosocial behavior, was positively related to costly donating or helping in preadolescence and adolescence, mothers' reports of helpfulness in mid- to late adolescence, self-reported helping/prosocial tendencies in mid-adolescence and early adulthood (until twenty-seven to thirty-two), sympathy in adolescence and adulthood, and friend-reported sympathy in the twenties and thirties (sometimes at $p < 0.10$). In addition, self-reported sympathy in adolescence predicted spontaneous prosocial behavior in adulthood. Preschool spontaneous sharing generally was *not* related to low-cost helping in adolescence or to self-reported personal distress. The other types of prosocial behavior were infrequently related to later prosocial responding. The exception was that preschoolers high in frequency of compliant sharing sometimes reported being prosocial in adolescence and adulthood and were marginally higher in internalized and stereotypic prosocial moral reasoning (but lower in rudimentary needs-oriented reasoning) in the late twenties to early thirties (see discussion later in this chapter; Eisenberg, Guthrie et al. 2002; Eisenberg et al. 2014). Thus, they seemed to have developed a prosocial self-conception.

In summary, empathy-related responding, especially sympathy, tends to be associated with higher levels of prosocial behavior; moreover, early-occurring prosocial behavior that is costly and related to attention to others' needs predicts individual differences in prosocial tendencies across adolescence into adulthood. It is likely that the other-oriented concern that is inherent in sympathy frequently provides the motivation for prosocial behavior intended to alleviate others' negative emotional state or need. Some altruistic behaviors appear to be motivated by moral values devoid of sympathy (see Eisenberg, VanSchyndel, & Spinrad, 2016). Moreover, sometimes prosocial behaviors are motivated by non-other-oriented motivations (e.g., the desire for approval, rewards, or reciprocity) rather than sympathetic concern or values. However, the latter types of prosocial behaviors are generally not considered moral in their motivation.

3. Empathy-Related Responding and Prosocial Moral Reasoning

Given that sympathy seems to motivate other-oriented prosocial behavior and includes an orientation to others' needs, it would seem likely to also affect people's reasoning about moral conflicts. However, there has been debate regarding the degree to which emotion, including sympathetic concern, affects moral reasoning.

In fact, Kohlberg (1981), the cognitive developmental theorist who made the most influential contributions to an understanding of moral reasoning in psychology, argued that cognition (e.g., perspective taking, abstract reasoning) is responsible for advances in moral reasoning and in the quality of moral behavior. In contrast, consistent with the view that emotion is important for moral reasoning, Hoffman (1987) argued that sympathy/empathy stimulates the development of internalized moral reasoning reflecting concern for others' welfare. Eisenberg (1986) further argued that sympathy in a given situation might prime the use of preexisting other-oriented moral cognitions and, thus, affect moral reasoning.

A modest association has sometimes been found between empathy and/or sympathy and moral reasoning about dilemmas pertaining to justice (Underwood and Moore 1982; see Eisenberg 1986). However, the association between empathy/sympathy and moral reasoning is more consistent for prosocial moral judgment – reasoning about moral dilemmas in which one person's needs or desires conflict with those of others in a context in which the role of prohibitions, authorities' dictates, and formal obligations is minimal (Eisenberg 1986). We have found relations between sympathy and higher-level prosocial moral reasoning in adolescence and adulthood in longitudinal and concurrent analyses (see Eisenberg 1986; e.g., Eisenberg, Miller et al. 1991; Eisenberg, Carlo et al. 1995; Eisenberg, Guthrie et al. 2002), and in research in Brazil (Eisenberg, Zhou and Koller 2001; for a review, see Eisenberg 1986; Eisenberg, Fabes, and Spinrad 2006). It is likely that sympathy contributes to the quality of prosocial moral reasoning, although the relation between the two might be bidirectional. Certain moral principles, for example, might direct attention to others' needs and, hence, foster sympathy.

4. Relations of Empathy-Related Responding with Aggression/Externalizing Problems versus Social Adjustment

Physically harming others generally is viewed as an immoral action, as is other externalizing behavior such as stealing, lying, and destroying others' property. Thus, one would expect individuals high in sympathy, compared to less sympathetic people, to be less likely to engage in aggression and other externalizing problem behaviors. Indeed, decades ago, Feshbach (1982) and others (e.g., Mehrabian and Epstein 1972) suggested that empathy-related responding reduces or inhibits aggressive or antisocial actions because the feedback from viewing harm to others is aversive. Consistent with this perspective, deficits in empathy and remorse are common in people with psychopathic traits (e.g., Frick 1998; Blair 1999).

In a meta-analytic review of research conducted before 1988, Miller and Eisenberg (1988) examined the relation of measures of empathy-related responding, broadly defined, to measures of aggression and externalizing problems. They found that questionnaire measures of empathy/sympathy (the two were seldom differentiated) were negatively related to aggression/ externalizing behaviors. In contrast, they found no significant relations when empathy/sympathy was assessed with facial/ gestural reactions or self-reports in reaction to experimental stimuli, but there were few such studies. However, as previously noted, there were methodological issues with early measures of empathy, and researchers seldom differentiated among various modes of empathy-related responding (e.g., empathy, sympathy, and personal distress) or between empathy with positive and negative emotions. Furthermore, in a different metaanalysis, Eisenberg and Miller (1987) found a weak, positive relation between empathy and social competence, but again, the measures of empathy-related responding used in the analyses generally were undifferentiated, and there were few studies using measures of sympathy.

Since the 1980s, evidence has accumulated supporting an association of empathy-related responding, and especially sympathy, with low aggression/externalizing and relatively high social competence (see Eisenberg, Fabes, and Spinrad 2006; Eisenberg, Spinrad, and Knafo-Noam 2015). For example, in a longitudinal study, teachers' reports and self-reports of elementary school children's dispositional sympathy related to measures of adult-reported maladjustment (e.g., externalizing) and socially appropriate behavior (measured in multiple ways) assessed concurrently and across multiple years (Eisenberg, Fabes, Murphy et al. 1996; Murphy et al. 1999). Moreover, Eisenberg, Liew, and Pidada (2001; 2004) also found similar concurrent relations between Indonesian third graders' sympathy (especially as reported by teachers) and their adult- and peer-reported adjustment and/or popularity, as well as some significant relations within time in sixth grade and from third to sixth grade, especially for boys in sixth grade. Sometimes the findings in the aforementioned studies were stronger for one sex than the other, but in general, associations between children's sympathy and low levels of externalizing problems or high levels of social competence have been obtained.

In most of the research, dispositional measures of sympathy were used. In a study of children's facial and self-reported empathy to emotionally evocative slides, Zhou et al. (2002) found that empathy (but not self-reported reactions) in response to viewing slides that depicted negative emotions was negatively related to adults' reports of children's externalizing problems in midelementary school. Two years later, both children's facial empathy in response to negative emotion slides and their reported empathy with both positive and negative emotion slides were related to high levels of social skills and relatively few externalizing problems. In a structural equation model across both assessments, children's empathy with the negative emotion slides had stronger unique predictive relations with maladjustment than did their empathy with positive emotion slides.

In contrast to sympathy and empathy, children's personal distress may be positively related to aggression. In a study of elementary school children, mothers' reports of children's aggressive coping were positively associated with markers of boys' (but not girls') personal distress (i.e., heart rate acceleration and facial distress) when reacting to a crying infant (Fabes, Eisenberg et al. 1994b). However, personal distress in response to empathy-inducing films also was related to unassertive behavior that appeared to reflect a lack of social competence (Eisenberg, McCreath, and Ahn 1988; Eisenberg, Fabes et al. 1990). Thus, the relation of personal distress to children's externalizing problems and social competence requires more examination.

The results in the aforementioned studies, as well as other results (see Eisenberg, Fabes, and Spinrad 2006; e.g., Jolliffe and Farrington 2011; Carlo et al. 2012;), demonstrate associations of sympathy and sometimes empathy with low levels of morally problematic externalizing problems and with relatively high socially competent behavior. These relations are likely to be partly due to the other-orientation inherent in sympathy that appears to motivate prosocial behavior – a socially competent type of behavior – and undermines aggression. However, the relation may also be due in part to individual differences in self-regulation affecting both sympathy and moral or social functioning.

5. Empathy-Related Responding and Self-Regulation

Eisenberg and colleagues have argued that emotion-related self-regulatory skills play an important role in whether people experience sympathy or personal distress. We define emotion-related self-regulation as processes used to manage and change if, when, and how (e.g., how intensely) one experiences emotions and emotion-related motivational and physiological states, as well as how emotions are expressed behaviorally (Eisenberg and Spinrad 2004). These self-regulatory capacities are based partly on temperamental effortful control (EC), defined as "the efficiency of executive attention, including the ability to inhibit a dominant response and/or to activate a subdominant response, to plan, and to detect errors" (Rothbart and Bates 2006). EC includes skills that can be used for managing the experience and expression of emotion, as well as other aspects of cognition and behavior.

Eisenberg and colleagues hypothesized that if empathic overarousal involving negative emotion often leads to an aversive emotional state that results in self-focused personal distress, those individuals who are unable to maintain their emotional reactions within a tolerable range would be prone to experience personal distress. In contrast, people who can maintain their vicarious arousal at a moderate level (that is not overarousing) were predicted to be more likely to experience sympathy (Eisenberg, Fabes et al. 1994; Eisenberg, Fabes, Murphy et al. 1996). Thus, we predicted that processes involved in the self-regulation of emotion (e.g., EC) would be positively related to sympathy, and that low levels of self-regulatory capacities, especially those involved in modulating emotional arousal (e.g., through allocation of attention), would be related to personal distress. In addition, individual differences in self-regulatory capacities and emotionality were expected to interact when predicting sympathy.

In addition to its role in modulating emotional arousal, the executive attention involved in EC is likely to contribute to integrating information, planning, and executing other cognitive activities that help interpret information relevant to others' emotions and well-being, as well as to feeling competent to deal with negative vicarious emotion. In addition, self-regulation might contribute to the tendency to enact sympathy-based prosocial behavior when there is a cost to the self.

There is mounting evidence that self-regulatory capacities, including EC, are related to individual differences in empathy-related responding (Eisenberg, Fabes et al. 1996; Eisenberg, Liew et al. 2001; Valiente et al. 2004; Davidov and Grusec 2006; see Eisenberg, Fabes and Spinrad 2006; Eisenberg, Michalik et al. 2007). In studies of college students and elderly adults, Eisenberg and colleagues found that personal distress was negatively related to self-reported self-regulation and/or to friends' reports of their coping. Conversely, dispositional sympathy was positively related to regulation in zero-order correlations or when the effects of negative emotional intensity were controlled (Eisenberg, Fabes et al. 1994; Eisenberg and Okun 1996; Okun, Shepard, and Eisenberg 2000). (Note, however, that findings in regard to sympathy and personal distress in a specific context are more complicated, likely in part because it is difficult to differentiate situational reports of distress from concern; see Eisenberg, Fabes et al. 1994).

Somewhat similar findings have been obtained when examining children's dispositional sympathy and personal distress. In a longitudinal study of school children, children's dispositional sympathy related to adults' reports of children's effortful control, within time and across two to four years. Children's physiological arousal (e.g., heart rate acceleration, skin conductance) when exposed to others in distress was also negatively related to children's (sometimes only boys') dispositional sympathy (Eisenberg, Fabes et al. 1996; 1998).

Moreover, there was a statistical interaction between individual differences in temperamental emotionality and effortful control when predicting sympathy. The most sympathetic children were those high in effortful control and prone to intense emotions in general (i.e., regardless of valence). Children who were low in effortful control were low in sympathy regardless of their level of emotionality (Eisenberg, Fabes et al. 1996; 1998).

In a different longitudinal sample, both four-and-a-half- to seven-year-olds reported sympathy in response to an empathy-inducing film and their self-reported dispositional sympathy were associated with relatively high effortful control as reported by parents and teachers. In contrast, children's reported personal distress in response to the film was related to low adult-reported effortful control (Valiente et al. 2004). Moreover, adults' reports of children's effortful control predicted sympathy up to eight years later, even across reporters, especially for boys, and behavioral measures of persistence and sitting still when asked (indices of regulation) often were positively related to children's concurrent or future sympathy (Eisenberg, Michalik et al. 2007).

In a third longitudinal sample, we recently found that children's effortful control at fifty-four months of age predicted their parent- and non-parental caregiver–reported sympathy at seventy-two and eighty-four months (combined), even when statistically controlling for their level of sympathy at forty-two months, albeit reported by only mothers (Taylor et al. 2015). Therefore, effortful control appeared to predict change in sympathy across time. Moreover, a positive relation between school children's adult-reported sympathy and their effortful control was also found in Indonesia (Eisenberg, Liew and Pidada 2001; 2004). Thus, it appears that the ability to regulate emotions could be involved in the experience of sympathy versus personal distress and perhaps in the association between sympathy and positive developmental outcomes. Self-regulation could contribute to both.

6. The Origins of Empathy-Related Responding

Empathy-related responding and prosocial behavior clearly have a genetic basis (see Eisenberg, Spinrad and Knafo-Noam, 2015), perhaps through the effects of genetics on children's temperamental emotionality and self-regulation. Nonetheless, socialization also seems to play a role in the development of empathy-related reactions. For example, researchers have argued that warm and supportive parents would be expected to have children prone to sympathy for a variety of reasons. Such a relation is expected, for instance, because sensitive, warm parenting provides modeling of sympathetic, prosocial behavior; sensitive parenting fosters a secure attachment as well as children's receptivity to parental desires, teachings, and values; and supportive parenting helps children to learn to manage their emotions (see Eisenberg, Fabes and Spinrad 2006, and the papers cited below).

In fact, there is considerable research consistent with these ideas (see Eisenberg, Fabes and Spinrad 2006; Eisenberg, Spinrad and Knafo-Noam, 2015). For example, level of parents' warmth/positive affect, encouragement, and low negative affect while doing a puzzle with their child was related to children's self-reported empathy/sympathy (Spinrad et al. 1999). In addition, Swiss children who were high and stable in trajectories of self-reported sympathy from age six to nine years reported more maternal support than those who exhibited low and increasing or low and stable trajectories for sympathy (Malti et al. 2013). In longitudinal research, Feldman (2007) found that mother–infant synchrony in the first year of life (indicative of sensitivity) predicted empathy in Israeli adolescents and Eisenberg, vanSchyndel et al. (2015) found that maternal warmth/support during childhood predicted friends' reports of sympathetic concern and caring in the late twenties and early thirties.

Eisenberg and colleagues have argued that parental practices/behaviors that help children to manage their emotions are likely to foster sympathy rather than personal distress (e.g., Eisenberg, Cumberland, and Spinrad 1998). Consistent with this view, parental preference for using instrumental problem solving to deal with children's emotions (e.g., helping the child find a concrete solution to a problem) related to boys' comforting behavior (Eisenberg, Fabes, and Murphy 1996) and markers of boys' sympathy (low skin conductance; high reported sympathy/sadness) in response to an empathy-inducing video (Eisenberg, Fabes et al. 1991a). Furthermore, mothers' reports of encouraging their children to express their own negative emotions at eighteen months predicted child empathy at twenty-four months (Taylor et al. 2013).

Emotion-related parenting practices/behaviors that expose children to moderate levels of emotional arousal may promote sympathy and reduce proneness to personal distress, perhaps by providing opportunities to learn about emotions and how to optimally regulate them. In a study of young school children (about five to seven years), sympathy was measured with children's self-reported reactions to an empathy-inducing film and parents' reports of children's typical (dispositional) sympathy. Parents' expression of emotion with their children was assessed with parents' reports and observations of parents' positive or negative expressivity when interacting with their child. Sympathy was highest for children exposed to moderate levels of either parental positive and negative expressivity (Valiente et al. 2004). Relatively young children may learn from parental expression of emotion but may be overaroused if it is too intense (which might undermine their self-regulation). In contrast, personal distress was related to high parental negative expressivity and to low parental positive expressivity (Valiente, Eisenberg et al. 2004). The children in this study were not from a sample with clinical problems; the findings might have been quite different if a clinical sample were used in which parents expressed very intense emotions. For example, in such a sample, there might be a linear, negative relation between parental intensity of negative emotion and children's sympathy.

Some potential effects of parental emotion socialization on sympathy may be mediated by children's regulation – that is, parenting may affect children's abilities to self-regulate, which in turn affect their sympathy. In a sample of Indonesian children, Eisenberg, Liew et al. (2001) found evidence that parental negative expressivity predicted low regulation, which in turn predicted low sympathy. Moreover, Taylor et al. (2015) found that authoritative parenting (warm, supportive parenting with optimal control) observed in mothers with children of forty-two months predicted children's effortful control at fifty-four months, which in turn predicted sympathy at seventy-two to eighty-four months.

Individual differences in children's self-regulation also might moderate the relation of degree of parental expression of emotion to young children's empathy-related responding. Valiente et al. (2004) found that young school children's effortful control and parental expressivity interacted statistically when predicting children's dispositional sympathy and situational sympathy (i.e., in reaction to a film). There was a positive relation of sympathy to relatively high levels of parents' expression of negative emotions for children who were higher in regulation and a negative relation for their less regulated peers. Less regulated children were prone to personal distress regardless of their parents' expression of negative emotion whereas regulated children were high in personal distress only if their parents expressed high levels of negative emotion. Thus, children's regulation seemed to affect their reactions to parents' expression of negative emotion. Similar relations were not found when the children were older, perhaps because most of those assessed in this nonclinical sample developed a reasonably high level of self-regulation with age (so fewer were likely to be especially vulnerable to typical levels of parental expression of emotion).

Parental reactions to their children's emotions and parents' expressivity with their children are probably partly affected by children's regulation and emotionality. Such child-effects on parental behavior likely result in bidirectional relations between parents' and children's behavior that, in turn, affect children's empathy-related responding. As evidence of such processes, Fabes, Eisenberg et al. (1994a) found that mothers of kindergartners viewed their children as more emotionally reactive than did mothers of second graders. Moreover, mothers displayed a greater amount of positive versus negative emotion when telling emotional stories (from picture books with empathy-inducing themes but presented without words) if their children were in kindergarten rather than second grade, particularly if they viewed their children as emotionally reactive. Mothers who viewed their children as reactive seemed to try to reduce the level of negative emotion experienced by their children who were vulnerable to distress. Moreover, mothers who displayed more positive versus negative emotion when telling stories to kindergartners had children who were more prosocial.

In contrast to the findings for kindergartners, mothers who viewed second graders as emotionally reactive, in comparison to mothers who viewed their children as less reactive, were less involved and warm when telling the potentially arousing stories; rather, they seemed to refrain from actively involving their reactive children in stories with distressing content. This may have been unfortunate because, across all second graders, maternal attempts to direct their child's attention to the story material, when combined with warmth, were related to high levels of prosocial behavior and sympathy and low levels of personal distress. Perhaps such maternal behavior served to direct their children's attention to the stories and highlighted the emotions of story protagonists, a maternal behavior believed to induce empathy/sympathy. The overall pattern of results in this study suggests that mothers' behavior varied with the perceived vulnerability of their children to negative emotions (which was affected by both grade level and perhaps temperament) and that certain maternal behaviors were associated with higher levels of children's sympathy and prosocial behavior. More research is needed to verify this pattern of joint child and parent effects, which could build on existing research already documenting a bidirectional relation over time between positive (i.e., authoritative) parenting and children's prosocial behavior (Padilla-Walker et al. 2012).

7. Conclusions

In general, empirical findings support the conclusion that empathy (e.g., Zhou et al. 2002) and sympathy (more consistently for the latter) contribute to prosocial behavior, prosocial moral reasoning, and social competence, as well to low levels of aggression/externalizing (see Eisenberg, Spinrad, and Knafo 2015). Moreover, individual differences in self-regulatory processes seem to play a role in empathy-related responding.

Although heredity is undoubtedly involved in individual differences in empathy-related responding, some parental socialization practices appear to foster sympathy and, thus, are likely to promote moral behavior and cognitions. Examples of such research are provided in this chapter, although there are also some inconsistencies in the larger body of research; thus, replication and extension of prior studies are merited. In addition, further genetically informed longitudinal studies are needed to examine the joint effects of heredity (likely partially mediated through aspects of temperament/personality such as emotionality and effortful control) and home or extrafamilial socialization on the development of empathy, sympathy, prosocial behavior, and other aspects of morality.

References

Batson, C. D. 1991. *The Altruism Question*. Hillsdale, NJ: Erlbaum & Assoc.

Blair, R. J. R. 1999. Responsiveness to Distress Cues in the Child with Psychopathic Tendencies. *Personality and Individual Differences*, 27, 135–45.

Blum, L. A. 1980. *Friendship, Altruism and Morality*. London: Routledge and Kegan Paul.

Carlo, G.; Mestre, M. V.; McGinley, M. M.; Samper, P.; Tur, A. and Sandman, D. 2012. The Interplay of Emotional Instability, Empathy, and Coping on Prosocial and Aggressive Behaviors. *Personality and Individual Differences*, 53, 675–80. doi:10.1016/j.paid.2012.05.022

Davidov, M. and Grusec, J. E. 2006. Untangling the Links of Parental Responsiveness to Distress and Warmth to Child Outcomes. *Child Development*, 77 (1), 44–58. doi: 10.1111/j.1467-8624.2006.00855.x.

Eisenberg, N. 1986. *Altruistic Emotion, Cognition, and Behavior*. Hillsdale, N.J: Erlbaum.

Eisenberg, N. and Fabes, R. A. 1990. Empathy: Conceptualization, Assessment, and Relation to Prosocial Behavior. *Motivation and Emotion*, 14, 131–49.

Eisenberg, N. and Lennon, R. 1983. Sex Differences in Empathy and Related Capacities. *Psychological Bulletin*, 94 (1), 100. doi:10.1037/0033-2909.94.1.100

Eisenberg, N. and Miller, P. 1987. The Relation of Empathy to Prosocial and Related Behaviors. *Psychological Bulletin*, 101, 91–119. doi:10.1037/0033-2909.101.1.91

Eisenberg, N. and Okun, M. A. 1996. The Relations of Dispositional Regulation and Emotionality to Elders' Empathy-Related Responding and Affect while Volunteering. *Journal of Personality*, 64, 157–83. doi:10.1111/j.1467-6494.1996.tb00818.x

Eisenberg, N. and Spinrad, T. L. 2004. Emotion-Related Regulation: Sharpening the Definition. *Child Development*, 75, 334–9. doi:10.1111/j.1467-8624.2004.00674.x

Eisenberg, N.; Cameron, E.; Tryon, K. and Dodez, R. 1981. Socialization of Prosocial Behavior in the Preschool Classroom. *Developmental Psychology*, 17, 773–82. doi:10.1037/0012-1649.17.6.773

Eisenberg, N.; Carlo, G.; Murphy, B. and Van Court, P. 1995. Prosocial Development in Late Adolescence: A Longitudinal Study. *Child Development*, 66, 1179–97. doi:10.2307/1131806

Eisenberg, N.; Cumberland, A. and Spinrad, T. L. 1998. Parental Socialization of Emotion. *Psychological Inquiry*, 9, 241–73. doi:10.1207/s15327965pli0904_1

Eisenberg, N.; Fabes, R. A.; Bustamante, D.; Mathy, R. M.; Miller, P. and Lindholm, E. 1988. Differentiation of VicariouslyInduced Emotional Reactions in Children. *Developmental Psychology*, 24, 237–46. doi:10.1037/0012-1649.24.2.237

Eisenberg, N.; Fabes, R A.; Carlo, G., et al. 1992. The Relations of Maternal Practices and Characteristics to Children's Vicarious Emotional Responsiveness. *Child Development*, 63, 583–602. doi:10.2307/1131348

Eisenberg, N.; Fabes, R. A.; Miller, P. A., et al. 1989. The Relations of Sympathy and Personal Distress to Prosocial Behavior: A Multimethod Study. *Journal of Personality and Social Psychology*, 57, 55–66. doi:10.1037/0022-3514.57.1.55

Eisenberg, N.; Fabes, R. A.; Miller, P. A.; Shell, C.; Shea, R. and May-Plumlee, T. 1990. Preschoolers' Vicarious Emotional Responding and Their Situational and Dispositional Prosocial Behavior. *Merrill-Palmer Quarterly*, 36, 507–29.

Eisenberg, N.; Fabes, R. A. and Murphy, B. C. 1996. Parents' Reactions to Children's Negative Emotions: Relations to Children's Social Competence and Comforting Behavior. *Child Development*, 67, 2227–47. doi:10.2307/1131620

Eisenberg, N.; Fabes, R. A.; Murphy, B. et al. 1994. The Relations of Emotionality and Regulation to Dispositional and Situational Empathy-Related Responding. *Journal of Personality and Social Psychology*, 66, 776–97. doi:10.1037/0022-3514.66.4.776

Eisenberg, N.; Fabes, R. A.; Murphy, B.; Karbon, M.; Smith, M. and Maszk, P. 1996. The Relations of Children's Dispositional Empathy-Related Responding to Their Emotionality, Regulation, and Social Functioning. *Developmental Psychology*, 32, 195–209. doi:10.1037/0012-1649.32.2.195

Eisenberg, N.; Fabes, R. A.; Schaller, M.; Carlo, G. and Miller, P. A. 1991a. The Relations of Parental Characteristics and Practices to Children's Vicarious Emotional Responding. *Child Development*, 62, 1393–1408. doi:10.2307/1130814

Eisenberg, N.; Fabes, R. A.; Schaller, M.; et al. 1991b. Personality and Socialization Correlates of Vicarious Emotional Responding. *Journal of Personality and Social Psychology*, 61, 459–70. doi:10.1037/0022-3514.61.3.459

Eisenberg, N.; Fabes, R. A.; Shepard, S. A.; Murphy, B. C.; Jones, J. and Guthrie, I. K. 1998. Contemporaneous and Longitudinal Prediction of Children's Sympathy from Dispositional Regulation and Emotionality. *Developmental Psychology*, 34, 910–24. doi:10.1037/0012-1649.34.5.910

Eisenberg, N.; Fabes, R. A. and Spinrad, T. L. 2006. Prosocial Behavior. In: N. Eisenberg (vol. ed.) and W. Damon and R. M. Lerner (series eds.), *Handbook of Child Psychology*, 6th edn. New York: Wiley, vol. III: *Social, Emotional, and Personality Development*, 646–718.

Eisenberg, N.; Guthrie, I. K.; Cumberland, A. et al. 2002. Prosocial Development in Early Adulthood: A Longitudinal Study. *Journal of Personality and Social Psychology*, 82, 993–1066. doi:10.1037//0022-3514.82.6.993

Eisenberg, N.; Guthrie, I. K.; Murphy, B. C.; Shepard, S. A.; Cumberland, A. and Carlo, G. 1999. Consistency and Development of Prosocial Dispositions: A Longitudinal Study. *Child Development*, 70, 1360–72. doi:10.1111/1467-8624.00100

Eisenberg, N.; Hofer, C.; Sulik, M. J. and Liew, J. 2014. The Development of Prosocial Moral Reasoning and a Prosocial Orientation in Young Adulthood: Concurrent and Longitudinal Correlates. *Developmental Psychology*, 50, 58–70. doi: 10.1037/a0032990

Eisenberg, N.; Liew, J. and Pidada, S. 2001. The Relations of Parental Emotional Expressivity with the Quality of Indonesian Children's Social Functioning. *Emotion*, 1, 116–36. doi:10.1037/1528-3542.1.2.116

2004. The Longitudinal Relations of Regulation and Emotionality to Quality of Indonesian Children's Socioemotional Functioning. *Developmental Psychology*, 40, 790–804. doi:10.1037/0012-1649.40.5.790

Eisenberg, N.; McCreath, H. and Ahn, R. 1988. Vicarious Emotional Responsiveness and Prosocial Behavior: Their Interrelations in Young Children. *Personality and Social Psychology Bulletin*, 14, 298–311. doi:10.1177/0146167288142008

Eisenberg, N.; Michalik, N.; Spinrad, T. L. et al. 2007. Relations of Effortful Control and Impulsivity to Children's Sympathy: A Longitudinal Study. *Cognitive Development*, 22, 544–67. doi:10.1016/j.cogdev.2007.08.003

Eisenberg, N.; Miller, P. A.; Shell, R.; McNalley, S. and Shea, C. 1991. Prosocial Development in Adolescence: A Longitudinal Study. *Developmental Psychology*, 27, 849–57. doi:10.1037/0012-1649.27.5.849

Eisenberg, N.; Schaller, M.; Fabes, R. A. et al. 1988. The Differentiation of Personal Distress and Sympathy in Children and Adults. *Developmental Psychology*, 24, 766–75. doi:10.1037/0012-1649.24.6.766

Eisenberg, N.; Shea, C. L.; Carlo, G. and Knight, G. 1991. Empathy-Related Responding and Cognition: A 'Chicken and the Egg' Dilemma. In: W. Kurtines and J. Gewirtz (eds.), *Handbook of Moral Behavior and Development*. Hillsdale, NJ: Erlbaum, vol. II: *Research*, 63–88.

Eisenberg, N.; Spinrad, T. L. and Knafo-Noam, A. 2015. Prosocial Development. In: M. Lamb (ed.) and R. M. Lerner (vol. ed.), *Handbook of Child Psychology and Developmental Science*, 7th edn. New York: Wiley, vol. III: *Socioemotional Processes*, 610–56.

Eisenberg, N.; VanSchyndel, S. K. and Hofer, C. 2015. The Association of Maternal Socialization in Childhood and Adolescence with Adult Offspring's Sympathy/Caring. *Developmental Psychology*, 51, 7–16. doi:10.1037/a0038137

Eisenberg, N.; VanSchydel, S. K. and Spinrad, T. L. 2016. Prosocial Motivation: Inferences from an Opaque Body of Work. *Child Development*, 87(6), 1668–78. doi: 10.1111/cdev.12638

Eisenberg, N.; Zhou, Q. and Koller, S. 2001. Brazilian Adolescents' Prosocial Moral Judgment and Behavior: Relations to Sympathy, Perspective Taking, Gender-Role Orientation, and Demographic Characteristics. *Child Development*, 72, 518–34. doi:10.1111/1467-8624.00294

Eisenberg-Berg, N. and Hand, M. 1979. The Relationship of Preschoolers' Reasoning about Prosocial Moral Conflicts to Prosocial Behavior. *Child Development*, 50, 356–63. doi:10.2307/1129410

Fabes, R. A.; Eisenberg, N.; Karbon, M.; Bernzweig, J.; Speer, A. L. and Carlo, G. 1994a. Socialization of Children's Vicarious Emotional Responding and Prosocial Behavior: Relations with Mothers' Perceptions of Children's Emotional Reactivity. *Developmental Psychology*, 30, 44–55. doi:10.1037/0012-1649.30.1.44

Fabes, R. A.; Eisenberg, N.; Karbon, M.; Troyer, D. and Switzer, G. 1994b. The Relations of Children's Emotion Regulation to Their Vicarious Emotional Responses and Comforting Behavior. *Child Development*, 65, 1678–93. doi:10.2307/1131287

Feldman, R. 2007. Mother–Infant Synchrony and the Development of Moral Orientation in Childhood and Adolescence: Direct and Indirect Mechanisms of Developmental Continuity. *American Journal of Orthopsychiatry*, 77, 582–97. doi:10.1037/0002-9432.77.4.582

Feshbach, N. D. 1982. Sex Differences in Empathy and Social Behavior in Children. In: N. Eisenberg (ed.), *The Development of Prosocial Behavior*. New York: Academic Press, 315–38.

Feshbach, N. D. and Feshbach, S. 1969. The Relationship between Empathy and Aggression in Two Age Groups. *Developmental Psychology*, 1, 102–7. doi:10.1037/h0027016

Frick, P. J. 1998. *Conduct Disorders and Severe Antisocial Behavior*. New York: Plenum.

Hoffman, M. L. 1987. The Contribution of Empathy to Justice and Moral Judgment. In: N. Eisenberg and J. Strayer (eds.), *Empathy and Its Development*. Cambridge: Cambridge University Press, 47–80.

Hume, D. 1777. *Enquiries Concerning the Human Understanding and Concerning the Principles of Morals*. Oxford: Clarendon Press, 2nd edn, 1966.

Jolliffe, D. and Farrington, D. P. 2011. Is Low Empathy Related to Bullying after Controlling for Individual and Social Background Variables? *Journal of Adolescence*, 34, 59–71. doi:10.1016/j.adolescence.2010.02.001

Knafo, A.; Zahn-Waxler, C.; Van Hulle, C.; Robinson, J. L. and Rhee, S. H. 2008. The Developmental Origins of a Disposition toward Empathy: Genetic and Environmental Contributions. *Emotion*, 8, 737–52. doi:10.1037/a0014179

Kohlberg, L. 1981. *The Philosophy of Moral Development: Moral Stages and the Idea of Justice*. San Francisco, CA: Harper and Row.

Lennon, R.; Eisenberg, N. and Carroll, J. 1983. The Assessment of Empathy in Early Childhood. *Journal of Applied Developmental Psychology*, 4, 295–302. doi:10.1016/0193-3973(83)90024-2

Malti, T.; Eisenberg, N.; Kim, H. and Buchmann, M. 2013. Developmental Trajectories of Sympathy, Moral Emotion Attributions, and Moral Reasoning: The Role of Parental Support. *Social Development*, 22, 773–93. doi: 10.1111/sode.12031

Mehrabian, A. and Epstein, N. 1972. A Measure of Emotional Empathy. *Journal of Personality*, 40, 525.

Miller, P. A. and Eisenberg, N. 1988. The Relation of Empathy to Aggressive and Externalizing/Antisocial Behavior. *Psychological Bulletin*, 103, 324–44. doi:10.1037/0033-2909.103.3.324

Murphy, B. C.; Shepard, S. A.; Eisenberg, N.; Fabes, R. A. and Guthrie, I. K. 1999. Contemporaneous and Longitudinal Relations of Dispositional Sympathy to Emotionality, Regulation, and Social Functioning. *Journal of Early Adolescence*, 19, 66–97. doi:10.1177/0272431699019001004

Okun, M. A.; Shepard, S. A. and Eisenberg, N. 2000. The Relations of Emotionality and Regulation to Dispositional Empathy-Related Responding among Volunteers-in-Training. *Personality and Individual Differences*, 28, 367–82. doi:10.1016/S0191-8869(99)00107-5

Padilla-Walker, L. M.; Carlo, G.; Christensen, K. J. and Yorgason, J. B. 2012. Bidirectional Relations between Authoritative Parenting and Adolescents' Prosocial Behaviors. *Journal of Research on Adolescence*, 22, 400–8. doi:10.1111/j.1532-7795.2012.00807.x

Rothbart, M. K. and Bates, J. E. 2006. Temperament. In: W. Damon and R. M. Lerner (eds.), *Handbook of Child Psychology*, 6th edn. Hoboken, NJ: Wiley, vol. III: *Social, Emotional, and Personality Development*, 99–166.

Spinrad, T. L.; Losoya, S.; Eisenberg, N.; Fabes, R. A.; Shepard, S. A.; Cumberland, A.; Guthrie, I. K. and Murphy, B. C. 1999. The Relation of Parental Affect and Encouragement to Children's Moral Emotions and Behaviour. *Journal of Moral Education*, 28, 323–37. doi:10.1080/030572499103115

Taylor, Z. E.; Eisenberg, N. and Spinrad, T. L. 2015. Respiratory Sinus Arrhythmia, Effortful Control, and Parenting as Predictors of Children's Sympathy across Early Childhood. *Developmental Psychology*, 61, 17–25. doi: 10.1037/a0038189

Taylor, Z. E.; Eisenberg, N.; Spinrad, T. L.; Eggum, N. D. and Sulik, M. J. 2013. The Relations of Ego-Resiliency and Emotion Socialization to the Development of Empathy and Prosocial Behavior across Early Childhood. *Emotion*, 13, 822–31. doi 10.1037/a0032894.

Trommsdorff, G.; Friedlmeier, W. and Mayer, B. 2007. Sympathy, Distress, and Prosocial Behavior of Preschool Children in Four Cultures. *International Journal of Behavioral Development*, 31, 284–93. doi:10.1177/0165025407076441

Underwood, B. and Moore, B. 1982. Perspective-Taking and Altruism. *Psychological Bulletin*, 91, 143–73. doi:10.1037/0033-2909.91.1.143

Vaish, A.; Carpenter, M. and Tomasello, M. 2009. Sympathy through Affective Perspective Taking and Its Relation to Prosocial Behavior in Toddlers. *Developmental Psychology*, 45, 534–43. doi:10.1037/a0014322

Valiente, C.; Eisenberg, N.; Fabes, R. A.; Shepard, S. A.; Cumberland, A. and Losoya, S. H. 2004. Prediction of Children's Empathy-Related Responding from Their Effortful Control and Parents' Expressivity. *Developmental Psychology*, 40, 911–26. doi:10.1037/0012-1649.40.6.911

Zahn-Waxler, C.; Robinson, J. L. and Emde, R. N. 1992. The Development of Empathy in Twins. *Developmental Psychology*, 28, 1038–47. doi:10.1037/0012-1649.28.6.1038

Zhou, Q.; Eisenberg, N.; Losoya, S. H. et al. 2002. The Relations of Parental Warmth and Positive Expressiveness to Children's Empathy-Related Responding and Social Functioning: A Longitudinal Study. *Child Development*, 73, 893–915. doi:10.1111/1467–8624.00446

8 An Interdisciplinary Perspective on the Origins of Concern for Others

Contributions from Psychology, Neuroscience, Philosophy, and Sociobiology

Carolyn Zahn-Waxler, Andrew Schoen, and Jean Decety

1. Introduction

The Enlightenment was a movement in the eighteenth century, concerned with critical examination of previously accepted doctrines in religion, governments, and social institutions, from the point of view of rational inquiry. The very nature of morality in humans underwent intensive analysis. Much of psychological theory and research have deeply embedded roots in philosophical theories. So it is not surprising that major themes of these philosophies reappeared much later in history, beginning in the midtwentieth century, when scientific methods were developed to investigate core human attributes relevant to moral feelings, actions, cognitions, and judgments. These research methods have evolved to include the study of emotions as part of our moral nature, as well as cognitions and prosocial acts thought to support acts of conscience and commitment to others in need.

It is important to continue to seek through science both basic and pragmatic knowledge of how social conflicts become resolved or exacerbated; how cooperation and generosity become heightened or diminished; how positive human potentials, especially concern for the well-being of others, becomes more fully realized or conversely how this can become undermined through acts of cruelty and indifference to the suffering of others. Biology, culture, and socialization all play roles in shaping these alternative developmental pathways. Methods of behavioral science have become more refined, enabling more sensitive, systematic analysis of qualities that underlie and motivate our moral and caring attitudes and actions. Methods in neuroscience and functional neuroimaging revolutionized work in this area regarding neurobiology of empathy and prosocial/moral judgments and actions. Evolutionary theories highlight ultimate mechanisms of morality, providing explanations as to how human sociality is the product of gene-culture coevolution, and how certain building blocks of prosocial behaviors are conserved across species (Decety et al. 2016).

In this chapter, we consider the early development of concern for others in humans. Concern for others is thought to be a critical component of morality. We emphasize developments in the first three years of life. This is when emotions, behaviors, and cognitions relevant to caring for others in need emerge and begin to consolidate children's social repertoires. Others have used constructs that are similar to (or components of) concern for others: they include sympathy, empathic concern, affective empathy, and cognitive empathy. These emotions are commonly embedded in caring acts that are also referred to as prosocial behaviors or altruism. What they have in common is that they are outer- and other-directed, focusing on others' needs and suffering. One advantage of the term "concern for others" is that it incorporates and separates affective, behavioral, and cognitive components in ways that can be directly observed and measured.

Concern for others has two opposites beginning early in development. These include both active disregard and passive disregard for the suffering of others. In the extreme, both opposites are reflected in certain forms of psychopathology and psychiatric disorders. The same is true of an excess of concern for others. There are methods that allow concern, active disregard, and passive disregard to be studied within the same research design (Hastings et al. 2000; Van Hulle et al. 2013). Both natural observations and experimental probes for reactions to another in distress can be used to examine children's orientations toward others in need (Zahn-Waxler and Radke-Yarrow 1982). Sometimes children show facial and vocal expressions of concern, caring actions, and efforts to understand the other's plight (concern for others). Other times, children can be aggressive and judgmental, even taking pleasure in the other's plight (active disregard); or they appear to be unaware of the problem (passive disregard). For many children, both concern and disregard for others become traitlike qualities early in development (Knafo et al. 2008; Knafo, Israel, and Ebstein 2011; Rhee, Friedman et al. 2013). It is important to bear in mind the strength of early individual differences, as they have been ignored in developmental theories.

We begin by examining early conceptions of human nature. We consider how religious beliefs and philosophical theories influenced psychological research in later eras. Then we describe research on the early development of concern for others. We identify typical expressions of concern for others, and later consider examples of biological and environmental factors (and their interactions) that influence individual differences. We then look at less examined aspects of children's responses to others in distress. That is, we describe ways in which extremes in concern for others can lead to emotional problems, as well as the two opposites, that is, active and passive disregard and the roles they play in the development of psychopathology. Finally, we discuss implications for future theory, research, and application of knowledge. It will be valuable, indeed essential, to find ways to inculcate positive morality in young children, at a time in brain development when there is heightened malleability and potential for change.

2. Historical Considerations

Western philosophy and theories of moral development were strongly influenced by Judeo-Christian heritage. Views ranged from the assumption that human beings come into the world, flawed and sinful, to a belief in their inherent goodness. Often these were seen as fixed qualities present in all humans. Some traditions focused on the importance of the "thou shalt nots," that is, inhibitory morality or internalizations of prohibitions while (less often) others focused on the "thou shalls," that is, positive morality that emphasized sympathy and concern for the welfare of others. The philosopher Thomas Hobbes believed that human behavior is motivated by egoism and self love: selfishness may lead to prosocial actions, but the motivation would be to alleviate one's own discomfort or to enhance one's own gain. Jean-Jacques Rousseau, on the other hand, believed that humans have a natural sensitivity toward others, including a strong sense of moral obligation that begins early in development. These views are still taught for their historical significance, as well as Rene Descartes' position that infants come into the world completely impressionable, as life experiences solely shape development of character and conduct. These views were not evidence-based, nor was there a developmental focus. But the themes carried into later psychological theory and research.

Immanuel Kant, David Hume, and Adam Smith all took exception to Hobbes' doctrine of self-interest but in different ways. Kant represented a prevailing view whereby cognition and active effort determined the nature of human morality. Moral behaviors essentially involved will and self-control, stemming from universal, impartial principles that are detached from emotion. A distinction was made between "pure" rational altruism and helping behavior motivated by sympathy and love. These emotions were viewed as contaminating factors, tainting the purity of the acts performed. Kohlberg's stage theory of moral reasoning in the twentieth century, which initially dominated research on morality, was strongly influenced by Kant, since stages that involved emotions as a motivating factor were relegated to a lower level of development. Kohlberg's highest stage of moral reasoning was based on principles of justice, uncluttered by emotion.

David Hume and Adam Smith shared a different view. Both argued that emotions such as empathy or sympathy are central to morality. They serve as innate, fundamental motivators of caring, benevolent behaviors. Adam Smith believed that sympathy resulted from perceptions of others' adverse conditions and a desire to see them happy purely for altruistic reasons. This is close to the Buddhist view of compassion. Darwin also believed that concern for others emerged early in life. His classic book on emotions included observations of his five-month-old son showing sympathy toward his nurse, who pretended to cry (Darwin 1872).

Adam Smith's monograph on the moral sentiments was written over two and a half centuries ago and rings true today (Smith 1759/1790). He viewed concern for the well-being of others as an essential feature of positive morality. This conception is now well represented in several contemporary research programs. Smith described "sympathy" as the ability to understand another's perspective and to have a visceral/somatic or emotional reaction to others. He focused on a triad of components of morality: (a) affective expression (i.e., an emotional joining in), (b) cognitive elements (apprehending or understanding the other's experience, also known as perspective taking), and (c) physiological substrates. Smith also saw these elements as motives for (d) caring actions toward others in distress. His theory was articulated in a way that was amenable to measurement. The construct of concern for others, used in longitudinal studies of early development, captures well the multiple components of Smith's original conception of empathy.

The different views of human nature wove their way into scientific theories and research on human morality in the twentieth and twenty-first centuries. Three themes would predominate: (1) the roles of reason and emotion, (2) the motives that underlie the way we treat one another, and (3) the roles of nature and nurture. Early polarization of ideas about the importance of cognition versus emotion became translated into two distinct areas of inquiry: (a) moral reasoning and judgments, that is, cognitive processes; and (b) moral emotions and behaviors. With few exceptions, there was little overlap in theories and research in these two domains, though this has now changed (Decety and Cowell 2014). The debate over whether prosocial acts are based on self-interest or motivated by concern for others became a topic of scientific inquiry. The roles of nature and nurture were examined in studies of genetic and environmental influences.

Research on children's morality began with a focus on conscience development, which was presumed to be slow in development. Most theories converged on the assumption that young children were immoral or amoral and incapable of experiencing concern for the well-being of others until around the age of seven years. Psychoanalytic theory was premised on a view of humans as sensation seeking, irrational, egocentric, exploitive, and cruel. Freud emphasized the taming of sexual and aggressive impulses as necessary for the development of conscience. Inhibitory morality was based on internalization of prohibitions, where feelings of guilt motivate restraint from wrongdoing. In Piaget's cognitive developmental theory, too, the young child was viewed as motivated to maintain pleasure and avoid pain and lacking a capacity for symbolic representation and perspective taking. Still other developmental theories emphasized the demanding, dependent and egocentric nature of young children.

Much has changed with the accumulation of new multidisciplinary empirical evidence (including evolutionary theories, biology, developmental science, and behavioral economics) about the cognitive, behavioral, social, and emotional competencies of children beginning early in life. But it is important to acknowledge this backdrop, as a reminder of the initial difficulty in achieving the level of knowledge of early morality that most of us now take for granted.

3. Developmental Origins of Concern for Others

Sociobiological Considerations

Many of the early sociobiological theories, while differing on specifics, shared the belief that all altruistic actions can be reduced to self-serving (perpetuation of the species) or self-destructive actions (altruism as self-sacrifice). Altruism viewed this way ignores the continuum on which it occurs and hence the many acts of kindness and concern that are part of everyday life. There is strong research evidence now for the very early origins of these aspects of positive morality. This was anticipated by an evolutionary perspective, unique at that time, on the development of responsibility and caring rooted in the evolution of mammalian species (MacLean 1985). Paul MacLean proposed that empathy emerged with the evolution of mammals and what he termed "a family way of life." This way of life brought with it processes of extended caregiving, attachment, sensitivity to suffering, and responsiveness to the distress cries of the young. MacLean emphasized interconnections of the limbic system with the prefrontal cortex, linked to parental concern for the young that provided the basis for the emergence of a more generalized sense of responsibility for the welfare of others. This suggests a deeply embedded capacity for concern for others that is part of our evolutionary heritage and history. Strong emotions of caring and connection in mammals played an essential role in their thrival as well as their survival.

Neurobiological Considerations

The human capacity for caring for others is then a biological adaptation that conferred a selective advantage by enhancing social cohesion and cooperation, and thus survival. From a neuroscience perspective (Decety 2015a; 2015b), there is substantial evidence that in mammalian species, including humans, emotion plays a causal role in eliciting several prosocial behaviors such as attachment, parental care, and empathy. In humans, these behaviors may originate in the early years of life. Affective aspects of empathy are tied to limbic and paralimbic circuits that develop earlier in ontogeny, whereas cognitive aspects of empathy may rely on prefrontal and temporal cortices, which are slower to mature (Singer 2006; Decety et al. 2016). Our ability to share affective states thus is based on phylogenetically old mechanisms that develop very early in ontogeny. The many interconnections between the limbic system and neocortex provide an important interface between affective and cognitive empathy over the course of development, thus affirming MacLean's earlier hypotheses.

Decety (2011) has described these early processes as components implemented by a complex network of distributed, often recursively connected, interacting neural regions, including the superior temporal sulcus, insula, medial and orbitofrontal cortices, amygdala, and anterior cingulate cortex, as well as autonomic and neuroendocrine processes implicated in (pro-)social behaviors and emotional states (also see Decety and Michalska 2010; Decety 2015a; 2015b, for an elaboration of an evolutionary and neurodevelopmental perspective). There is now a rapidly growing body of literature that examines neural, genetic, psychophysiological, and endocrine components of concern for others and caring behavior (also see Grossmann and Johnson 2007; Hastings et al. 2014).

4. A Theory of the Development of Empathy in Humans

Martin Hoffman (1975) proposed a developmental theory of empathy in childhood. It made use of MacLean's ideas regarding brain connections between the limbic system and prefrontal cortex that integrate primitive emotional responses with higher-order awareness. This can lead to empathic arousal that predisposes individuals toward altruism as they mature (or what we call concern for others).

Hoffman described four stages of empathic development.

> Stage 1. Global empathy. This consists of infants' reflexive, contagious crying in response to the cries of other infants. In

global empathy, which prevails in the first year of life, the distress of self and other are seen as fused, as the infant cannot distinguish between its own and another's distress. This can also be seen a form of personal distress or self-distress.

Stage 2. Egocentric empathy. Here children are aware of the fact that they are physically distinct beings, separate from others. But there is still confusion about internal states, and children's empathic, comforting responses are attuned to the child's own needs rather than those of the person in distress. This emphasis on self-as-distinct as a prerequisite for true concern for others (Stage 3) would appear in later research on explicit, overt expressions of self–other differentiation and self-recognition. Egocentric empathy was thought to begin around the age of one. By around eighteen months, when children begin to distinguish between self and other, they are moving toward the next stage of development.

Stage 3. Other-oriented empathy. This begins later in the second year of life and continues through the preschool years. By now, children can respond to someone else's particular needs, in ways that show empathic concern for the victim, cognitive awareness of the other's circumstances, and prosocial or altruistic actions. These response patterns are still restricted to familiar settings and social contexts for these young children.

Stage 4. Capacity for generalized empathy. This begins at around seven years as children become able to recognize abstract conditions of distress such as orphans, war victims, and other conditions of suffering outside the everyday lives of children.

Hoffman's stage theory was compelling because it was the first mention in developmental psychology of the possibility that empathic arousal could evolve into what we would call concern for others in the first years of life. However, the stages were based on a few anecdotes and hypotheticals rather than empirical data. Around the same time this theory emerged, investigators began to conduct longitudinal studies of the emergence of empathy and prosociality in early childhood (Zahn-Waxler and Radke-Yarrow 1982). This work was carried out at the National Institute of Mental Health (NIMH) in the United States at a time when longitudinal studies were uncommon; empathy was seen as a questionable, amorphous construct; and funding for its research was not perceived as a high priority. It was one thing to develop a theory but another to find a means to conduct research on the topic. At that time, the Intramural Research Program of the NIMH in Bethesda, Maryland, provided opportunities for what they viewed as exploratory but innovative research. This led to the beginnings of a research program on concern for others.

The longitudinal studies had been preceded by experimental work at the NIMH on socialization processes hypothesized to influence three- to five-year-old preschool children's concern for others (Yarrow, Scott, and Waxler 1973). It became clear from this work that concern for others originates even earlier in development; hence it was critical to study these processes in the first years of life. In the decades to follow, there would be a proliferation of research on social-emotional competencies in the first few years of life, as well as on moral judgments and complex understanding of others' motives and behaviors (Hamlin, Wynn, and Bloom 2007; Gopnik 2009; Hamlin 2015; Vaish 2016; Van de Vondervoort and Hamlin 2016). Future research would affirm the core features of early concern for others and extend it in exciting new directions.

5. The Development of Concern for Others in Humans: Empirical Evidence

It was necessary to develop procedures for studying young children's responses to others in distress. Because expressions of others' distress (i.e., the stimuli for concern for others) are infrequent and unpredictable, in the first studies mothers were carefully trained to provide detailed, tape-recorded accounts of observations of their children's responses to others' distress emotions. This included when children observed distress as bystanders (a hungry baby cries) and when they were the cause of the distress (a child bites its mother). In addition to this use of naturalistic observation, experimental probes were used where others enacted distress and children's responses were videotaped in the home (Zahn-Waxler and Radke-Yarrow 1982; Zahn-Waxler, Radke-Yarrow et al. 1992). Mothers also simulated a specific distress each week (e.g., they would pretend to be sad, hurt, or tired). Every three weeks, a home visitor simulated distress. In later studies, children's responses to simulated distress were videotaped both in the home and laboratory. This made it possible to establish the reliability and validity of mothers' observations. Distress simulations are now used routinely in studies of empathy-related responding children across a wide age range.

By using such procedures, different components of concern for others then can be coded separately and objectively. The longitudinal research emphasized measures of emotion, behavior, and cognition that could be inferred from observations of children's reactions. Emotions reflecting empathic concern for the victim consisted of facial, vocal, and postural/gestural expressions (e.g., cocking the head, cooing, sympathetic sounds and statements, concerned looks coded through discrete facial muscle movements). Concern for others can also be manifest in behaviors and cognitions. Behaviors consisted of prosocial acts of helping, sharing, comforting, protecting, and defending. Cognitions were nonverbal and verbal efforts to understand the problem that we referred to hypothesis testing or inquiry that explored the nature of the other's distress (e.g., looking back and for between the injury and its cause, and verbal expressions of concern such as "Owie?" or, "Did you pinch it?" These affective, behavioral, and cognitive components of concern for others were each rated on four-point scales to assess the degree of their presence. Self-distress (i.e., frets, whimpers, cries) was similarly rated.

Typical Development of Concern for Others

Typically, children were one year of age when the research started and were followed through the second and third years of life (Zahn-Waxler, Radke-Yarrow, and King 1979; Zahn-Waxler, Radke-Yarrow et al. 1992; Zahn-Waxler, Robinson, and Emde 1992; Knafo et al. 2008). Based on the ages of the children studied, it was possible to examine characteristics of stages 2 and 3 proposed by Hoffman. Neither theory nor research at that time suggested a reason to study children before the age of one. We found, however, that empathic concern was already present by age one, indicating the early existence of an other-oriented affective response toward someone in distress. This affective component of concern did not increase with age. By one year of age, self-distress or personal distress in response to another's distress was present but infrequent. It diminished further between twelve and twenty-four months of age.

By one year of age, most children could comfort another in distress, through simple nonverbal, mostly physical gestures and postures (touching, patting, hugging, affectionately leaning in) (Zahn-Waxler, Radke-Yarrow et al. 1992). These responses were not common, but they were present by this time. From the onset such actions, though simple in form of expression, appeared to reflect concern for the other in distress. That is, there was no suggestion that these early expressions represented egocentric empathy, thought to predominate in Stage 2. Language began to play a role between eighteen and twenty-four months, as some children expressed verbal sympathy. Since then, we also have learned that early language predicts concern for others during the first three years of life (Rhee, Boeldt et al. 2013).

Cognitive exploration of the other's distress also increased during this time period as children made efforts to understand the nature of the other's problem and the impact on the victim. The development of language during this period contributed to increases in children's cognitive inquiries and perspective taking. This early cognitive ability is consistent with later research indicating cognitive capacities of infants related to developing moral codes and making moral judgments about wrongdoing in harming others in this time period (Hamlin et al. 2007; Gopnik 2009; Cowell and Decety 2015b).

Behavioral expressions of concern for others became more frequent and more varied over the second and third years of life. Young children helped, shared, comforted, sympathized, protected, and defended persons in distress. The naturalistic observations obtained occurred primarily within the family home and neighborhood settings, often involving parents, siblings, and other relatives but also playmates and neighbors. Concern for others sometimes was directed to strangers. For example, a child seeing a man in a store who seemed unhappy told his mother, "I want to make that man happy." Caring actions were seen in most children, though to varying degrees. Increasingly, over time the actions took more nuanced and sophisticated forms of expression (e.g., making multiple attempts, sensitive attunements, and adjustments if a particular prosocial act did not work).

While prosocial actions and cognitive understanding increased with age, the affective component, that is, empathic concern, did not (Knafo et al. 2008). Concern for others was already present to a substantial degree and did not change over time. These early hallmarks of our humanity remind us that we enter this world with a capacity to care for others (some more than others), or as has also been said, "wired to be social." In a study of twins in utero, each twin reached out to the other in apparent nonrandom patterns, the authors using the term "caressed" to describe the actions (Castiello et al. 2010).

These affective, behavioral, and cognitive qualities that constitute concern for others are illustrated in the following description by a mother reporter of a complex set of caring responses by her eighteen-month-old daughter toward a crying infant:

A neighbor asked me to watch her child. After she left the baby began to shriek. He was very upset by my efforts to comfort him, so I put him in a high chair and gave him a cookie. As soon as he began to cry, Julie looked very startled and worried. Her body stiffened. She bent toward him and cocked her head, reaching toward him. He began to throw the cookies. She tried to return them, which surprised me because usually she tries to eat everyone's cookies. She put the pieces on the tray and looked very worried. Her eyebrows were up and her lips were pursed. Then I put him back on the floor. She hovered over him whimpering herself and looking at me questioningly. I put him in the playpen and he continued to cry once in a while. She began to stroke his hair, and she reached into the playpen and patted his shoulder. I could hear her cooing and making concerned sounds. Then she came into to the kitchen, took my hand and led me to the living room. She kept looking at me with a very concerned, worried look. Then she took my hand and tried to put it on top of Brian's head.

The finding of little or no developmental change for the affective component, of concern for others, in contrast to the increase with age in the behavioral and cognitive components has been found in other studies (see review by Davidov et al. 2013). In one study of children ranging in age from preschool to sixth grade, empathic concern/sympathy they felt for a crying baby remained constant over age. Children reported far more sympathy than anger or fear, affirming its strong presence in children's social repertoires (Zahn-Waxler, Friedman, and Cummings 1983).

This research illustrates the importance of distinguishing different elements of concern for others or what was termed empathy in Hoffman's stage theory. Affective, behavioral, and cognitive components are interrelated, but only to a degree, and the components may function differently, as was the case for the affective component. It may emerge full-blown in some children and be more moderate, minimal, or nonexistent in other children. As noted earlier, it shows a traitlike quality that shows stability over time (Knafo et al. 2008). Like several other emotions, it does not necessarily grow or diminish with time on its own, that is, as a function of development per se. Emotions may become more regulated, but there is no reason to think that they automatically increase with age. Decety (2011; 2015b) has presented a strong argument for the need to parse different aspects of empathy, and this is one example of the importance of doing so.

6. Expansions of Research on Concern for Others

Developments in the First Year of Life

With regard to Hoffman's theory there was not a good fit with respect to stages 2 and 3, either in terms of the nature of phenomena observed or developmental progressions identified using a longitudinal research design. More recent research provides an opportunity to consider the viability of Stage 1.

There is now a growing body of work regarding young infants' implicit capacity for self–other differentiation (see review by Davidov et al. 2013), which is present in the first year of life. This suggests that awareness of others, and hence the potential for concern for them, also could be present at that time. While efforts to examine empathic concern in such young infants have been rare, some evidence exists. Evidence also suggests that self-distress in response to others' distress does not result from infants' confusion between their own and another's distress (i.e., global empathic arousal, hypothesized by Hoffman as Stage 1) but rather reflects difficulty with emotion regulation.

Hay, Nash, and Pederson (1981) observed pairs of six-month-old infants in a playroom and examined responses to the spontaneous crying and fussing of the peer. Self-distress responses were very rare; instead, young infants typically responded in an other-focused manner: the large majority directed their attention to the crying peer, and many oriented toward the other infant by leaning, gesturing, or touching. Thus, other-oriented responses to another's distress can already be observed well before the second year of life, contrary to existing theory. A recent study of eight-month-old babies observed with peers (Liddle, Bradley, and Mcgrath 2015) confirms the findings of Hay et al. (1981); it identified expressions of empathic concern and prosocial behavior, and also found that the other-oriented responses helped to settle down and comfort fussy and crying babies.

Roth-Hanania, Davidov, and Zahn-Waxler (2011) followed a small sample of young infants' responses to distress before and after their first birthday. They examined responses to maternal distress simulations and to a video of a crying infant from eight to sixteen months, using an accelerated longitudinal design. Again, contrary to theory, concern for others emerged *prior* to the second year of life. Moderate levels of both affective and cognitive components of concern for others were already present at eight and ten months. And both components predicted prosocial behaviors in the second year of life when children are able to engage in caring actions. Here also, while the cognitive element increased gradually during the transition to the second year, the affective element did not. This again highlights the need to distinguish between the different components of concern for others. A follow-up longitudinal study of a larger sample of infants at three, six, twelve, and eighteen months is ongoing. Preliminary analyses reveal similar patterns (Davidov et al. 2017). Darwin's observation of sympathy in his five-month-old son was prophetic in this regard.

Reflexive (contagious) crying in infants, originally termed global empathic arousal in Hoffman's theory, is increasingly thought to be part of an entirely different system that involves difficulty in regulating emotion (Davidov et al. 2013; Decety 2016). Thus, another interpretation is that rather than being an empathic contagious response to another baby crying, as often conceived, this reaction in fact reveals another function that is anything but empathic. It could be that the function of this cry is to compete for caregiver attention, a call for the mother to come and nurse rather than a response to someone else's infant (Campos et al. 2008;

Decety and Cowell, 2017). In studies of contagious crying in infants of different ages in the first year of life, crying does not occur immediately but only when the (intense) cry stimulus is sustained over a minute or two (Geangu et al. 2010). In addition, this reflexive behavior is no longer observed at five months of age. Contagious crying does not gradually give way to empathic concern during the first year of life.

We propose based on the recent research of Davidov and colleagues that *two separate affective response systems* are active from the early months of life when children are exposed to another's distress. The one system (self-distress), we would argue, signals a *need for caregiving* by others as the child becomes dysregulated by another's distress. The other system signals the presence of the potential for *provision of caregiving*. The two systems are diametrical opposites in what they represent in terms of needing from others versus providing for others. We would expect the neural and other biological manifestations to differ as well. In summary, research on the origins of concern for others indicates that (a) it occurs much earlier in development than hypothesized; (b) there are two quite different systems in play almost from the onset of life; and (c) there are multiple ways in which it may manifest itself, hence casting doubt on the viability of Hoffman's stage theory.

Empathic Happiness and Empathic Cheerfulness

Because empathy, as typically construed, is a response to another's suffering, emotions experienced are negatively toned. If one feels another's sorrow, one also feels sad. If one winces while witnessing another's pain, it becomes part of one's own experience. However, this captures only one aspect of empathy. Other more positively toned forms may also occur early in development. According to Darwin (1872), expressions of empathy toward someone in distress involve the quality of tenderness. For him, components of tenderness included affection, joy, and sympathy, thus bringing in the importance of positive emotions. Collectively, *empathic concern, empathic happiness,* and *empathic cheerfulness* are "empathy subtypes" that may play both common and unique roles in children's caring actions. Relatively little research has been done on empathic happiness and empathic cheerfulness. Most of what has been done is with older children, but these phenomena are likely to occur much earlier as well (Light and Zahn-Waxler 2011).

Empathic happiness is in play when others' expressions of pleasure and joy elicit parallel responses in those who witness the happiness of others. As with *empathic concern,* there is a presumed mirroring or neural resonance with the other's emotions, along with an other-oriented feeling of goodwill. Sallquist et al. (2009) found that empathic happiness in preschool children was associated with what they termed greater empathy/sympathy toward another in distress. Empathic cheerfulness does not involve a mirroring or neural resonance to the other's emotions, but it does involve the use of a basic positive emotion.

It has been known for some time that empathic happiness emerges very early in development. Infants can respond to the positive affect of others by showing vicarious happiness. Ten-week-old infants' responses to images of happy, sad, and angry faces made by their mothers' elicited distinct matching responses (Haviland and Lelwica 1987), most frequently in response to mothers' expressions of joy. The active use of positive emotion to relieve another's distress, that is, empathic cheerfulness, has roots in infancy too. Infants as young as four months attempt to reengage their mothers using positive affect when the mother makes a still-face display (Cohn, Campbell, and Ross 1991). Also, the study by Liddle et al. (2015) found that six-month-old peers' smiling responses to playmates in distress appeared to provide comfort. Caring and helping behaviors are associated with activation of the reward and pleasure circuits in both nonhuman animals and in humans (Decety 2011). Giving (treats) to others makes young children happy, even happier than when they receive treats themselves (Aknin, Hamlin, and Dunn 2012).

General positive emotion and *empathic happiness* may facilitate both *empathic concern* and *empathic cheerfulness*, which are interrelated in older children (Light et al. 2009). Young children who are friendly and cheerful and enjoy the company of others are also likely to resonate to the pleasure of others. Sociability (e.g., Volbrecht et al. 2007), dispositional cheerfulness, and positive hedonic tone (Robinson et al. 1994) are associated with empathic concern in the first three years of life. In one longitudinal study, positive affect observed in four-month-olds predicted concern for others at two years of age (Young, Fox, and Zahn-Waxler 1999). Future research on concern for others in distress would benefit from including assessment of positive affective states, empathic cheerfulness in particular, because it can be a powerful means of lifting another out of state of distress.

7. Maladaptive Responses to Others in Distress

Three extremes of concern for others, that is, surfeits, active deficits, and passive deficits, emerge in the first years of life. These extremes have been associated with later psychological and psychiatric problems. Caring too much for others in distress is more commonly associated with internalizing problems such as depression and anxiety. Lack of concern for others is associated with disorders such as conduct problems/antisocial behavior, psychopathy, and autism spectrum. Both within the range of typical development (McClure 2000) and at the extremes, girls show higher concern for others than boys, and boys show more disregard than girls (Hastings et al. 2000). This parallels sex differences in psychopathology from childhood and adolescence through adulthood. Conduct problems and autism-spectrum problems show a marked male preponderance, while anxiety and depression show a marked female preponderance (Zahn-Waxler, Shirtcliff, and Marceau 2008). Empathy deficits are symptoms that help define male-related problems. Empathy surfeits are correlates and sometimes causes of female-related problems. Gender differences in concern and disregard, in conjunction with gender differences in child temperament (Else-Quest et al. 2006) and socialization experiences (Zahn-Waxler, Shirtcliff and Marceau 2008), may provide a better window into our understanding of etiologies of these different psychological and psychiatric problems (Rutter, Caspi and Moffitt 2003).

Surfeits of Concern for Others in Distress

Concern for others can have negative consequences if it becomes extreme, inappropriate, or dysregulated. It can be a risk factor for depression. Depression is multidetermined, with familial transmission in play due both to genetic and environmental factors. One form of extreme concern that may have consequences for the development of depression (and anxiety as well) begins early in life. Some young children come to believe that they are responsible for hurting others when in fact they have not caused the problems. Often at an early age it is difficult for them to distinguish between these two sets of circumstances. The fact that they also sometimes do cause pain and distress in others further compounds the confusion. We have seen toddlers apologize for their actions even when they had done nothing wrong. This was sometimes done in a way that reflected negative self-judgment, seen in such statements as "Sorry, I bad. I be nice."

Guilt proneness may be part of some children's nature (Zahn-Waxler, Kochanska et al. 1990) or they may be socialized to feel responsible even when innocent of wrongdoing. Child-rearing practices that focus on guilt-induction (psychological induction gone awry), that is, making the child feel responsible for the problems of others, can have adverse consequences. Family environments where children are exposed to extreme and chronic distress in parents are especially pernicious. Toddlers who witness marital fights between parents and preschool children exposed to parental depression are more likely to become overinvolved and eventually depleted by trying to take care of the problems of others (who are supposed to be taking care of them) (Cummings, Zahn-Waxler and Radke-Yarrow 1981; Zahn-Waxler, Kochanska et al. 1990; Radke-Yarrow et al. 1994). These are children who show high levels of concerned actions (e.g., trying to comfort a depressed mother; trying to break up a fight between parents). They assume more responsibility and a burden of guilt than is appropriate for their age.

These overly high levels of concern thus can become fused with feelings of guilt, blameworthiness, and helplessness. Depression can be observed in children as young as three years and it is marked by self-conscious emotions of guilt and shame (Luby et al. 2009). These conditions have been implicated in the development of learned helplessness that is a key element in depression. Individuals begin to make attributions of self-responsibility that are internal, global, and stable ("It's my fault, it happens all the time, and it will always be that way"). Substantial research now supports associations between high levels of caring for others (especially in adverse environments) and symptoms of anxiety and depression in children and adolescents, especially for girls (see the review by Zahn-Waxler and Van Hulle 2011). This is one example of how surfeits in caring for others in distress can contribute to psychopathology, internalizing problems in particular (Zahn-Waxler and Schoen 2016). For children who show too much concern, interventions exist to improve social functioning by reducing children's sense of responsibility (Beardslee et al. 2003).

Deficits in Concern for Others in Distress

Active Disregard The ability to empathize mediates prosocial behavior when sensitivity to others' distress is paired with a drive toward their welfare (Decety 2015a). Disruption or atypical development of the neural circuits that process distress cues and integrates them with decision value leads to callous disregard for others, in the case of psychopathy. Active disregard emerges in the second year of life, slightly later than concern for others. By then, some young children appear to enjoy others' suffering and show anger and judgmental reactions (Zahn-Waxler, Radke-Yarrow et al. 1992). This occurs less often than concern for others, is seen in fewer children, and like the affective component of concern for others does not increase with age during this time period as do prosocial actions. But it is a potent, maladaptive reaction that bodes poorly for future relationships. It is seen in children raised in hostile environments. Maltreated toddlers show more active disregard and less concern for peers in distress than nonmaltreated toddlers (e.g., Klimes-Dougan and

Kistner 2001). Active disregard at this age may be a precursor of later active devaluation of others that is part of psychopathic traits.

The importance of (observed) active disregard for others in early development is highlighted in two recent studies of children in the second and third years of life (Rhee, Boeldt et al. 2013; Rhee, Friedman et al. 2013). Early active disregard predicted antisocial behavior in childhood and adolescence based on mother, teacher, and child reports. Early language predicted less disregard and greater concern, suggesting the possible protective role and the need to encourage language from the first years of life. In another study (Hastings et al. 2000), children at high risk for later conduct problems did not differ from low-risk children on concern for others at age five, but the high-risk boys did show more active disregard. High-risk children at age five showed a decrease in observed concern for others by age seven. They also showed less concern for others than their counterparts according to their own reports as well as those of their mothers and teachers. By age seven, active disregard was linked to maternal authoritarian parenting (controlling for initial level of behavior problems), suggesting the role of socialization experiences as well as intrinsic factors (also see Waller et al. 2013 and Wagner et al. 2015 regarding the role of parenting and child characteristics in the expression of callous-unemotional traits).

With regard to biological markers, there is ample research on physiological correlates of active deficits and antisocial behavior (Ortiz and Raine 2004). Measures of physiological underarousal (e.g., low heart rate, low skin conductance) are often associated with callous/psychopathic traits and antisocial behavior (Lahey et al. 1993). Such traits and behaviors eventually become inversely related to empathic concern and prosocial behavior (Eisenberg et al. 2007). Physiological underarousal can be seen in aggressive children as young as three years (Ortiz and Raine 2004), though this is not invariable. In one study, aggressive/disruptive toddlers showed heightened rather than diminished physiological reactivity and they did not show lower concern for others than controls (Gill and Calkins 2003). At least in the early years of life, concern for the welfare of others can exist in conjunction with behaviors that violate the rights of others. Negative relations between concern for others and aggression (and their physiological correlates) may develop over time, suggesting the value of early interventions as concern is still preserved in some young aggressive children (Hastings et al. 2000).

Atypical processes are also present at the neural level in adolescents with conduct disorder and psychopathic traits. A study using electroencephalogram (EEG) examined this phenomenon by assessing how callous-unemotional traits in juvenile psychopaths are related to empathetic arousal deficits (Cheng, Hung, and Decety 2012). In this study, juvenile offenders with high callous-unemotional traits, juvenile offenders with low callous-unemotional traits, and age-matched typically-developing adolescents were shown stimuli of people in pain while EEG/event-related brain potentials (ERPs) were recorded. Results demonstrated that youth with high callous-unemotional traits exhibit atypical neural dynamics of pain empathy processing in the early stages of affective arousal. This abnormality was exemplified by a lack of the early EPR response (120 ms), thought to reflect an automatic aversive reaction to negative stimuli, and was coupled with relative insensitivity to actual pain (as measured with the pressure pain threshold). Nevertheless, their capacity to understand intentionality was not impaired, nor was their sensorimotor resonance.

Functional magnetic resonance imaging (MRI) studies have reported that adolescents with disruptive psychopathic traits show reduced activity to increasing perceived pain intensity within structures typically implicated in affective responses to others' pain, including the rostral anterior cingulate cortex, insula, and amygdala (Marsh et al. 2008). Youths appeared to show no neural response deficits in pain-experiencing regions when viewing others in distress. However, those with conduct disorder showed less coupling compared to controls between the amygdala, a key region in emotion processing, and the ventromedial prefrontal cortex, a region thought to be involved in behavioral responses (Decety et al. 2009). Another study with adolescents with conduct disorder also found structural neural deficits associated with lack of empathy (Sterzer et al. 2007). By adolescence, these processes have crystallized, affirming the need to study active disregard as a precursor of psychopathic traits at the neural level early in development.

Passive Disregard for Others Laboratory research using structured distress probes documents deficits in empathy and prosocial behavior in young children on the autism spectrum (Hobson et al. 2009; Hutman et al. 2012) consistent with parent reports. One longitudinal study of empathic concern and active disregard for others in twins at fourteen and twenty months of age also included a measure of unresponsiveness to another's distress (similar to passive disregard). It was more common in boys than girls and did not increase, on average, in frequency between fourteen and twenty months, though a subset of children who had had positive socialization experiences at fourteen months began to show empathic concern by twenty months (Zahn-Waxler, Robinson, and Emde 1992; Robinson et al. 1994). As with concern and active disregard, unresponsiveness showed some heritable influence. In three recent studies, toddlers at greater genetic risk for autism spectrum disorder (ASD) by virtue of having an older sibling with ASD showed little empathic concern relative to low-risk toddlers (Hutman et al. 2010; McDonald and Messinger 2012; Campbell et al. 2015). Hutman et al. (2010) showed that such genetically high-risk children not only showed lack of concern compared low-risk participants, as well as high-risk participants for other reasons, they were also more likely to be diagnosed later with ASD. The response to distress paradigm is now considered to be a worthwhile target for early intervention.

It is not clear why some children consistently show a lack of concern for others that is passive in its form of expression. They may be on the autism spectrum, where unresponsiveness reflects core deficits in empathy and related abilities to express more positively toned affect. They may show high sensitivity to environmental stressors, seen in high internal arousal indexed by high levels of cortisol (Putnam et al. 2015). Lack of communicative skills associated with neurological deficits may blunt empathy in some children. Since language plays a significant role in the expression of empathy even in the first years (Hutman et al. 2012; Rhee, Boeldt et al. 2013), the study of variations in language in autistic children may help to explain why empathy is more preserved in some of them. (Scheeren et al. 2013).

In humans, exposure to high levels of prenatal androgens may result in masculine behavior and abilities. Simon Baron-Cohen has proposed an extreme male brain of autism whereby fetal testosterone, more common in males than females, creates a hypermasculinized brain, associated with autism/Asperger's, difficulty in social relationships, and restricted interests (Baron-Cohen 2002). This may also be true at a subsyndromal level. In typically developing four-year-olds, high fetal testosterone predicted problems in empathy, social relationships, and restricted interests, for both boys and girls (Knickmeyer et al. 2005). Similar patterns were observed in other research, with fetal testosterone, showing an inverse relationship with empathy (Chapman et al. 2006; Knickmeyer et al. 2006). More male-typical behaviors and fewer female-typical behaviors, including empathy (Constantinescu and Hines 2012), have been found in females exposed to high levels of testosterone prenatally because of the genetic disorder congenital adrenal hyperplasia (CAH) or because mothers were prescribed hormones during pregnancy.

Passive deficits occur on a continuum; low concern does not necessarily reflect psychopathology but can still create interpersonal problems. Some of these children may be shy/behaviorally inhibited, hence uncomfortable in new situations (which is typically the case with laboratory studies and meeting new people). We know little, though, about when low empathic concern reflects a problem or the degree to which it is amenable to modification. For children on the autism spectrum, in particular, this will be quite difficult. Physiological and gene-related effects have been associated with low empathic concern. For example, low empathy in preschool children of depressed mothers is associated with right frontal EEG asymmetry (Jones, Field, and Davalos 2000). Also, the AVPR1A gene variant is associated with preschooler's low altruistic behavior (Avinun et al. 2011).

8. Reflections and Future Directions

There is a propensity to assume that most important aspects of development, in addition to physical growth, also increase with age as we become cognitively more complex, emotionally more regulated, and socially more sophisticated in our interactions with others. We begin life as very simple creatures compared with where we end up as adults. Because emotions occur at the onset of life and appear to show primacy in early development, they are viewed by some as more primitive (and less trustworthy) than our (higher-order) thought processes, the latter being a more reliable guide for navigating our lives in general and moral lives in particular (Bloom 2014). But adults are not necessarily more caring than children and can do harm that far exceeds anything that children could conceive of or do. Adults as well as children can be selfish, egocentric, and aggressive. Physical violence and sexual abuse are common within and outside of family settings, and wars continue to create great suffering, despite Steven Pinker's (2011) compelling argument that we have become less violent and more peaceful over the course of civilization. We return then to the scientific questions prompted by early philosophers, who were also sometimes protopsychologists.

Motives for Prosocial Behavior

Earlier philosophical debates about motives for altruism were played out in research that began in the 1980s. Batson and Shaw (1990) argued for a pluralism of prosocial motives (altruistic and egoistic) in adults, some of which have their origins in empathically based concern. Cialdini (1990) argued, in contrast, that all prosocial behaviors can be explained most parsimoniously by egoistically based motives, that is, such behaviors are ultimately motivated by desire for reward, fear of punishment, or need to reduce aversive arousal experienced in response to another's distress. Batson and Shaw conducted a series of elegantly designed studies that provided a plausible case for the possibility that prosocial, caring acts under certain conditions are grounded in empathic concern and do not simply result from reward/punishment contingencies or efforts to reduce personal distress.

Since this time, some psychologists have attempted to examine similar kinds of questions from a developmental perspective. A recent special section of the journal *Child Development* (Davidov et al. 2016), for example, focuses on the various motives and potential explanatory mechanisms that underlie prosocial behaviors in children. Empathic concern is one core motive. It may at once intermingle with and be separate in nature from other motives. There are many contemporary research venues for addressing issues previously restricted to the domains of theology and philosophy. It remains a question, however, as to whether science alone can ever fully determine whether prosocial behavior in humans is ultimately guided by altruistic, egoistic, or manipulative motives.

Nature and Nurture

Philosophers' theories about the roles of nature and nurture in positive morality were faithfully played out in research on constitutional and environmental influences on empathic concern and prosociality. One of the first experimental studies of concern for others followed young children in a nursery school setting over a six-week period (Yarrow, Scott, and Waxler 1973). Four groups of children received different kinds of training in real and symbolic distress situations. Two of these four groups were treated by the experimenter (who also functioned as a nursery school teacher) in a warm, nurturant manner. In the other two groups, the adult was more distant and did not behave in a nurturant manner. Only the condition that combined nurturance toward the child and generalized training (through instruction, perspective taking, and modeling prosocial behaviors in both real and symbolic distress situations) resulted in generalized concern for others. These findings were replicated and extended using other research designs (Zahn-Waxler, Radke-Yarrow, and King 1994; Robinson, Zahn-Waxler, and Emde 1994). A very recent study (Eisenberg et al. 2015) is notable in that it followed children into adulthood and found an effect of maternal socialization over time (controlling for earlier levels of children's concern for others). Adult children whose mothers were warm and supportive during childhood (and showed little negative affect) showed the most sympathy and concern for others in distress. While many other studies have also reported beneficial effects of such socialization practices on children's concern for others, there are always a number who are unaffected.

Constitutional or temperament differences have been implicated both in why some children are not responsive and conversely why others are highly sensitive to positive socialization experiences. Cowell and Decety (2015) remind us of the complex interplay among neural, socioenvironmental, and behavioral facets for understanding early manifestations of morality in development and of some ways this can be studied. A recent neurodevelopmental study of moral sensitivity (Decety and Cowell 2015b) identifies direct links between implicit moral evaluations and actual moral behavior (generosity) in young children (three to five years) and identifies specific neuromarkers of each. A study of twelve- to twenty-four-month olds found strong individual differences in moral evaluations that were reflected in neural differences, linked to their own generosity and predicted by parents' sensitivity to justice (Cowell and Decety 2015a). Several other studies now focus on interactions between genetics (and other biological factors) and environment to help us understand individual differences in early expressions of concern for others as well as other signs of early positive morality (e.g., Bakermans-Kranenburg and van IJzendoorn 2008; 2011; Knafo et al. 2011; McDonald et al. 2016; Apter-Levy et al. 2013; DiLalla et al. 2015).

Cognition and Emotion

Scientific and conceptual progress has put us in a better position than our forefathers to speak to the roles of both emotion and reason in the moral lives of children. One wonders whether theories would have differed and whether it would have taken so long if societies had allowed for the possibility of analytic foremothers; women as caregivers would have had more experience and arguably more sensitivity to the role of emotions in positive morality in young children. Cumulatively, research points to the vital roles of emotion *and* cognition in supporting our caring actions toward others. Both are present very early in life in children's responses to the distress of others and commonly work in synchrony.

There is no reason to choose between cognitive and affective processes, one being more vital to positive morality than the other. But the role of emotion, empathy in particular, has a growing body of critics. Bloom (2014) claims that empathy is fragile and can misguide us. According to Bloom, empathy is a "parochial, narrow-minded" emotion, one that "will have to yield to reason if humanity is to have a future." Such arguments against empathy rely on an outdated view of emotion as a beast that needs to yield to sober reason (Cameron, Inzlicht, and Cunningham 2015). Sober reason sounds good in the abstract. But it is often hard to come by for most people and arguably is as "fragile" as empathy. Moral judgments and evaluations of fairness and justice are often in the eyes of the beholder. There may be universals but it is often difficult to agree upon and enact them.

A functionalist theory of emotion stresses the adaptive value of all basic emotions. When they become extreme and dysregulated, they will cause problems. But they are all there for a reason. In the case of empathy, it will indeed fail sometimes when it starts to exhaust the individual, but excess of concern is not commonly seen. Much more problematic, both for the individual and society than an excess of concern, is the failure to experience emotional arousal and concern for others. These are the opposites of empathy that we now know are also present in the first years of life. Most studies of responses to others' suffering have not emphasized these opposites seen both in active and passive disregard. It would be better to direct our efforts here "if humanity is to have a future," rather than on an excess of concern for others.

We come full circle back to the minority view of Adam Smith in his theory of moral sentiments (Smith 1759/1790). He well knew the need for dispassion and the role of self-interest in human affairs. But he also reminded us that morality is not always calculating. Human beings are social creatures, born with natural empathy; and concern for the well-being of others is essential to morality. Both affective and cognitive empathy must be in play if our moral potentials are to be fully realized.

Kith, Kin, and Beyond

Kith are our neighbors and kin are our relatives. It is most natural for us to extend ourselves to family members and others who are close to us, those who are similar, those who are familiar, those with whom we have had a great deal of experience, and those from whom we know what to expect. Most theories predict that we show more empathic concern toward those we know than toward strangers for both biological and environmental reasons, and that this begins early in life. Often the longitudinal studies of concern for others that consistently examine children's concerned responses both toward mothers and strangers (which, in fact, are positively correlated) are cited by others to make the point that young children's caring is parochial, confined mainly to family and little to strangers. It is the case that children show more *prosocial behavior* to their mothers than to an adult stranger. But they do not invariably show less *empathic concern* (i.e., the affective component) toward the stranger, and sometimes they show more to the stranger than to their mothers (Knafo et al. 2008). Rather than focusing solely on the differences, it is important to (a) recognize that some children do show concern toward strangers even at a very young age; and (b) consider how to foster this in others who don't, as part of an effort to widen their social worlds and recipients of their caring and concern, as they grow older. We've seen that some caregivers are able to create these wider worlds for their children. This will always be a challenge given that the capacity for empathy is not limitless (Cameron et al. 2015), but this should not limit us from trying to help parents expand their children's social networks as well as their own to include greater diversity.

It is valuable then for parents, teachers, and other caregivers to encourage children's social competence, including expressions of concern for others, and to begin early in life. Several programs are available, though still more often for older than younger children, and there is considerable research to guide additional programs (see the review by Zahn-Waxler and Schoen 2016). Recent classroom interventions with preschool and older children focus on mindfulness and loving-kindness practices to increase attention and self-regulation, heighten compassion, and reduce bullying and other forms of aggression (Flook et al. 2015). Practices to increase mindfulness are now used with parents (Coatsworth et al. 2015) to heighten empathy for their offspring and themselves.

Debates about human nature are likely to continue throughout time. Each generation will strive to understand factors that contribute to compassion, caring, and commitment to others' suffering, as well as those that predict insensitivity, hostility, and the placing of one's needs at the expense of others. These debates can continue to provide a constructive forum for addressing these questions. Because science and the research designs it generates are not perfect, the conclusions we draw will have limitations. For those who have often had the opportunity to observe young children's unadulterated and unsullied expressions of concern for others, it is both plausible and essential to assume that human prosocial actions have empathic as well as egoistic motives. Folk wisdom and an abundance of scientific data indicate that people vary considerably in their capacities to establish empathic ties. It may be time to focus less on developmental change per se in concern for others, and more on conditions that contribute to why we vary, not only in concern but also in our inabilities to care for one another. Only then will we be in a better position to identify means to inculcate positive morality in children, especially for those who find it difficult to empathize, help, comfort, share, and care for one another.

References

Aknin, L. B., J. K. Hamlin and E. W. Dunn. 2012. Giving Leads to Happiness in Young Children. *PLoS One*, 7, e39211. doi: 10.1371/journal.pone.0039211.

Apter-Levy, Y., M. Feldman, A. Vakart, R. P. Ebstein and R. Feldman. 2013. Impact of Maternal Depression across the First 6 Years of Life on the Child's Mental Health, Social Engagement, and Empathy: The Moderating Role of Oxytocin. *American Journal of Psychiatry*, 170, 1161–8. doi: 10.1176/appi.ajp.2013.12121597.

Avinun, R., S. Israel, I. Shalev, et al. 2011. AVPR1A Variant Associated with Preschoolers' Lower Altruistic Behavior. *PLoS One*, 6, e25274. doi: 10.1371/journal.pone.0025274.

Bakermans-Kranenburg, M. J. and M. H. van IJzendoorn. 2008. Oxytocin Receptor (OXTR) and Serotonin Transporter (5-HTT) Genes Associated with Observed Parenting. *Social Cognitive and Affective Neuroscience*, 3, 128–34. doi: 10.1093/scan/nsn004.

2011. Differential Susceptibility to Rearing Environment Depending on Dopamine-Related Genes: New Evidence and a Meta-Analysis. *Development and Psychopathology*, 23, 39–52. doi: 10.1017/S0954579410000635.

Baron-Cohen, S. 2002. The Extreme Male Brain Theory of Autism. *Trends in Cognitive Sciences*, 6, 248–54. doi: 10.1016/S13646613(02)019046.

Batson, C. D. and L. L. Shaw. 1990. Evidence for Altruism: Toward a Pluralism of Prosocial Motives. *Psychological Inquiry*, 2, 107–22. doi: 10.1207/s15327965pli0202_1.

Beardslee, W. R., T. R. Gladstone, E. J. Wright and A. B. Cooper. 2003. A Family-Based Approach to the Prevention of Depressive Symptoms in Children at Risk: Evidence of Parental and Child Change. *Pediatrics*, 112, e119–31. doi: 10.1542/peds.112.2.e119.

Bloom, P. 2014. Against Empathy. *Boston Review*. bostonreview.net/forum/paul-bloom-against-empathy (accessed November 2016).

Cameron, D., M. Inzlicht and W. Cunningham. 2015. Empathy Is Actually a Choice. *New York Times*. nyti.ms/1GcEOYR (accessed November 2016).

Campbell, S. B., N. B. Leezenbaum, E. N. Schmidt, T. N. Day and C. A. Brownell. 2015. Concern for Another's Distress in Toddlers at High and Low Genetic Risk for Autism Spectrum Disorder. *Journal of Autism and Developmental Disorders*, 45, 3594–605. doi: 10 1007/s10803-015-2505-7.

Campos, J. J., D. Witherington, D. I. Anderson, C. I. Frankel, I. Uchiyama and M. Barbu-Roth. 2008. Rediscovering Development in Infancy. *Child Development*, 79, 1625–32. doi: 10.1111/j.1467-8624.2008.01212.x.

Castiello, U., C. Becchio, S. Zoia, et al. 2010. Wired to Be Social: The Ontogeny of Human Interaction. *PloS one*, 5, e13199. doi: 10.1371/journal.pone.0013199.

Chapman, E., S. Baron-Cohen, B. Auyeung, R. Knickmeyer, K. Taylor and G. Hackett. 2006. Fetal Testosterone and Empathy: Evidence from the Empathy Quotient (EQ) and the "Reading the Mind in the Eyes" Test. *Social Neuroscience*, 1, 135–48. doi: 10.1080/17470910600992239.

Cheng, Y., A. Y. Hung and J. Decety. 2012. Dissociation between Affective Sharing and Emotion Understanding in Juvenile Psychopaths. *Development and Psychopathology*, 24, 623–36. doi: 10.1017/S095457941200020X.

Cialdini, R. B. 1991. Altruism or Egoism? That Is (Still) the Question. *Psychological Inquiry*, 2, 124–6. doi: 10.1207/s15327965pli0202_3.

Coatsworth, J. D., L. G. Duncan, R. L. Nix, et al. 2015. Integrating Mindfulness with Parent Training: Effects of the Mindfulness-Enhanced Strengthening Families Program. *Developmental Psychology*, 51, 26–35. doi: 10.1037/a0038212.

Cohn, J. F., S. B. Campbell and S. Ross. 1991. Infant Response in the Still-Face Paradigm at 6 Months Predicts Avoidant and Secure Attachment at 12 Months. *Development and Psychopathology*, 3, 367–76. doi: 10.1017/S0954579400007574.

Constantinescu, M. and M. Hines. 2012. Relating Prenatal Testosterone Exposure to Postnatal Behavior in Typically Developing Children: Methods and Findings. *Child Development Perspectives*, 6, 407–13. doi: 10.1111/j.17508606.2012.00257.x.

Cowell, J. M. and J. Decety. 2015a. Precursors to Morality in Development as a Complex Interplay between Neural, Socioenvironmental, and Behavioral Facets. *Proceedings of the National Academy of Sciences*, 112, 12657–62. doi: 10.1073/pnas.1508832112.

2015b. The Neuroscience of Implicit Moral Evaluation and Its Relation to Generosity in Early Childhood. *Current Biology*, 25, 93–7. doi: 10.1016/j.cub.2014.11.002.

Cummings, E. M., C. Zahn-Waxler and M. Radke-Yarrow. 1981. Young Children's Responses to Expressions of Anger and Affection by Others in the Family. *Child Development*, 52, 1274–82. doi: 10.2307/1129516.

Darwin, C., 1872. *The Expression of the Emotions in Man and Animals*. London: John Marry.

Davidov, M., A. Vaish, A. Knafo-Noam and P. D. Hastings. 2016. The Motivational Foundations of Prosocial Behavior from a Developmental Perspective: Evolutionary Roots and Key Psychological Mechanisms. Introduction to Special Section. *Child Development*, 87(6), 1655–67.

Davidov, M., C. Zahn-Waxler, R. Roth-Hanania and A. Knafo. 2013. Concern for Others in the First Year of Life: Theory, Evidence, and Avenues for Research. *Child Development Perspectives*, 7, 126–31. doi: 10.1111/cdep.12028.

Davidov, M., C. Zahn-Waxler, R. Roth-Hanania, Y. Paz, J. Orlitsky and F. Uzefovsky. 2017. Links between Affective and Cognitive Empathy in Infancy and Later Prosocial Behaviors. Symposium presentation at the Biennial Meetings for the Society for the Society for Research on Child Development. Austin, Texas, April 5–8, 2017.

Decety, J. 2011. The Neuroevolution of Empathy. *Annals of the New York Academy of Sciences*, 1231, 35–45. doi: 10.1159/000317771.

2015a. How Evolutionary Theory and Neuroscience Contribute to Understanding the Development of Prosociality: Commentary. *Prosocial Behaviour*. www.child-encyclopedia.com/prosocial-behaviour/according-experts/how-evolutionary-theory-and-neuroscience-contribute (accessed November 2016).

2015b. The Neural Pathways, Development and Functions of Empathy. *Current Opinion in Behavioral Sciences*, 3, 1–6. doi: 10.1016/j.cobeha.2014.12.001.

Decety, J. and J. M. Cowell. 2014. The Complex Relation between Morality and Empathy. *Trends in Cognitive Sciences*, 18, 337–9. doi: 10.1016/j.tics.2014.04.008.

Decety, J. and J. M. Cowell. 2017. Interpersonal Harm Aversion as a Necessary Foundation for Morality: A Developmental Neuroscience perspective. *Development and Psychopathology*, epub ahead of print.

Decety, J., I. B. A. Bartal, F. Uzefovsky and A. Knafo-Noam. 2016. Empathy as a Driver of Prosocial Behaviour: Highly Conserved Neurobehavioural Mechanisms across Species. *Phil. Trans. R. Soc. B*, 371, 20150077. doi: 10.1098/rstb.2015.0077.

Decety, J. and L. H. Howard. 2013. The Role of Affect in the Neurodevelopment of Morality. *Child Development Perspectives*, 7, 49–54. doi: 10.1111/cdep.12020.

Decety, J. and K. J. Michalska. 2010. Neurodevelopmental Changes in the Circuits Underlying Empathy and Sympathy from Childhood to Adulthood. *Developmental Science*, 13, 886–99. doi: 10.1111/j.1467-7687.2009.00940.x.

Decety, J., K. J. Michalska, Y. Akitsuki and B. B. Lahey. 2009. Atypical Empathic Responses in Adolescents with Aggressive Conduct Disorder: A Functional MRI Investigation. *Biological Psychology*, 80, 203–11. doi: 10.1016/j.biopsycho.2008.09.004.

Decety, J. and M. Svetlova. 2012. Putting Together Phylogenetic and Ontogenetic Perspectives on Empathy. *Developmental Cognitive Neuroscience*, 2, 1–24. doi: 10.1016/j.dcn.2011.05.003.

DiLalla, L. F., K. Bersted and S. G. John. 2015. Evidence of Reactive Gene-Environment Correlation in Preschoolers' Prosocial Play with Unfamiliar Peers. *Developmental Psychology*, 51, 1464–75. doi: 10.1037/dev0000047.

Eisenberg, N., R. A. Fabes and T. L. Spinrad. 2007. *Handbook of Child Psychology*, vol. III, *Prosocial Development*. doi: 10.1002/9780470147658.chpsy0311.

Eisenberg, N., S. K. VanSchyndel and C. Hofer. 2015. The Association of Maternal Socialization in Childhood and Adolescence with Adult Offsprings' Sympathy/Caring. *Developmental Psychology*, 51, 7–16. doi: 10.1037/a0038137.

Else-Quest, N. M., J. S. Hyde, H. H. Goldsmith and C. A. Van Hulle. 2006. Gender Differences in Temperament: A Meta-Analysis. *Psychological Bulletin*, 132, 33–72. doi: 10.1037/0033-2909.132.1.33.

Flook, L., S. B. Goldberg, L. Pinger and R. J. Davidson. 2015. Promoting Prosocial Behavior and Self-Regulatory Skills in Preschool Children through a Mindfulness-Based Kindness Curriculum. *Developmental Psychology*, 51, 44–51. doi: 10.1037/a0038256.

Geangu, E., O. Benga, D. Stahl and T. Striano. 2010. Contagious Crying beyond the First Days of Life. *Infant Behavior and Development*, 33, 279–88. doi: 10.1016/j.infbeh.2010.03.004.

Gill, K. L. and S. D. Calkins. 2003. Do Aggressive/Destructive Toddlers Lack Concern for Others? Behavioral and Physiological Indicators of Empathic Responding in 2-Year-Old Children. *Development and Psychopathology*, 15, 55–71. doi: 10.1017.S095457940300004X.

Gopnik, A. 2009. *The Philosophical Baby: What Children's Minds Tell Us about Truth, Love and the Meaning of Life*. New York: Random House.

Grossmann, T. and M. H. Johnson. 2007. The Development of the Social Brain in Human Infancy. *European Journal of Neuroscience*, 25, 909–19. doi: 10.1111/j.1460-9568.2007.05379.x.

Hamlin, J. K. 2015. The Infantile Origins of Our Moral Brains. In: J. Decety and T. Wheatley (eds), *The Moral Brain – Multidisciplinary Perspectives*. Cambridge, MA: MIT Press, 105–22.

Hamlin, J. K., K. Wynn and P. Bloom. 2007. Social Evaluation by Preverbal Infants. *Nature*, 450, 557–9. doi: 10.1038/nature06288.

Hastings, P. D., J. G. Miller, S. Kahle and C. Zahn-Waxler. 2014. The Neurobiological Bases of Empathic Concern for Others. In: M. Killen and J. G. Smetana (eds.), *Handbook of Moral Development*, second edition. New York/London: Psychology Press, 411–34.

Hastings, P. D., C. Zahn-Waxler, J. Robinson, B. Usher and D. Bridges. 2000. The Development of Concern for Others in Children with Behavior Problems. *Developmental Psychology*, 36, 531–46. doi: 10.1037//OO12 1649.36.5.531.

Haviland, J. M. and M. Lelwica. 1987. The Induced Affect Response: 10-Week-Old Infants' Responses to Three Emotion Expressions. *Developmental Psychology*, 23, 97–104. doi: 10.1037/0012-1649.23.1.97.

Hay, D. F., A. Nash and J. Pedersen. 1981. Responses of Six-Month-Olds to the Distress of Their Peers. *Child Development*, 52, 1071–5. doi: 10.2307/1129114.

Hobson, J. A., R. Harris, R. García-Pérez and R. P. Hobson. 2009. Anticipatory Concern: A Study in Autism. *Developmental Science*, 12, 249–63. doi: 10.1111/j.14677687.2008.00762.x.

Hoffman, M. L. 1975. Developmental Synthesis of Affect and Cognition and its Implications for Altruistic Motivation. *Developmental Psychology*, 11, 607–22. doi: 10.1037/0012-1649.11.5.607.

Hutman, T., A. Rozga, A. D. DeLaurentis, J. M. Barnwell, C. A. Sugar and M. Sigman. 2010. Response to Distress in Infants at Risk for Autism: A Prospective Longitudinal Study. *Journal of Child Psychology and Psychiatry*, 51, 1010–20. doi 10.1111/j.1469-7610.2010.02270.x.

Hutman, T., A. Rozga, A. DeLaurentis, M. Sigman and M. Dapretto. 2012. Infants' Pre-Empathic Behaviors Are Associated with Language Skills. *Infant Behavior and Development*, 35, 561–9. doi: 10.1016/j.infbeh.2012.05.007.

Jones, N. A., T. Field and M. Davalos. 2000. Right Frontal EEG Asymmetry and Lack of Empathy in Preschool Children of Depressed Mothers. *Child Psychiatry and Human Development*, 30, 189–204. doi: 10.1023/A:1021399605526.

Killen, M. and J. Smetana (eds.) 2005. *Handbook of Moral Development*. New York: Psychology Press.

Klimes-Dougan, B. and J. Kistner. 2001. Physically Abused Preschoolers' Responses to Peers' Distress. *Developmental Psychology*, 26, 599–602. doi: 10.1037/00121649.26.4.599.

Knafo, A., S. Israel and R. P. Ebstein. 2011. Heritability of Children's Prosocial Behavior and Differential Susceptibility to Parenting by Variation in the Dopamine Receptor D4 Gene. *Development and Psychopathology*, 23, 53–67. doi: 10.1017/S0954579410000647.

Knafo, A., C. Zahn-Waxler, C. Van Hulle, J. L. Robinson and S. H. Rhee. 2008. The Developmental Origins of a Disposition toward Empathy: Genetic and Environmental Contributions. *Emotion*, 8, 737–52.

Knickmeyer, R., S. Baron-Cohen, P. Raggatt and K. Taylor. 2005. Fetal Testosterone, Social Relationships, and Restricted Interests in Children. *Journal of Child Psychology and Psychiatry*, 46, 198–210. doi: 10.1111/j.1469 7610.2004.00349.x.

Knickmeyer, R., S. Baron-Cohen, P. Raggatt, K. Taylor and G. Hackett. 2006. Fetal Testosterone and Empathy. *Hormones and Behavior*, 49, 282–92. doi: 10.1016/j.yhbeh.2005.08.010.

Lahey, B. B., E. L. Hart, S. Pliszka, B. Applegate and K. McBurnett. 1993. Neurophysiological Correlate of Conduct Disorder: A Rationale and a Review of Research. *Journal of Clinical Child Psychology*, 22, 141–53. doi: 10.1207/s15374424jccp2202_2.

Liddle, M. J. E., B. S. Bradley and A. Mcgrath. 2015. Baby Empathy: Infant Distress and Peer Prosocial Responses. *Infant Mental Health Journal*, 36(4), 446–58. doi: 10.1002/imhj.21519.

Light, S. and C. Zahn-Waxler. 2011. Nature and Forms of Empathy in the First Years of Life. In: J. Decety (ed.), *Empathy: From Bench to Bedside*. Cambridge, MA: MIT Press, 109–30.

Light, S. N., J. A. Coan, C. Zahn-Waxler, C. Frye, H. H. Goldsmith and R. J. Davidson. 2009. Empathy Is Associated with Dynamic Change in Prefrontal Brain Electrical Activity during Positive Emotion in Children. *Child Development*, 80, 1210–31. doi: 10.1111/j.1467-8624.2009.01326.x.

Luby, J., A. Belden, J. Sullivan, R. Hayen, A. McCadney and E. Spitznagel. 2009. Shame and Guilt in Preschool Depression: Evidence for Elevations in Self-Conscious Emotions in Depression as Early as Age 3. *Journal of Child Psychology and Psychiatry*, 50, 1156–66. doi: 10.1111/j.14697610.2009.02077.x.

MacLean, P. D. 1985. Brain Evolution Relating to Family, Play, and the Separation Call. *Archives of General Psychiatry*, 42, 405–17. doi: 10.1001/archpsyc.1985.01790270095011.

Marsh, A. A., E. C. Finger, K. A. Fowler, et al. 2013. Empathic Responsiveness in Amygdala and Anterior Cingulate Cortex in Youths with Psychopathic Traits. *Journal of Child Psychology and Psychiatry*, 54, 900–10. doi: 10.1111/jcpp.12063.

Marsh, A. A., E. C. Finger, D. G. Mitchell, et al. 2008. Reduced Amygdala Response to Fearful Expressions in Children and Adolescents with Callous-Unemotional Traits and Disruptive Behavior Disorders. *American Journal of Psychiatry*, 165, 712–20. doi: 10.1176/appi.ajp.2007.07071145.

McClure, E. B. 2000. A Meta-Analytic Review of Sex Differences in Facial Expression Processing and Their Development in Infants, Children, and Adolescents. *Psychological Bulletin*, 126, 424–53. doi: 10.1037/0033 2909.126.3.424.

McDonald, N. M. and D. S. Messinger. 2012. Empathic Responding in Toddlers at Risk for an Autism Spectrum Disorder. *Journal of Autism and Developmental Disorders*, 42, 1566–73. doi: 10.1007/s10803-011-1390-y.

McDonald, N. M., J. K. Baker and D. S. Messinger. 2016. Oxytocin and Parent-Child Interaction in the Development of Empathy among Children at Risk for Autism. *Developmental Psychology*, 52, 735–45. doi: 10.1037/dev0000104.

Ortiz, J. and A. Raine. 2004. Heart Rate Level and Antisocial Behavior in Children and Adolescents: A Meta-Analysis. *Journal of the American Academy of Child and Adolescent Psychiatry*, 43, 154–62. doi: 10.1097/00004583 20040200000010.

Pinker, S. 2011. *The Better Angels of Our Nature: Why Violence Has Declined*. New York: Viking.

Putnam, S. K., C. Lopata, M. L. Thomeer, M. A. Volker and J. D. Rodgers. 2015. Salivary Cortisol Levels and Diurnal Patterns in Children with Autism Spectrum Disorder. *Journal of Developmental and Physical Disabilities*, 27, 453–65. doi: 10.1007/s1088201594282.

Radke-Yarrow, M., C. Zahn-Waxler, D. T. Richardson, A. Susman and P. Martinez. 1994. Caring Behavior in Children of Clinically Depressed and Well Mothers. *Child Development*, 65, 1405–14. doi: 10.1111/j.1467 8624.1994.tb00825.x.

Rhee, S. H., D. L. Boeldt, N. P. Friedman, R. P. Corley, J. K. Hewitt, S. E. Young, A. Knafo, J. Robinson, I. D. Waldman, C. A. Van Hulle and C. Zahn-Waxler. 2013. The Role of Language in Concern and Disregard for Others in the First Years of Life. *Developmental Psychology*, 49, 197–214. doi: 10.1037/a0028318.

Rhee, S. H., N. P. Friedman, D. L. Boeldt, R. P. Corley, J. Hewitt, A. Knafo, B. B. Lahey, J. Robinson, C. A. Van Hulle, I. D. Waldman, S. E. Young and C. Zahn-Waxler. 2013. Early Concern and Disregard for Others as Predictors of Antisocial Behavior. *Journal of Child Psychology and Psychiatry*, 54, 157–66. doi:10.1111/j.14697610.2012.02574.x.

Robinson, J. L., Zahn-Waxler, C., Emde, R. N. 1994. Patterns of Development in Early Empathic Behavior: Environmental and Child Constitutional Influences. *Social Development*, 3, 125–46. doi: 10.1111/j.1467–9507.1994.tb00032.x.

Roth-Hanania, R., M. Davidov and C. Zahn-Waxler. 2011. Empathy Development from 8 to 16 Months: Early Signs of Concern for Others. *Infant Behavior and Development*, 34, 447–58. doi: 10.1016/j.infbeh.2011.04.007.

Rutter, M., A. Caspi and T. E. Moffitt. 2003. Using Sex Differences in Psychopathology to Study Causal Mechanisms: Unifying Issues and Research Strategies. *Journal of Child Psychology and Psychiatry*, 44, 1092–115. doi: 10.1111/14697610.00194.

Sallquist, J., N. Eisenberg, T. L. Spinrad, N. D. Eggum and B. M. Gaertner. 2009. Assessment of Preschoolers' Positive Empathy: Concurrent and Longitudinal Relations with Positive Emotion, Social Competence, and Sympathy. *Journal of Positive Psychology*, 4, 223–33. doi 10.1080/17439760902819444.

Scheeren, A. M., H. M. Koot, P. C. Mundy, L. Mous and S. Begeer. 2013. Empathic Responsiveness of Children and Adolescents with High-Functioning Autism Spectrum Disorder. *Autism Research*, 6, 362–71. doi: 10.1002/aur.1299.

Singer, T. 2006. The Neuronal Basis and Ontogeny of Empathy and Mind Reading: Review of Literature and Implications for Future Research. *Neuroscience and Biobehavioral Reviews*, 30, 855–63. doi: 10.1016/j.neubiorev.2006.06.011.

Smith, A. 1759/1790. *The Theory of Moral Sentiments*, edited by D. D. Raphael and A. L. Macfie. Indianapolis: Liberty Fund 1982.

Sterzer, P., C. Stadler, F. Poustka and A. Kleinschmidt. 2007. A Structural Neural Deficit in Adolescents with Conduct Disorder and Its Association with Lack of Empathy. *Neuroimage*, 37, 335–342. doi: 10.1016/j.neuroimage.2007.04.043.

Vaish, A. 2016. Flexible Concern: The Development of Multidetermined and Context-Dependent Empathic Responding. *Child Development Perspectives*, 10, 143–8. doi: 10.1111/cdep.12178.

This volume. Sophisticated Concern in Early Childhood.

Van de Vondervoort, J. W. and J. K. Hamlin. 2016. Evidence for Intuitive Morality: Preverbal Infants Make Sociomoral Evaluations. *Child Development Perspectives*, 10, 149–54. doi: 10.1111/cdep.12175.

Van Hulle, C., C. Zahn-Waxler, J. L. Robinson, S. H. Rhee, P. D. Hastings and A. Knafo. 2013. Autonomic Correlates of Children's Concern and Disregard for Others. *Social Neuroscience*, 8, 275–90. doi: 10.1080/17470919.2013.791342.

Volbrecht, M. M., K. Lemery-Chalfant, N. Aksan, C. Zahn-Waxler and H. H. Goldsmith. 2007. Examining the Familial Link between Positive Affect and Empathy Development in the Second Year. *Journal of Genetic Psychology*, 168, 105–30. doi: 10.3200/GNTP.168.2.105-130.

Wagner, N. J., W. R. Mills-Koonce, M. T. Willoughby, B. Zvara and M. J. Cox. 2015. Parenting and Children's Representations of Family Predict Disruptive and Callous-Unemotional Behaviors. *Developmental Psychology*, 51, 935–48. doi: 10.1037/a0039353.

Waller, R., F. Gardner and L. W. Hyde. 2013. What Are the Associations between Parenting, Callous-Unemotional Traits, and Antisocial Behavior in Youth? A Systematic Review of Evidence. *Clinical Psychology Review*, 33, 593–608. doi: 10.1016/j.cpr.2013.03.001.

Yarrow, M. R., P. M. Scott and C. Z. Waxler. 1973. Learning Concern for Others. *Developmental Psychology*, 8, 240–60. doi: 10.1037/h0034159.

Young, S., N. Fox and C. Zahn-Waxler. 1999. The Relations between Temperament and Empathy in 2-Year-Olds. *Developmental Psychology*, 35(5), 1189–97. doi: 10.1037/00121649.35.5.1189.

Zahn-Waxler, C. and M. Radke-Yarrow. 1982. The Development of Altruism: Alternative Research Strategies. In: N. Eisenberg (ed.), *The Development of Prosocial Behavior*. New York/London: Academic Press, 109–37.

Zahn-Waxler, C. and A. Schoen. 2016. Empathy, Prosocial Behaviour and Adjustment: Clinical Aspects of Surfeits and Deficits in Concern for Others. *Prosocial Behaviour*. www.child-encyclopedia.com/prosocial-behaviour/according-experts/empathy-prosocial-behaviour-and-adjustment-clinical-aspects (accessed November 2016).

Zahn-Waxler, C. and C. Van Hulle. 2011. Empathy, Guilt and Depression: When Caring for Others Becomes Costly to Children. In: B. Oakley et al. (eds.), *Pathological Altruism*. New York: Oxford University Press, 243–59.

Zahn-Waxler, C., S. L. Friedman and E. M. Cummings. 1983. Children's Emotions and Behaviors in Response to Infants' Cries. *Child Development*, 54, 1522–8. doi: 10.2307/1129815.

Zahn-Waxler, C., R. J. Iannotti, E. M. Cummings and S. Denham. 1990. Antecedents of Problem Behaviors in Children of Depressed Mothers. *Development and Psychopathology*, 2, 271–91. doi: 10.1017/S0954579400000778.

Zahn-Waxler, C., G. Kochanska, J. Krupnick and D. McKnew. 1990. Patterns of Guilt in Children of Depressed and Well Mothers. *Developmental Psychology*, 26, 51–9. doi: 10.1037/00121649.26.1.51.

Zahn-Waxler, C., M. Radke-Yarrow and R. A. King. 1979. Child Rearing and Children's Prosocial Initiations toward Victims of Distress. *Child Development*, 50, 319–30.

Zahn-Waxler, C., M. Radke-Yarrow, E. Wagner and M. Chapman. 1992. Development of Concern for Others. *Developmental Psychology*, 28, 126–36. doi: 10.1037/00121649.28.1.126.

Zahn-Waxler, C., J. L. Robinson and R. N. Emde. 1992. The Development of Empathy in Twins. *Developmental Psychology*, 28, 1038–47. doi: 10.1037/00121649.28.6.1038.

Zahn-Waxler, C., E. A. Shirtcliff and K. Marceau. 2008. Disorders of Childhood and Adolescence: Gender and Psychopathology. *Annu. Rev. Clin. Psychol.*, 4, 275–303. doi: 102.10.1146/annurev.clinpsy.3.022806.0913.

9 Sophisticated Concern in Early Childhood

Amrisha Vaish

The ability to respond empathically to and care about others is a fundamental human capacity. Empathic responding will be used here as an umbrella term for empathy, which is an affective response that stems from the apprehension or comprehension of another's emotional state and is similar to what the other is feeling (though with the awareness that the source of the emotion is the other rather than the self), as well as the related process of sympathy (or empathic concern), which is the feeling of concern or compassion for a person in need (Hoffman 1981; Eisenberg 1986; Batson 1991; Eisenberg et al. 1991).[1] These forms of fellow feeling have long been recognized as a critical source of morality, emphasized most prominently by philosophers such as David Hume (1776) and Adam Smith (1759). Hume, for instance, argued that sympathy, benevolence, and a "feeling for humanity" are the true moral motivations. Indeed, empirically, empathy and especially sympathy have been extensively shown to lead to prosocial behaviors and away from antisocial behaviors from early in development (e.g., Eisenberg and Miller 1987; Miller and Eisenberg 1988; Batson 1998; Hoffman 2000).[2] Given its

---

[1] For the purposes of this chapter, empathic responding will refer to empathy, sympathy, and personal distress (to be described later), which are fundamentally affective experiences that can result from or be influenced by more cognitive processes (Hoffman 1984; Eisenberg et al. 1991). It will not include what is often referred to as "cognitive empathy" or Theory of Mind (e.g., Blair 1995; Shamay-Tsoory 2011), which includes fundamentally cognitive processes that can but need not impact empathic responding (see Singer 2006).

[2] I will not distinguish here between the roles of empathy versus sympathy in motivating prosocial or moral behavior. This is primarily because in the psychological literature, empathy and sympathy have not always been clearly distinguished, either conceptually (in the way that I, following Eisenberg, am doing here) or empirically, making it difficult to ascertain the distinct roles that the two processes might play in moral motivations. Nonetheless, the distinction is likely important for understanding moral motivations more fully. Specifically, it may be argued that empathy (i.e., feeling similar to or mirroring what the other is feeling) is not other-oriented and is thus not by itself sufficient to motivate prosocial behavior; rather, it is sympathy (the feeling of other-oriented concern and desire for the other's negative state to be alleviated) that should be more closely associated with prosocial behavior (see Eisenberg et al. 1991; Eisenberg 2000). Whether this proposal holds up to empirical investigation remains an open question, however.

crucial role in prosociality and morality, it becomes imperative to understand the nature of early empathic responding.

Although a vast literature already exists on this topic, I will argue here that two vital aspects of empathic development have been largely overlooked. To preview, these concern the multidetermined and the context-dependent aspects of early empathic responding. Yet it is critical to understand these aspects because they add enormous scope and thus render empathic concern a particularly powerful social tool. In what follows, I first spell out these two aspects of empathic responding. I then review some recent social neuroscience literature on empathic responding in adults that provides a helpful framework for the developmental project at hand. Following this, I review recent developmental studies that have begun to examine the two new aspects of empathic responding (see also Vaish, 2016). I end with a discussion of developmental mechanisms and proposals for future work.

1. Multidetermined Empathic Concern

Perhaps the most far-reaching and influential theory of empathy development comes from Martin Hoffman. According to Hoffman (1975; 1984; 2000), infants are born with the capacity to automatically experience empathic distress. This *global empathy* connects humans as social beings to the emotional plight of others and is thus a vital affective component of empathic concern; yet it is not "true" (or "proper") empathic concern because infants do not possess a critical cognitive component required for empathic concern, namely, self–other discrimination (Hoffman 2000; 2007). True empathy emerges in the second half of the second year, when children are able to differentiate between self and other (Lewis et al. 1989; Butterworth 1992; Moore 2007). Toddlers now realize that others have independent inner states, and when they experience affective resonance with another's distress, they recognize that response as stemming from the other rather than the self. They now show increasing empathic responses to others' distress as well as appropriate, other-directed comforting and prosocial behaviors (Hoffman 2000; 2007).

Hoffman argues for multiple modes of empathic arousal (Hoffman 2000). The most basic modes are preverbal, automatic, and essentially involuntary, and include processes such as motor mimicry and emotional contagion. These processes arouse an involuntary affective response and require only a shallow level of cognitive processing (see also Eisenberg et al. 1991). Coupled with the ability to differentiate between self and other, however, they are effective routes to empathic responding. These modes are crucial for arousing empathy in early childhood but also throughout life, especially in ordinary, face-to-face situations in which the victim's distress is directly perceptible.

Importantly, Hoffman (2000) argues that in the absence of observable cues, higher-level cognitive processes can also lead to empathic responses. One such process involves activating and accessing elaborated cognitive networks (made up of social scripts in which extensive information about situations and people in general is embedded). These networks develop out of direct or vicarious experiences, and once created, can be informative about similar experiences in the future. A second higher-level process is affective perspective taking, which involves viewing a target's situation from his perspective and thereby making an inference about his affective state (Feshbach 1978; Hoffman 1982; 1984; Eisenberg et al. 1991). As these modes involve more sophisticated levels of cognition than the simpler processes, they are expected to emerge later in development (around two to three years of age; Hoffman 1982; 1984; Eisenberg et al. 1991; Decety and Svetlova 2012). Critically, these are the modes that contribute scope to a person's empathic capability, as they expand "the importance of empathic morality beyond the face-to-face encounters of children and members of primary groups, which has been the focus of most of the research. [They expand the] model to encompass a variety of situations limited not by the victim's presence but by the observers' imagination" (Hoffman 2000, 8).

Empirical Examination of Hoffman's Theory

Those aspects of Hoffman's theory of empathy development that concern early affective resonance and the emergence of empathic responding in the first two years have received a great deal of empirical attention. It is well established that newborn infants respond by crying when they hear another infant in distress (Simner 1971; Sagi and Hoffman 1976; Dondi, Simion, and Caltran 1999; see also Geangu et al. 2010). Decades of research also show that young children respond with empathic concern and prosocial behavior toward others. Typically, infants see a parent or stranger experiencing a negative situation (e.g., bumping her knee) and overtly showing pain, distress, or sadness. In these situations, toddlers show concern in their facial and vocal expressions and often attempt to alleviate the victim's distress by comforting, helping, or sharing with her (e.g., Eisenberg et al. 1989; Zahn-Waxler, Radke-Yarrow, et al. 1992; Zahn-Waxler, Robinson, and Emde 1992; Svetlova, Nichols, and Brownell 2011). Moreover, children's concern for the victim in these overt distress situations relates positively with their prosocial behavior (Hoffman 1982; Eisenberg and Miller 1987) and negatively with their antisocial and aggressive behavior (Miller and Eisenberg 1988). This work provides evidence for an early capacity to experience empathic concern based on affective resonance.

Hoffman's proposal regarding self–other discrimination has also received support. In particular, a reflective sense of self as tested by mirror self-recognition (MSR) coincides with the beginning of other-directed and appropriate prosocial behavior (Bischof-Köhler 1991; Zahn-Waxler, Radke-Yarrow, et al. 1992). However, some authors have recently proposed that a simpler, more implicit form of self-recognition may be sufficient for empathic concern, and that this form (based on infants' subjective experience of their own sensory perception and self-generated actions) is present from birth (Davidov et al. 2013; see also Lewis and Brooks-Gunn 1979; Rochat 2003). The suggestion is that from the very beginning, humans are not only affectively tuned to others' states but, with the aid of implicit social-cognitive tools, are able to experience true concern for them (see Nichols, Svetlova, and Brownell 2009; Roth-Hanania, Davidov, and Zahn-Waxler 2011).

Importantly, because all of this work has examined empathic responding primarily in the context of observable perceptual cues, we cannot know the degree to which affective resonance versus other (more sophisticated and cognitive) modes are at work. Though it is certainly possible that more cognitive processes are involved even when observable perceptual cues are present, we cannot conclude that they are – and the more parsimonious account would be that they are not. Thus, the principal method used with infants and young children thus far has taught us that empathic concern grounded in affective resonance has deep ontogenetic roots, but has not permitted conclusions about other potential modes of empathic responding in development. As a result, we know very little about the scope of early empathic responding. Yet understanding the development of multidetermined empathic responding is essential to our understanding of the nature of early concern.

2. Context-Dependent Empathic Concern

As important as empathic responding is, it also needs to be regulated. Just as experiencing too little empathy can be maladaptive – leading, for instance, to problems in social interactions and relationships – so too can experiencing too much empathy. An influential view in this regard is that of Eisenberg (e.g., Eisenberg 2000; Eisenberg, Spinrad, and Sadovsky 2006; Eisenberg and Eggum 2009), who has proposed that a person who experiences too much empathy may instead end up experiencing personal distress, which is an aversive affective reaction to the apprehension of another's emotion and associated with the desire to alleviate one's own rather than the other's distress (e.g., Batson 1991; Hoffman 2000). This is maladaptive because unlike empathic concern, which promotes an other-focus, personal distress promotes a self-focus and is negatively related or unrelated to prosocial behavior (Batson 1991; Eisenberg et al. 2006). Moreover, too much concern for others can be a risk factor for depression (Zahn-Waxler and Hulle 2012; see Oakley et al. 2012, for a broader perspective on pathological altruism and its pitfalls).

Eisenberg proposes that there are individual differences in the degree to which people experience sympathy versus personal distress, due in part to individual differences in proneness to empathic arousal and ability to regulate emotional reactions (Eisenberg 1992; Eisenberg and Eggum 2009). The capacity to regulate one's emotions varies across individuals, starting in childhood and stemming in part from temperamental differences (Rothbart and Bates 2006). Individuals most likely to experience empathy are those who are prone to at least moderate levels of vicarious emotion and are well regulated. An individual who is prone to intense emotions but is not well regulated is more likely to experience personal distress.

The developmental research has generally supported this proposal. For instance, personal distress seems to be linked to higher levels of physiological arousal than sympathy (Eisenberg et al. 2006; see Eisenberg, Valiente, and Champion 2004, for a review). Moreover, higher levels of children's emotion regulation correlate with high empathic concern and low personal distress (Eisenberg et al. 1996; Valiente et al. 2004). Individual variation in this regard is highly relevant because it predicts children's later prosocial tendencies and general social adjustment (Eisenberg et al. 1997).

Eisenberg's proposal and the resulting empirical research have been vital to our understanding of empathic responding both as a process and at the level of individual variation. Moreover, this work draws attention to a broader issue that is extremely important in the study of empathic responding, namely, that more is not always better. After all, empathic responding and the prosocial behavior it motivates can be costly in terms of cognitive, emotional, and material resources (Hodges and Klein 2001; Hodges and Biswas-Diener 2007; Keysers and Gazzola 2014). Moreover, too much empathic responding can be a hindrance. For example, empathizing greatly with someone in pain can exhaust one's emotional resources, leaving one less able to provide appropriate care (Hodges and Biswas-Diener 2007). Competitive situations also require empathic regulation, as one may be best served by empathizing with members of one's own group but *not* as much with members of the other group. The ability to regulate empathic concern is thus invaluable for directing our emotional and prosocial energies selectively and flexibly depending on context. As Hodges and Biswas-Diener (2007, 404) put it, "Like fire, empathy is a powerful and valuable tool available to our species, made infinitely more useful when we know how to manage it."

Yet almost nothing is known about the development of such selective and context-dependent management of empathic responding. When and how do children regulate their empathic responses *flexibly*, that is, depending on context, the victim, and/or their own situation? This question focuses not on the optimal level of empathic arousal required to respond prosocially, nor on individual differences in the ability to attain that optimal arousal; at issue here is a different aspect of empathic regulation, namely, that the degree of empathic regulation that is required (in the sense of appropriate for the individual) can itself vary by context *even for a given individual* (always assuming individual differences).[3] This sort of context-dependent concern has received little attention in developmetal work.

I am thus arguing for the need to examine the development of multidetermined and context-dependent empathic concern. Interestingly, social neuroscience has been exploring and providing fascinating insights into multidetermined and context-dependent empathy in adults. I briefly review this work next, as it provides a useful framework for developmental research.

3. Adult Empathic Responding: Bottom-Up and Top-Down Processes

Adults regularly empathize and sympathize with victims in a wide variety of situations (Batson et al. 1981; 1991; Decety and Jackson 2006; Singer and Lamm 2009). Social neuroscientists have been studying the nature of and mechanisms underlying empathic responding for some time now.

---

[3] Note here that my focus is not on how much empathic regulation is *morally* required but on how much is required or appropriate for the agent herself. One may, for instance, argue that an agent is morally required to experience the highest possible level of empathic responding that allows her to engage in the greatest possible amount of moral action. Yet, across contexts that vary in who the needy individual is, what (and how plausible) the source of the individual's distress is, what the agent's own physical, emotional, and/or material capacities are, and so forth, it may in fact often be more practical or even beneficial, for the agent to reduce her empathic responding. A prime example of this tension is a competitive situation wherein an agent may need to dramatically dampen her empathic responding toward the opponent in order to compete well, and yet may be criticized on moral grounds for not responding empathically toward someone in need. With this in mind, I will focus here only on the degree of empathic regulation required for the agent herself rather than morally required.

This work has resulted in a framework in which mature, adult empathic responding is a multilevel, multifaceted construct comprising of both *bottom-up* and *top-down* information processing mechanisms, with top-down processes being responsible for multidetermined and flexible empathic responses. I consider each of these processes in turn.

Bottom-Up Empathic Processes

Adults are expert emotion sharers. When we view facial expressions of emotions, for example, we display corresponding facial expressions ourselves (see Dimberg and Öhman 1996, for a review), even when the emotions are presented outside of conscious recognition (Dimberg, Thunberg, and Elmehed 2000). This facial mimicry is correlated with the observer's empathic responding (Sonnby-Borgström, Jönsson, and Svensson 2003). Similarly, observing someone in pain or distress activates part of the same neural network that is activated when we ourselves are in pain (see Decety and Lamm 2006; Singer and Lamm 2009). The greater the similarity and familiarity between two individuals, the easier is the observer's identification with the other, and thus the more enhanced and accurate is the state matching (Preston and de Waal 2002; de Waal 2008). Such empathic responses are thought to occur involuntarily, through perception-driven, *bottom-up* information processing mechanisms such as mimicry and emotional contagion, which operate primarily on sensory input and require relatively little cognitive processing (for definitions and reviews, see Hoffman 2000; Preston and de Waal 2002; Decety and Lamm 2006; Singer and Lamm 2009).

Importantly, these bottom-up processes result in a simple matching of affective states (akin to the emotional contagion seen in newborn infants) but they do not by themselves lead to true empathy (Preston and de Waal 2002; Preston and Hofelich 2012). For this, some fundamental *top-down* information processing mechanisms (i.e., mechanisms that involve more cognitive, conceptual, or deliberate processes) are also needed. If bottom-up processes are to create strong affective resonance, for instance, an observer must attend to the target's state (Preston and de Waal 2002). Moreover, as noted previously, true empathic responding requires a rudimentary self–other discrimination. Indeed, research with adults shows that experiencing affect that is resonant with another's affect does not involve a complete overlap between self and other (Hoffman 2000; Decety and Sommerville 2003; Jackson et al. 2006). Bottom-up processes in conjunction with these essential top-down processes help us quickly and automatically apprehend or comprehend the emotional states of others, potentially leading to empathic concern and thereby to prosocial behavior (e.g., Batson et al. 1991; 1997; Eisenberg et al. 1991; Hoffman 2000; Stel and van den Bos 2010).

Automatically sharing others' emotional states in these ways enables us to have forceful and immediate responses to others' suffering. This serves vital functions, ranging from caring for our offspring, regulating our social interactions, acting prosocially toward those in need, coordinating activities, and cooperating toward shared goals (de Waal 2008). Yet, as discussed previously, empathic responding is particularly powerful if it is multidetermined and flexible. Indeed, adults' empathic responding exhibits both of these features, and it does so by relying on a wide variety of more sophisticated top-down processes.

Top-Down Processes

Numerous top-down information processing mechanisms, including perspective taking, social scripts, attention, contextual appraisal, regulation, and executive control, have been found to contribute to adults' empathic responding (Decety and Lamm 2006; the first two of these mechanisms – perspective taking and social scripts – have also been extensively considered by Hoffman, Eisenberg, and other developmental theorists, as discussed earlier). This is true in two ways. First, *top-down processes can generate empathic responding* even in the absence of bottom-up processes; in other words, they facilitate multidetermined empathic responding. For instance, in the absence of overt distress cues from a victim, we can rely on affective perspective taking (imagining how the other feels) (Stotland 1969; Feshbach 1978; Krebs and Russell 1981; Batson, Fultz, and Schoenrade 1987; Eisenberg 1991). Indeed, when adults are presented with descriptions or pictures of situations likely to induce emotions (such as pain or shame) and asked to imagine how another individual would feel in those situations, their brains show activation in areas implicated in processing the relevant emotions, indicating that taking another's perspective elicits empathic responding (Ruby and Decety 2004; Decety and Jackson 2006; Jackson et al. 2006). A simpler top-down process that can generate empathic concern is the use of elaborated cognitive networks, including social scripts in which extensive information about other situations and people in general is stored (Karniol 1982; Eisenberg et al. 1991).

The degree to which observers rely on perspective taking proper versus on social scripts presumably depends on how familiar the situation is to the observer and how similar the observer's own viewpoint, characteristics, or feelings are to those of the target individual: greater familiarity and similarity result in greater reliance on social scripts whereas less familiarity and similarity require greater reliance on the cognitively more demanding process of perspective taking (see Eisenberg et al. 1991). Thus, although both top-down processes can generate empathic responding in the absence of overt perceptual cues, perspective taking likely provides greater flexibility than social scripts as it opens up the possibility of responding empathically even in relatively unfamiliar scenarios.

In sum, even when we have no perceptual access to the other's emotional state, we can employ top-down processes to apprehend or comprehend the other's state, which can engender empathic processes. This function of top-down processes may not be required in ordinary face-to-face social interactions in which an individual is harmed and displays distress, but it becomes vital if, for instance, an individual is harmed but does not display any distress, or if the harmed individual is absent and we only hear or read about her negative situation. This is consistent with (though rarely discussed in relation to) Hoffman's proposal that empathic responding needs to be multidetermined in order to be a reliable social and prosocial motivator (Hoffman 1981; 2000).

In addition to generating empathic responding in the absence of bottom-up processes, *top-down processes modulate and regulate the extent of empathic responding*; in other words, they facilitate flexible empathic responding. One such process is attention. As noted previously, in order for bottom-up processes to induce affective resonance, the observer must attend to the target's state (Preston and de Waal 2002). This suggests that those aspects of a scene to which we pay attention should increase or decrease our empathic responding. The empirical evidence supports this idea. When adults evaluated the consequences of painful situations depicted in pictures (e.g., cutting one's finger), their brains showed activation in regions generally implicated in pain processing, whereas when adults were asked to count the number of hands in the pictures (in order to distract attention from the pain-related aspects of the pictures), the activation in those regions was significantly reduced (Gu and Han 2007).

Contextual appraisal also exerts an influence on the degree of our empathic responding. In one study, participants viewed images of hands being injected with needles. On some trials, participants were led to believe that the hands had been anesthetized, whereas on other trials, they were not. Participants showed very similar levels of initial activation in the brain's pain matrix regardless of whether or not they believed the hands had been numbed, suggesting an automatic affective response to the perceptually aversive stimuli. However, there was greater activation in areas of the brain involved in appraisal processes (such as evaluating valence and distinguishing self from other) when participants believed that the hands were anesthetized than when they did not (Lamm, Nusbaum, et al. 2007; see also Lamm, Batson, and Decety 2007). These top-down processes likely enabled participants to distinguish between their automatic response to the aversive stimuli and the knowledge that such a response was not in fact appropriate given the contextual information that the hands were anesthetized. This suggests that the initial automatic response to aversive stimuli might be down-regulated by cognitive mechanisms of top-down control, resulting in a dampened empathic response.

The perspective we adopt also modulates our empathic responding. When viewing videos of patients undergoing painful treatment, for example, participants were instructed either to imagine how they would feel if they were in the other's situation (imagine self) or to imagine how the other would feel (imagine other). Participants reported (in a behavioral experiment assessing self-reported emotional responses) feeling lower empathic concern and greater personal distress in the imagine-self than imagine-other condition (Lamm, Batson, and Decety 2007; see also Batson, Early, and Salvarini 1997; Ruby and Decety 2004; Jackson et al. 2006). Moreover, participants showed higher activity in brain areas involved in the affective response to threat or pain (such as the amygdala, the insula, and the anterior medial cingulate cortex) when imagining themselves in the other's place, consistent with the idea that the imagine-self perspective led to a greater level of personal distress.

Our relationship with and evaluation of the other can also impact our empathic responding considerably. Thus, being in a competitive situation can result in counterempathic responses, that is, joy when the other loses and sadness when the other wins (Lanzetta and Englis 1989), and seeing an unfair individual in a painful situation greatly reduces empathic responses in the brain (at least in men; Singer et al. 2006). Finally, group membership has an impact, as we show greater empathic concern and prosocial behavior toward ingroup versus outgroup members (e.g., Xu et al. 2009; see Cikara, Bruneau, and Saxe 2011).

The fact that top-down processes can modulate and inhibit empathic responses induced primarily by bottom-up processes lends great flexibility and sophistication to empathic concern. The important implication is that in ordinary and familiar situations, bottom-up processes (in conjunction with some essential top-down processes) give us forceful and direct access to the other's feelings and the possibility to act fast, yet we have the capacity to control, modulate, and inhibit our empathic responses depending on various aspects of the situation, the victim, and the self. As discussed previously, empathic responding and the prosocial behavior it motivates can be extremely costly (Hodges and Klein 2001; Hodges and Biswas-Diener 2007). Top-down processes such as those discussed in the preceding give us the ability to regulate our emotional responses and direct our energies to those who truly need them and those whom we care about, particularly in situations in which we are able and willing to become involved and act prosocially.

To summarize, social neuroscience research convincingly shows that mature empathic responding is comprised of both bottom-up and top-down processes, which work together to provide adults with a multidetermined and context-dependent mechanism with which to "feel into" others very effectively but also flexibly.[4] These qualities make adult empathic responding an especially powerful and valuable social tool. Yet we know almost nothing about the development of multidetermined and context-dependent empathic responding. Some recent work has begun to fill this gap, however, and this is what I turn to now.

4. Multidetermined and Context-Dependent Empathic Responding in Development

Based on the social neuroscience work, there are two ways in which top-down processes can play a role in empathic responding. First, they can generate empathic responses in the absence of overt emotional cues (making them multidetermined). Second, they can modulate empathic responses generated primarily by bottom-up processes (lending flexibility). I will consider the developmental work related to each of these in turn.

Can Top-Down Processes Generate Empathic Responses in Children?

Some early work tackled this question using picture and story assessments (Feshbach and Roe 1968; Eisenberg-Berg and Lennon 1980; Iannotti 1985), in which the child heard stories and saw pictures of hypothetical protagonists in emotion-eliciting situations (e.g., a child has lost her dog) but was provided no information about the protagonists' feelings. The child was then asked to indicate verbally or by pointing to pictures of facial expressions how she herself felt, under the assumption that the child had responded empathically if her reported emotion was similar to the presumed emotion of the protagonist. These studies

---

[4] Importantly, my argument is not that adults always have complete control over their empathic responses. We often go along with an emotional response to another's situation despite our best efforts to prevent it. What this likely means is that our top-down, emotional regulation processes are not always sufficiently powerful to control the bottom-up processes (and of course individuals will vary greatly in how well they are able to regulate and modulate their emotional and empathic responses; Eisenberg and Eggum 2009).

found that young children do often report feelings consistent with an empathic response. However, these assessments create strong demand characteristics, tapping children's inclination to provide socially appropriate responses rather than their empathic responses (Eisenberg and Miller 1987; Eisenberg et al. 2006).

More recent work provides direct evidence of top-down processes generating empathic responses. One study tested eleven-year-olds with autism, eleven-year-olds with learning disabilities, and typically developing six-year-olds (Hobson et al. 2009). In this study, participants and two experimenters each drew a picture. Then, in the harm condition, the "perpetrator" experimenter unexpectedly tore up the "victim" experimenter's drawing, or, in the control condition, the first experimenter tore up a blank sheet of paper. In both cases, the victim observed the first experimenter neutrally and did not display any emotion. Nevertheless, in the harm condition, a significantly higher percentage of children without autism than children with autism looked immediately and spontaneously to the victim and showed concern for the victim. These differences did not emerge in the control condition. These findings suggest that by six years of age, typically developing children who observe someone being harmed show concern for her even in the absence of any distress.

A further study adapted and extended Hobson et al.'s (2009) task for use with much younger children (Vaish, Carpenter, and Tomasello 2009). In this study, eighteen- and twenty-five-month-old children viewed an adult either harming another adult by destroying or taking away her possessions (harm condition) or else doing something similar that did not harm her (neutral condition). Again, the "victim" simply watched the harmful or harmless actions without displaying any emotions. Following these *sympathy situations*, children were given the opportunity to act prosocially toward the victim in a subsequent, unrelated *prosocial situation*. The results revealed that during the sympathy situations, children showed greater concern in their facial expressions when they saw the victim being harmed than not being harmed, despite the fact that the victim showed no overt emotions. Children were also subsequently more prosocial toward the victim if they had previously observed her being harmed than not being harmed. Furthermore, individual children's concern during the sympathy situations correlated positively with their subsequent prosocial behavior. Thus, by the middle of the second year, children can respond empathically toward a person in a distressing situation *even if* that person does not display overt distress, and this empathic response, like the response that prior work had documented to overt emotional signals, likely motivates children's prosocial behavior. What the precise nature of this empathic response is – whether it is purely other-oriented concern or whether it also typically involves some empathy (arrived at through cognitive means rather than affect matching) – is an interesting question for future research.

Concern in these studies clearly did not result directly from perception-driven processes such as mimicry or emotional contagion, as no perceptible cues of distress were provided. Instead, children needed to at least partly rely on more cognitive, top-down processes such as affective perspective taking to generate an empathic response. Depending on how familiar children were with situations like the ones used in this study, they might additionally have relied on social scripts to infer the victim's affect and to thus respond empathically (see Hobson et al. 2009; Vaish et al. 2009, for detailed discussions).

To summarize, the developmental studies reviewed in the preceding provide initial evidence that top-down processes can generate empathic concern even in young children, and thus that empathic concern is multidetermined from early in ontogeny (see also Vaish and Warneken 2012). Next, I consider the second role of top-down processes – that of modulation.

Can Top-Down Processes Modulate Empathic Responses in Children?

There are two lines of developmental research that are relevant here. The first has focused on whether cognitive appraisal of the context can modulate children's empathic concern. One study addressed the question indirectly, by examining young children's moral judgments (Leslie, Mallon, and Dicorcia 2006). In this study, four-year-old typically developing children and children with autism heard stories in which two individuals each have a cookie that the teacher permits them to eat. Children were asked whether it was permissible for one individual to eat her own cookie even if this made the other individual, who wanted both cookies, cry. Both groups judged the action to be permissible. In contrast, when the story involved one individual hitting another individual and the victim thus being justifiably sad, both groups judged the action to be wrong. These findings show that even early in ontogeny, moral judgments are not primarily reflexive reactions to cues of distress but take into account the context as well. However, this study left unclear whether contextual cues only impact children's moral judgments or also their empathic responses.

A further study directly tested this question by presenting three-year-olds with *sympathy situations*, during which an adult displayed distress in response to either (a) substantial harm, such as getting his hand caught in a box, in which case his distress was justified; (b) very minor harm, such as getting his sleeve caught in a box, in which case his distress was unjustified; or (c) no perceivable harm, in which children were looking away when the adult was purportedly harmed and so they did not perceive the harm, only his subsequent distress (Hepach, Vaish, and Tomasello 2012b). The logic was that if children respond to distress cues primarily through automatic, bottom-up processes and do not take context into account, then their concern should be similar across all conditions, since the recipient displayed the same distress in all conditions. Alternatively, if children respond primarily to the degree of perceived harm, then they should show the greatest concern in the substantial-harm case, less in the minor-harm case, and least in the no-perceivable-harm case. However, if children's concern is modulated by contextual appraisal, then they should show substantially reduced concern in the minor-harm case, when the unjustified distress does not call for much concern.

The data supported this last alternative. Children who witnessed the adult being substantially harmed showed high levels of concern in their facial expressions, and children in the no-perceivable-harm condition showed substantial checking behavior, that is, looking to the adult to assess the situation and to anticipate what might happen next (similar to "cognitive empathy" as used, for instance, by Zahn-Waxler, Radke-Yarrow, et al. 1992; Roth-Hanania et al. 2011). Children in both conditions also attempted to assist the adult during the sympathy situations. Moreover, they checked on the adult when he later expressed distress out of their view. Strikingly, children in the minor-harm condition showed lower concern than in the substantial-harm case and lower checking behavior than in the no-perceivable-harm case (though these differences were not statistically significant). Children in the minor-harm condition were also less likely to assist the adult during the sympathy situations and to check on him when he later expressed distress out of view. Finally, as in Vaish et al. (2009), the greater the concern that children showed during sympathy situations, the faster they were to help the adult in a separate prosocial task.

A further recent study demonstrated that even eighteen-month-olds look longer at an actor displaying distress in an inappropriate context (she achieved her goal of playing with a ball) than an appropriate context (she hurt her finger), and show more concern and checking looks toward the justifiably distressed adult (Chiarella and Poulin-Dubois 2013). Together, these studies reveal that young children cognitively appraise the context within which distress occurs, and this contextual appraisal impacts the degree of concern that they feel for distressed individuals. By the middle of the second year, then, top-down processes modulate children's empathic responses, allowing them to regulate their arousal and direct their concern (and prosocial behavior) to those who truly need it.

In addition to the work on contextual appraisal as it impacts children's empathic concern, a different line of work is exploring the development of flexible empathic responding in intergroup contexts. Some research has suggested, for instance, that young children show greater empathic responding toward gender ingroup members than gender outgroup members (Feshbach and Roe 1968; Theimer, Killen, and Stangor 2001). Note, however, that to the degree that such findings emerge from factors such as greater familiarity or a greater sense of comfort interacting with one's own gender, they may not necessarily reflect the effects of complex top-down processes such as conceptualizing the distinctions between one's ingroup versus outgroup. Indeed, similar objections could be raised about findings that infants show greater concern and prosocial behavior toward their mothers than toward unfamiliar adults (e.g., Zahn-Waxler, Radke-Yarrow, et al. 1992). A more recent study, however, employed the minimal group paradigm (in which children were randomly assigned to an arbitrary "red team" or "blue team") and found that children between six and eight years of age reported feeling greater empathic concern for ingroup members than for outgroup members who were socially rejected (Masten, Gillen-O'Neel, and Brown 2010). Thus, at least by middle childhood, group membership begins to modulate empathic responding. Importantly, because the minimal group paradigm, by definition, does not rely on preestablished groups or categories that participants are more familiar or comfortable with or have preconceived notions about, Masten et al.'s (2010) study provides stronger evidence that there is at least some top-down construal of group membership that can modulate empathic responding toward ingroup versus outgroup members (though how complex such construal is remains an open question).

In sum, developmental research has begun to provide insights into the ontogenetic emergence of and the mechanisms underlying flexible empathic responding. This research suggests that at least two top-down processes – contextual appraisal and group membership – modulate and thereby add great flexibility to children's empathic responding. As children develop and become more active participants in and recipients of their social worlds, their empathic responding keeps pace by becoming more multidetermined and flexible, allowing them to engage in more complex, selective, and sophisticated interactions and relationships.

5. The Mechanisms of Development

Evidence for top-down processes generating and modulating empathic concern in early ontogeny naturally raises a fascinating mechanistic question: how and under what circumstances do top-down processes begin playing a role in early empathic responding? Answers to this mechanistic question will necessarily be found at multiple levels. At the neural level, we can ask about changes in the brain that would allow top-down, cognitive capacities to bring about empathic responding. In particular, the prefrontal cortex (PFC), which is thought to be the seat of executive control and higher-order cognitive processes in the brain, has long been thought to be silent during most of infancy and to follow an extremely protracted development (Decety and Meyer 2008; Decety and Svetlova 2012). If this is right, then the top-down processes necessary for a multidetermined and flexible empathic system may simply not be available in early development, with the implication that early empathic responding is driven primarily by bottom-up processes (which are supported by early-developing limbic and paralimbic structures; Decety 2010; Hastings et al. 2014). Interestingly, though, recent work suggests that the PFC is active from early in infancy (see Grossmann 2013, for a review), but that it may not be connected or functionally integrated with other regions of the brain (Singer 2006; Johnson, Grossmann, and Kadosh 2009; Decety 2010). The implication is that some relevant top-down processes may be present in infancy but may not play a significant role in empathic responding until later in development when the connectivity is substantially increased (Light and Zahn-Waxler 2012). Developmental structural and functional neuroimaging can thus help us understand the changing nature of empathic responding in early ontogeny.

Advances in children's emotional and cognitive capacities also contribute to the emergence of multidetermined and flexible empathic responding (see Eisenberg and Eggum 2009).[5] For one, an increase in children's own emotional repertoires likely enhances their ability to understand others' diverse emotional responses (Eisenberg, Murphy, and Shepard 1997). At the same time, improvement in effortful control and executive attention improves children's ability to control and regulate their emotional and thus empathic responses. Specifically, infants possess very limited effortful control, but this capacity improves to some degree during

---

[5] The inclusion of both emotional and cognitive advances here should make it clear that I view empathic responding as involving and integrating both of these domains, and view the increasing flexibility in children's empathic responding as resulting not only from advances in the cognitive domain but from advances in both (often intricately bound) domains (cf. Bell and Wolfe 2004; Pessoa 2008).

the second year and substantially during the third year (Kochanska, Murray, and Harlan 2000; Rueda, Posner, and Rothbart 2004).

The development of the imagination (in particular, the ability to imagine other possibilities than those one currently perceives) as well as language also gives children the capacity to understand and contextualize others' perspectives. In addition, children's developing awareness of their own internal states (metacognition or meta-emotion) allows them to monitor their own empathic responses and the various cognitive processes that impact those responses; this sort of awareness may greatly increase the control that children can exert on their empathic responding. Finally, all of these emotional and cognitive advances go hand-in-hand with the increased experiences involving different people and situations that children gather over development, all of which presumably enhance their ability to understand or imagine others' inner states in a flexible and multidetermined way.

In addition, socialization plays a vital role in the emergence of sophisticated empathic responding. By the second year of life, for instance, maternal displays of emotion and control as well as their affectively toned explanations partially account for children's empathic and caring behavior (Zahn-Waxler, Radke-Yarrow, and King 1979; Robinson, Zahn-Waxler, and Emde 1994; see also Kochanska 1991). More generally, Hoffman (2000) has argued that one of the most effective parenting strategies for changing children's harmful behavior and eliciting prosocial behavior is induction, wherein parents draw the child's attention to the feelings, needs, thoughts, and intentions of the other as well as the child's role in causing those internal states. Hoffman argues that inductive parenting taps children's natural empathic proclivity and thus enhances empathic responding. I would add that inductive parenting might also highlight for children the possibility and the importance of using perspective taking in order to empathize and sympathize with others. Over time, children might internalize this connection and begin to take others' perspectives spontaneously as a way of engendering empathic concern for others – not only when children are themselves the cause of others' emotions but also when they are the observers.

Needless to say, the various aforementioned factors are not mutually exclusive and likely work closely together. Moreover, several other factors undoubtedly play a role. Children's temperament, for example, has an influence on the effectiveness of parenting strategies (Kochanska 1995), and cultural context greatly impacts children's development such as via its impact on parents' socialization goals (Kärtner, Keller, and Chaudhary 2010). It is thus important to keep in mind that empathic responding is a complex and dynamic system.

I turn now to consider the links between early multidetermined and flexible sympathy and early prosocial behavior.

6. Multidetermined and Context-Dependent Prosocial Behavior

Empathic concern plays a vital role in motivating prosocial behavior, and so charting the development of empathic concern necessarily has implications for our understanding of prosocial behavior. In particular, the ontogenetic emergence of multidetermined and flexible empathic responses might be reflected in increasingly sophisticated prosocial responses. It has been argued that children start out as indiscriminate helpers, and only as they develop preferences, become sensitive to context, and acquire norms do their early prosocial impulses become more deliberate, selective, and morally informed (Hay and Cook 2007; Warneken and Tomasello 2009). I would add that the developmental transition to increasingly flexible empathic concern should also increase the flexibility and selectivity of prosocial behavior.

The scant evidence supports this idea. For instance, the studies by Vaish et al. (2009) and Hepach et al. (2012b) both revealed that children were more prosocial toward true victims than toward those who were not harmed or were unjustifiably distressed, respectively. The correlation that both studies found between children's concern and subsequent prosocial behavior suggests that it was the flexibility in children's concern that (at least partially) explained the flexible prosocial behavior. Along similar lines, Vaish, Missana, and Tomasello (2011) showed that three-year-old children were more helpful toward puppets that had been harmed than toward nonvictim puppets. Flexible concern thus seems to increase the flexibility and sophistication of children's prosocial behavior.

Note, however, that sympathy and prosocial behavior are not always so closely tied and indeed are dissociable (Eisenberg and Fabes 1990). That is, sympathy can occur without leading to prosocial behavior, and prosocial behavior can occur in the absence of sympathy (Eisenberg and Strayer 1987). We may feel strong concern for others but not have the know-how, the means, or the time to assist them. Conversely, we may act prosocially toward others not out of concern for them but out of a sense of duty or to enhance our own reputation. This applies to flexible prosocial behavior as well. To illustrate, young children are less likely to help a harmful than a helpful individual (Vaish, Carpenter, and Tomasello 2010; Dahl, Schuck, and Campos 2013; Kenward and Dahl, 2011). It is possible that this reduced helping results from reduced empathic responding toward the harmful individual, which would suggest that moral evaluations impact children's empathic responses (in line with work with adults; Singer et al. 2006). Equally, it is possible that children reduce their helping toward harmful individuals because they are afraid of them or out of a desire to punish them (which may in turn require reduced empathic concern for those individuals). It is thus critical to explore the mechanisms underlying children's prosocial behavior in order to clarify when and under what circumstances empathic responding and/or other factors motivate such behavior (see Hepach, Vaish, and Tomasello 2012a; 2013). More generally, as the work on the development of empathic responding expands, we must keep in mind both the association and the dissociation between empathic responding and prosocial behavior.

7. Future Directions and Conclusions

Given that the ability to respond with empathic concern in a multidetermined yet flexible way is so vital to our social interactions, understanding the ontogenetic origins of such responding is undeniably important. Research in this direction has begun to provide valuable insights, but much more work lies ahead. Most obviously, future work will need to broaden the scope of our understanding by examining other processes such as actively changing perspective (e.g., taking one's own versus another's perspective), changing the focus of attention, and the relationship with and evaluation of the other, which have all been shown to modulate the degree of empathic arousal in adults (see Decety and Lamm 2006; Hein and Singer 2008; Singer and Lamm 2009). This descriptive work will open up a much broader space within which to ask more detailed and mechanistic questions. However, even the little that we currently know points the way to fascinating future directions.

One open question – related to the question of mechanisms – concerns the nature of top-down processes, namely, how complex top-down processes need to be to render empathic responding substantially multidetermined and flexible. As discussed earlier, even when primarily bottom-up processes engender affective resonance, some top-down processes are involved in bringing about empathic responding. One such process is self–other discrimination, which is necessary for affective resonance to result in empathic responding. Although a fundamental and implicit self-awareness exists in infancy and may allow for empathic concern at even the youngest ages (see Davidov et al. 2013), a more reflective sense of self emerges later in development and persists into adulthood. How does the emergence of this sophisticated sense of self change the scope and nature of empathic responding? Future work on such questions can significantly improve our understanding of what is needed for children to begin perceiving, understanding, and responding to others' plight in a reliable yet flexible way.

It will also be important for future work to consider individual variation. After all, children, like adults, are not all equally empathic. Indeed, individual differences in empathic concern to others' distress can be detected as early as fourteen months of age (Zahn-Waxler, Robinson, et al. 1992). Similar individual differences certainly exist in more multidetermined and flexible empathic concern as well. What explains this variation?

Numerous factors are known to account for individual differences in empathic responding. These include biological factors such as genes, brain development, and neuroendocrine development; developmental processes such as emotion regulation, the emergence of language, and the development and consolidation of a self; parenting and disciplining styles; and socialization and cultural practices (e.g., Bischof-Köhler 1991; Hoffman 2000; Trommsdorff, Friedlmeier and Mayer 2007; Knafo et al. 2008). Given what we now know about the top-down processes involved in empathic responding, future research will need to consider additional factors. For instance, social and cognitive abilities such as taking others' perspectives, children's acquaintance with a variety of social and emotional experiences, and the degree to which caregivers or cultures promote the display of emotions may all play a role in determining which top-down processes impact empathic responding and to what extent.

To conclude, developmental theories and empirical work over the past decades have provided us with significant insights into the bases and structure of early empathic responding. In order to further advance our understanding, the field needs to expand to include the study of multidetermined and flexible empathic responding. Such sophisticated empathic responding is central to the kinds of complex and selective social interactions that humans engage in, yet we know almost nothing about its emergence over the course of development. Some recent empirical work has begun to fill this gap. This research indicates that even in young children, empathic responding is multidetermined such that it can be generated from both bottom-up and top-down information processing mechanisms. Moreover, it is flexible such that top-down processes can regulate bottom-up processes to give rise to a context- and individual-appropriate (though not necessarily morally required) response. Though this work provides some first insights, it raises many more questions for future work. By moving further in these new directions, we can gain enormous insight into the nature of early empathic responding and, ultimately, into human sociality.

References

Batson, C. D. 1991. *The Altruism Question: Toward a Social-Psychological Answer.* Hillsdale, NJ: Erlbaum.

1998. Altruism and Prosocial Behavior. In: D. T. Gilbert, S. T. Fiske and G. Lindzey (eds.), *The Handbook of Social Psychology.* Boston: McGraw-Hill, vol. II, 282–316.

Batson, C. D.; Batson, J. G.; Slingsby, J. K.; Harrell, K. L.; Peekna, H. M. and Todd, R. M. 1991. Empathic Joy and the Empathy-Altruism Hypothesis. *Journal of Personality and Social Psychology,* 61 (3), 413–26.

Batson, C. D.; Duncan, B. D.; Ackerman, P.; Buckley, T. and Birch, K. 1981. Is Empathic Emotion a Source of Altruistic Motivation? *Journal of Personality and Social Psychology,* 40 (2), 290–302.

Batson, C. D.; Early, S. and Salvarini, G. 1997. Perspective Taking: Imagining How Another Feels versus Imagining How You Would Feel. *Personality and Social Psychology Bulletin,* 23 (7), 751–8.

Batson, C. D.; Fultz, J. and Schoenrade, P. A. 1987. Adults' Emotional Reactions to the Distress of Others. In: N. Eisenberg and J. Strayer (eds.), *Empathy and Its Development.* Cambridge: Cambridge University Press, 163–85.

Batson, C. D.; Sager, K.; Garst, E.; Kang, M.; Rubchinsky, K. and Dawson, K. 1997. Is Empathy-Induced Helping Due to Self-Other Merging? *Journal of Personality and Social Psychology,* 73 (3), 495–509.

Bell, M. A. and Wolfe, C. D. 2004. Emotion and Cognition: An Intricately Bound Developmental Process. *Child Development,* 75 (2), 366–70.

Bischof-Köhler, D. 1991. The Development of Empathy in Infants. In: M. E. Lamb and H. Keller (eds.), *Infant Development: Perspectives from German Speaking Countries.* Hillsdale, NJ: Lawrence Erlbaum Associates, 245–73.

Blair, R. J. R. 1995. A Cognitive Developmental Approach to Morality: Investigating the Psychopath. *Cognition,* 57 (1), 1–29.

Butterworth, G. 1992. Origins of Self-Perception in Infancy. *Psychological Inquiry,* 3 (2), 103–11.

Chiarella, S. S. and Poulin-Dubois, D. 2013. Cry Babies and Pollyannas: Infants Can Detect Unjustified Emotional Reactions. *Infancy,* 18 (suppl. 1), E81–E96. doi: 10.1111/infa.12028

Cikara, M.; Bruneau, E. G. and Saxe, R. R. 2011. Us and Them: Intergroup Failures of Empathy. *Current Directions in Psychological Science,* 20 (3), 149–53. doi: 10.1177/0963721411408713

Dahl, A.; Schuck, R. K. and Campos, J. J. 2013. Do Young Toddlers Act on Their Social Preferences? *Developmental Psychology,* 49 (10), 1964–70.

Davidov, M.; Zahn-Waxler C.; Roth-Hanania, R. and Knafo, A. 2013. Concern for Others in the First Year of Life: Theory, Evidence, and Avenues for Research. *Child Development Perspectives,* 7 (2), 126–31. doi: 10.1111/cdep.12028

de Waal, F. B. M. 2008. Putting the Altruism Back into Altruism: The Evolution of Empathy. *Annual Review of Psychology,* 59, 279–300.

Decety, J. 2010. The Neurodevelopment of Empathy in Humans. *Developmental Neuroscience,* 32 (4), 257–67.

Decety, J. and Jackson, P. L. 2006. A Social-Neuroscience Perspective on Empathy. *Current Directions in Psychological Science*, 15 (2), 54–8.

Decety, J. and Lamm, C. 2006. Human Empathy through the Lens of Social Neuroscience. *Scientific World Journal*, 6, 1146–63.

Decety, J. and Meyer, M. 2008. From Emotion Resonance to Empathic Understanding: A Social Developmental Neuroscience Account. *Development and Psychopathology*, 20 (special iss. 04), 1053–80. doi: 10.1017/S0954579408000503

Decety, J. and Sommerville, J. A. 2003. Shared Representations between Self and Other: A Social Cognitive Neuroscience View. *Trends in Cognitive Sciences*, 7 (12), 527–33.

Decety, J. and Svetlova, M. 2012. Putting Together Phylogenetic and Ontogenetic Perspectives on Empathy. *Developmental Cognitive Neuroscience*, 2 (1), 1–24.

Dimberg, U. and Öhman, A. 1996. Behold the Wrath: Psychophysiological Responses to Facial Stimuli. *Motivation and Emotion*, 20 (2), 149–82.

Dimberg, U.; Thunberg, M. and Elmehed, K. 2000. Unconscious Facial Reactions to Emotional Facial Expressions. *Psychological Science*, 11 (1), 86–9.

Dondi, M.; Simion, F. and Caltran, G. 1999. Can Newborns Discriminate between Their Own Cry and the Cry of Another Newborn Infant? *Developmental Psychology*, 35 (2), 418–26.

Eisenberg, N. 1986. *Altruistic Emotion, Cognition, and Behavior*. Hillsdale, NJ: Erlbaum.

   1991. Meta-Analytic Contributions to the Literature on Prosocial Behavior. *Personality and Social Psychology Bulletin*, 17 (3), 273–82.

   1992. *The Caring Child*. New York: Cambridge University Press.

   2000. Emotion, Regulation, and Moral Development. *Annual Review of Psychology*, 51, 665–97.

Eisenberg, N. and Eggum, N. D. 2009. Empathic Responding: Sympathy and Personal Distress. In: J. Decety and W. Ickes (eds.), *The Social Neuroscience of Empathy*. Cambridge, MA: MIT Press, 71–83.

Eisenberg, N. and Fabes, R. A. 1990. Empathy: Conceptualization, Measurement, and Relation to Prosocial Behavior. *Motivation and Emotion*, 14 (2), 131–49.

Eisenberg, N. and Miller, P. A. 1987. The Relation of Empathy to Prosocial and Related Behaviors. *Psychological Bulletin*, 101 (1), 91–119.

Eisenberg, N. and Strayer, J. 1987. Critical Issues in the Study of Empathy. In: N. Eisenberg and J. Strayer (eds.), *Empathy and Its Development*. New York: Cambridge University Press, 3–13.

Eisenberg, N.; Fabes, R. A.; Miller, P. A. et al. 1989. Relation of Sympathy and Personal Distress to Prosocial Behavior: A Multimethod Study. *Journal of Personality and Social Psychology*, 57 (1), 55–66.

Eisenberg, N.; Fabes, R. A.; Murphy, B.; Karbon, M.; Smith, M. and Maszk, P. 1996. The Relations of Children's Dispositional Empathy-Related Responding to Their Emotionality, Regulation, and Social Functioning. *Developmental Psychology*, 32 (2), 195–209.

Eisenberg, N.; Fabes, R. A.; Shepard, S. A. et al. 1997. Contemporaneous and Longitudinal prediction of Children's Social Functioning From Regulation and Rmotionality. *Child Development*, 68 (4), 642–64.

Eisenberg, N.; Guthrie, I. K.; Murphy, B. C.; Shepard, S. A.; Cumberland, A. and Carlo, G. 1990. Consistency and Development of Prosocial Dispositions: A Longitudinal Study. *Child Development*, 70 (6), 1360–72.

Eisenberg, N.; Murphy, B. and Shepard, S. 1997. The Development of Empathic Accuracy. In: W. Ickes (ed.), *Empathic Accuracy*. New York: Guilford Press, 73–116.

Eisenberg, N.; Shea, C. L.; Carlo, G. and Knight, G. P. 1991. Empathy-Related Responding and Cognition: A "Chicken and the Egg" Dilemma. In: W. Kurtines and J. Gewirtz (eds.), *Handbook of Moral Behavior and Development*. Hillsdale, NJ: Lawrence Erlbaum Associates, vol. II: *Research*, 63–88.

Eisenberg, N.; Spinrad, T. L. and Sadovsky, A. 2006. Empathy-Related Responding in Children. In: M. Killen and J. G. Smetana (eds.), *Handbook of Moral Development*. Mahwah, NJ: Lawrence Erlbaum Associates, 517–49.

Eisenberg, N.; Valiente, C. and Champion, C. 2004. Empathy-Related Responding: Moral, Social, and Socialization Correlates. In: A. G. Miller (ed.), *The Social Psychology of Good and Evil: Understanding Our Capacity for Kindness and Cruelty*. New York: Guilford Press, 386–415.

Eisenberg-Berg, N. and Lennon, R. 1980. Altruism and the Assessment of Empathy in the Preschool Years. *Child Development*, 51 (2), 552–7.

Feshbach, N. D. 1978. Studies of Empathic Behavior in Children. In: B. A. Maher (ed.), *Progress in Experimental Personality Research*. New York: Academic Press, vol. VIII, 1–47.

Feshbach, N. D. and Roe, K. 1968. Empathy in Six- and Seven-Year-Olds. *Child Development*, 39 (1), 133–45.

Geangu, E.; Benga, O.; Stahl, D. and Striano, T. 2010. Contagious Crying beyond the First Days of Life. *Infant Behavior and Development*, 33 (3), 279–88.

Grossmann, T. 2013. Mapping Prefrontal Cortex Functions in Human Infancy. *Infancy*, 18 (3), 303–24.

Gu, X. and Han, S. 2007. Attention and Reality Constraints on the Neural Processes of Empathy for Pain. *NeuroImage*, 36 (1), 256–67.

Hastings, P. D.; Miller, J. G.; Kahle, S. and Zahn-Waxler, C. 2014. The Neurobiological Bases of Empathic Concern for Others. In: M. Killen and J. G. Smetana (eds.), *Handbook of Moral Development*, 2nd edn. New York/London: Psychology Press, 411–34.

Hay, D. F. and Cook, K. V. 2007. The Transformation of Prosocial Behavior from Infancy to Childhood. In: C. A. Brownell and C. B. Kopp (eds.), *Socioemotional Development in the Toddler Years*. New York: Guilford Press, 100–31.

Hein, G. and Singer, T. 2008. I Feel How You Feel but Not Always: The Empathic Brain and Its Modulation. *Current Opinion in Neurobiology*, 18 (2), 153–8.

Hepach, R.; Vaish, A. and Tomasello, M. 2012a. Young Children Are Intrinsically Motivated to See Others Helped. *Psychological Science*, 23 (9), 967–72.

Hepach, R.; Vaish, A. and Tomasello, M. 2012b. Young Children Sympathize Less in Response to Unjustified Emotional Distress. *Developmental Psychology*, 49 (6), 1132–38.

Hepach, R.; Vaish, A. and Tomasello, M. 2013. A New Look at Children's Prosocial Motivation. *Infancy*, 18 (1), 67–90.

Hobson, J. A.; Harris, R.; García-Pérez, R. and Hobson, P. 2009. Anticipatory Concern: A Study in Autism. *Developmental Science*, 12 (2), 249–63.

Hodges, S. D. and Biswas-Diener, R. 2007. Balancing the Empathy Expense Account: Strategies for Regulating Empathic Response. In: T. F. D. Farrow and P. W. R. Woodruff (eds.), *Empathy in Mental Illness*. New York: Cambridge University Press, 389–407.

Hodges, S. D. and Klein, K. J. K. 2001. Regulating the Costs of Empathy: The Price of Being Human. *Journal of Socio-Economics*, 30 (5), 437–52.

Hoffman, M. L. 1975. Developmental Synthesis of Affect and Cognition and Its Implications for Altruistic Motivation. *Developmental Psychology*, 11 (5), 607–22.

   1981. Is Altruism Part of Human Nature? *Journal of Personality and Social Psychology*, 40 (1), 121–37.

   1982. Development of Prosocial Motivation: Empathy and Guilt. In: N. Eisenberg (ed.), *The Development of Prosocial Behavior*. New York: Academic Press, 281–338.

   1984. Interaction of Affect and Cognition in Empathy. In: C. E. Izard, J. Kagan and R. B. Zajonc (eds.), *Emotion, Cognition, and Behavior*. New York: Cambridge University Press, 103–31.

   2000. *Empathy and Moral Development: Implications for Caring and Justice*. Cambridge: Cambridge University Press.

   2007. The Origins of Empathic Morality in Toddlerhood. In: C. A. Brownell and C. B. Kopp (eds.), *Socioemotional Development in the Toddler Years: Transitions and Transformations*. New York: Guilford Press, 132–45.

Hume, D. 1776. *An Enquiry Concerning the Principles of Morals*. Notre Dame, IN: University of Notre Dame Press, 1965.

Iannotti, R. J. 1985. Naturalistic and Structured Assessments of Prosocial Behavior in Preschool Children: The Influence of Empathy and Perspective Taking. *Developmental Psychology*, 21 (1), 46–55.

Jackson, P. L.; Brunet, E.; Meltzoff, A. N. and Decety, J. 2006. Empathy Examined through the Neural Mechanisms Involved in Imagining How I Feel versus How You Feel Pain. *Neuropsychologia*, 44 (5), 752–61.

Johnson, M. H.; Grossmann, T. and Kadosh, K. C. 2009. Mapping Functional Brain Development: Building a Social Brain through Interactive Specialization. *Developmental Psychology*, 45 (1), 151–9.

Karniol, R. 1982. Settings, Scripts, and Self-Schemata: A Cognitive Analysis of the Development of Prosocial Behavior. In: N. Eisenberg (ed.), *The Development of Prosocial Behavior*. New York: Academic Press, 251–78.

Kärtner, J.; Keller, H. and Chaudhary, N. 2010. Cognitive and Social Influences on Early Prosocial Behavior in Two Sociocultural Contexts. *Developmental Psychology*, 46 (4), 905–14.

Kenward, B. and Dahl, M. 2011. Preschoolers Distribute Scarce Resources According to the Moral Valence of Recipients' Previous Actions. *Developmental Psychology*, 47 (4), 1054–64.

Keysers, C. and Gazzola, V. 2014. Dissociating the Ability and Propensity for Empathy. *Trends in Cognitive Sciences*, 18 (4), 163–6.

Knafo, A.; Zahn-Waxler, C.; Van Hulle, C.; Robinson, J. L. and Rhee, S. H. 2008. The Developmental Origins of a Disposition toward Empathy: Genetic and Environmental Contributions. *Emotion*, 8 (6), 737–52.

Kochanska, G. 1991. Socialization and Temperament in the Development of Guilt and Conscience. *Child Development*, 62 (6), 1379–92.

1995. Children's Temperament, Mother's Discipline, and Security of Attachment: Multiple Pathways to Emerging Internalization. *Child Development*, 66 (3), 597–615.

Kochanska, G.; Murray, K. T. and Harlan, E. T. 2000. Effortful Control in Early Childhood: Continuity and Change, Antecedents, and Implications for Social Development. *Developmental Psychology*, 36 (2), 220–32.

Krebs, D. L. and Russell, C. 1981. Role-Taking and Altruism: When You Put Yourself in the Shoes of Another, Will They Take You to Their Owner's Aid? In: J. P. Rushton and R. M. Sorrentino (eds.), *Altruism and Helping Behavior*. Hillsdale, NJ: Erlbaum, 137–65.

Lamm, C.; Batson, C. D. and Decety, J. 2007. The Neural Substrate of Human Empathy: Effects of Perspective-Taking and Cognitive Appraisal. *Journal of Cognitive Neuroscience*, 19 (1), 42–58.

Lamm, C.; Nusbaum, H. C.; Meltzoff, A. N. and Decety, J. 2007. What Are You Feeling? Using Functional Magnetic Resonance Imaging to Assess the Modulation of Sensory and Affective Responses during Empathy for Pain. *PLoS One*, 2 (12), e1292.

Lanzetta, J. T. and Englis, B. S. 1989. Expectations of Cooperation and Competition and Their Effects on Observers' Vicarious Emotional Responses. *Journal of Personality and Social Psychology*, 56 (4), 543–54.

Leslie, A. M.; Mallon, R. and Dicorcia, J. A. 2006. Transgressors, Victims, and Cry Babies: Is Basic Moral Judgment Spared in Autism? *Social Neuroscience*, 1 (3–4), 270–83.

Lewis, M. and Brooks-Gunn, J. 1979. *Social Cognition and the Acquisition of Self*. New York: Plenum Press.

Lewis, M.; Sullivan, M. W.; Stanger, C. and Weiss, M. 1989. Self Development and Self-Conscious Emotions. *Child Development*, 60 (1), 146–56.

Light, S. and Zahn-Waxler, C. 2012. Nature and Forms of Empathy in the First Years of Life. In: J. Decety (ed.), *Empathy: From Bench to Bedside*. Cambridge, MA: MIT Press, 109–30.

Masten, C. L.; Gillen-O'Neel; C. and Brown, C. S. 2010. Children's Intergroup Empathic Processing: The Roles of Novel Ingroup Identification, Situational Distress, and Social Anxiety. *Journal of Experimental Child Psychology*, 106 (2–3), 115–28.

Miller, P. A. and Eisenberg, N. 1988. The Relation of Empathy to Aggressive and Externalizing/Antisocial Behavior. *Psychological Bulletin*, 103 (3), 324–44.

Moore, C. 2007. Understanding Self and Others in the Second Year. In: C. A. Brownell and C. B. Kopp (eds.), *Socioemotional Development in the Toddler Years*. New York: Guilford Press, 43–65.

Nichols, S. R.; Svetlova, M. and Brownell, C. A. 2009. The Role of Social Understanding and Empathic Disposition in Young Children's Responsiveness to Distress in Parents and Peers. *Cognition, Brain, Behavior: An Interdisciplinary Journal*, 13 (4), 449–78.

Oakley, B.; Knafo, A.; Madhavan, G. and Wilson, D. S. (eds.) 2012. *Pathological Altruism*. New York: Oxford University Press.
Pessoa, L. 2008. On the Relationship between Emotion and Cognition. *Nature Reviews Neuroscience*, 9 (2), 148–58.
Preston, S. D. and de Waal, F. B. M. 2002. Empathy: Its Ultimate and Proximate Bases. *Behavioral and Brain Sciences*, 25 (1), 1–72.
Preston, S. D. and Hofelich, A. J. 2012. The Many Faces of Empathy: Parsing Empathic Phenomena through a Proximate, Dynamic-Systems View of Representing the Other in the Self. *Emotion Review*, 4 (1), 24–33.
Robinson, J. L.; Zahn-Waxler, C. and Emde, R. N. 1994. Patterns of Development in Early Empathic Behavior: Environmental and Child Constitutional Influences. *Social Development*, 3 (2), 125–45.
Rochat, P. 2003. Five Levels of Self-Awareness as They Unfold Early in Life. *Consciousness and Cognition*, 12 (4), 717–31.
Roth-Hanania, R.; Davidov, M. and Zahn-Waxler, C. 2011. Empathy Development from 8 to 16 Months: Early Signs of Concern for Others. *Infant Behavior and Development*, 34 (3), 447–58. doi: dx.doi.org/10.1016/j.infbeh.2011.04.007
Rothbart, M. K. and Bates, J. E. 2006. Temperament. In: W. Damon and R. M. Lerner (eds.), *Handbook of Child Psychology*, 6th edn. Hoboken, NJ: Wiley, vol. III: *Social, Emotional, and Personality Development*, 99–166.
Ruby, P. and Decety, J. 2004. How Would *You* Feel versus How Do You Think *She* Would Feel? A Neuroimaging Study of Perspective-Taking with Social Emotions. *Journal of Cognitive Neuroscience*, 16 (6), 988–99.
Rueda, M. R.; Posner, M. I. and Rothbart, M. K. 2004. Attentional Control and Self-Regulation. In: R. F. Baumeister and K. D. Vohs (eds.), *Handbook of Self-Regulation: Research, Theory, and Applications*. New York: Guilford Press, 283–300.
Sagi, A. and Hoffman, M. L. 1976. Empathic Distress in Newborns. *Developmental Psychology*, 12 (2), 175–6.
Shamay-Tsoory, S. G. 2011. The Neural Bases for Empathy. *Neuroscientist*, 17 (1), 18–24.
Simner, M. L. 1971. Newborns' Response to the Cry of Another Infant. *Developmental Psychology*, 5 (1), 136–50.
Singer, T. 2006. The Neuronal Basis and Ontogeny of Empathy and Mind Reading: Review of Literature and Implications for Future Research. *Neuroscience and Biobehavioral Reviews*, 30 (6), 855–63.
Singer, T. and Lamm, C. 2009. The Social Neuroscience of Empathy. *Annals of the New York Academy of Sciences*, 1156, 81–96.
Singer, T., Seymour, B., O'Doherty, J. P., Stephan, K. E., Dolan, R. J. and Frith, C. D. 2006. Empathic Neural Responses are Modulated by the Perceived Fairness of Others. *Nature*, 439 (7075), 466–9.
Smith, A. 1759. *The Theory of Moral Sentiments*. Mineola, NY: Dover, 2006.
Sonnby-Borgström; M., Jönsson; P. and Svensson, O. 2003. Emotional Empathy as Related to Mimicry Reactions at Different Levels of Information Processing. *Journal of Nonverbal Behavior*, 27 (1), 3–23.
Stel, M. and van den Bos, K. 2010. Mimicry as a Tool for Understanding the Emotions of Others. Paper presented at the Proceedings of Measuring Behavior, Eindhoven, Netherlands.

Stotland, E. 1969. Exploratory Investigations of Empathy. In: L. Berkowitz (ed.), *Advances in Experimental Social Psychology*. New York: Academic Press, vol. IV, 271–314.

Svetlova, M.; Nichols, S. R. and Brownell, C. A. 2011. Toddlers' Prosocial Behavior: From Instrumental to Empathic to Altruistic Helping. *Child Development*, 81 (6), 1814–27.

Theimer, C. E.; Killen, M. and Stangor, C. 2001. Young Children's Evaluations of Exclusion in Gender-Stereotypic Contexts. *Developmental Psychology*, 37 (1), 18–27.

Trommsdorff, G.; Friedlmeier, W. and Mayer, B. 2007. Sympathy, Distress, and Prosocial Behavior of Preschool Children in Four Cultures. *International Journal of Behavioral Development*, 31 (3), 284–93.

Vaish, A. 2016. Flexible Concern: The Development of Multidetermined and Context-Dependent Empathic Responding. *Child Development Perspectives*, 10 (3), 149–54.

Vaish, A.; Carpenter, M. and Tomasello, M. 2009. Sympathy through Affective Perspective-Taking and Its Relation to Prosocial Behavior in Toddlers. *Developmental Psychology*, 45 (2), 534–43.

Vaish, A.; Carpenter, M. and Tomasello, M. 2010. Young Children Selectively Avoid Helping People with Harmful Intentions. *Child Development*, 81 (6), 1661–9.

Vaish, A.; Missana, M. and Tomasello, M. 2011. Three-Year-Old Children Intervene in Third-Party Moral Transgressions. *British Journal of Developmental Psychology*, 29 (1), 124–30.

Vaish, A. and Warneken, F. 2012. Social-Cognitive Contributors to Young Children's Empathic and Prosocial behavior. In: J. Decety (ed.), *Empathy: From Bench to Bedside*. Cambridge, MA: MIT Press, 131–46.

Valiente, C.; Eisenberg, N.; Fabes, R. A.; Shepard, S. A.; Cumberland, A. and Losoya, S. H. 2004. Prediction of Children's Empathy-Related Responding from Their Effortful Control and Parents' Expressivity. *Developmental Psychology*, 40 (6), 911–26.

Warneken, F. and Tomasello, M. 2009. The Roots of Human Altruism. *British Journal of Psychology*, 100 (3), 455–71.

Xu, X.; Zuo, X.; Wang, X. and Han, S. 2009. Do You Feel My Pain? Racial Group Membership Modulates Empathic Neural Responses. *Journal of Neuroscience*, 29 (26), 8525–9.

Zahn-Waxler, C. and Hulle, C. V. 2012. Empathy, Guilt, and Depression: When Caring for Others Becomes Costly to Children. In: B. Oakley, A. Knafo, G. Madhavan and D. S. Wilson (eds.), *Pathological Altruism*. New York: Oxford University Press, 321–44.

Zahn-Waxler, C.; Radke-Yarrow, M. and King, R. A. 1979. Child Rearing and Children's Prosocial Initiations toward Victims of Distress. *Child Development*, 50 (2), 319–30.

Zahn-Waxler, C.; Radke-Yarrow, M.; Wagner, E. and Chapman, M. 1992. Development of Concern for Others. *Developmental Psychology*, 28 (1), 126–36.

Zahn-Waxler, C.; Robinson, J. L. and Emde, R. N. 1992. The Development of Empathy in Twins. *Developmental Psychology*, 28 (6), 1038–47.

V

Empathy and Morality

10 Is Empathy Required for Making Moral Judgments?

John Deigh

1. Hume's Account of Our Moral Sensibilities

The problem I'll be discussing in this chapter begins with Hume. At any rate, Hume's ethics is as far back as I have traced it. Hume, in *A Treatise of Human Nature*, asks at the beginning of book III whether moral distinctions derive from reason or feeling (Hume 1739). The chief distinction that interests him is that between virtue and vice, and the way he puts the question is to ask whether we distinguish between virtue and vice by means of our ideas or our impressions (Hume 1739, 456). Nonetheless, we can be certain, given the argument in part 1 of book III, that Hume in asking this question understands ideas and impressions as proxies for reason and feeling. His principal question, then, is whether we distinguish between virtue and vice by relying on the deliverances of reason or those of feeling. Asking it in terms of ideas and impressions suits his using, to answer it, apparatus and results that he had previously introduced and derived in books I and II.

In asking the question, Hume presupposed that the human mind has certain sensitivities or powers that enable its possessor to distinguish between virtue and vice. For answering it requires determining which of the mind's sensitivities and powers are stimulated or exercised when its possessor concludes of an action that it is noble and exhibits virtue or, alternatively, that it is depraved and springs from vice. Hence, in asking the question, he fastened on us, if not for the first time, then at least much more securely than any predecessor who gave a similar answer, the idea that to understand the nature of moral judgment requires understanding the distinctive mechanisms of the mind that produce such judgments. On this idea, moral judgment is a type of judgment that we distinguish from other types, not by its subject, but rather by the peculiar operations of the mind that produce its tokens. That is, on this idea, we distinguish moral judgments from other types in the same way as we distinguish visual judgments from tactile ones and not in the way we distinguish arithmetic judgments from geometric ones. The idea fits Hume's project of applying the methods of natural science, what he calls experimental philosophy, to the subject of morals since it focuses on the mechanisms of the mind that produce moral judgments. Such a focus lends itself to a scientific search for the natural causes and conditions that explain the phenomenon in question. This focus, I believe, is problematic, and in the discussion to follow I will lay out the trouble it causes in the study of moral judgment.

Let us begin the discussion with an explanation of the answer Hume gave to the question with which he opens book III. His answer is that moral distinctions derive from feeling. And he argues for this answer by excluding ideas from being the means by which we distinguish between virtue and vice. Summarizing his argument, he writes, "Our decisions concerning moral rectitude and depravity are evidently perceptions; and as all perceptions are either impressions or ideas, the exclusion of the one is a convincing argument for the other. Morality, therefore, is more properly felt than judg'd of ..." (Hume 1739, 470).

His project going forward, then, is to identify the impressions by which we distinguish between virtue and vice and to explain how they arise in the mind. Those impressions, he tells us, are certain qualitatively distinct pleasant and unpleasant feelings that follow ideas that have a specific type of content. The objects of those feelings are human beings, either oneself or others, and the ideas the feelings succeed represent features of their objects the thought of which we find satisfying or displeasing. Hume abstracts this schema from observing that we take pleasure in contemplating or witnessing generous, heroic, and patriotic actions and are distressed when we see or hear about cruel, duplicitous, and cowardly actions. The former and similar acts of moral rectitude or goodness gladden our hearts and lift our spirits; the latter and similar acts of moral degeneracy and weakness unsettle and displease us. In the former cases, the pleasure we take gives way to sentiments of moral approbation or esteem; in the latter, the displeasure gives way to sentiments of moral disapprobation or blame. These sentiments are a distinct or, as Hume says, "*peculiar* kind" of pleasure and pain, which "makes us praise or condemn" (Hume 1739, 472).

Moral approbation and disapprobation, Hume goes on to observe, are not restricted to ourselves or those near to us. The heroism of our enemies as well as that of our friends can elicit our esteem. The cruelty of tyrants who ruled centuries ago and over people unrelated to us can arouse our disgust. And because they can, our feelings of approbation and disapprobation do not depend on any personal interest we take in how the objects of these sentiments, by their actions, benefit or harm us. Thus, to explain how these sentiments arise in the mind, Hume concludes, one must look to mental operations that do not come from self-love. To explain them, that is, one must look to mental operations that occur when one views things generally and disinterestedly.

Hume's explanation is complicated. It is based on two facts about human psychology. First, Hume writes, "The minds of men are similar in their feelings and operations" (Hume 1739, 575). Second, he observes immediately afterward, "As in strings equally wound up, the motion of one communicates to the rest; so all the affections readily pass from one person to another, and beget correspondent movements in every human creature" (Hume 1739, 576). The communication of feeling to which Hume refers in stating this second fact takes place through the workings of sympathy. Sympathy, as Hume understands it, is not a distinct passion, like pity or benevolence. Rather, it is a principle of the mind whose operation turns an idea of another's feeling into that very feeling. Thus, when one sees in another's face or posture or infers from his conduct that he is feeling pain, pleasure, anger, joy, sadness, or the like, one forms an idea of what he is feeling. And then, as a result of the influence of sympathy, this idea is enlivened into the feeling itself. Hume, accordingly, constructs from this principle of sympathy and his premiss that the minds of human beings are all similar an explanation of how feelings that are concordant with the feelings of another and that result from the workings of sympathy give rise to esteem or blame for whoever brought pleasure or pain, as the case may be, to the object of one's sympathy.

The details of this explanation need not concern us. What matters is Hume's making sympathy its pivotal factor. The conversion that sympathy brings about of an idea of another's feeling into the feeling itself connects one with that person in a way that makes his feelings matter to one when, as feelings of pleasure or pain, they serve as tokens of his happiness or unhappiness. Having those feelings, Hume holds, yields favorable or unfavorable sentiments toward whoever's actions brought pleasure or pain to that person. In other words, the sentiments of approbation and disapprobation, esteem and blame, result from one's first being so connected to another's pleasure or pain and then taking the party or parties responsible for it as the sentiments' objects. Hume, thus, in attributing this mechanism of connection to the human mind, gave an account of the phenomena of having feelings in common with another that we now typically explain as resulting from empathy. His explanation of how we make moral distinctions – distinctions between virtue and vice, in particular – thus represents a view of moral judgment as requiring empathy.[1] And what is more

---

[1] Hume allows one small exception: when one finds another's witty conversation or charming demeanor, for instance, immediately agreeable, the pleasure of his company can produce the sentiment of approbation directly. In this case, the sentiment and so one's

important is that it represents more generally an explanation on which the ability to make these distinctions is due to certain native sensitivities and tendencies of mind that are distinct from the mental powers by which we make other distinctions, like those between sweet and sour, rain and snow, night and day.

At the same time, this feature does not alone distinguish Hume's explanation of moral judgment from the traditional explanations against which he was arguing. The prevailing tradition at the time was that of Christian ethics. In this tradition, the seat of moral knowledge is located in conscience, and we determine whether an act is one of virtue or vice by exercising this knowledge. Hence, given the Christian tradition's understanding of conscience as a distinct power, native to the mind, its explanation is like Hume's. It too attributes our ability to make distinctions between virtue and vice to a certain mental power that is distinct from mental powers by which we make other distinctions.

Nonetheless, there is a significant difference between them. On the traditional explanation, because the judgments of virtue and vice are exercises of moral knowledge, the location of that knowledge in conscience, however important that may be to the broader theory of moral agency, is not essential to the ability of men and women to make these judgments. If moral knowledge were located in some other organ of thought than conscience, they could still exercise it. They would still, therefore, have the ability to determine whether an action was virtuous or vicious, and the power in virtue of which they would have this ability would then be the distinct mental power to which moral judgments were attributed. On Hume's explanation, by contrast, such judgments could not be made if men and women lacked sympathy and were unable to view things disinterestedly, that is, from a view uninformed by self-love or other kinds of partiality, since without sympathy or the ability to take this disinterested view, human beings would be incapable of the sentiments of approbation and disapprobation that are the vehicles of moral opinion.

The difference, then, between the two explanations rests on a difference between the content of moral judgments, on the one hand, and their psychological profile, on the other. On the traditional explanation, one makes these judgments using knowledge of moral laws or precepts, the typical exposition of which reduces them to one or a few basic precepts of right and wrong. These basic precepts supply, then, the content

discernment of virtue arise without the intermediation of empathy since one does not need to enter empathically into anyone else's mind to experience the pleasure that elicits the sentiment. Noting these exceptions, Hume then quickly moves on to observe that taking such conduct as virtuous in other cases "has a considerable dependence on the principle of *sympathy* so often insisted on." Hume, 1978, p. 590.

of morality and consequently the content of moral judgments. If, for instance, the sole basic precept were the Golden Rule, then the content of morality would be conduct among human beings that promoted reciprocity in their relations with each other. On Hume's explanation, by contrast, one makes moral judgments by means of viewing things disinterestedly and under the influence of sympathy. Given his understanding of sympathy as a mechanism that works to convert an idea of another's feeling into that very feeling and the subsequent favorable or unfavorable sentiment that results from that feeling as representing moral judgment, the determinant of moral judgment is its psychological profile and not its content.

It will be useful, at this point, to distinguish moral judgment from other moral opinion. Hume suggests this distinction when he declares in the passage I earlier quoted that "Morality is more properly felt than judg'd of" (Hume 1739, 470). Plainly, this declaration implies that Hume takes judgments to be exercises of reason, for his point is to affirm that moral distinctions derive from feeling and not from reason. Accordingly, in deference to Hume, I propose to take moral judgments to be those moral opinions that one reaches by applying moral knowledge or, more exactly, moral beliefs that if true and well founded, would be knowledge to the events or facts before one, and to understand that in so applying such knowledge or beliefs, one exercises reason. Thus, the explanandum of the traditional explanation is moral judgment. The explanandum of Hume's explanation, by contrast, is not, or at least not in the first instance. Hume, indeed, denies that the opinions one forms directly about people's virtues and vices are judgments since he denies that they are exercises of reason.[2]

Hume, to be sure, allows that to be consistent in one's moral opinions of people who engage in actions of a given type sometimes requires that one adjust one's feelings to conform to the opinions one forms of them when one's view of those actions is clear and undistorted. It is possible, then, to interpret him, as some commentators do, as having thereby introduced moral judgments into his theory and, as a result, gone

---

[2] Hume, despite implying that our discernment of moral distinctions consists in feeling rather than judgment, nonetheless sometimes uses "judgment" to describe it. For example, immediately after introducing the subject of book III in its opening paragraphs, he refers to "those judgments by which we determine moral good and evil" (Hume 1739, 456). And later in his discussion of natural virtue, he writes of the two ways in which a person's motives or character gives rise to sentiments of approbation or disapprobation, "My opinion is, that both these causes are intermix'd in our judgments of morals; after the same manner as they are in our decisions concerning most kinds of external beauty" (Hume 1739, 589–90). I take these occurrences of "judgment" as showing a lack of consistency in Hume's use of "judgment" and not deviation from his thesis about the means by which we make moral distinctions. On his use of "judgment" in such contexts, see Stroud 1977, 172n1.

against his thesis that we distinguish between virtue and vice by means of our feelings. These commentators' argument is that such adjustments require one to judge what feelings one would have if one were viewing the actions from a clear and undistorted view, and such judgments follow from applying what, on Hume's theory, would amount to moral knowledge or beliefs (Sayre-McCord 1994). But I do not believe such an interpretation is necessary. The adjustments to feeling Hume allows are like the adjustments we make to our visual perceptions of objects of a given type to bring them in line with how such objects appear to us from a similarly clear and undistorted view. That we perceive an object as having, say, the same hue through various changes in light is due to the way the mind transforms the images of the object on the retina into perceptions of the object's color, and it seems better to suppose that such transformations are built into the machinery of perception than that they consist in exercises of reason in which we apply beliefs about color and light to the objects before us. In general, therefore, Hume's explanation represents the view that what makes one's favorable or unfavorable response to someone a moral opinion is its consisting in qualitatively distinct pleasant and unpleasant feelings that accompany the idea of that person and that occur when one views things disinterestedly and under the influence of sympathy. It thus represents the view that the determinant of moral opinion is its psychological profile and not its content.

2. A Problem with Hume's Account

A view like Hume's is obviously untenable without further explanation. One cannot, after all, deny that people make judgments about duties they have and do so by applying a set of beliefs they hold to the facts or events before them. G. E. M. Anscombe's example of owing a grocer money as a result of his both supplying one with potatoes and sending one a bill nicely makes the point (Anscombe 1958a; 1958b). Defenders of the view must therefore give some explanation of these judgments as either not really moral or not really judgments. Hume, plainly, accepts them as judgments. He too sees that when we are presented with certain facts or events, we apply a set of beliefs to those facts or events in determining that someone has trespassed on another's land or otherwise invaded his property or that someone has gone back on his word or otherwise reneged on a promise. What Hume denies is that these judgments are moral judgments. To be sure, he observes that they do produce in the mind of people who view these facts or events disinterestedly and under the influence of sympathy the sentiment of blame, the object of which is the trespasser or promise breaker. But in a mind that views them self-interestedly, they do not. His famous worry about the sensible knave who acts justly contrary to his own selfish interests only when his omitting to do so would cause "a considerable breach in the social union" implies as much (Hume 1751, 81). In this way, Hume keeps separate judgments that can give rise to moral sentiments from the sentiments themselves. Of course, these judgments, being judgments about people's rights and duties, are moral judgments in a perfectly ordinary sense of the word "moral." They concern matters of justice, and judgments about matters of justice are moral judgments. So, to defend a view like Hume's, one must justify taking the word "moral" in a different sense.

The justification comes from the argument in book III, part 1, of the *Treatise* whose summarization by Hume we earlier noted. Hume rests this argument on his thesis that morality is essentially practical (Hume 1739, 475). Let us call this thesis "Hume's internalist thesis." In saying that morality is essentially practical, he means that it is in the nature of morality to have influence on our passions and actions. Accordingly, Hume takes the word "moral," when used to qualify names of mental states, to restrict the mental states that those names denote to states that have an influence on our passions and actions. His internalist thesis is thus what supports his use of "moral" in this way. It justifies, that is, his taking "moral" in a different sense from the one on which judgments concerning matters of justice are *ipso facto* moral. To defend a view like Hume's, then, one must offer a similar justification.

The dispute over Hume's internalist thesis, as he understood it, has engaged the interest of moral philosophers for over a half-century. It arose in metaethics when specialists in the field came to realize that the question the thesis raises about the motivational influence of moral judgments is independent of questions about the definability of ethical terms and the deducibility of ethical sentences from sentences that are not ethical (Frankena 1958). As a result of this realization, studies in metaethics expanded into areas of psychology that had previously been at most tangential to the inquiries into the semantics of ethical language and the logic and epistemic status of ethical arguments that had been the primary preoccupations of moral philosophers in the analytic tradition. This expansion corresponded to a shift from treating questions about the analysis of moral judgments as questions about their content, that is, whether the basic terms expressing this content were definable in naturalistic terms, indefinable, or noncognitive, to treating them as questions about the psychological profile of moral judgments, whether motivation was built into them and, if so, by virtue of which operations of the mind. This shift helped to entrench Hume's idea that to understand the nature of moral opinions requires determining the sensitivities and powers of the mind whose stimulation and workings produce them. At the same time, because many philosophers still held to the use of the word "moral" in the ordinary sense in which the only criterion of application is the content of the cognition or affect one uses the word to describe, the dispute in metaethics over the question Hume's internalist thesis raises reached, after several decades of fierce debate, an impasse. To date, philosophers have not found a way out of this impasse (Enoch 2011, 249–52).

3. A Proposal

In a paper I wrote some years ago, *Empathy and Universalizability*, I proposed, in view of this impasse, to study the question that Hume's thesis raises as a question in psychology rather than as a question in metaethics (Deigh, 1995). My proposal was to accept the common description of psychopaths as people who know the difference between right and wrong but are nonetheless amoral in the sense of lacking such marks of moral agency as compunctions of conscience and a liability to feelings of guilt, and to ask whether their amorality, while consistent with their being competent to make moral judgments of one type, is due at bottom to a cognitive deficit and therefore to an inability to make moral judgments of a different type. My thought was that an affirmative answer could vindicate Kant's supposition of the possibility of our making judgments of the type he characterized as categorical imperatives, that is, judgments of duty that, on their own, influence their makers to act in accordance with them. The cognitive deficit I attributed to psychopaths was their lacking the capacity for empathy, where I understood empathy to be a state of understanding what is going on in another's mind that one attains by taking that other person's perspective. Accordingly, my hypothesis was that having a capacity for empathy in addition to the cognitive capacities that people who bear the marks of moral agency have in common with psychopaths gives a person the capacity to make judgments of the type Kant characterized as categorical imperatives. And I understood the examination of this hypothesis to lie outside of metaethics since one could undertake it, as I had proposed, independently of questions about the nature of moral judgment.

Subsequent criticism of my hypothesis has convinced me that I did not go far enough in proposing to treat the question that Hume's internalist thesis raises as a question in psychology rather than metaethics. One criticism, due to Jeanette Kennett, rests on a comparison of psychopathy with autism (Kennett 2002). While both conditions, according to Kennett, include a lack of empathy, only psychopathy is a condition of amorality. Autism, by contrast, is a disorder whose severity varies from

Is Empathy Required for Making Moral Judgments? 253

the extremes of mental retardation to more mild forms that are not so disabling as to make those subject to them incapable of functioning productively in society, and such people can have a conscience and be guided by it. Hence, Kennett concludes, having a conscience is consistent with being incapable of empathy. This conclusion, Kennett argues, supports Kant's conception of moral judgment and motivation as products of reason. Taking empathy to be essential to Hume's account of our moral sensibility and inessential to Kant's, she then finds that Kant's account, but not Hume's, fits the moral judgments of high-functioning autistics who have a conscience. In other words, vindication of Kant's thesis about the possibility of judgments that qualify as categorical imperatives cannot come from our capacity for empathy.

Oddly, Kennett takes the need that high-functioning, conscience-driven autistics have for order and their intolerance of inconsistency as evidence of this fit between Kant's account and the moral judgments they make. Drawing on anecdotal and personal descriptions of them as both applying and following moral rules rigidly and expecting similar behavior from others, Kennett maintains that such behavior manifests a "reverence for reason" indicative of Kant's conception of moral judgment (Kennett 2002, 355). Typically, though, such rigid adherence to rules is seen as symptomatic of some emotional disturbance that the agent is keeping in check through such rigidity. Someone who punctiliously arranges the books on his shelves alphabetically by author and vigilantly restores the arrangement whenever it is altered is not usually thought to be moved by reason alone but rather by anxieties about disruptions to an inviolate order. Yet Kennett offers no argument to distinguish such rigidity in the adherence to a common rule for organizing written materials from the similar rigidity in the adherence to moral rules on which she bases her argument for Kant's conception of moral judgment (de Vignemont and Frith 2008; Maibom 2008; McGeer 2008).

Be this as it may, the problem ultimately with Kennett's argument is her using the comparison of psychopaths with high-functioning autistics to make it. Her assumption is that the comparison will throw light on the determinants of moral judgment given the amorality of psychopaths and the possession of a conscience by high-functioning autistics. Thus, her case against including empathy among the determinants rests on this assumption together with the observation that neither psychopaths nor autistics are capable of empathy.[3] And her rationale for favoring Kant's

---

[3] The problem occurs as well in Sean Nichols' argument for excluding empathy from the determinants of moral judgment (Nichols 2004, 8–11). Nichols uses a different comparison, one between psychopaths and small children before they have developed a capacity for empathy, but his strategy is the same as Kennett's. The small children Nichols compares

conception of moral judgment over Hume's similarly presupposes that what determines whether someone's judgments of duty are moral judgments is their psychological profile and not their content. This presupposition is at the root of her criticism. Consequently, the most effective answer to the criticism is to challenge its presupposition about the

> with psychopaths have the same role in his argument as the high-functioning autistics have in Kennett's: they exemplify people who are capable of making moral judgments despite lacking the capacity for empathy. Comparing them with psychopaths, who also lack the capacity for empathy, serves to fix the features of these small children's capacity for making moral judgments as the determinants of moral judgments. Like Kennett, then, Nichols also assumes that the comparison with psychopaths throws light on the determinants of moral judgment. At the same time, since the children with whom Nichols compares psychopaths are too young to have developed the powers of reason that Kant's conception of moral judgment implies, the conclusion he reaches about the nature of moral judgment is the opposite of Kennett's conclusion about the nature of moral judgment. No matter; his argument suffers from problems that are as serious as the ones affecting hers.
>
> Specifically, Nichols bases his attribution of a capacity for moral judgment to small children who lack the capacity for empathy on studies that use a test that educational psychologists devised for determining whether a person recognizes a distinction between what these psychologists label "moral rules" from what they label "conventional rules." He similarly bases his excluding psychopaths from the class of people who are capable of making moral judgments on studies using the same test. The latter studies use a personality inventory – the Hare checklist – to divide their subjects, incarcerated felons, into psychopaths and nonpsychopaths. Unless one defines a psychopath as someone whose score on the Hare checklist indicates the presence of psychopathy, the use of the checklist will produce some false positives, people who have a conscience but nonetheless count as psychopaths, and false negatives, people who do not count as psychopaths even though they lack a conscience. The first problem with Nichols' argument, then, is that a statistically significant difference between the prisoners who were grouped by the Hare checklist as psychopaths – the test group – and those who were not – the control group – in their sensitivity to the distinction between "moral" rules and "conventional" ones does not imply that the difference between the prisoners who have a conscience and the prisoners who lack one in their sensitivity to this distinction (given the possibility of correcting for the false positives and the false negatives) is statistically significant. Of course, if the validity of the Hare test – the correlation between those it scores as psychopaths and true psychopaths – is high, then the seriousness of this problem diminishes as the difference between the test group and the control group widens. But without knowing either the validity of the Hare test or the statistical results of the studies, one can draw no conclusions from them.
>
> Even if one allows that the Hare checklist yields an insignificant number of false positives and false negatives, there is a second problem with Nichols' argument. The studies he cites found a statistically significant difference between how psychopaths do on the recognition test for the "moral"/"conventional" distinction and how nonpsychopaths do on it. Nichols, however, treats the test as if it were a litmus test for psychopathy, whereas at most these studies establish a significant association between being a psychopath and being unable to draw the distinction. It is statistically significant in the same sense in which the association of heart disease with high blood pressure is statistically significant. And just as it is possible for one to have heart disease without having high blood pressure, so too it is possible for a psychopath to draw the distinction. After all, nothing about lacking a conscience implies an inability to give the answers on a paper and pencil test or in an interview that show that one recognizes what is "moral" from what is "conventional." Hence, one cannot conclude from these studies that psychopathy excludes the capacity for making moral judgment. At most, one can conclude from them that it is statistically associated with the lack of that capacity.

determinants of moral judgment. Such a challenge requires a more clear-cut division between metaethics and psychology than I drew in proposing to study Hume's thesis about internalism as a question within the latter and exclusive of the former. And drawing this more clear-cut division means recovering the field of metaethics as it stood before its studies expanded into areas of psychology as a consequence of the special interest that philosophers came to take in the question Hume's thesis raises.

4. Metaethics

Anglo-American philosophers originally used the word "metaethics," it is reasonable to suppose, to mean a kind of study in ethics that was roughly analogous to the studies in mathematics and logic of metamathematics and metalogic.[4] These studies emerged in the 1920s and 1930s. Metamathematics came first. David Hilbert invented it to advance his investigations into the consistency of arithmetic. His idea was to abstract from arithmetic a formal symbolic system that could, when the symbols were assigned meanings, express its axioms and theorems and be used to display the proofs of the latter. Hilbert then took this formal system as what metamathematics, or proof theory, as he also called it, studies. The study's uppermost goal was to show that within the system, no string of symbols of the form $p \mathbin{.\sim} p$, a form that represents a contradiction, could be the last line of a proof. Subsequently, Alfred Tarski extended Hilbert's program beyond arithmetic to an area of study he called semantics. Tarski, to capture Hilbert's idea of taking a formal symbolic system as itself an object of study, called the system the object language and called the language in which the study was conducted the meta-language. Where Hilbert's program was narrowly focused on foundational questions of mathematics, specifically those of the consistency and completeness of arithmetic, Tarski's was more broadly focused on modeling the notions of truth and reference in formalized languages generally. Hence, he dubbed his program "metalogic."

Metalogic was, in turn, adapted by Rudolph Carnap for the purpose of advancing logical positivism. Carnap, in his *Logische Syntax der Sprache*,

---

[4] The Oxford English Dictionary (OED) cites a 1938 article in *The Philosophical Review* as the source of the earliest occurrence of "meta-ethics" or a cognate in English. This citation, however, is misleading. The article, "Philosophy in France 1936–37," by André Lalande, is a translation from the French, and "meta-ethics" is the translator's translation of "métamorales," a French term from the writings of the anthropologist Lucien Lévy-Bruhl. The earliest use of "meta-ethics" or a cognate by an Anglo-American philosopher that I have found occurs in Edel (1942, 141). Edel's program for expounding Moore's ethics is roughly modeled on studies in metamathematics and metalogic, and his use of "meta-ethical" reflects that model.

expounded, with this purpose in mind, a program of study whose main project was to construct formalized languages for expressing the arguments and conclusions of science (Carnap 1937). His idea was that these languages, once constructed, could serve as object languages for the study of the logic of science. Such a study, Carnap held, would serve to substantiate the doctrines of logical positivism. Metaethics, conceived as a study analogous to metamathematics and metalogic, was a child of this program.

Carnap argued, in the last chapter of his book, for replacing traditional philosophy with the sort of study of which he intended these formalized languages to be the object. He argued, that is, for the abandonment by philosophers of their traditional inquiries in metaphysics and for their taking up instead the logical analysis of the syntax of these languages when they were enriched with symbols whose interpretation made them suitable for expressing the knowledge found in a branch of science. Because Carnap expounded his program in the service of logical positivism, he treated ethics, when undertaken as a normative discipline, as continuous with metaphysics. He therefore denied that it was a branch of science. Or, what came to the same thing for him, he denied that it was a study that contributed to knowledge. Consequently, the languages whose syntax he took to be the proper object of philosophical study had no symbols whose interpretation would yield ethical sentences, since in his view there were no conceptual or epistemological questions on which the logical analysis of a language enriched with such symbols would throw light.

Carnap's adherence to logical positivism, however, is inessential to the program he expounded in the service of it. One can therefore apply his program to ethics just as one applies it to any of the special sciences when one conceives of ethics as a branch of knowledge. Accordingly, one can engage in a study that consists in the logical analysis of the syntax of a language enriched with symbols whose interpretation makes it suitable for expressing ethical arguments and their conclusions. Such a study would go beyond the analysis of the syntax of the language only in its identifying certain symbols of the language as distinctly ethical and its focusing on the relation of formulae that contain those symbols to other formulae of the language. The study would therefore correspond to the understanding of metaethics as the study of the formal nature of ethical language and the logic and epistemic status of ethical arguments.

Suppose, then, a formalized language, EL, suitable for expressing ethical arguments and their conclusions. This language can serve as an object language for studies in metaethics. The symbols whose interpretation makes EL suitable for this purpose are, in effect, ethical predicates, and one can accordingly take the sentences of EL in which they occur as ethical sentences.[5] Using this notion of an ethical sentence, we can then define a moral judgment as the mental act of affirming a proposition or propositionlike thought that matches the speech act of asserting an ethical sentence. We need to include in this definition that the mental act it identifies as a moral judgment may be the affirmation of a propositionlike thought rather than of a proposition so as to accommodate noncognitivist interpretations of the symbols of EL that correspond to ethical predicates. To be sure, some noncognitivist theories of the meaning of ethical predicates imply that ethics is not a branch of knowledge, but this implication does not exclude them from being used to interpret symbols of EL in studies that consist in the logical analysis of the language's syntax. While Carnap had no interest in the question of how to enrich a formalized language with symbols whose interpretation would make that language suitable for expressing ethical arguments and their conclusions, his younger contemporaries, A. J. Ayer and Charles Stevenson, who argued for taking ethical terms as having a distinctive noncognitive meaning, gave theories of this meaning that one could use to interpret the symbols of EL that correspond to ethical predicates. Consequently, we can understand their studies too as fitting the conception of metaethics that results from applying Carnap's program to ethics. Their studies too are compatible with defining moral judgments as the mental acts of affirmation that match the speech acts of asserting ethical sentences.

This definition represents an understanding of moral judgments on which the only mental powers whose exercise is necessary to making such judgments are those required for affirming propositions or propositionlike thoughts. Since every judgment consists in the exercise of such powers, it follows that anyone who is capable of making judgments is capable of making moral judgments. Only unfamiliarity with the concepts or conceptlike thoughts expressed by the symbols of EL that on a given interpretation of the language correspond to ethical predicates could render such a person incapable of making moral judgments. Hence, what determines, according to this definition, whether a judgment someone makes is a moral judgment is the concept or conceptlike thought she applies. In other words, what determines, on this definition, whether a judgment someone makes is a moral judgment is the content of that judgment and not its psychological profile. On the understanding of moral judgment that the definition represents, one can then study how different operations of the mind yield the same moral judgment. Such

---

[5] For example, if the formalized language contains a first order, monadic functional constant E whose English translation is the predicate "is evil" and an individual constant N whose English translation is the name "Nero," then "E(N)" is an ethical sentence of the language whose translation is "Nero is evil."

a study, being a study in psychology as distinct from metaethics, avoids the stalemated controversies that are born of Hume's idea that to understand the nature of moral opinions requires understanding the distinctive mechanisms of the mind that produce them.

5. Two Ways of Making Moral Judgments

The upshot is that the study is open to the possibility that minds make moral judgments in different ways, that is, in ways that involve the stimulation of different mental sensitivities and the exercise of different mental powers. This possibility is well illustrated by different ways of making geometric judgments. These different methods of geometry were the inspiration for Hilbert's popular book, coauthored with Stefan Cohn-Vossen, *Anschauliche Geometrie* (Hilbert and Cohn-Vossen 1932). Hilbert, in the book's preface, writes,

> In mathematics, as in any scientific research, we find two tendencies present. On the one hand, the tendency toward *abstraction* seeks to crystalize the *logical* relations inherent in the maze of material that is being studied and to correlate the material in a systematic and orderly manner. On the other hand, the tendency toward *intuitive understanding* fosters a more immediate grasp of the objects one studies, a live *rapport* with them, so to speak, which stresses the concrete meaning of their relations.
>
> As to geometry, in particular, the abstract tendency has here led to magnificent systematic theories of Algebraic Geometry, of Riemannian Geometry, and of Topology; these theories make extensive use of abstract reasoning and symbolic calculation in the sense of algebra. Notwithstanding this, it is still as true today as it ever was that *intuitive* understanding plays a major role in geometry. And such concrete intuition is of great value not only for the research worker, but also for anyone who wishes to study and appreciate the results of research in geometry (Hilbert and Cohn-Vossen 1932, iii).[6]

Hilbert then goes on, in the chapters that follow, to present these results intuitively by means of visual constructions and commentary that enable

---

[6] In the original, the passage reads, "In der Mathematik wie in aller wissenschaflichen Forschung treffen wir zweierlei Tendenzen an: die Tendenz zur Abstraktion – sie sucht die *logischen* Gesichtspunkte aus dem vielfältigen Material herauszuarbeiten und dieses in sstematischen Zusammenhang zu bringen – und die andere Tendenz, die der Anschaulichkeit, die vielmehr auf ein lebendiges Erfassen der Gegenstande und ihre *inhaltlichen* Beziehungen ausgeht.

"Was insbesondere die Geometrie betrifft, so hat bei ihr die abstrackte Tendenz zu den grossartigen systematischen Lehrgebäuden der algebraschen Geometrie, der Riemannschen Geometrie und der Topologie geführt, in denen die Methoden der begriffflichen Überlegung, der Symbolik und des Kalküls in ausgiebigem Masse zur Verwendung gelangen. Dennoch kommt auch heute dem *anschaulichen* Erfassen in der Geometrie eine hervorragende Rolle zu, und zwar nicht nur als einer überlegenen Kraft des Forschens, sondern auch für die Auffassung und Würdigung der Forschungsergebnisse."

the reader to see and understand propositions pictorially that one could also come to understand and affirm abstractly by means of the equations with which one works in algebraic geometry.

In ethics, too, there is something like this difference between tendencies to abstract and intuitive thought. On the one hand, there is the tendency to take moral precepts abstractly as formulae that individually express inflexible principles of action and that jointly represent order in the world, deviation from which is a serious offense against its authority. On the other, there is the tendency to take them pragmatically as rules that reflect mutual agreement among people about how to conduct their lives together and whose underlying rationale is the production of a common good in which all can share. The first tendency is manifested in stricter compliance with moral precepts and greater concern with their exact formulation. It fosters a more legalistic conception of morality. The second tendency is manifested in compliance with moral precepts from a sense of one's having some latitude in determining what actions satisfy them and thus in a view of them as open to interpretation so as best to suit them to the ends they serve. It fosters a more instrumental conception of morality. Each yields moral judgments, of course, but the sensitivities and powers of the mind whose stimulation and exercise produce such judgments differ according as the first or second of these tendencies characterizes the thinking behind them.

The difference between taking moral precepts as inflexible principles of action and taking them as rules reflecting mutual agreement among those whom they govern figures importantly in Jean Piaget's study of the development of moral thought in children (Piaget 1965). Piaget locates the first tendency in the thought of children at a younger age, whose way of relating to moral rules he refers to as "the morality of constraint" (Piaget 1965, 197). Children, Piaget explains, come to the understanding of moral rules that the morality of constraint implies as a result of their being subject to their parents' supervision and discipline. Accordingly, the child sees the rules its parents impose as fixed limits on its behavior, limits that require obedience by virtue of its parents' authority. As children grow older and leave the shelter of their parents' domain, they enter into social relations with peers and engage with them in activities that are free of close adult supervision and regulated by rules whose adjudication and enforcement they manage themselves. Piaget locates the second tendency in the thought of children at this later stage. He refers to the way they relate to moral rules as "the morality of cooperation" (Piaget 1965). The new understanding of moral rules children acquire at this stage, he suggests, comes from their taking responsibility for how the rules that regulate the activities in which they are cooperatively engaged are to be applied and for what to do when someone breaks or ignores these rules. It thus consists, on Piaget's account of this later development in moral thought, in a child's abandoning an egocentric understanding of the world on which rules are fixed, structural parts, put in place by adults, and its coming instead to see rules as more variable in view of their being based in mutual agreement among all who participate in the activities they regulate.

This later development includes as well the child's learning to take the perspectives of others who are coparticipants in activities that are regulated by rules. Presumably, the development of this skill is due at least in part to the child's engaging in these activities independently of close adult supervision. Presumably, that is, it is due at least in part to the child's taking, in cooperation with others, responsibility for adjudicating and enforcing the rules that regulate their joint activities. To exercise this skill requires empathy with those whose perspective one is taking. To be sure, empathy emerges in children earlier in their lives. Piaget does not suggest otherwise. But children's exercise of their capacity for empathy in judging the moral quality of their own or others' rule-following and rule-breaking conduct is unnecessary at an earlier stage, given an understanding of moral rules as elements of a morality of constraint. When that understanding changes, however, and children come to see moral rules as elements of a morality of cooperation, then they acquire as well the habit of taking the perspective of the other participants in the activities in which they are engaged. Such perspective taking is essential to the success of these activities, for it is essential that each participant in them relate to every other as a cooperating partner in a joint enterprise, and they could not do so successfully if they were unable to comprehend either the views that each of their fellow partners has of his or her own situation within the enterprise or the beliefs, intentions, and motives with which their fellow partners act as participants in it. So too the child's exercise of its capacity for empathy in judging the moral quality of rule-following and rule-breaking conduct is essential to the success of the enterprise.

Empathy, then, is necessary for making moral judgments that reflect an understanding of moral rules as elements of a morality of cooperation. That is, while it is unnecessary for making moral judgments in which rules are taken abstractly as formulae to be applied to the facts at hand and followed to the letter as their authority requires, it is necessary for making moral judgments in which rules are taken pragmatically as instruments for achieving a common good made possible by cooperation with others in activities the rules regulate. In the former, one's thought is concentrated on the rule's formulation as an authoritative proscription or prescription and on the conduct required for conformity to it. In the latter, one's thought is directed toward one's relations with others as the object of the rule's regulation, and through empathy with those with whom one shares these relations one comes to a more concrete understanding of the rule's import and how it should be applied. Here Hilbert's description of the tendency toward an intuitive understanding of the objects of judgment as yielding a live rapport ("ein lebendiges Erfassen")[7] with them seems especially apt as does his subsequent emphasis on the visual aspect of the intuitive understanding of geometry that he and his coauthor present. Empathy too is a kind of visualization, at least when it includes an understanding of its object as a whole person engaged in projects that give structure to his or her life and not simply as a site of emotions whose present feelings one shares (Deigh 1995, 759–61). Such visualization alone fixes the difference in psychological profile of moral judgments that require empathy from those that do not.

6. A Kantian Objection

The hypothesis I advanced in my earlier paper, the hypothesis that through the exercise of the capacity for empathy one could make moral judgments of the type Kant characterized as categorical imperatives, is viable, I explained, only on the assumption that the empathy that informs the judgments includes an understanding of its object as a whole person, someone with projects and concerns that give structure to his or her life. The visualization that such empathy entails plausibly explains how a cognition alone could move one to action since it is plausible that one could be moved to further someone's ends in life or alleviate his or her concerns just from seeing how those ends and concerns matter to him or her. On this supposition, one may be so moved independently of any emotional identification with the person who is the object of one's empathy. The visualization of what he or she is thinking and feeling with regard to ends and concerns that matter to him or her would be sufficient. It is not yet, of course, a moral judgment since the cognition would have to comprise more than visualization for it to be an affirmation of a proposition corresponding to the assertion of an ethical sentence. Still, it offers the possibility of moral judgments of the type Kant characterized as categorical imperatives. Or so I argued.

Students of Kant might object at this point. The hypothesis, after all, is part of an account of moral judgment on which some judgments are moral judgments despite their lacking the character of categorical

[7] See fn. 5.

imperatives, and in Kant's ethics categorical imperatives are the bases of all moral judgments. Though Kant opposes Hume on the question of whether moral distinctions derive from reason or feeling, his opposition does not include rejection of Hume's idea that to understand the nature of moral judgment requires understanding the distinctive mechanisms of the mind that produce such judgments. To the contrary, Kant's argument for the possibility of categorical imperatives is an argument for morality's having its grounding solely in the operations of reason. Specifically, it is an argument for identifying moral judgments with exercises of what Kant described as pure practical reason, and his endorsement of Hume's idea is unmistakable in this identification. Hume may have been the first to treat the nature of moral judgment as a question for psychology, but the treatment received a powerful second from Kant.

Yet one should not so hastily regard Kant as a backer of Hume's campaign to treat the nature of moral judgment as a question for psychology. Kant's attribution of moral judgments to the operations of reason is not the result of a psychological study. Kant does not adduce observational evidence gathered through such a study for it. Rather, he follows traditional Christian ethics in taking morality as an object of study that stands apart from the actual conduct and customs of human beings and that one applies in critically judging that conduct and those customs. It is, in this respect, an ideal. Kant expounds the ideal through analysis of the concepts of duty and practical law (or law that determines the will). He concludes from this analysis that the fundamental principle of morality is a precept requiring that lawfulness itself determine the will. One could not, he then argues, follow this precept in determining one's will from natural desire or passion, for in that case the object of one's desire or passion and not lawfulness itself would be what determines one's will. Hence, morality – the ideal that stands apart from human conduct and customs – can be realized in human life only if the human mind is equipped with a power that can determine the will independently of natural desire and passion. If there is no such power, Kant says, morality is "a mere phantom of the brain" (Kant 1785, 112).

Such a power cannot, *mutatis mutandis*, be subject to natural causes. Else natural events and not lawfulness itself would determine the will. In other words, the mental power that Kant holds men and women must possess if morality is to be realized in human life necessarily operates outside of the natural world, even if the effects of its operation occur within that world. Its possession and exercise by human beings, if they do possess and exercise it, cannot, then, be known empirically. Consequently, Kant does not come to his understanding of moral judgment as by nature the product of such a power through empirical study of the sensitivities and powers of the mind that produce such judgment. Specifically, he does not come to understand the nature of moral judgment as a product of pure practical reason through observation of the workings of reason. Rather, he posits, as a necessary condition of a judgment's being a moral judgment, the power to determine the will independently of natural causes. Unless a judgment of duty issues from an exercise of that power, it is not a moral judgment. Thus, his procedure, which starts with the exposition of an ideal and then moves to explaining the conditions for its being realized, is the reverse of Hume's. Hume assumes at the start that people actually discern moral distinctions, that they are in fact capable of such discernment. He never questions the reality of this capacity. His interest, rather, is in whether its exercise is rooted in reason or feeling, and he concludes that it is rooted in the latter by observing its workings. The irony, then, of citing Kant as endorsing Hume's idea that to understand the nature of moral judgment requires understanding the distinctive mechanisms of the mind that produce it is that the endorsement is inseparable from Kant's denying the possibility of acquiring such understanding through scientific study.

References

Anscombe, G. E. M. 1958a. On Brute Facts. *Analysis*, 18, 69–72.
   1958b. Modern Moral Philosophy. *Philosophy*, 33, 1–19.
Carnap, R. 1937. *The Logical Syntax of Language* (A. Smeaton, trans.). Patterson, NJ: Littlefield, Adams & Co. 1959.
Deigh, J. 1995. Empathy and Universalizability, *Ethics*, 105, 743–63.
Edel, A. 1942. The Logical Structure of G. E. Moore's Ethical Theory. In: P. Schilpp (ed.), *The Philosophy of G. E. Moore*. New York: Tudor, 137–76.
Enoch, D. 2011. *Taking Morality Seriously*. Oxford: Oxford University Press.
Frankena, W. 1958. Obligation and Motivation in Recent Moral Philosophy. In: A. I. Melden (ed.), *Essays in Moral Philosophy*. Seattle: University of Washington Press, 40–81.
Hilbert, D. and Cohn-Vossen, S. 1932. *Anschauliche Geometrie*. Berlin: J. Springer (English translation: *Geometry and the Imagination* (P. Nemenyi, trans.). New York: Chelsea. 1952).
Hume, D. 1739. *A Treatise of Human Nature*, 2nd edn. (L. A. Selby-Bigge, ed.). Oxford: Oxford University Press 1978.
   1751. *Enquiry into the Principles of Morals* (J. B. Schneewind, ed.). Indianapolis, IN: Hackett. 1983.
Kant, I. 1785. *Groundwork of the Metaphysics of Morals* (H. J. Paton, trans.). New York: Harper & Row, Inc. 1964.
Kennett, J. 2002. Autism, Empathy, and Moral Agency, *Philosophical Quarterly*, 52, 340–57.
Maibom, H. 2008. The Will to Conform. In: W. Sinnott-Armstrong (ed.), *Moral Psychology: The Neuroscience of Morality: Emotion, Brain Disorders, and Development*. Cambridge, MA: MIT Press, 266–72.

McGeer, V. 2008. Varieties of Moral Agency: Lessons from Autism (and Psychopathy). In: W. Sinnott-Armstrong (ed.), *Moral Psychology: The Neuroscience of Morality: Emotion, Brain Disorders, and Development.* Cambridge, MA: MIT Press, 227–57.

Nichols, S. 2004. *Sentimental Rules: On the Natural Foundations of Moral Judgment.* New York: Oxford University Press.

Piaget, J. 1965. *The Moral Judgment of the Child* (M. Gabain, trans.). New York: Free Press.

Sayre-McCord, G. 1994. On Why Hume's "General Point of View" Isn't Ideal – and Shouldn't Be. *Social Philosophy and Policy*, 11, 202–28.

Stroud, B. 1977. *Hume.* London: Routledge & Kegan Paul.

Vignemont, F. de and Frith, U. 2008. Autism, Morality, and Empathy. In: W. Sinnott-Armstrong (ed.), *Moral Psychology: The Neuroscience of Morality: Emotion, Brain Disorders, and Development.* Cambridge, MA: MIT Press, 273–80.

11 The Empathy in Moral Obligation
An Exercise in Creature Construction

Neil Roughley

In his Tanner Lectures on Human Values (de Waal 2006), Frans de Waal claims that there is only a gradual difference between systems of behavioural control in the great apes and human morality, both motivational systems working primarily by mechanisms of empathy. In her response to de Waal, Christine Korsgaard argues that the emergence of the 'ability to be motivated by an ought' is the decisive step on the way to the human life form, and that this is a saltatory development without precursors in the life forms of our nearest living relatives (Korsgaard 2006, 117). Korsgaard's phylogenetic claim corresponds to a generally held systematic view according to which prosocial behaviour is one thing, acting because you (believe you) ought to another. Empathy, it seems clear, may play a significant role in generating intrinsic desires to help, protect or support others. But, even if one rejects the Kantian claim that such desires cannot count as moral motivators (Kant 1785, 397ff.; Batson 2014, 45–7), it seems obvious that action thus motivated is not the entirety of morally praiseworthy action. And it seems equally clear that we don't only regard moral criticism as legitimate when it concerns a lack of helping, protecting or supporting behaviour. At least under some circumstances, lying, not keeping a promise, not treating others according to their deserts, failure to honour a contract and favouritism are all forms of behaviour that merit moral condemnation, although the relevant behaviour may not be explained by a lack of empathy, but may even conceivably result from empathy that is morally inappropriate.

Empathy, then, it may seem, is at most only relevant for an understanding of a part of morality, perhaps for cases of the kind that Hume subsumed under the 'natural virtues'. The step to the moral ought introduces a new kind of motivation, a point of orientation for our action that is independent of what we are intrinsically motivated to do. Empathy, surely, is irrelevant here.

I will be arguing that this conclusion is misguided. Certainly, empathy is not the only source of moral motivation. But, as I hope to show, this does not mean that empathy may not be centrally involved in generating moral obligation itself. I shall argue that this is indeed the case. It does not follow from the way this is the case that morality is equally accessible to other animals. Empathy is only one contributory factor among others. Although it is – fairly obviously – not sufficient, it is, I shall claim, necessary.

1. Semantic and Methodological Preliminaries

Before developing the argument, there are three points that should be made. The first two concern talk of moral obligation, the third concerns methodology.

Moral Obligation

First, some remarks on the relationship between the concept of moral obligation and that of the moral 'ought'. If someone ought to do something, it isn't necessarily the case that they are obliged, or 'obligated' to do it. You aren't under an obligation to go to the dentist's regularly just because you ought to do so. This, someone might think, is simply because obligations are at home in morality and not in prudence. Certainly, it is unclear what it might mean to say that someone is under an obligation of prudence. There are, of course, obligations of a legal nature, which may or may not correspond to moral obligations. So, obligation is a concept that only corresponds to 'oughts' within certain spheres of reasons. It seems likely that understanding obligation will be facilitated by asking what features those spheres of reasons have in common that are missing in other spheres.

For our purposes here, it is important to see that, even within morality, you may not be obligated to do everything that you ought to do. I will assume that the fact that an agent ought to do something necessarily corresponds to her reasons conclusively speaking for her doing it.[1] What tradition called 'imperfect duties' may, if 'duty' and 'obligation' are equated, only be duties up to a certain point. That is, giving aid, for example, may be something we have an obligation to do up to, but only up to a certain point, although we may beyond that point still have stronger reasons to give more aid than not to. If that is correct, or even just a coherent possibility, and if the adduced correspondence between conclusive reasons and ought holds, then it may be that, in such cases, we ought to φ, although we are under no obligation to φ. Those of us who

---

[1] This might be so because 'ought' is defined in terms of conclusive reasons or because 'reason' is defined in terms of ought (cf. Broome 2013, 63f.).

earn more than a certain amount no doubt have strict obligations to contribute to aiding those in need, obligations presumably most easily fulfillable by giving to charity. It seems not implausible that those obligations run considerably further than most of us live up to, but still stop short of prescribing everything there is conclusive reason for us to do. Moreover, as Raz points out,[2] even were this intuition to be false, it would be odd to claim that someone advancing it is guilty of incoherence.[3]

The plausibility of there being such cases, or at least of their coherence, opens up a gap between moral ought and moral obligation. In what follows, it is the latter concept for which I propose an analysis. I take it that standard applications of negation allow simple extensions to moral prohibitions and moral permissions.

Morality

A second point about talk of moral obligation concerns the adjectival qualifier 'moral'. A number of authors think that, when carrying out analyses of concepts such as moral judgement and moral obligation, we should be working with a concept of morality that is applicable to all human cultures, possibly to all conceivable cultures (e.g., Prinz 2007). It follows from this assumption that the concept of the moral should be content-free. One initially plausible reason that has been advanced for such an approach is that it is a necessary condition for a coherent discussion of who is morally right where cultures conflict (Tugendhat 1993, 32f.). Without a formal concept of the morally right, so the thought goes, representatives of the cultures will inevitably be talking past each other in any dispute.

However, this turns out not to be a good reason where we are dealing with a culture that has standards radically different from our own: where some other culture is separated from our own by a gulf of sufficient breadth, such a condition is irrelevant for the question of whether we are talking past each other. Perhaps the members of some group believe that anyone who has even slightly different opinions or action proclivities than they should have their heads sawn off or be thrown from a high

---

[2] Raz thinks that such cases of supererogation are explained by what he calls 'exclusionary permissions' (Raz 1990, 91ff.).

[3] Broome suggests that someone advancing it may be mistaking incommensurate reasons for a gap between the balance of reasons and permissibility (Broome 2013, 61). However, his example, of someone having to decide whether to take guests sightseeing or to meet a deadline, seems to be a perfectly good example of a conflict between altruism and self-interest. If such reasons are incommensurate, it is difficult to understand why we think that moral judgements in many standard cases, where moral reasons outweigh those of self-interest, are fairly clear.

building. Now imagine that they speak English and dignify their activities by characterising them as 'morally right'. And assume that representatives of the group are prepared, for the duration of a discussion, to desist from sawing off other discussants' heads. I submit that a conversation with these people about what is 'morally right' will not involve representatives of our and their culture talking about the same thing under that predicate.

Certainly, there will be a substantive disagreement about what people in many situations ought, all in all, to do or what they have conclusive reasons to do. However, the sources of the reasons will be different. Prima facie, the source of the throat-cutters' putative reasons are sentences in some scripture or perhaps the interpretation of those sentences by some authoritative figure. If the group members take those sentences or interpretations to issue from a deity, then the source of their putative reasons is a religion. Whether a set of religious precepts has subset of norms that count as moral will depend on further conditions being met. I think that the key condition here is that the relevant norms function[4] in ways that are at least minimally transparent to those involved, to protect individual humans from forms of negative impact made possible by our nature as physically and psychologically vulnerable entities. Religious or other action-guiding systems that don't require that this condition be met may be thought to stand alongside moral systems as potential competitors in the provision or exclusion of reasons.

Insistence on the condition I have named, call it the *vulnerability constraint*, seems to me to reconstruct the way people of all sorts of convictions in many cultures would think of the moral. But the constraint sets limits. Indeed, that is precisely the point. And setting those limits involves rejecting the claim that the concept of the moral is helpfully thought of as content-free.

The criticism that Philippa Foot directed at Richard Hare's prescriptivism in the 1950s (Foot 1958–9, 84) has a certain similarity to the point I am making, but only a certain one. Foot argued that Hare's theory cannot be right because it doesn't account for the fact, as she saw it, that the topic of moral judgements is the conditions of human 'flourishing', a point she went on to argue is enshrined in the use of terms such as 'morally good'. The constraint that Foot thus imposes on what she takes to be the correct use of the term 'moral' is considerably stronger than the one I have proposed. We should, I think, reject it for various reasons. The one I want to mention here picks up on the reason certain authors

---

[4] Particularlists might want to replace the last five words with 'that the relevant judgements express (cognitive or noncognitive) attitudes that function ...'.

have advanced for a completely content-free characterisation: it has to allow us to conceptualise moral disagreement. Call this the *disagreement constraint*.

It seems to me to be an obvious further adequacy condition on any attempt to make sense of how moral agents understand moral obligation that such an account allows a coherent description of a genuine deontic dispute between X and Y. X and Y have a deontic dispute where X takes φ-ing in some situation to be morally obligatory and Y takes φ-ing in the same situation to be morally proscribed. If, for instance, X means by his deontic claim that φ-ing contributes to human flourishing and Y means by hers that it doesn't maximise expected utility, then there is obviously no genuine dispute. But the interlocutors are, it seems clear, in genuine disagreement, even if the one is judging in terms of human flourishing and the other in terms of utility maximisation. An analysis of moral obligation should tell us why.

A number of authors, following Richard Hare (1952, 49; 1963, 28f., 97ff.), have taken it that the disagreement constraint can only or at least can best be accounted for within an expressivist moral semantics. I will be proposing a different way in which it can be met. One thing that I think has been missed is that the disagreement constraint and the vulnerability constraint can both be met together.

Methodology

A final preparatory point concerns my approach to the analysis of the metaphysics of moral obligation. My procedure will involve the adaptation of a proposal advanced by Paul Grice, which he entitled *creature construction* (Grice 1974–5, 36ff.). Under this title, Grice proposed the construction in the imagination of progressively complex creatures, according to what he took to be Aristotle's procedure in understanding 'the soul', where the structure of each new type of creature is an 'extension' of the structure of its predecessor type (Grice 1974–5, 38f.). However, whereas the constructions proposed by Grice aim at highlighting ever more complex explanatory structures as means to understanding complex psychological laws, the constructions I will make use of here aim to show that such a procedure can help us make sense of the very special type of metaphysical relations to which moral judgements have recourse. Behind the adoption of this method lies the conviction that morality is the product of the phylogenesis of certain kinds of psychological structure, before the development of which moral categories quite simply had no purchase. Put simply, prior to the genesis of certain mental structures, there was no right or wrong about which members of the relevant *homo* lineage did what to other members of that lineage.

Like Aristotle, Grice was impressed by the continuity between the psychology of nonhuman animals and humans. He believed that, by constructing creatures that build on psychologically less rich variants of themselves, we can build models of agents, comparison with which allows us to understand better key features of human psychology. According to the Gricean version of this method, the theory of the more complex creature is not only an extension of but also 'includes' the theory of its less complex relative. In what follows, I will discuss cases of creatures a specific augmentation of whose psychological complexity leads to the generation of moral agents. Here, there is an important sense in which it would be misleading to see the structure of the more complex agent types as 'including' that of their less complex relatives. Some psychological additions can remove or reduce the capacity for certain kinds of actions, as well as generating the capacity for others. This is because the decisive psychological steps involve the genesis – or, if you like, the 'construction' – of reasons that don't exist for entities with endowments of lesser complexity.

A final difference from the Gricean version is that my creature constructionist endeavours make use of some empirical material from primatology and psychopathology, rather than being a matter of pure imaginative model building. The relevant empirical data provide pointers to possible constructions and help us to keep those constructions sufficiently close to the way things are in our world. Nevertheless, the procedure used here remains that of the construction of models intended to illuminate our psychology and its preconditions, rather than being a direct description of our mental life. As such, the model is not directly falsifiable by empirical data. However, should the empirical facts turn out to be very different from those from which the construction takes its lead, the model could end up being simply irrelevant.

My construction of the psychology of agents capable of generating and upholding the category of moral obligation will have four stages. The first two, which introduce the decisive basic capacities, will require a somewhat more extensive discussion than stages III and IV, which can, on the basis of stages I and II, be developed fairly straightforwardly.

2. The Emotional Construction of Moral Obligation, Stage I

As in contractarianism, let us begin from agents in a world without morality. In doing so, however, we should reject the contractarian assumption that agents without morality will in all relevant respects be psychologically identical to moral agents. Instead, I assume that moral agents will not only be the bearers of psychological states with different contents to those of corresponding states in nonmoral agents (i.e., that they want different things), but that moral agents will also play host to psychological states of types unavailable to human agents who live their lives outside of moral practices. For this reason, there is something importantly right about the claim, advanced by Thomas Nagel in *The Possibility of Altruism*, that we need to do moral psychology in order to develop a comprehensive understanding of the forms of motivation available to humans (Nagel 1970, chs. I, II). According to the contrasting conception, we can do motivational or social psychology independently of how morality moves us and from there work out what the deep psychological structure of morality must be. But if moral agents have a substantively different psychology than nonmoral agents, then this latter conception is seriously flawed. That this is indeed the case will hopefully be one lesson of the discussion that follows.

The construction that I shall be proposing also differs from that of the contractarian as regards the psychological starting point.[5] According to the standard contractarian model, the relevant agents have interests, understood as wants, which are relevant insofar as other agents have wants with similar contents. For the structure of the theory, it is reciprocity, not the contents of the wants, that is decisive, although, of course, the contents of the norms that are generated depend on the wants' contents. According to my proposal, in contrast, what we need to get the construction going is an attitude with a specific content. It needs to be anthropologically basic, i. e. generally shared by human persons. We also need to exclude its being the product of a moral upbringing.

The starting point I want to take is given by an attitude which according to Peter Strawson is ascribed to human persons by a 'central commonplace': that it matters to people a great deal whether the actions of others that affect them are the result of good will, indifference or ill will towards them on the part of those others. The way in which this matters is in turn expressed in emotional reactions of specific kinds we are disposed to play host to. Strawson says we are disposed to 'resent' action which (at

---

[5] Contractarian theory also tends to proceed from a nonmoral normative premise, i.e. that it is rational for agents to pursue their own interests, a premise frequently expressed by the adoption of a rational choice framework (cf. Gauthier 1986, 3). In as far as the contractarian claims to derive moral obligation from cooperative structures taken to be indirectly rational (Gauthier 1986, 207), the step thus taken appears to be from one dimension of normativity to another. In contrast, the construction of moral obligation I am proposing doesn't proceed from any such normative premise.

least potentially) affects us negatively and which we take to express either the ill will or indifference of the agent (Strawson 1962, 5f.). There are two claims here about the human life form, both of which seem to me to be correct. The first concerns a very basic orectic disposition that is the motor of a great deal of our behaviour. The second concerns a specific form of emotional behaviour that expresses that disposition.

Now, according to certain authors (e.g., Tugendhat 1993, 59ff.; Darwall 2006, 17, 67ff.), any emotion we rightly label 'resentment' presupposes the existence of morality, in particular, that the action resented is taken by the resenter to be one the agent was under a moral obligation to omit. Jay Wallace has disputed this, arguing that there may be forms of nonmoral resentment, which are based on beliefs that some nonmoral requirement, for instance, a requirement of etiquette, has been contravened (Wallace 1994, 36). John Deigh has gone further, arguing that there are reactions appropriately labelled 'resentment' that presuppose no beliefs about requirements, indeed no propositional attitudes at all (Deigh 2011, 208f.).

I think that Deigh is right that the emotional phenomena we pick out with the term don't require beliefs on the part of the emoter concerning requirements. However, it is fairly obvious that most cases of resentment involve us taking it that the object of our reaction was morally required not to do what she did. Accordingly, talk of 'resentment' carries the association of a moral emotion, so that the use of the term for my purposes is likely to trigger worries about circularity. For this reason, I will use an artificial term to pick out the basic emotional reaction to actions of others that affect us negatively and appear to display ill will or indifference. I will call the relevant reaction *resentment**. Resentment* is not a moral emotion or even an emotion that presupposes requirements of any sort, but rather an emotion in which the very idea of moral obligation grounds. Or so I claim.

Our first constructed creature, then, is an agent with the disposition to resent* certain actions of other agents. But in what precisely does resentment* consist? Like resentment, it is an essentially affective state which, I take it, has a certain feel. Moreover, it is a reaction of its bearer to her doxastic, or at least protodoxastic, construal of its object as having behaved in a certain way. Thus far, resentment* and resentment as analysed by Wallace don't differ. The decisive difference concerns the way the attitude's object is construed as having behaved. Whereas according to Wallace the description under which the resenter subsumes the agent's action is normative, according to my construction, the description, or protodescription, with which the resenter* operates has no normative content. What is resented* – like what is resented according to

Strawson – is action that is taken to (potentially) affect the resenter*
and to express the agent's ill will or indifference. The decisive content
concerns what Strawson calls the quality of the agent's will (Strawson
1962, 15).

But why precisely does the resenter* react as she does to her registering the agential expression of a negative or indifferent quality of will?
Answering this question turns out to require a number of steps.

As I remarked, the decisive condition of the reaction for Strawson is
that the quality of the will of agents whose actions (potentially) affect us
matters to us a great deal.[6] I will turn in a moment to a further specification of the attitudinal mode described here as 'mattering'. First, it
should be noted that the attitude is a standing attitude, comparable in
this respect to the attitude we have towards our own survival. We don't go
around thinking about the importance to us of our survival, but we are
so disposed that, if it is thrown into doubt, a strong optative attitude is
activated in a way that is generally both conscious and has a whole range
of possible direct behavioural consequences. Similarly, the question of
the quality of will of others is something that frequently doesn't cross
our mind or guide behaviour until we are given evidence of its negative
or indifferent character.

In the survival and the quality of will cases, then, mattering grounds
in a dispositional attitude. The mode of mattering is, however, different
in the two cases. Although both involve a strong, indeed peremptory,
optative attitude, only in the quality of will case is that peremptoriness
directed back towards the source of the problem, that is, the other agent.
Strawson makes this point by means of a formulation that recurs in his
text, according to which the omission of actions that express a negative
or indifferent quality of will is something we 'demand' (Strawson 1962,
6, 8, 15ff.). That we do so is, importantly, a feature of the standing attitude; however, this feature only becomes manifest when that attitude is
triggered.

What, now, is the relationship between the triggering of this dispositional 'demand' and the triggering of the emotional reaction I am calling
'resentment*'? Both occur simultaneously and both have the disposition
as their precondition. One difference concerns the content of the triggered demand and the emotion. The former is general in two dimensions: neither the specific ways in which a negative or indifferent quality

---

[6] The complete set of conditions elaborated in Strawson's article importantly add the absence of features that either temporarily or permanently prevent the agent from participating in normal human relationships, features that undercut the capacity for 'interpersonal regard'. These points, which are essential to the primary responsibility-theoretic thrust of Strawson's argument, can safely be put to one side for my purposes here.

of will can manifest itself nor the particular persons who might do so are distinguished. Resentment* picks out specific instantiations of these two dimensions: we resent* particular actions of particular agents.

Should we perhaps think of resentment* as the affective registering that the dispositional demand has not been met? This conception would fit in with a general cognitive theory of emotions as forms of affective registering (e.g., Prinz 2004, 66ff.). As I am not convinced that the states we think of as emotions are of a unitary kind, I don't take this to be a strong argument for understanding resentment* in purely cognitive terms. Certain authors have, on the contrary, taken it that the phenomenology of resentment reveals the emotion as itself involving demands. Darwall, for instance, describes moral resentment as involving 'implicit' demands (Darwall 2006, 72, 76).

This seems to me to be correct. Like hope, which is surely at core an affectively toned form of wanting, resentment* is, I think, an affective state that has a world-to-content direction of fit. Unlike hope, it also has the opposite direction of fit. It consists of three components: the registering that the dispositional demand has been flaunted in a specific way by a specific agent; the rearticulation of that demand, now addressed to that specific agent;[7] and an affective colouring of these two features. Phenomenologically, the affective component binds the former two components together to give their conjunction the feel of a single whole.[8]

The last question to which we need an answer in order to get clear on the character of resentment* concerns the justification for talk of 'demands'. As a demand is first and foremost a kind of speech act, that is, a type of directive, we need to know why an attitude should be characterised in terms of a speech act. There are two parts to the answer. The first concerns the understanding of the attitude in terms of a speech act, specifically as a directive;[9] the second concerns the specific type of directive at issue, namely a demand.

Why a directive, then? The decisive point here, one that has been emphasized by Darwall, is that demands are addressed to the agent represented in their content – whereas mattering, however strong and whatever its content, is not. Resentment*, so the claim goes, is an emotion

---

[7] The fact that the content of the demand concerns any action that expresses the agent's quality of will means that Coleen Macnamara's worry about unrealisable, backwards-directed demands (Macnamara 2013, 155) is unfounded for the construction I am developing.

[8] This is, if you like, an add-on theory of resentment* (Goldie 2000, 40). It doesn't feel as though there are separate components, but that's because they're fused together.

[9] I have argued at length (Roughley 2016, ch. 4) that the basic attitudes can only be made sense of in terms of their expressive articulation in language. In contrast to what some authors have claimed, mere wants are not linguistically articulated in imperatives, but in optatives (Roughley 2016, 89ff.).

addressed to an agent who has seen to it that the content of the dispositional demand has gone unfulfilled. But how are we to understand the claim that an emotion is addressed?

I suggest that the imperatival address of an attitude consists in the satisfaction of two conditions. First, its bearer is disposed to give voice to it as a directive speech act under accommodating conditions. Note, however, that in certain cases accommodating conditions may never be plausibly forthcoming in view of the character of the relevant interpersonal relationships. Second, the natural behavioural expressions of the attitude are such as to engage the target agent of the attitude in a way that naturally provokes her to respond to the attitude expressed, a response that consists either in *seeing to it that* the attitude's content is realised, in *explaining why* the attitude was not fulfilled in this case or in *rejecting* the attitude.[10]

What, finally, justifies thinking of resentment* as involving the specific kind of directive we call a demand? It has been claimed that what distinguishes demands from other imperatives is that they require 'authority' (Macnamara 2013, 151). If this were correct and equally applicable to demands understood as attitudes, then the demand I am following Strawson in seeing as basic would at the very least have normative preconditions: authority is a normative status and would appear to require some normative source of its conferral. Moreover, the most plausible candidate source appears to be morality.

However, it is simply false that demands require authority. There are other features that can confer on a directive the status of a demand. A highwayman declaiming 'Stand and deliver!' is certainly demanding something, as is someone demanding to be let in or a child demanding attention. It seems that either physical power or urgency from the point of view of the speaker can justify talk of a demand. The peremptoriness conferred in the cases of the latter kind is what is at work in the demands contained in resentment*.[11]

Creature construction step 1 is the production of an agent with the disposition to resentment*, where the latter is a nonmoral emotion. With Strawson, I take it that the emotion is also natural for humans. If it isn't, there are problems with seeing why the constructive steps that build on

---

[10] Compare the remarks by Victoria McGeer on the way the reactive attitudes engage their addressees' dispositions to react to the quality of will of others, particularly where that quality itself 'purports to comment on' the quality of will expressed in their own actions (McGeer 2013, 179f., 181f.).

[11] In the course of arguing that moral resentment entails demands grounded in authority, Darwall distinguishes them from 'naked demands', the kind that I need to get my construction going (Darwall this volume, 301).

it are relevant for understanding our morality. But there are certainly difficulties in making it clear that creatures such as us might play host to such a phenomenon independently of any preexisting normative or deontic structures. Requirements are ubiquitous in our social world, and attempting to peel them off may look doomed to failure.

However, there are natural phenomena which look very much like expressions of resentment*. For the reason just given, these are not easily distinguished among normal humans. However, evidence from psychopathology and comparative psychology gives us good reason to believe that resentment* exists in deontically uncontaminated forms.

Psychopaths appear to provide one kind of case. Take the following examples reported by Robert D. Hare and Simon Baron-Cohen. Baron-Cohen tells of a psychopath who murdered someone with a broken bottle because he felt the latter had been looking at him across the bar (Baron-Cohen 2011, 44). Hare recounts the example of a psychopathic prison inmate who threatened to kill his wife when she told him she couldn't visit him the following weekend because she hadn't found anyone to look after their children (Hare 1993, 60). The agent in the first case seems to impute ill will to his victim; the agent in the second case ascribes indifference to his wife. Both the attributions and the reactions are obviously seriously askew. Nevertheless, the pattern of reaction seems to be precisely one that manifests resentment minus any deontic dimension that may be thought to be presupposed in normal cases. The agents in these examples clearly demand certain forms of behaviour from others, forms of behaviour which, importantly, they wouldn't be prepared to accept as required of themselves.

Certain examples from comparative psychology at least look to be equally compelling. In experiments with the token-exchange paradigm on capuchin monkeys and chimpanzees, two animals in adjacent cages are offered food – cucumber slices or grapes (the latter being valued more highly than the former) – in exchange for tokens that been handed out to them immediately before. Whereas the exchange is generally accepted, the condition under which one animal's neighbour is offered a grape and the first animal is 'only' offered a cucumber slice frequently leads to refusals, sometimes to screaming and agitation that looks like protest behaviour. Although Sarah Brosnan and Frans de Waal, who first carried out the experiments, have argued that such reactions may demonstrate a sense of fairness in the animals (Brosnan and de Waal 2003; de Waal 2006, 44ff.), there is, as with the psychopaths, no evidence that the reactions are anything but egoistic (cf. Bräuer, Call and Tomasello 2009). What the animals' behaviour does plausibly express are demands that the experimenter not treat them worse than they obviously could, along with the concomitant bodily disturbances characteristic of emotional reactions.[12]

Both of the adduced natural phenomena, then, appear to provide evidence that there is such a thing as resentment*. It is on this psychological foundation that my construction of moral obligation will build.

3. The Emotional Construction of Moral Obligation, Stage II

At the second stage of construction, we add a further emotional capacity that normal humans possess, but which appears to be missing in psychopaths and primates. As at the first stage, opportunities for conceptual confusion abound. Confusion is nigh because the term most appropriate for the relevant capacity, 'empathy', appears to be, if not ambiguous in everyday usage, then to at least refer to a variety of only partly overlapping phenomena.[13] Accordingly, theories of empathy tend to propose significantly varying criteria.

To mark the concept required for my purposes, I shall talk of *Smithian empathy*, as its workings were described in some detail by Adam Smith in his *Theory of Moral Sentiments* (Smith 1759/90). There are, however, three reasons why the label is anything but sufficient for unequivocality. First, Smith called the mechanism that does the relevant work 'sympathy'. Second, he himself doesn't distinguish sufficiently between several different mechanisms that can be thus labelled.[14] Third, the decisive feature of his central concept itself needs conceptual sharpening before we can make use of it.

The decisive feature of the mechanism I am picking out with the expression is that it results in an emotion felt *on behalf of* another sentient being. Clearly, this involves something other than 'mind reading',

---

[12] There is an important question about the primate cases that could be advanced as an objection: can we plausibly take the animals to be demanding not merely behaviour with certain consequences, but behaviour that manifests specific qualities of will? John Deigh quotes Oliver Wendell Holmes Jr.'s remark that 'even a dog distinguishes between being stumbled over and being kicked' (Deigh 2011, 208f.). Deigh takes this to support the claim that resentment does not require the capacity for propositional thought. My analysis of resentment* requires thoughts with propositional structure, but I am not convinced that higher animals have no such capacity. A further question concerns the capacities of social cognition possessed by the animals – capacities some form of which are implied by Holmes' remark. Call and Tomasello have argued that the jury is still out on whether chimpanzees have a 'theory' of mind (Call and Tomasello 2008). However, capuchins are undoubtedly a different matter. Perhaps mechanisms that operate below those responsible for a full theory of mind might be at work here.

[13] Cf. Batson 2011, 11ff. For an example of such confusion, see my discussion of Slote's misunderstanding of Batson (Roughley 2015, 30f.).

[14] This is also argued by Darwall (this volume, 293f.).

which is essentially a doxastic process (and is therefore, even in the simulation variant, misleadingly labelled 'cognitive em*pathy*'). Cognition of some form, however, is essential to empathy as I understand it here: an empathiser needs some sort of capacity to understand both that the target of her empathy is a distinct sentient being and that that being is the bearer of a particular emotion. Emotion contagion, it has been claimed, is distinct from empathy in that it may come into play where no such capacities are given, as in Sagi and Hoffman's well-known example of one- to two-day-old babies' crying on hearing another infant's crying.[15] Adult examples, in which the latter of these two capacities is not activated, include cases in which a father becomes worried about the health of his child as a result of sensing, but not doxastically registering, the worry of his partner. Cases of contagion can even include catching the emotion of another without catching its particular content. For instance, the worry of the father's partner may turn out to concern not their child, but the performance of her football team.

In contrast, Smithian empathy requires at least some measure of similarity of both emotion type and emotion content, as well as the triggering of the empathic emotion via a cognitive process that focuses on relevant features of, or related to, the empathisee. What is relevant follows from type and content of the empathiser's emotion. This is, however, still insufficient. If empathising involves feeling an emotion on behalf of someone else, merely feeling what another is feeling as a result of taking it that that is what they are feeling will not necessarily be a case of empathising. If X adores celebrity C, reads in the magazine *Celebrity* that C loves pink clothes and, as a result, starts to love pink clothes himself, this need not be a case of Smithian empathy.[16] It would be if X were to think of himself as in some way representing C. Perhaps X thinks of himself as a mini-incarnation of C-ism in the face of the petty-mindedness of the small town he is stuck in. More usual cases of empathy in the sense I am after are feeling joy for someone who has won something or feeling frustrated for someone who has just failed to achieve something through bad luck.[17] Note that such empathic reactions generally kick in on the

---

[15] Batson has pointed out that this is not the only possible interpretation of the data (Batson 2011, 16).

[16] It would, however, appear to be a case of one kind of 'sympathy' for Smith. 'We feel', he says, 'a peculiar sympathy with the satisfaction of those who are in [the condition of the great]. We favour all their inclinations [...]' (Smith 1759/90, I.iii.2, 52).

[17] Smith devotes an entire chapter of the *Theory* to arguing not only that there are both negative and positive variants of 'sympathy', but also that the psychological dynamics are significantly different in the two cases: whereas we tend to empathise with strong negative emotions, but tend not to take particularly seriously minor emotional discomforts of others, it is their less weighty positive emotions, he claims, that tend to strike a

basis of a preexisting emotional bond. That bond might be part-constitutive of a personal relationship or it might be a one-way bond someone maintains toward a celebrity or royalty. Empathy with what Smith calls 'deep afflictions' may, however, be triggered in the absence of such a precondition.

It is the capacity for vicarious emoting, that is, for feeling emotions on behalf of another, that we need to add to the capacity for resentment* in the second stage of moral creature construction. Although the phenomenon is one we are all familiar with, it is not easy to say what 'on-behalfness' precisely consists in. Smith's way of expressing the point is to say that the empathiser 'adopts', 'makes his own', 'goes along with' or 'enters into' the emotion of the empathisee (Smith 1759/90, 9, 17, 35, 44, 70ff.). An important and again familiar effect of this way of emotionally relating is that the empathisee will at least sometimes see the empathiser as 'sharing' her emotion, a conceptualisation that, where the emotion in question is a form of suffering, can, as Smith puts it, be felt by the empathisee to 'disburthen' her (Smith 1759/90, I.1.2, 15). Again, the mere fact that another person may have caught my contagious emotion will not suffice to alleviate my suffering. Emotional unburdening seems to result from a process that in some way parallels the alleviation of physical effort when another agent takes the strain.

There are two explicatory proposals that might count as attempts to capture this point. However, both seem to me to be inadequate. They are in different ways both too strong.

De Waal has spoken of 'identification' as a necessary feature of full empathy. He explains his concept of identification in terms of a reduction of the difference between self and other (de Waal 2008, 286ff.; 2009). I take it that he means that this is how things appear to the empathiser in empathising. This might be right in the X and C example: perhaps X strolls through his home town fantasising that he is C. But this is far too strong for the case of feeling joy or frustration for another person. The relevance of talk of 'identification' for Smithian empathy actually seems to be the converse: people who have no doubt about the distinction between themselves and some other might be said to 'identify' with that other person insofar as they feel some emotion on their behalf. Vicarious emoting is then the explanans, not the explanandum.

Darwall's analysis takes us further, although the concept in terms of which he explicates that of vicarious emoting still misses its target. His explicit attempt to makes sense of Smith's proposal proceeds in two steps,

---

chord with us, whereas our ability to go along with their joyous reactions to life-changing events tends to be restricted by the disposition to envy (Smith 1759/90, I.ii.5, 40ff.).

the first of which I think is right, whereas the second takes us beyond what I think we should say. According to Darwall, the relation of on-behalfness is established by the empathiser 'seconding or endorsing' the attitude of the empathisee. The question is now whether anything more informative can be said about what seconding consists in. He claims that it is a matter of taking the emotion to be fitting in the situation (Darwall this volume).[18] If this were right, empathy would itself involve a normative component. There is, however, a clear difference between a psychological or agential event being brought about on behalf of another entity in some situation and that event being, or appearing appropriate to the situation. This can be seen fairly easily where we are dealing with actions. If I perform some action on your behalf, say an action you would have performed had you been able to be in the situation yourself, that provides no reason to think, or to think that I think that the action is appropriate to the situation. You might have a completely idiotic conception of the situation, something I might be aware of, but I might still for some reason want or feel obliged to perform the action in your stead.

The same gap is conceivable in the emotional case. For this reason, I propose to understand 'going along with an emotion' in terms of the willingness of an empathiser to take on the perspective on the emotion's object that is entertained by the empathisee. To use and extend Smith's own metaphor, the Smithian empathiser puts herself in the empathisee's shoes and is prepared to wander around in them for a bit – even though the shoes may not fit terribly well and may even be ill suited to the terrain. Willingness here is nonnormative, as can be seen from the fact that one reason for such acceptance may be the kind and quality of the bond linking empathiser and empathisee. A father may involuntarily go along with his daughter's fear of flying, although he doesn't think that such fear is justified and wouldn't empathise with fear with this content in anyone else. Empathy can be misplaced and known by the empathiser to be so.

There is one final step we need to take in order to complete the sketch of empathy required here. Careful attention to the way I described the empathic joy and empathic frustration cases reveals that these contain no description of any emotion that the empathisee actually feels, but rather a characterisation of the situation in which she finds herself.

---

[18] As a matter of Smith interpretation, this is a tricky point. Smith explicitly identifies 'sympathetic' emoting with taking the emotion to be proper or fitting of its object. I take it that Smith is, at least in the early part of the *Theory*, attempting to reduce the latter to the former. Slote has explicitly argued that this attempt fails (Slote 2004, 5). The claim of Darwall's I am disputing in the main body of this text is that Smith needs the latter to make sense of the former. I agree with Slote that the reductive claim is false. My systematic point here is that Smithian empathy is a nonnormative mechanism, one which, for that reason, can play the role required in the process of creature construction.

This corresponds to one of Smith's programmatic statements, according to which 'sympathy [...] does not arise so much from the view of the passion as from the situation that excites it' (Smith 1759/90, I.i.1, 12). According to Smith's and Martin Hoffman's proposals, it is possible to react empathically where the empathiser doesn't believe that the empathisee is playing host to the empathically felt emotion. A central case for Hoffman is that of feeling empathic anger for the victim of a physical attack, although the victim may only feel sad or disappointed (Hoffman 2000, 30). Smith thinks we can feel empathic sadness at the loss of reason of someone suffering from dementia, although the person is actually perfectly content. We do so by counterfactual means, by imagining how the person who has lost her reason would feel if, *per impossibile*, she were at the same time fully conscious of the fact. I suspect that Smith's basic idea here is not foreign to everyday understanding. But whatever the person on the street would think, this is the concept I am making use of in my exercise of creature construction.

4. The Emotional Construction of Moral Obligation, Stage III

The next step involves our putting together the resources we have built up in steps I and II. Creatures disposed to feel resentment* and to undergo processes subserved by the mechanisms of Smithian empathy are disposed to feel vicarious resentment*. Such resentment* on behalf of another can be labelled *indignation**. Indignation* involves an expansion of the demand at work behind resentment*: whereas the latter demand concerns the quality of will expressed in actions that (potentially) affect the emotion's bearer, the former concerns the quality of will expressed in actions that (potentially) affect others.

However, the expansion of the circle of those covered by the demand is not simply an addition to the demand's content. Rather, it results from the disposition to vicarious emoting on behalf of those individuals. An indignant* agent demands on behalf of a further agent the eschewal of agential ill will or indifference towards that agent. This is not simply to demand that the further agent be treated in a certain way on the basis of certain motivational constraints; it is to demand this from her perspective.

Which further agents are covered by someone's dispositions to indignation* will depend on varying factors, none of which are relevant to the question of whether an emotion counts as indignation*. An agent has the capacity for indignation* once the circle of those for whom resentment* is felt is expanded, however minimally, by means of Smithian empathy.

So, an agent *A* who feels indignation* at the action of some other agent *B* demands from the perspective of some third subject *C* that actions expressing ill-will or indifference towards *C* be eschewed, takes *B*'s action to express ill-will or indifference towards *C* and experiences an emotion that conjoins the vicarious demand specifically addressed to *B* with the affect felt in the face of the construal of her action as contravening the demand.

It seems likely that indignation* thus understood is beyond the capacity of both psychopaths and primates, because neither seem to be able to give their resentment* a vicarious twist that would afford them corresponding experiences on behalf of others.[19]

5. The Emotional Construction of Moral Obligation, Stage IV

Even if primates were capable of indignation*, that would still not, pace Brosnan and de Waal, mean that they had what in the eighteenth century was known as a 'moral sense'. Indignation* may be felt for a highly restricted group of others – for reasons such as their possession of certain bodily features or social standing which we take to be morally irrelevant. This possibility is overlooked by Strawson in 'Freedom and Resentment', who moves from the 'personal' reactive attitudes to variants he characterises as 'impersonal or vicarious', adding that the latter feature qualifies the attitudes thus generated as 'moral' (Strawson 1962, 15). However, the latter is not a single feature, but two features. Only when we introduce a standpoint that is in some sense impersonal or, as Strawson also puts it, 'disinterested' do we arrive at a structure that really does qualify as moral.

I think, however, that there is an important insight concealed in Strawson's nondifferentiation of the two steps beyond resentment*. This is that the move to the 'impersonal' level needs to retain its structural connection to vicarious emoting if it is to count as arriving at the level of morality. What Strawson thinks of as the impersonal analogues of the personal reactive attitudes remain participant attitudes even as they abstract from the action-guiding interests of their bearers. As I interpret Adam Smith, this point is the key to understanding his introduction of the so-called impartial spectator. Insofar as talk of 'spectating' entails what Strawson calls 'the objective attitude (or range of attitudes)', Smith's label is seriously misleading for his own purposes. Smithian

---

[19] But see Roughley in press, section 7, for an attempt to understand how close chimpanzees might come.

'impartial spectators' are agentially removed, but emotionally involved, an involvement that runs via empathy. The decisive step in stage IV of our construction is building into our creatures the capacity for impartial empathy.

The role of impartial empathy is that of regulating indignation*. An agent with this capacity is endued with a standpoint from which to criticise indignant* reactions, be they her own or the reactions of others. There is, of course, a serious, indeed often insurmountable, epistemic problem of knowing whether we are really dealing with impartiality. This practical problem is a theoretical advantage, as it mirrors our difficulties in knowing whether moral judgements are true.

According to the Smithian construction I am canvassing, the disposition to play host to a further layer of affectively embedded demands is added to the disposition to experience indignation*, itself a consequence of the dispositions to Smithian empathy and to resentment*. According to the construction, it is agents with this psychological makeup who are the bearers of moral obligation. The idea of creature construction is particularly appropriate here not only because the third capacity presupposes the first and the second, but also because the decisive final capacity in turn also presupposes the three on which it is built. If you don't know what it is to resent* the actions of another, if you are unable to feel emotions on behalf of another and if you are in particular incapable of feeling vicarious resentment*, you will have no conception of what it might mean to feel impartial indignation*. An agent with these emotional and correlative epistemic deficits will therefore be able to play no role in generating and upholding the practice in which the concept of moral obligation is embedded. An agent missing any of these capacities, who lives in a social world in which they are developed and made the basis of moral practice, may be able to mouth the words that correspond to deontic moral judgements in appropriate situations. Such an agent will not, however, know what she is talking about. There is, then, an important sense in which she will be unable to make genuine moral judgements.

6. Moral Obligation

The concept of moral obligation can now be given a succinct analysis: X is morally obligated to φ in situation s iff an impartial empathiser would be indignant* at X's eschewal of φ-ing in s.

Alongside the reference to impartiality, which often features centrally in normative moral theories, this analysis makes use of two emotional concepts, that of empathising and that of indignation*. Why, precisely, do we need them? Put another way, what is the rationale for the emotional dimension of the construction of moral obligation?

The first part of the answer focuses on the fact that moral obligation is essentially subjection to a demand. Assuming it is correct that we ought to do something if conclusive reasons speak for our doing it, the question remains what it means to say that there is a moral obligation to do what we ought. The answer that seems most phenomenologically appropriate is that we are the addressees of corresponding demands. This explains the move to the psychological phenomena we identified as the demands at the core of resentment* and indignation*. However, as these cannot be mere empirical psychological phenomena, we need to move to the counterfactual demands contained in impartial indignation*.

Empathy, secondly, makes possible the first step beyond the self-interested perspective expressed in resentment*. It does so by enabling its subject to play host to demands on behalf of others. What is decisive here is that those demands do not simply concern the treatment of others, but are brought forward on their behalf. Thus understood, vicarious emoting sets us on a path that binds moral obligation to the (potential) psychological condition of those subjects for whose sake the relevant obligations exist. In this role, Smithian empathy ensures that moral obligations are not the consequences of mere social norms or conventions. In contrast to moral obligations, social or conventional requirements need not meet the vulnerability constraint. Empathy ensures that the constraint is met.

It is perhaps helpful here to contrast the way Hume in the *Treatise* attempts to solve what I take to be the same problem. For Hume, our 'sympathy' with the usual effects attending character dispositions leads us to feel a specific sort of pleasure in view of those dispositions where those effects are themselves pleasurable or useful. Hume takes the relevant kind of pleasure to be equivalent to approval (Hume 1739–40, III. iii.1). This is the basis of what he terms the 'natural virtues'. This is, however, not how we get to obligation, which is established within social practices or agreements whose stable functioning is in the long-term interest of the society as a whole. For Hume, then, the 'artificial virtues' are dispositions to conform to certain socially established norms. It thus appears unclear why we should think of them as as much a part of morality as the natural virtues. Hume sees the unifying feature in the approval also felt here on the basis of 'sympathy'. However, as the disposition to uphold social practices such as promising and property may involve unpleasant short-term effects, the question arises as to what the object of sympathy might be here. Hume's answer is that it is 'sympathy with public interest' (Hume 1739–40, III. ii.3, 500).

As has been repeatedly pointed out, Hume's sympathy is not the phenomenon that goes under the same name in Smith. It ought to be clear that no sense can be made of the idea that we might feel some emotion on behalf of the public interest. What we feel vicariously must be felt for other individuals. Smith negotiates the problem of the negative emotions that obligations generate by having impartial empathisers consider the psychology of both perpetrator and victim and eventually come down on one side or the other emotionally. X has an obligation to eschew φ-ing where the reasons Y has for resenting* X's φ-ing move an impartial empathiser to indignation* on Y's behalf in view of X's reasons for φ-ing.

In contrast, Hume constructs an objective measure, the public interest, and then attempts to tie conformity to this measure back to approval through a form of 'sympathy' that presumably involves a general positive feeling in view of the overall effects of the relevant practice. However, approval thus understood is given without any view to the fate of particular individuals to whom the practice may not give protection or support. Thus construing obligation as a matter of subjection to a practice that is approved all-in-all involves abandoning the participant attitude that in a Smithian view structures moral obligation all the way down. The intuition captured by the Smithian model is that, although political, legal or other social duties may be generated by the requirements of approved social practices, moral obligation is a matter of what we are interpersonally answerable for. The counterfactual twist added by the qualification of impartiality means that the persons to whom an obligated agent is answerable may be unknown to her, indeed may at the limit not even exist.

One unusual feature of the model I am proposing is that, although it is developed via a construction of the psychologies of relevant creatures, it aims not primarily at a model of the psychology of deontic moral judgement, but rather at a conception of the metaphysics of moral obligation. As I remarked at the beginning of this piece, the adoption of the method of creature construction to this end seems appropriate because of the unintelligibility of the concept of moral obligation in the complete absence of certain psychological structures of sentient beings. If early hominids possessed no such psychological structures, there was, it seems, no question as to whether doing horrible things to other sentient beings was morally impermissible. Moral obligation requires a 'bearer' or agential substrate. This has the consequence that if all humans were to lose the capacities responsible for the existence of the concept, there would be no more obligatory or impermissible human actions.[20]

---

[20] To be precise, these formulations should be hedged by the concession that tying the construction to the capacities of humans is not strictly necessary. It is, as Kant insisted,

286 Neil Roughley

This is no cause for concern. Compare the worries once expressed by Simon Blackburn about response-dependent conceptions of moral permissibility. As he points out, if the sensibility of everyone were to change so that we all come to see some dubious practice as morally in order, that would not mean that the practice is OK. Rather, it would only show that 'everyone has deteriorated' (Blackburn 1985, 160). Note that what worries Blackburn is the content of moral permissions, not whether there are such things as moral permissions in the first place. The model proposed here for the mind-dependence of deontic moral categories works at a psychologically and conceptually deeper level than that of the worries Blackburn rightly articulates. Whereas the content of permissions is a matter of how impartial empathisers would react when confronted with specific forms of behaviour, the existence of the category of moral permissions is, I am claiming, dependent, among other things, on agents possessing the capacity for impartial empathy. Independently of whether I have identified the right psychological structures, I find it inconceivable that no such structures constitute necessary conditions for the existence of morally deontic properties.

7. Some Consequences for Deontic Moral Judgements

Although the model is metaphysical, not psychological, it does have consequences for an understanding of moral judgement. There are various ways in which such a conception could be developed, between which I don't want to adjudicate here. However, it seems appropriate to conclude by noting three points that would be pertinent for an analysis of deontic moral judgement that aims at compatibility with the metaphysics of obligation we have constructed.

First, the model doesn't require that someone judging an action morally proscribed actually empathise with the (potential) victim of the action. The empathy at issue is counterfactual and its bearer is an impartial emoter. However, as indicated at the end of section 5, it follows from the model that someone making genuine moral judgements at least have the capacity for Smithian empathy, alongside the capacity for resentment*. Absent such capacities, it seems appropriate to disqualify the producer of even true moral sentences as the maker of moral judgements. For our

conceivable that other beings somewhere else in the universe might have the relevant capacities (Kant 1785, 410ff.). Against Kant, I am insisting that the relevant capacities must have an emotional dimension. Whether relevant emotional capacities of other beings might be in some way functionally equivalent without being identical, that is, whether some other path of creature construction might be equally viable, is a further question that can be left open here.

purposes, it can remain an open question whether this disqualification is merely the refusal to confer a psychological predicate or whether it also counts as a semantic claim. A compatible theory of deontic moral judgement, it seems, will have some 'hybrid' dimension, as it will pick out both a cognitive relation to the dispositions to indignation* of an impartial empathiser and also require emotional preconditions on the part of the judger.[21]

Second, a compatible theory of moral judgement is well placed to meet the disagreement constraint. The reference to the indignation* of an impartial empathiser leaves plenty of room for varying conceptions of the kinds of reasons that such empathisers would countenance and take to be decisive. This room results from a significant level of indeterminacy in the truth conditions that would be specified by reference to empathisers' dispositions.[22] This indeterminacy may be thought to be a problem, rather than an advantage of the theory. However, it should be noted that the dispositions to indignation* and empathy on the part of the impartial emoter both involve clear restrictions on what might be taken to be the object of the relevant reaction. Moral obligation has to be essentially a matter of measures that protect or support our physically and psychologically vulnerable nature, as this vulnerability is registered in our sensitivity to the ill-will or indifference of other agents where their behaviour potentially affects us. Indignation* of an impartial empathiser picks up on precisely these features. Plausibly, this gives us just the right amount of leeway to explain basic normative disagreement whilst confining the disagreement to an area which we take to be that of morally significant possibilities.

The final point relevant for an understanding of moral judgement is empirical. Shaun Nichols, in arguing for his sentimentalist conception, dismisses the suggestion that empathy may be constitutively necessary for moral judgement because, whereas children begin to make a clear distinction between moral and conventional norm violations around

---

[21] On hybrid metaethical theories, see Fletcher and Ridge 2014.
[22] In the method of meeting the disagreement constraint, the model is a distant relative of Moore's conception according to which the decisive moral property is 'non-natural' (cf. Moore 1903, §11, 10ff.). Both strategies involve the claim that there is a relevant moral property that can be descriptively ascribed, a property that is unusual in leaving open what features of the empirical world may fall under the corresponding concept. Clearly, the construction developed here involves a rejection of any Moorean claim that the concept's openness for empirical satisfaction entails its lack of complexity. Moreover, the specificity of the features out of which the property is constructed ensures that the corresponding concept is not completely open. It is for this reason that the construction also meets the vulnerability constraint.

their third birthday, perspective taking, as measured by the false belief test, is not developed until about a year later (Nichols 2004, 9f.).

The appropriate reply here involves a number of moves. The first is of a general nature and concerns children's acquisition of concepts. The fact that children use words in a way that approximates to the way in which adults use them may only be an indication that the children are on the way to the acquisition of the concepts named by the terms in adults' usage, not that they actually possess those concepts. The claim that the capacity for empathy is required for the possession of the concept of moral obligation does not entail that infants may not begin to use words such as 'allowed' and 'got to' in simple moral contexts before they have developed the capacities necessary for understanding what they are talking about. Children's capacities to say things in structured contexts without being able to think the corresponding thought plausibly provides a complex case of their behaviour within what Vygotsky called 'the zone of proximal development' (Vygotsky 1930–4, 84ff.). This is the developmental period within which they may be able to do certain things when provided with social scaffolding, but during which they are unable to behave in the relevant way autonomously. It seems likely that the zone of proximal development for moral concepts will be fairly extended.[23]

If the model I have delineated here is correct, the most demanding feature of the concept of moral obligation is likely not to be the one that involves empathy, but rather that of impartiality. What children who distinguish between moral and conventional norms may well be doing in the moral case is expressing their indignation*, independently of what they may think that other 'spectators' are likely to think of their own emotional state. If this were correct, we would have an explanation of one dimension in which young children's use of moral concepts falls short of their full use. It would, however, pace Nichols, still require that they are capable of something like Smithian empathy. Importantly, the claim that this is impossible in view of three-year-olds' inability to pass the false belief task has no particularly strong support.

First, evidence has been accumulating that the false belief task may be so difficult to pass because of the demanding cognitive and linguistic abilities it presupposes that have no necessary connection to 'theory of mind'. Indeed, the use of implicit, nonlinguistic parameters seems to show that a primitive theory of mind may be present during the second year (Onishi and Baillargeon 2005; Southgate, Senju and Cisbra

---

[23] The importance of a semantic zone of proximal development was impressed on me by Mike Tomasello in discussion.

2007). Moreover, once one ceases to focus primarily on doxastic states, but instead looks at children's reactions to the behaviour of others that manifests or is appropriate to their having specific goals or emotions, there can be no question that infants under three can attribute mental states to others. Infant helping and comforting that has been elicited in various experimental situations doesn't seem plausibly explained in any other way. In important experiments carried out by Amrisha Vaish, eighteen-month-old children developed concerned facial expressions and subsequently helped adults who had been harmed but who didn't react emotionally to the hurt. As the experimental situations are likely to have been novel for the children, simulation of the victim's mental state looks like the most plausible explanation (Vaish et al 2007).

Might such simulation involve Smithian empathy, that is, the infant taking on the relevant emotions on behalf of the victim? It certainly seems that it might. The capacity for instrumental helping, demonstrated where children spontaneously pick up objects accidentally dropped or open a cupboard door for an adult whose hands are full (Warneken and Tomasello 2007), is precisely the capacity to *act* on behalf of another. And perhaps the phenomenon of so-called paternalistic helping has a Smithian explanation (Tomasello 2016, 49). Here, three-year-olds reject an experimenter's request, instead performing an action better suited to fulfilling what can be assumed to be the experimenter's goal in making the request (Martin and Olson 2013). Whether the mechanisms that subserve these forms of helping behaviour might – all? – run without any such 'mentalising' on behalf of others is, at present, an empirically open question. What is, pace Nichols, clear is that the empirical data certainly don't exclude phenomena of Smithian empathy already being in place when young children begin to distinguish moral from conventional judgements.[24]

Bibliography

Baron-Cohen, S. 2011. *Zero Degrees of Empathy. A New Theory of Human Cruelty*. London: Penguin.
Batson, D. D. 2011. *Altruism in Humans*. New York: Oxford University Press.
  2014. Empathy-Induced Altruism and Morality: No Necessary Connection. In: H. Maibom (ed.), *Empathy and Morality*. Oxford: Oxford University Press, 41–58.
Blackburn, S. 1985. Errors and the Phenomenology of Value. In: *Essays in Quasi-Realism*. New York/Oxford: Oxford University Press 1995, 149–65.

---

[24] I'd like to thank Stephen Darwall and Thomas Schramme for helpful comments on earlier drafts of this chapter.

Bräuer. J., J. Call and M. Tomasello. 2009. Are Apes Inequity Averse? New Data on the Token-Exchange Paradigm. *American Journal of Primatology*, 71, 175–81.

Broome, J. 2013. *Rationality through Reasons*. Chichester: Wiley Blackwell.

Brosnan, S. F. and F. B. M. de Waal. 2003. Monkeys Reject Equal Pay. *Nature*, 425, 297–9.

Call, J. and M. Tomasello. 2008. Does the Chimpanzee Have a Theory of Mind? 30 Years Later. *Trends in Cognitive Science*, 12, 187–92.

Darwall, S. 2006. *The Second-Person Standpoint. Morality, Respect and Accountability*. Cambridge, MA: Harvard University Press.

de Waal, F. B. M. 2006. *Primates and Philosophers: How Morality Evolved*. Princeton, NJ: Princeton University Press.

  2008. Putting the Altruism Back into Altruism: The Evolution of Empathy. *Annual Review of Psychology*, 59, 279–300.

  2009. Comment on Batson 'Empathic Concern and Altruism in Humans'. *On the Human. A Product of the National Humanities Center*. onthehuman.org/2009/10/empathic-concern-and-altruism-in-humans/ (accessed November 2016)

Deigh, J. 2011. Reactive Attitudes Revisited. In: C. Bagnoli (ed.), *Morality and the Emotions*. New York: Oxford University Press. 197–216.

Fletcher, G. and M. Ridge. 2014. *Having It Both Ways: Hybrid Theories and Modern Metaethics*. Oxford: Oxford University Press.

Foot, P. 1958–9. Moral Beliefs. *Proceedings of the Aristotelian Society* (New Series), 59, 83–104.

Gauthier, D. 1986. *Morals by Agreement*. Oxford: Oxford University Press.

Goldie, P. 2000. *The Emotions: A Philosophical Exploration*. Oxford: Oxford University Press.

Grice, H. P. 1974–5. Method in Philosophical Psychology (from the Banal to the Bizarre). *Proceedings and Addresses of the American Philosophical Association*, 48, 23–53.

Hare, R. D. 1993. *Without Conscience: The Disturbing World of the Psychopaths among Us*. New York: The Guildford Press.

Hare, R. M. 1952. *The Language of Morals*. Oxford: Clarendon Press.

  1963. *Freedom and Reason*. Oxford: Clarendon Press.

Hoffman, M. L. 2000. *Empathy and Moral Development: Implications for Caring and Justice*. Cambridge: Cambridge University Press.

Hume, D. 1739–40. *A Treatise of Human Nature*, edited by L. A. Selby-Bigge. Oxford: Clarendon Press 1978.

Kant, I. 1785. *Grundlegung zur Metaphysik der Sitten*. Kants gesammelte Schriften, edited by Königlich Preussische Akademie der Wissenschaften. Berlin: Georg Reimer 1911, vol. IV, 385–463.

Korsgaard, C. 2006. Morality and the Distinctiveness of Human Action. In: F. B. M. de Waal (ed.), *Primates and Philosophers: How Morality Evolved*. Princeton, NJ: Princeton University Press, 98–119.

Macnamara, C. 2013. Taking Demands out of Blame. In: D. J. Coates and N. A. Tognazzini (eds.), *Blame: Its Nature and Norms*. New York: Oxford University Press, 141–61.

Martin, A. and K. R. Olson. 2013. When Kids Know Better: Paternalistic Helping in 3-Year-Old Children. *Developmental Psychology*, 49, 2071–81.

McGeer, V. 2013. Civilizing Blame. In: D. J. Coates and N. A. Tognazzi (eds.), *Blame: Its Nature and Norms*. New York: Oxford University Press, 162–88.

Moore, G. E. 1903. *Principia ethica*. Cambridge: Cambridge University Press 1999.

Nagel, T. 1970. *The Possibility of Altruism*. Princeton, NJ: Princeton University Press.

Nichols, S. 2004. *Sentimental Rules: On the Natural Foundations of Morality*. Oxford University Press.

Onishi, K. H. and R. Baillargeon. 2005. Do 15-Month-Old Infants Understand False Beliefs? *Science*, 308, 255–8.

Prinz, J. 2004. *Gut Reactions: A Perceptual Theory of Emotions*. New York: Oxford University Press.

2007. *The Emotional Construction of Morals*. Oxford: Oxford University Press.

Raz, J. 1990. *Practical Reason and Norms*. Princeton, NJ: Princeton University Press.

Roughley, N. 2015. On the Objects and Mechanisms of Approval and Disapproval. In: N. Roughley and T. Schramme (eds.), *On Moral Sentimentalism*. Newcastle: Cambridge Scholars. 28–40.

2016. *Wanting and Intending: Elements of a Philosophy of Practical Mind*. Dordrecht: Springer.

In press. Moral Obligation from the Outside In: K. Bayertz and N. Roughley (eds.), *The Normative Animal: On the Anthropological Significance of Social, Moral and Linguistic Norms*. Oxford: Oxford University Press.

Slote, M. 2004. Moral Sentimentalism. *Ethical Theory and Moral Practice*, 7, 3–14.

Smith, A. 1759/1790. *The Theory of Moral Sentiments*, edited by D. D. Raphael and A. L. Macfie. Indianapolis: Liberty Fund 1982.

Southgate, V., A. Senju and G. Csibra. 2007. Action Anticipation through Attribution of a False Belief in Two-Year-Olds. *Psychological Science*, 18, 587–92.

Strawson, P. F. 1962. Freedom and Resentment. In: *Freedom and Resentment and Other Essays*. Abdingdon: Routledge 2008, 1–28.

Tomasello, M. 2016. *A Natural History of Human Morality*. Cambridge, MA/London: Harvard University Press.

Tugendhat, E. 1993. *Vorlesungen über Ethik*. Frankfurt a. M.: Suhrkamp.

Vaish, A., M. Carpenter and M. Tomasello. 2007. Sympathy through Affective Perspective Taking and Its Relation to Prosocial Behaviour in Toddlers. *Developmental Psychology*, 45, 534–43.

Vygotsky, L. S. 1930–4. *Mind in Society*, edited by M. Cole et al. Cambridge, MA/London: Harvard University Press 1978.

Wallace, R. J. 1994. *Responsibility and the Moral Sentiments*. Cambridge, MA: Harvard University Press.

Warneken, F. and M. Tomasello. 2007. Helping and Cooperation at 14 Months of Age. *Infancy*, 11, 271–94.

12 Empathy and Reciprocating Attitudes

Stephen Darwall

It is a familiar feature of emotions and attitudes that they present us with a "take" on their objects that appears to justify our attitudes as "fitting" responses to their objects (D'Arms and Jacobson 2000). If I resent someone for having done something, then, from the perspective of my anger, the thing she has done will seem to have wronged me and make my resentment fitting. And if you come to see things the same way, it will be to you as well, as though what she did justifies my resentment as a response that "fits" her resentable deed.

You can come to share my emotional or attitudinal view through a form of empathy called "perspective taking." You can try to imagine being "in my shoes" and share my anger from my perspective. Of course, even when you do take up my point of view, you may find it difficult or impossible to share my angry outlook. Even as you try to see things from my standpoint, my anger may nonetheless seem unfitting to you. More about this kind of case presently.

Perspective taking need not involve a voluntary act of the imagination, however. Philosophers such as Robert Gordon and Alvin Goldman have argued that we frequently attribute states of mind to others through unconscious, involuntary "simulation" of their perspectives (Goldman 1992; 1993; 2009; Gordon 1986).

An experiment by Kahneman and Tversky illustrates the point (Kahneman and Tversky 1982). Subjects were told a story of two individuals, A and B, who are traveling together in a cab to the airport to catch two different flights scheduled to leave at the same time. They encounter traffic and arrive thirty minutes late. A goes to his gate and is told that his flight left on time, thirty minutes before. B is also told that her flight has left, but only a few minutes before. When asked who is more upset, A or B, 96 percent of the subjects answer B, as I assume you would also. How do we come to this conclusion? It seems implausible that we survey past similar situations and hazard an inductive generalization. You probably thought more or less instantly that B would be more upset. An explanation of how came to your conclusion might be that you unconsciously simulated A and B in their respective situations (which you might have done implicitly while hearing the story anyway) and then reported the result of your involuntary imaginative projection.

Whether voluntary or involuntary, perspective taking differs from a more primitive form of empathy known as "emotional contagion," where one person "catches" another's feeling, but not necessarily "in her shoes." The phenomenon is perfectly familiar. Walking among happy families and children, one feels happy oneself. Coming into a room where everyone is downcast, one tends to feel down also. This is the form of empathy that children develop first, which seems to involve mimicry, perhaps "mirror neurons," and perhaps facial feedback of some kind. The ancients identified the phenomenon, though they did not, of course, understand the underlying mechanisms. "The human countenance ... borrows smiles or tears from the human countenance," Hume quotes Horace as saying (Hume 1978, 220).[1]

Contagion is what Hume himself usually means by "sympathy": "the propensity we have to receive by communication [the] inclinations and sentiments" of others (Hume 1978, 316). An important difference between contagion and perspective taking is that when a "caught" feeling has an object, it need neither be, nor be thought to be, the same as the object of the feeling from which it is caught. If A is angry with C and approaches B with an angry face, B may catch A's anger. But so far as the mechanism of contagion goes, B's anger need not have the same object as A's, namely C. Contagion simply induces anger in B, and something else must supply anger's object. In pure contagion cases, the anger that A induces in B is as likely to be with *A* (and *his* angry face) as it is to be with anyone else. B may have no idea, indeed, with whom A is angry and still catch A's anger by contagion. Emotional contagion involves no tendency to feel others' feelings from their perspective. We feel them from our own and tend to supply objects that make sense from that point view.

When, however, we share someone's attitude or emotion through perspective taking, we generally have the same object in view. But even here, empathic sharing of someone's affective state of mind through perspective taking is a genus that admits of different species. Here are four; there may be others: (1) the mostly cognitive process Gordon and Goldman describe in which we attribute a state of mind to someone; (2) an affect-laden process in which we appreciate "what it's like" for that person to be in that mental state;[1] (3) a different affect-laden state that we call having or feeling "empathy *with* someone," irrespective of any judgment of her

---

[1] This is what I call "proto-sympathetic empathy" in Darwall 2002.

attitude's fittingness;[2] and (4) a state of mind that is part of the process of judging whether a person's attitude or emotion is fitting.

Hume's compatriot and friend, Adam Smith, is the *locus classicus* here. Smith is the source, first, of the simulation theory of folk psychology advanced by Gordon and Goldman, since Smith holds that it is primarily through perspective taking that we attribute mental states to others (process 1 in the preceding). "We can form no idea of what other men feel," Smith writes, "but by conceiving what we ourselves should feel in the like situation." "By the imagination, we place ourselves in [the other's] situation," and attribute the feeling we imagine feeling in that situation to the other (Smith 1790, 9).

But in addition to attributing mental states to others, Smith holds that we can also have "sympathy" with them, which he defines as "our fellow-feeling with any passion whatever" (Smith 1790, 10). Smithian "sympathy," however, is not Humean. It is no form of contagion, but sharing others' feelings (at least as we believe them to be) when we imaginatively take up their perspective.

Reflection on Smith's *Theory of Moral Sentiment*, however, reveals that he actually includes a variety of phenomena under this head. To begin, even attribution must involve *some* imaginative sharing of the state we attribute to the other, if only "offline," since according to the simulation theory we attribute mental states to others by attributing those we imaginatively have ourselves in their shoes. However, Smith famously holds also that we judge the fittingness (what he calls the "propriety") of others' attitudes and emotions through taking up their perspective as well (process 4 in the preceding).

> To approve of the passions of another, therefore, as suitable to their objects is the same thing as to observe that we entirely sympathize with them; and not to approve of them as such is the same thing as to observe that we do not entirely sympathize with them (Smith 1790, 16).

But if *this* sympathy is also the result of an imaginative projection into the other's point of view, it clearly cannot result from the *same* projection that makes us aware of what the other's passion is. For then we could not distinguish seeing someone as having a certain attitude and judging it to be suitable or fitting to its object. The latter must involve a different imaginative process through which we can somehow *second* or endorse what we take the other's passion to be. Only then do we judge the passion "proper," that is, "suitable" or fitting to its object.

---

[2] Unlike (2), this involves some feeling for the person like compassion. See Blum this volume.

In assessing what the other's passion actually is and what it is like for that person to have it, we imaginatively take on as many features of the individual as we can "In imagination we become the very person," Smith says (Smith 1790, 75). More realistically: we ignore or abstract from none of his or her features. It is misleading for Smith to say that to figure out what others are feeling, we imagine "what *we ourselves* should feel in the like situation" (emphasis added, Smith 1790, 9). It's more like we imagine what we would feel if we were *the other* in her situation ("we become the very person").

When, however, we judge whether the other's feeling or passion in that situation is fitting or *proper*, there will be features of the other that, though relevant to what she actually feels, are irrelevant to what she *should* feel in the situation that confronts her. The question of what someone actually feels, or what it is like for her to feel it, is irreducibly particular; it is about *her*, the particular individual she is. So to judge it, we have imaginatively to "become the very person" she is. The question of whether her passion or feeling is proper is not, however, irreducibly particular; it concerns what it would be proper for *someone* to feel in the situation she confronts.[3]

For example, I might have an irrational fear of flying; my fear might be out of proportion to and an unfitting response to the dangers that flying actually involves. If you are to either grasp or appreciate my fear *epistemically*, then, you must imagine what you would feel if you were I, if you became my very person, along with all my irrational foibles. But some of my features, my foibles, will not be features I would have if my fear were fitting or proper.

So, to judge the propriety of someone's attitudes, we cannot imaginatively become his "very person"; neither do we imaginatively "play" *ourselves* in the person's situation (that would be relevant to judging what *we* would feel, not what either of us *should* feel in the normative sense). Rather, and this is where Smith's idea of the "impartial spectator" comes in, we imagine being *someone* in the other's situation and work out what *to feel* from that perspective.[4] If the passion or feeling that results seconds what we take to be the other's in fact, with the latter knowledge perhaps coming from an imaginative projection of the first sort, then this constitutes sympathy or fellow feeling with the other's feeling, and we judge her feeling proper. If not, we judge it improper.[5]

---

[3] To which, we can assume, not every aspect of her, as the particular individual she is, is relevant.
[4] As I see it, Smith's idea of the "impartial spectator" is simply a heuristic to focus on the normative question of what feeling is *proper*, of what is the thing *to feel*.
[5] Of course, a person's situation can be defined in more or less fine-grained ways, and some fine-grained ways will include features of the individual person. But that just means

I have gone into these niceties of Smith's moral psychology to illustrate two points. The first is the role of perspective taking in coming to share others' emotions and attitudes in a way that, unlike emotional contagion, retains their objects. And the second is the intimate tie between sharing someone's attitude "in their shoes" and thinking their attitude a fitting response to the object. As we have just seen, the two are not exactly identical, since you may come to share my attitude by imaginatively taking on features of me as I confront my situation, including the object in question, that are irrelevant to whether my response is fitting to the relevant object(s) in the situation I confront. To judge the latter, you have to ignore these features and (impartially) project yourself as *someone* facing my situation. But even if you do not, the emotion or attitude you come to have by taking my perspective will present itself, as it does to me, as a fitting response to its object. In sharing my resentment, its object will at least *seem* to be a resentable injury or wrong.

My main object in this chapter is to show how perspective taking and feeling the propriety of someone's attitude toward one through taking her standpoint on one are implicated in the distinctive attitudes through which we hold one another (and ourselves) morally *accountable* or answerable, which Strawson famously dubbed "reactive attitudes" (Strawson 1968). I will be arguing that a distinctive feature of reactive attitudes is that they are *reciprocating attitudes*. Reciprocating attitudes are attitudes that seek reciprocation from their object persons, which the latter do when they place themselves imaginatively in the perspective of the person holding them accountable and hold themselves accountable to that person.

1. Reciprocal Attitudes

In this section, I want to explore a phenomenon I shall call *reciprocal* attitudes or emotions. These are pairs of mental states in which when the first is an attitude someone fittingly has toward someone, the second is the attitude that the person who is the object of the first attitude would fittingly have toward herself. I shall be arguing that reciprocating attitudes seek reciprocation through their reciprocals, but that not all attitudes that have reciprocals seek reciprocation and are therefore reciprocating attitudes. But all reciprocal attitudes, whether they are reciprocating or not, are apt to be transformed into their reciprocals through empathic perspective taking.

that there are different normative questions of propriety for situations defined in these different ways.

Consider admiration or esteem, on the one hand, and pride, on the other. Suppose I admire your ease and grace in interpersonal relations. Then it will be to me as if your ease and grace (as I take it) are admirable – fitting objects of my admiration (as my admiration is a fitting response to them). If you come to share my view of your attributes by empathically taking my perspective, you may feel pride.[6] In feeling pride, your attributes will seem to you estimable or admirable features, things of which to be proud. It is essential to pride, however, that it can only be felt by someone who takes herself to *have* the estimable features (or to be somehow identified with her). In admiring your grace and ease, I can only be proud of these if I take them somehow to reflect on me.

To a first approximation, we might try saying that admiration and pride are reciprocal emotions because they share a common evaluation of an object and differ in the relation of the person having the emotion to the object. However, although these aspects are necessary for the relation of reciprocal emotions I have in mind, they are not sufficient.

To see why, consider the relation between resentment and moral blame. Both are examples of what Strawson famously called "reactive attitudes." Reactive attitudes have distinctive "second-personal" holding-answerable aspects that will be at the center of what I want to discuss later (Strawson 1968; Darwall 2006; 2013a; 2013b). What I want to focus on now, though, is that, like admiration and pride, blame and resentment share an evaluative take on a common object. However, blame and resentment are not reciprocal attitudes in the way that admiration and pride are. In calling the latter reciprocal emotions, I mean to highlight a further feature they share, but that is lacked by resentment and blame.

Admiration and pride do not merely share a common evaluative take on a common object. In addition, pride is the attitude that the person who is the object of admiration fittingly has *herself* if the admiration is fitting. If X fittingly admires Y, then Y's sense that she is fittingly admired shows itself in her (Y's) pride.

More generally, two attitudes of different type, A and B, are reciprocals if, and only if, for any two persons X and Y, if Y is (part of) a fitting object of X's attitude A, then B is an attitude it would be fitting for Y to have.

Blame and resentment are not reciprocal attitudes in this sense. Blame and resentment do share a common take on a common object. To someone with either attitude, it is as if the person who is the object of the attitude has done something culpable. The difference between blame and

---

[6] There is a complication, since pride is not simply a dual of esteem or admiration; it also seems to involve some enjoyment of, or willingness to enjoy, being *seen* in these ways. We can ignore this complication, however.

resentment is that whereas resentment is felt as if from the perspective of a *victim* of a culpable act, uninvolved third parties can appropriately feel blame. Blame is an example of what Strawson calls an "impersonal" reactive attitude, whereas resentment is a "personal" reactive attitude (Strawson 1968, 84–5). Personal reactive attitudes are held from the perspective of someone somehow involved in the target conduct, either as agent or as victim or beneficiary. Impersonal reactive attitudes are felt as if from the perspective of a disinterested or impartial third party.

But though blame and resentment share a common take on a common object, they are not reciprocals, because it is not the case that if X fittingly blames Y, then it would be fitting for Y to have the attitude of resentment. Of course, Y might resent being the object of blame, but Y's resentment cannot be fitting if the blame is. As we shall see, the reciprocal of blame is not resentment, but guilt.

Another pair of reciprocal attitudes is disesteem (or contempt) and shame. When we view someone with contempt, we see him as below us in some ordering of esteem or honor. Shame is the attitude that occupies the same conceptual space, but from the perspective of the person below who is fittingly viewed with contempt from above.

Shame has to do with what Erving Goffman called "the presentation of the self in everyday life" (Goffman 1959). When others accept or honor our social self-presentation, we are able to occupy social places or play social roles to which we aspire. If, however, they do not, if they show contempt for, ridicule, or otherwise discredit our self-presentation, they deny us the recognition our pretensions require. The response that fits in the shoes of someone who is the object of fitting contempt is shame.

Shame has to do with "face," both in self-presentation's social sense – loss of face – and in the countenance. The natural expression of shame is to hide the face and thereby lose its social expression. Someone who looks at another with contempt is sometimes said to "look him out of countenance," forcing him to alter his self-presentation.[7] Shame thus feels as if one is fittingly viewed with contempt, and in this way shame is a reciprocal of contempt.

Reciprocal attitudes are composed of an *other's-perspective attitude* and a *self-perspective attitude*. We can thus array our three examples as in Table 12.1.

One way someone can come to have a self-perspective emotion or attitude of a reciprocal pair is through empathic perspective taking with

---

[7] Oliver Goldsmith's Vicar of Wakefield remarks in the eponymous novel that his daughters "had early learnt the lesson of looking presumption out of countenance" (Goldsmith 1766, 52).

Table 12.1. *Some Reciprocal Attitudes*

Other's perspective	Self-perspective
Admiration (esteem)	Pride
Contempt	Shame
Blame	Guilt

its respective other's-perspective attitude. I admire your ease and grace, and if you can empathically take my perspective on you, your ease and grace will appear admirable to you too. So far, you are sharing my attitude toward you, perhaps not yet bringing it home as directed to *you* and features of yours. If you do, however, and if you take my attitude to heart, you will then feel the attitude as pride, the evident appreciation of one's own estimable features.

Similarly, if I am a would-be philosopher, you have contempt for my philosophical efforts, and I take your contempt to heart by internalizing your perspective on me, I will feel the self-perspective reciprocal emotion of shame. Finally, if you blame me for having inconsiderately interrupted you and cut you off without listening when you were trying to say something to me, and I empathically internalize your blame and own its target as actions of mine, I will feel the self-perspective reciprocal emotion of guilt.

This is true generally of reciprocal attitudes. The self-perspective attitude of a reciprocal pair is naturally generated when someone who is an object of an other's-perspective attitude of the pair internalizes or takes to heart the other's-perspective attitude through taking his perspective and feels its object in himself.

2. Reactive, Second-Personal Attitudes and Reciprocity

In the last section, I briefly introduced Strawson's idea of reactive attitudes in the process of giving examples to illustrate reciprocal attitudes and how they differ from other attitudes that share a common take on a common object. Blame, resentment, and guilt are all examples of reactive attitudes for reasons I will clarify presently. The point in the last section, however, was that although blame and resentment can share a common take on a common object, they are not reciprocal attitudes in the way that blame and guilt, and contempt and shame, are. Reciprocal attitude pairs don't merely share a common take on a common object. They are composed of an other's-perspective attitude and self-perspective attitude, where the second is the attitude that is fitting from the perspective of the person who is the fitting object of the first.

In the next section, I shall be arguing that although both contempt and shame, and blame and guilt, are reciprocal attitude pairs in this sense, there is a further sense in which guilt *reciprocates* blame, but shame does not reciprocate disesteem or contempt. The reason has to do with an essential aspect of reactive attitudes that will be the subject of this section. Reactive attitudes mediate relations of mutual accountability and reciprocity. Blame implicitly holds its object answerable and bids for her to take responsibility for her culpable misdeed. It implicitly *addresses* its object in a way that other critical attitudes such as disesteem or shame do not. It calls for response and therefore implicitly relates to its object from a second-person standpoint. Guilt is the response for which it calls – the sense that one is to blame for something one has done and should take responsibility. Indeed, feeling guilt and acknowledging culpability is itself part of holding oneself answerable and taking responsibility for one's actions. It implicitly acknowledges one's blameworthiness, and so holds oneself accountable, to anyone in a position to view one with justified blame.

Strawson introduced the category of "reactive attitudes" in *Freedom and Resentment* in the course of making an argument about freedom of the will (Strawson 1968). Strawson's discovery, as we might justly call it, can be described in three interrelated propositions. First, reactive attitudes play a distinctive role in holding people responsible (in the sense of accountable or answerable); indeed, they might best be described as "holding accountable" attitudes.[8] Second, these attitudes have an essentially "interpersonal" (second-personal) structure in that their objects are invariably persons of whom the attitudes implicitly make demands (Strawson 1968, 77, 92–3)[9]. Third, reactive attitudes are held from a second-personal perspective of "involvement or participation with others in inter-personal human relationships" (Strawson 1968, 79). They hold their objects accountable and tacitly demand that their objects hold

---

[8] This is the sense of "responsibility" that Watson calls "responsibility as accountability," which he contrasts with "responsibility as attributability" (roughly, the sense in play in Aristotle's and Hume's discussions of responsibility, in which what matters is whether someone's conduct can be attributed to a relatively durable trait of hers) (Watson 1996).

[9] Although this is true of reactive attitudes that are most frequently discussed – e.g., blame, resentment, and guilt – it is not true in all cases. For example, Strawson also lists gratitude and adult love as reactive attitudes. It is significant, however, that these examples are, like the more typical "juridical ones," reciprocating attitudes in the sense here discussed. For discussions of love and trust as non-juridical reactive "attitudes of the heart," see Darwall 2016 and 2017.

themselves accountable also. They come, as I sometimes put it, with an RSVP.[10]

Consider indignation or moral blame, for example. To feel indignation or blame toward someone is to feel that she is to blame for wrongful conduct and therefore appropriately held answerable for what she has done, even if only by being the object of reactive attitudes, including her own. Blame differs in this way from other forms of criticism that point out someone's faults; blame makes the charge that something someone did was not just faulty, but *his* fault, that *he* was at fault. And blame invariably includes a sense of authoritative demand that may be absent from other forms of criticism (Strawson 1968, 85). It implicitly calls its object to take responsibility for having violated a legitimate demand.

Or consider the reactive attitude that takes oneself as object, namely, guilt. To feel guilt is to feel as if one is appropriately blamed (to blame) and held responsible for something one has done. Guilt simultaneously involves a form of blame (blaming oneself) along with an acceptance of blame and therefore recognition of blameworthiness. Guilt's natural expressions are also second personal – confession, apology, making amends, and self-addressed reproach. Like any reactive attitude, guilt makes an implicit demand, here, of oneself (to take responsibility for what one has done). But since one is also the attitude's object, guilt also implicitly acknowledges the legitimacy of the demand and, in so doing, partly constitutes taking responsibility for oneself. This is why someone's feeling guilt can mitigate others' blame; the former already partly constitutes what the latter implicitly demands.

Compare guilt with shame. Like guilt, shame feels as if one is rightly regarded in a certain way. But here the relevant regard is third personal rather than second personal – one feels as if one is justifiably *seen* (as shameful) third personally. Whereas guilt is concerned with how one conducts oneself in relation to what is legitimately demanded of one second personally, shame is concerned with (social) self-presentation to a third-personal view, with "face." And whereas guilt's characteristic expression is second personal, the natural expression of shame is registered in the face one presents to a third-personal view. One "loses" the face one had, for example, by turning red, looking down, or staying out of view. One changes what there is of one to be seen in third-personal social space.

Earlier I adverted to Strawson's distinction between "personal" reactive attitudes, such as resentment and guilt, which we feel as if from the perspective of an involved party – that of victim and perpetrator,

---

[10] For an extended defense of the following claims, see Darwall 2006, 65–90.

respectively – and "impersonal" reactive attitudes, such as indignation or blame, that we hold as if from the standpoint of a disinterested third party, as I put it, the perspective of a representative person or member of the moral community (Strawson 1968, 72; Darwall 2013c). It is important to appreciate, however, that impersonal reactive attitudes are no less "inter-personal" in Strawson's terms, or "second personal" in mine, than personal reactive attitudes (in the relevant sense of expressing demands of, and so implicitly addressing them to, their objects). Any doubt about this should be dispelled by the realization that otherwise, impersonal reactive attitudes could not play the role they do in Strawson's argument about freedom of the will. Strawson's core point is that all reactive attitudes, whether personal or impersonal, are felt from the (second-person) perspective of "involvement or participation with others in inter-personal human relationships" (Strawson 1968, 79). That is what distinguishes them from third-personal "objective" attitudes and inescapably requires presuppositions about their objects' will and moral agency.

Similarly, although guilt is a first-personal attitude in an obvious sense, it is no less second personal for that, since it no less implicitly addresses a demand than do blame or resentment.[11] As I mentioned previously, guilt involves the simultaneous tacit address and acceptance of a demand; this is what enables it to play a role in *taking* responsibility. That is why sincere apologies that express guilt can lead to the diminishment of blame; they help to satisfy the demand for taking responsibility that blame expresses. So just as a third-party attitude can be second personal in the relevant sense, so a second-personal attitude requires no second person in the sense of a *second party*. Guilt is a second-personal attitude even though addresser and addressee are the same person.

The demands that reactive attitudes implicitly address are not naked demands; they are put forward as legitimate. We can see this, again, in the case of guilt. To feel guilt is to feel that one violated a *justified* demand and that one is therefore under a legitimate demand to hold oneself accountable, which one partly does in feeling guilt. The perspective from which one makes the demand cannot, however, be the very same as that from which one accepts it. The perspective *from* which we blame is that of a representative person or member of the moral community; but one receives blame as the very individual one is.

---

[11] It is worth bearing in mind that all second-personal attitudes are also first personal since, as Buber noted, when we view or address someone else as "you," the first-personal "I" is implicit also: "When one says You, the I of the I-You is said, too. Whoever says You does not have something for his object ... he stands in relation" (Buber 1970, 54). 'Relation is reciprocity. My You acts on me as I act on it' (Buber 1970, 67).

Again, Strawson's core point about reactive attitudes is that we hold them, whether personal or impersonal, from a second-personal perspective of relationship *to* someone, and that regarding someone from this point of view invariably commits us to various presuppositions about his or her volitional capacities. We cannot intelligibly hold someone accountable for complying with a demand to take responsibility unless we assume that he is capable of holding himself accountable for complying with it as well. But this requires that he have an ensemble of psychological capacities, crucially including the capacity for perspective taking, comprising what we might term *second-personal competence*, that is, the ability to take an impartial or "representative" second-person perspective on himself and to regulate his will by demands that are justified from that point of view.

Compare this with third-personal attitudes such as annoyance, disesteem, contempt, disgust, or shame. We can clearly have these attitudes toward someone without being committed to any assumption that the person toward whom we have them is capable of accepting our view or regulating himself by it. Take Hume's example of an "egregious blockhead" (Hume 1985, 314). Disdain or contempt for someone as an "egregious blockhead" carries no implicit demand that he stop being so stupid or answer for his stupidity. Neither is the disdain intelligible only on the assumption that he is capable of understanding what a blockhead he is. To the contrary, it may be even more intelligible, at least to someone who feels such disdain, on the assumption that he is not. Moreover, those who feel the disdain are far likelier to express it, whether actually *or* imaginatively, to other *cognoscenti* than to the supposed blockhead himself.

3. Blame and Guilt as Reciprocating Attitudes

Now that we have clarified the way in which reactive attitudes such as blame and guilt mediate relations of reciprocity and mutual accountability, we can see fairly easily the sense in which blame and guilt are not merely reciprocal, but *reciprocating* attitudes. Reactive attitudes such as resentment and moral blame call for reciprocation. They come with an RSVP, calling on their objects to hold themselves answerable and take responsibility for the culpable action.

Although "praise" and "blame" are frequently thought to express contrary attitudes, and are certainly used that way by Hume and in translations of Aristotle, "blame" in the distinctive holding-accountable sense that refers to a reactive attitude is actually not a contrary of "praise." First, blame in the latter sense is an *attitude*, whereas there is no attitude of praise. In its noun form, "praise" refers what is made actual by praising acts, whereas "blame" in our sense is an attitude that is *expressed* by an act of blaming. Without a praising, there is no praise, but someone can blame someone "in his heart" without ever expressing it overtly.

More important for our purposes, however, is the difference between the attitude that praise standardly expresses, esteem of some kind, and the attitude of blame. Neither esteem nor disesteem call for reciprocation, although it is essential to a Strawsonian analysis of reactive attitudes that they involve implicit address and are therefore committed to certain presuppositions as what Gary Watson calls "constraints of moral address" (Watson 1987, 263, 264; see also McKenna 2012). That, again, is the distinctive feature Strawson draws on in his argument about freedom of the will.

Even expressions of esteem or disesteem don't necessarily invite reciprocating response, although they do of course imply that their respective *reciprocal* attitudes are justified in D'Arms and Jacobson's sense of "fitting," or in Adam Smith's sense of "proper" (Smith 1790; D'Arms and Jacobson 2000). Perhaps it is ungrateful to fail to acknowledge praise that expresses esteem, but that is owing to a norm of gratitude, not to the nature of either praise or esteem. And plainly contempt does not call upon its object to acknowledge his contemptible state. To the contrary, that might be even more contemptible.

Blame, on the other hand, does not simply imply that its reciprocal attitude of guilt would be justified. In calling upon its object to take responsibility for her culpable action, it implicitly demands its object to reciprocate by feeling guilt. In this way, guilt is not merely the self-perspective reciprocal to the other's-perspective attitude of blame. Guilt is a reciprocating attitude to blame.

When we feel guilt, and own it not just as a feeling with which we are afflicted but as the fitting response to our culpable action, we hold ourselves accountable and (begin, at least, to) take responsibility for what we have done. In holding ourselves thus accountable, we acknowledge our culpability to others and ourselves as representative persons or members of the moral community. We blame ourselves from this perspective we share in common with them.

Blame and guilt are thus reciprocating attitudes that mediate a fundamental reciprocity as equal moral persons that we presuppose from the second-person standpoint we take up when we have either attitude. Unlike contempt, which views its object from above, reactive attitudes such as blame address their objects as equal members of the moral community who share a standing to hold one another accountable. Similarly, when we feel guilt, we feel not that we are justifiably viewed as low, base, or shameful, but that we have violated demands that everyone has the standing to make of everyone else.[12] Acknowledging our own culpability is thus a form of respect, simultaneously for others and their justified demands, but also for ourselves and our own demands of ourselves, as fellow representative persons or members of the moral community.

In conclusion, we should note empathy's role in mediating this mutual respect. We respect one another by acknowledging our independent points of view and that each of us has the authority and responsibility to live her own life in relations of mutual accountability with one another. Empathic perspective taking is what enables us to take up and appreciate one another's viewpoints, without which mutual respect and accountability would be impossible. Through empathy, we can feel blame as guilt, and guilt as the attitude that reciprocates blame.

Finally, when we judge actions to be fitting objects of blame and resentment, that is, blameworthy or resentable, we implicitly presuppose the legitimate demands such actions violate along with the authority to make the demands and to hold agents accountable for violations. The attitudes through which we hold one another accountable implicitly demand reciprocation, that is, that their objects hold themselves accountable through an attitude that reciprocates the blame or resentment, by empathically bringing it home as guilt.[13]

Bibliography

Buber, Martin. 1970. *I and Thou*, trans. Walter Kaufman. New York: Touchstone, Simon and Schuster.

D'Arms, J. and Jacobson, D. 2000. Sentiment and Value. *Ethics*, 110, 722–48.

Darwall, S. 2002. *Welfare and Rational Care*. Princeton, NJ: Princeton University Press.

  2006. *The Second-Person Standpoint: Morality, Respect, and Accountability*. Cambridge, MA: Harvard University Press.

  2013a. *Morality, Authority, and Law: Essays in Second-Personal Ethics I*. Oxford: Oxford University Press.

  2013b. *Honor, History, and Relationship: Essays in Second-Personal Ethics II*. Oxford: Oxford University Press.

  2013c. Bipolar Obligation. In: S. Darwall, *Morality, Authority, and Law: Essays in Second-Personal Ethics I*. Oxford: Oxford University Press, 20–39.

---

[12] More precisely, we feel as if we have justifiable demands (period). I am claiming in my own philosophical voice that these demands can be justified only from the standpoint of equal moral persons (Darwall 2006). It is of course possible for someone to think, mistakenly in my view, that they are justified on some other basis (for example, that they are commanded by God, who has superior authority over us).

[13] I am indebted to other participants in the *Forms of Fellow Feeling* Conference at Duisburg-Essen University, in March 2013 and to the editors of this volume for their very helpful comments and suggestions.

2016. Love's Second-personal Character Holding, Beholding, and Upholding. In K. Schaubroeck, *Love, Reason, and Morality*. New York Routledge, 93–109.

2017. Trust as a Second-personal Attitude of the Heart. In P. Faulker and T. Simpson, *The Hilosophy of Trust*. Oxford: Oxford University Press.

Goffman, E. 1959. *The Presentation of Self in Everyday Life*. New York: Anchor.

Goldman, A. 1992. In Defense of the Simulation Theory. *Mind and Language*, 7, 104–19.

1993. Ethics and Cognitive Science. *Ethics*, 103, 337–60.

2009. Mirroring, Mindreading, and Simulation. In: J. A. Pineda (ed.), *Mirror Neuron Systems*. New York: Humana Press, 311–30.

Goldsmith, O. 1766. *The Vicar of Wakefield*. Chicago: Scott, Foresman, 1901.

Gordon, David. 1978. Folk Psychology as Simulation. *Mind and Language*, 1, 158–71.

Hume, A. 1992. *A Treatise of Human Nature*, ed. L. A. Selby-Bigge, second edition, with rev. P. H. Nidditch. Oxford: Oxford University Press.

1985. An Enquiry Concerning the Principles of Morals. In: L. A. Selby-Bigge (ed.), *Enquiries Concerning Human Understanding and Concerning the Principles of Morals*, 3rd. ed., rev. P. H. Nidditch. Oxford: Clarendon Press.

Kahneman, D. and Tversky, A. 1982. The Simulation Heuristic. In: D. Kahneman, P. Slovic and A. Tversky (eds.), *Judgment under Uncertainty: Heuristics and Biases*. New York: Cambridge University Press, 201–8.

McKenna, M. 2012. *Conversation and Responsibility*. Oxford: Oxford University Press.

Smith, A. 1790. *The Theory of Moral Sentiments* (D. D. Raphael and A. L. MacFie, eds.). Indianapolis: Liberty Classics 1982.

Strawson, P. F. 1968. Freedom and Resentment. In: P. F. Strawson (ed.), *Studies in the Philosophy of Thought and Action*. London: Oxford University Press, 71–96.

Watson, G. 1987. Responsibility and the Limits of Evil: Variations on a Strawsonian Theme. In: F. D. Schoeman (ed.), *Responsibility, Character, and the Emotions: New Essays in Moral Psychology*. New York: Cambridge University Press, 256–86.

1996. Two Faces of Responsibility. *Philosophical Topics*, 24, 227–48.

13 The Role of Empathy in an Agential Account of Morality: Lessons from Autism and Psychopathy

Thomas Schramme

1. Introduction

Moral psychology these days is an interdisciplinary endeavour; or at least many philosophers would agree that it ought to be pursued in an interdisciplinary fashion. Yet, it is not quite clear whether there actually is a genuine interchange between the disciplines. To be sure, for moral philosophers it has become familiar to acknowledge empirical research and sometimes even to contribute to it. But, as we will see, there is also occasionally a rather uncritical and superficial stance towards empirical research by philosophers. They are frequently far too occupied to exploit such findings mainly as handy vehicles for supporting their theories – theories which are mostly developed in a purely armchair approach. Empirical researchers, on the other hand, are often not interested in the conceptual legwork performed by philosophers. A really interdisciplinary approach would not just require acknowledgement of the work done by other disciplines, but a real critical engagement. I believe the debate on the connections between empathy and morality can work as a good example for establishing both the merits and pitfalls of such an interdisciplinary effort, especially when considering the putative real-life test cases of autism and psychopathy.

In this chapter, I defend a constitutive role of empathy for morality. I will rely on a particular reading of the notion of morality that is often neglected. This interpretation of morality is not affected by sceptical discussions apparently undermining a constitutive role of empathy for morality. I will call the approach regarding morality put forward in this chapter *agential*. It focuses on mental and behavioural aspects of moral agents, not on moral codes. More specifically, I will discuss the notion of morality in terms of human capacities. In the first section, I explain why I am not interested in empathy tokens, individual instantiations of empathic response, but in the general capacity to empathise. This is important in order to get a clear grasp of the thesis that empathy has a constitutive role for morality. In the second section, I will introduce some results of the philosophical and psychological debate on autism and psychopathy in relation to empathy and morality. It will be seen that the currently best explanations of (severe forms of) autism and psychopathy point at deficits in either cognitive empathy or emotional empathy respectively. I will also argue that, whatever the empirical results, we need to conceptually clarify what it means to be a moral agent. This is vital because we need to decide whether we deem psychopaths and autists to be moral agents or impaired in terms of moral agency. Otherwise, we cannot establish a connection between empathy and agential morality via this route. Obviously, the question of what 'moral agency' means is not an empirical question. To be sure, it might be influenced by empirical considerations, but it cannot be decided without philosophical armchair reflection. I will therefore attempt to develop some steps towards a theory of moral agency in the third section. In conclusion, I believe we are justified in identifying a constitutive role of the capacity for empathy for the development of moral agency. We are justified in drawing this conclusion on the basis of our current scientific knowledge about the psychopathology of autism and psychopathy and on the basis of a philosophical account of human moral agency.[1]

How the (Possibly) Constitutive Role of Empathy for Morality Ought to Be Conceived

Empathy is here understood as sharing the present or normally expectable feelings or emotions of others. As we will later see, there are arguably aspects of empathy that do not involve feelings on the side of an empathiser and that are based on perspective taking. But for the purposes of this section, it will suffice to stick to a common and straightforward reading of empathy as shared or vicarious feeling. Empathy is instantiated in real interpersonal encounters, but we know, of course, of many aspects of morality where there is no such interpersonal feature involved. We are morally obliged, for instance, to respect things, such as property, which we cannot empathise with. We are morally required to do so even where the owner would not be harmed by its loss, so this aspect of morality apparently cannot be explained on grounds of empathy with another person. There are also abstract group-oriented normative considerations, such as the common good and social justice, which are part of morality. It seems impossible to ground these abstract moral concerns on a personal feeling such as empathy. It therefore seems that,

---

[1] In this chapter, I draw loosely on some thoughts I have published before (Schramme 2014a; 2014b; 2014c; 2014d).

if at all, empathy is only a possible basis for explaining *some* aspects of morality: the vicarious or shared experience of direct harm suffered by real people. Here, the connection between empathy and moral approbation and disapprobation seems straightforward. But in general, the role of empathy in explaining or even justifying morality seems limited in scope and relevance.

I believe that much of the scepticism towards the role of empathy in morality is based on particular readings of the concepts of morality and of empathy. When slightly changing the perspective on morality and on empathy, it will become clear that the phenomena can be seen as strongly linked and that the scepticism mentioned can be addressed. Opponents of the constitutive role of empathy in morality often talk about empathy as individual instantiations, as empathy tokens.[2] They point out that these occurrences can be affected by influences that are adverse to moral behaviour, such as biases, prejudices or egocentric attitudes, or by trivial circumstances of a situation, such as the mood or surroundings of an agent (Prinz 2011b, 221ff.; cf. Maibom 2014a, 35ff.). Empathy might therefore lead us astray, as judged from a moral point of view, either by epistemological failure or by motivational misguidance.

Indeed, similarly to other mental capacities, such as bravery or honesty, empathy can be influenced or undermined by circumstantial conditions. Yet this is not very exciting, philosophically speaking, since hardly any moral philosopher has claimed that empathy tokens are necessary or sufficient for moral behaviour. Neither would a proponent of military virtues assert that bravery tokens are necessary or sufficient for being a real soldier. Honesty tokens are also not necessary for truthfulness. The idea is rather that a certain capacity or disposition – to be empathic – might be necessary for morality. So, empathy needs to be interpreted as a capacity or a disposition when thinking about a possible constitutive role for morality.

In order to see such a connection between empathy – understood as a capacity – and morality, it is also important to be clear about the notion of morality. Often, morality is defined in relation to a practice, for instance as a system of rules or 'code of conduct' (Gert 2011). Here, morality is a kind of sociological term, referring to a particular normative account

---

[2] To provide just a few examples of such reference to tokens of empathy: 'Many cases of disapprobation arise without prior empathy. Consider a case in which you yourself are the victim of a crime; you feel moral outrage but not empathy' (Prinz 2011a, 219). '[W]e can experience real empathic concern based on a false perception of the other's internal state. This possibility highlights a danger' (Batson this volume, 61). 'Empathy and sympathy do not automatically entail the existence of altruistic desires ... It is possible to enter these emotional states by thinking about problems that have already been solved' (Sober and Wilson 1998, 236).

of right and good behaviour. In other words, it is a substantive account of morality. Now, it is indeed hard to see how empathy would have any role in determining such substance. Neither empathy tokens nor empathy dispositions seem to help, because they might at best explain certain aspects of a code of conduct, referring for instance to our aversion to suffering, pain and similar conditions we can emphasize with. Yet, as we have already seen, such a descriptive account cannot explain all aspects of morality, for instance impersonal immoralities, which do not really affect anyone. Hence empathy seems simply to be the wrong element to use in a justification of a code of conduct, because it does not provide the right kind of reasons. Empathy might provide motivating reasons, but for a normative justification of a code of conduct we would require justifying reasons, which are supposedly objective, not subjective. Empathy therefore seems at best to have a role within a descriptive account of certain elements of codes of conduct. Its role for morality therefore seems to be restricted in form and scope.

But the notion of morality has another important meaning, which is more to the point when discussing the pertinence of empathy for morality. In contrast to the sociological notion just mentioned, this other notion focuses on the mental reality of moral codes and its consequences in actions. It is not concerned with a particular code of conduct, but with a formal aspect of any such code, namely its normativity and its psychological and behavioural dimensions. I will call this an agential account of morality. Codes of conduct have the peculiar characteristic that they can steer our choices and behaviour – they have normative pull. 'Morality' understood as an agential notion refers to such moral sensitivity of agents (Wong 2013). To 'have morality' here means to be a moral person in the sense that one sees codes of conduct as relevant to one's deliberation and behaviour – or to one's agency, for short. When morality is interpreted as an agential notion, it is much easier to appreciate the role of empathy for its constitution, especially when also keeping to the dispositional reading of empathy. After all, as has been emphasised in many moral psychological theories and empirical findings, empathy helps us to develop a recognition of the normative significance of other people and eventually of the significance of codes of conduct (see, e.g., Hoffman 2000, 2011). For instance, Adam Smith discussed the role of empathy as a 'source of fellow-feeling' (Smith 1759 [1759–90], 12). Indeed, the notion of fellow feeling can be interpreted as a feeling that the other is a fellow person, which is arguably a constitutive element of acknowledging the normative pull of morality. The role of empathy is therefore developmental. Becoming a moral person is supported by (or possibly requires) the development of the capacity to empathise. This capacity does not need to be instantiated in any given moral situation, but forms a kind of psychological background to moral agency. It is similar to becoming a rational person: one does not need to act rationally in each situation in order to become a rational person, but one needs to develop certain capacities.

I follow Gary Watson in understanding moral agency as applying to 'an individual who can, to a significant extent, act effectively and competently in moral matters' (Watson 2013a, 3322). The notion of moral agency can cover different levels and aspects of relevant capacities and deficits (Rottschaefer 1998, 19f.), for instance moral understanding, judgement or knowledge, moral appreciation or care, moral motivation, moral intention, practical deliberation, control and also moral development. In addition, it can be linked to more general, that is, not specifically moral, capacities, such as decision-making or the formation of value judgements (cf. Prinz 2007, 270ff.). It also allows for the inclusion of self-regarding notions such as conscience, moral identity, self-evaluation and self-concern or, more generally, the moral self (Noam and Wren 1993; Glover 2000, 26ff.; Hitlin 2008; Lapsley 2008; Glenn et al. 2010; Watson 2013b).

Further, moral agency has a complementary facet: moral patiency (Reader 2007). Human beings regularly do not only act but are 'on the receiving end' of actions; they are moral patients as well as moral agents. Moral patiency involves an acknowledgement of our vulnerability and of our dependency on other people. It hence provides a normative reason to appreciate the necessity of morality as an instrument of coordinating behaviour and providing mutual support. It is hard to see how we could become moral agents without also being moral patients, since we need to understand what it means to be harmed or to suffer.

In order to test the thesis regarding the constitutive role of empathy for (agential) morality, we would have to look at groups of people who lack empathy or who are seriously impaired in this respect and study whether they are morally capable persons. Obviously, it would not be enough to only study instances of failure of the capacity, that is, empathy tokens and their lack. We need to identify exemplars with a missing mental trait: the capacity to empathise. Luckily, there is now a burgeoning empirical and philosophical literature on two mental pathologies that are relevant for answering the question at hand: psychopathy and autism. It has been claimed that both psychopaths and autists lack empathy (Baron-Cohen and Wheelwright 2004; Baron-Cohen 2012). So it is worth studying their capacity for moral agency. If it is true that they lack empathy and moral agency and if we can explain the possible connection between the two deficits, we would have a reason to conclude – via inference to the best explanation – that empathy is necessary for (agential) morality. But before we can draw such an inference, we need to study more thoroughly the pathological phenomena and the notion of empathy, which so far has been used in a loose way as sharing a feeling. As will become clear shortly, in order to provide an answer to the question under consideration, we also need to make at least some conceptual claims regarding moral agency. What, exactly, does it mean to act morally? Since this is a problem that cannot be answered without putting forward substantive normative claims, the whole issue will in the end continue to be contested.

2. Empathy and Morality in Autism and Psychopathy

Autism is not a single mental disorder, but a condition along a spectrum of psychopathological phenomena which involve different grades of impairment. There are less severe forms, such as Asperger's syndrome and so-called high-functioning autism, and there are obviously different grades of severity in individual cases as well. This makes it dubious, right from the start, to refer to autism as a general category. In the recent *Diagnostic and Statistical Manual of Mental Disorders*, DSM-5, different subtypes have been merged into one single diagnosis, autism spectrum disorder (ASD), with several specifiers. Such variability should make us wary in using empirical literature when pursuing our philosophical purpose of clarifying the role of empathy in moral agency. After all, in scientific research, individual cases and their differences are bound to be secondary, and so we might end up with overgeneralisations. Some people might want to draw the radical conclusion that we should not refer to autism and autists at all. Especially in the context of the debate on moral agency, such a reference might have negative social effects, undermining the moral and social status of people already disadvantaged by medical conditions. Against such scepticism, I will assume the usefulness of empirical research on psychopathological cases, including such complicated phenomena as autism and psychopathy. Still, the related worry needs to be taken very seriously, and we must not, in real life, reduce individual people to medical cases (Glover 2014).

For a long time, autists were regarded as clearly lacking in empathy. This was mainly due to the influential research done by Simon Baron-Cohen and his colleagues, especially Uta Frith (Frith 1989; Baron-Cohen 1995). Their principal area of research was the capacity, or its lack, of taking the perspective of other people, a mental function that is obviously quite important for social understanding and cooperation. Whether someone is able to take the perspective of someone else has been mainly established by the false-belief test. Here, a test person observes another person, call her Mary, putting an object somewhere, say in a drawer. She then leaves the room. Another person comes in and places the object somewhere else. Mary does not know about this change of places. The test person is supposed to explain where Mary will search for the object when she returns. If the answer is that Mary will look for the object where she has placed it originally and not where it really is, it is assumed that the participant is able to mentally take the perspective of other people. When we add the capacity to explain and predict actions of other people, we arrive at what is usually called a theory of mind. Empirical research has established – although there is some debate regarding the explanatory power of some findings – that autists tend to be impaired in such theory of mind capacity. More colloquially, this is sometimes referred to as 'mind-blindness', a term coined by Baron-Cohen.

This kind of research has been challenged on several accounts. In particular, some aspects of the methodology of the false-belief test have been criticized, as the setting is detrimental to subjects like autists, who are impaired in other respects, for instance in coping with stressful test situations. These other impairments might explain their failure in the specific task (Stubblefield 2013). More importantly, the notion of empathy developed in the framework developed by Baron-Cohen is obviously limited. To be able to take the perspective of another person, or to have a theory of mind, is possibly one aspect of empathy, but it does not even involve the element of shared feeling, a feature we have used as a defining criterion of empathy so far.

In the psychological as well as the philosophical debate on empathy, a more fine-grained categorisation has been developed. First, there is an aspect of empathy that seems to be working at a subconscious level and that does not require any effort on the part of the empathiser, and hence can be deemed a passive phenomenon. It is called 'emotional contagion', or sometimes 'motor mimicry'. This aspect of empathy is instantiated, for instance, when we pick up a mood or affect of another person or within a group. It is a disposition that humans have in common with many other species. Second, there is the already mentioned aspect of sharing the feeling of someone else, a phenomenon referred to as emotional (or affective) empathy. This kind of empathy, which involves feeling, is contrasted, third, with so-called cognitive empathy. Cognitive empathy is what we have just been discussing in relation to theory of mind and perspective taking. It might involve some conscious effort on the side of the empathiser, and it seems to clearly be a capacity that can be developed by training. Indeed, it is a capacity that seems to come with a standard of success, namely the level of accuracy in inferring others' mental states (Ickes 1997). A further distinction in cognitive empathy can be drawn. There are two different objects of a change in perspective: we can attempt to understand other persons' cognitive mental states, such as their beliefs, or to understand their affective mental states. The latter category, which can be called 'affective perspective taking' (Vaish et al. 2009), does not involve the matching of emotions between empathiser and target, but is a cognitive process of inferring affective states of another person. So altogether we have three broad categories that can be related to empathy:[3] emotional contagion, emotional empathy and cognitive empathy. Cognitive empathy can be further differentiated into cognitive and affective perspective taking.

With these distinctions in mind, we can easily see that Baron-Cohen's research has only tentatively established that autists are impaired in terms of cognitive empathy. More recent research has attempted to clarify the empathic capacities of autists from a more differentiated conceptual basis. One important finding – though again there is no unanimous consensus on this – is that autists are not deficient in terms of emotional empathy and that they might even be more sensitive in this respect (Dziobek et al. 2008; Smith 2009). One specific problem with this kind of research, however, is that it does not sufficiently distinguish between emotional empathy and emotional contagion (Minio-Paluello et al. 2009; Bons et al. 2013) and also personal distress, which is a self-oriented response to others' distress (Davis 1996, 106). Emotional empathy clearly requires a self–other distinction in the empathiser. In other words, empathisers are conscious of the fact that they are sharing the feeling of someone else and that their own emotion is caused by this other person (Sober and Wilson 1998, 234; Snow 2000). Emotional contagion does not require such self–other distinction; it is rather a kind of fusion between persons. Personal distress, again, does rarely, if ever, dispose to moral behaviour. It regularly results in flight responses, especially when escape is easy. It might also result in aggression. So altogether the level of emotional empathy in autists is not sufficiently clear, but there is some evidence for assuming that they are not incapacitated in this respect.

Psychopaths have also been used as test cases for theories regarding moral agency. Unfortunately, the philosophical debate has not only suffered from some uncritical acceptance of the very category and the related

---

[3] Many philosophers would say that emotional contagion is not empathy proper (e.g., Coplan 2011), and some psychologists say that perspective taking is not empathy (e.g., Bird and Viding 2014). Obviously, by allowing perspective taking to be called (cognitive) 'empathy', I have expanded the notion of empathy introduced at the beginning of this chapter, where feeling-with was the decisive element. Such a conceptual expansion is in line with much of the relevant literature and also empirical measures of empathy, such as the Interpersonal Reactivity Index.

empirical findings, but also from a lack of clarity regarding the distinctions in empathy just discussed (Aaltola 2014; Schramme 2014a). There are several ways to understand the construct of psychopathy, and all of them are heavily contested. Usually, psychopathy is deemed to be a severe personality disorder of an antisocial kind. The so-called Psychopathy Checklist, which is a diagnostic tool developed by the clinical psychologist Robert Hare, has had significant influence in forensic psychiatry, though psychopathy is not even an official psychiatric term. It is not a disorder listed in the *Diagnostic and Statistical Manual of Mental Disorders* or in the *International Classification of Diseases*. Still, somewhat oversimplifying, the notion of psychopathy can be understood as referring to the most severe cases of antisocial personality disorder (Hare 1998, 193; Widiger 2006, 157). The latter is an established psychiatric term. Still, in contrast to these attempts at terminological clarity, a recent survey of psychopathy literature concludes that 'there is a lack of consensus about what psychopathy really is' (Skeem et al. 2011, 136). Another study ends by stating that 'despite the large volume of accumulated research, theoretical understanding of psychopaths continues to be limited, and the answer to the question "What is psychopathy?" remains elusive' (Blackburn 2009, 128). Hence there is a real danger for philosophical theory to take empirical research regarding psychopathy for granted, or worse, to pick and choose whatever findings suit philosophers' pet theory.

Disregarding these psychiatric issues for the purposes of this chapter, it has often been argued that psychopaths lack fellow feeling, which was more or less identified with what we would now call emotional empathy. It seems fairly obvious that they do not lack cognitive empathy. After all, psychopaths get sadistic pleasure due to the very fact that they well understand the mental ordeal of their victims. It is no wonder, then, that some philosophers have doubted the philosophical reasoning for a strong connection between empathy and morality, since psychopaths have the capacity to empathise and still seem to be unable to act or think morally (Maibom 2014b). So it seems that a lack of morality cannot be explained by a lack of empathy after all, hence my proposed argument would be threatened. However, this objection can only be fairly assessed on the basis of a sufficiently developed account of empathy. As it stands, it mainly undermines the idea that cognitive empathy alone might play an important role for becoming or being a morally capable person. Perhaps lack of morality can be explained by a lack of emotional empathy after all. To back such a theoretical claim, it would be important to know whether psychopaths are deficient in this respect. Unfortunately, the empirical basis to decide whether psychopaths lack in emotional empathy is undecided. For some time, it was assumed that this is so (Blair 2008). However, in recent times empirical research has established that there is no clear evidence of a complete lack of emotional empathy in psychopaths (Meffert et al. 2013). There might also be ways to compensate for impairment in emotional empathy via cognitive routes (Decety et al. 2013). Still, there seems to be a marked impairment in spontaneous affective responses to the suffering of others.

Although I have repeatedly hinted at the fact that empirical findings regarding *the* autist or *the* psychopath are not forthcoming and that we need to be wary of the methodology and conceptual pitfalls of such research, we can nevertheless establish the following hypothesis on the basis of the current state of scientific research: autists are impaired in terms of cognitive empathy, and psychopaths have a reduced capacity for emotional empathy (cf. Blair 2008). Which aspect of empathy, if any, might be constitutive for morality? This depends on what is required to be a moral agent (Krahn and Fenton 2009). As we will see in the following section, this is a question that requires conceptual claims, which are also not straightforward.

3. Conceptual Issues Regarding Moral Agency

What exactly is required to be a moral agent? So far, I have discussed this notion mainly in relation to mental capacities, especially empathy. Although moral agents need not always act morally, they should regularly show moral behaviour. Otherwise, we could not find out what is needed to be able to act morally. After all, we can only formulate an empirically verifiable hypothesis about the requirements of moral agency when we create a link between the incapacity to be moral and certain missing or impaired mental features – features, such as empathy, that we find in healthy human beings. Our only evidence for assuming that certain persons are not able to act morally is that they never act or think morally; in other words, that they never take the moral point of view. Surely, this is one reason why psychopaths have been studied in the philosophical literature. They truly seem to be amoral persons – not simply immoral in the sense that they have a bad character or very often act wrongly.

But now we encounter a serious problem, as it is not straightforward what it means to act or think morally. For instance, is it enough to simply observe moral rules? Many philosophers would claim that proper moral behaviour requires a particular motivation, for instance to observe moral rules because one believes that it is right to act this way. According to this interpretation, agents cannot be called moral without considering their mental features, such as their beliefs or convictions. Similarly, it is often claimed that proper moral motivation has to be altruistic, that is, it must not be egoistic or self-interested. This would have consequences for some theories that use empirical test cases in order to support philosophical claims. Assuming that psychopaths or autists are able to observe rules – an assumption that seems straightforwardly true – it would still be unclear whether they are moral agents. Is following rules enough to be a moral agent? This question cannot be answered empirically, but is a (normatively laden) conceptual issue.

A good example of the potential confusion regarding the basic notion of (agential) morality is the debate on moral motivation. There are two competing philosophical theories, internalism and externalism. Many philosophers assume that moral judgements are 'practical' (Smith 1994, 6f.) in the sense that people are normally motivated to act in a certain way if they deem it the morally right thing to do – barring weakness of will and other possible intervening events or mechanisms influencing deliberation and action. This so-called motivational internalism assumes an internal connection between moral motivation and judgements regarding moral obligation (Falk 1947; Frankena 1958; Svavarsdottir 1999, 165). The opposing position, called externalism, denies this implication. It assumes the possibility that someone may deem something to be morally required without being motivated to act accordingly. It has been claimed that the case of psychopaths can help to solve this issue (Prinz 2007, 42ff.). After all, they apparently know what is morally required but lack the disposition to do it, a finding that seems to speak in favour of externalism (Roskies 2003). Yet it is not clear that psychopaths (or autists, for that matter) actually understand what it means that something is morally required. They certainly know the rules that apply within a society (Smith 1994, 66ff.), but does such a kind of knowledge amount to moral understanding? If psychopaths lack real understanding of the moral ought, the tables might be turned in favour of internalism, since it would then be implied that people who are not motivated to act according to moral codes are indeed also not making moral judgements. Accordingly, the case for motivational externalism versus internalism is still open (Bedke 2009, 191). This is where conceptual issues come into play, because we now have to conceptually decide whether psychopaths have moral understanding or can make moral judgements (Schramme 2014b).

There have been attempts to solve this issue empirically by testing psychopaths and autists for the capacity to draw a distinction between moral and conventional rules (Blair 1995; Blair et al. 2005; Levy 2007). There is an important difference between conventional and moral rules, as the former depend on a given authority who sets the rules and whose demands can be overridden in particular circumstances, whereas moral rules seem to obligate categorically. Children, from a very early age, are able to grasp the difference between conventional and moral rules. It can therefore be assumed that they have an understanding of morality. Interestingly, many findings establish that psychopaths, in contrast, indeed lack a proper understanding of the relevant difference. Psychopaths therefore seem to lack moral understanding, a finding that seems to underline internalism. However, other theorists claim that there are serious flaws in the relevant research, partly concerning its methodology (Kelly et al. 2007), but most notably in respect to its conceptual presumptions (Shoemaker 2014) regarding the distinction between moral and conventional rules. So again, the case seems to revolve around conceptual issues, since it is possible, on the one hand, to say that someone has moral understanding if they know the relevant code of conduct (as opposed to conventional rules), but it is also possible, on the other hand, to interpret moral understanding as an agential notion, where it requires an element of acknowledging the special pull of moral normativity. Altogether, this shows that we need some kind of conceptual resolution in order to use psychopathy or autism as a test case for moral philosophical theories. Whether morality is something a psychopath or autist has or lacks depends at least partly on what we mean by 'moral understanding' or 'moral judgement' (Kennett and Fine 2008, 218; Kennett 2010, 245; Sinnott-Armstrong 2014).

Autists are occasionally seen as moral agents because they are strongly rule-oriented. One might even go so far as to claim that autists take a kind of Kantian perspective, because they seem to follow rules for the rules' sake, not at all because of the consequences of their behaviour. Autists also follow rules even where it is against their own inclination (Jaarsma et al. 2012). It is important to be specific about the theoretical implications of the underlying account of moral agency. After all, it clearly seems wrong to claim that rule-orientation or following moral rules for the sake of their status as moral rules is the mark of agential morality. This would also be a misconception of the Kantian perspective. Indeed, to follow Kant's ideal is fairly demanding; it does not merely result in rigidly following rules. Agential morality seems to require, as a conceptual requirement, some understanding of the normativity of moral codes. Simply showing morally adequate behaviour is not enough to fulfil that criterion. Indeed, it might seem to be a mark of lacking agential morality to always follow rules without having the capacity to acknowledge circumstantial considerations. Consider the proverbial white lies. Autists regularly present offensive or insulting behaviour because of their high level of honesty. For instance, they might tell people the truth about their looks – 'Interesting moustache you are sporting there, Madam.' We know of similar unintended insults in the case of small children. Fully developed moral agents seem to be able to distinguish contexts in which they ought to lie or refrain from telling the truth by simply staying silent. So, a particular aspect of alleged moral competence – following rules – might after all undermine the assumption of full moral agency in autists. Still, it has to be acknowledged that autists, at least of the high-functioning type, are probably capable of assessing normative reasons and hence to take the moral point of view – even in Kant's relatively demanding interpretation (Kennett 2002).

Another important aspect of agential morality is showing helping behaviour, in addition to refraining from harming others. Many animals can abstain from harming others, and some may even help others, when they gain some level of understanding regarding the consequences of doing so. Being a moral agent seems to require, in the right circumstances, to be disposed to help others and not simply to avoid harming others. Admittedly, there are serious philosophical issues surrounding this claim, especially regarding the problem of altruism, which is often linked to helping behaviour. One might wonder if any real person is a moral agent if we stick to a demanding account of altruistic motivation, as is regularly found in the literature. Here the ultimate goal or desire for performing an action needs to be the concern for another person (Stich et al. 2010; Batson 2014). This seems unlikely to be found in reality. After all, when we develop a moral identity, something we might call a moral conscience, dispositions for moral behaviour first and foremost seem to serve our own interest in virtue of fostering our identity. So, on a demanding conception of altruism, helping, and hence altruistic behaviour might seem something over and above normal moral behaviour. Thus a lack of showing altruistic behaviour might not undermine the assumption of normal moral agency.

But be that as it may, it does not seem outlandish to require helping behaviour for a fully developed capacity to act morally, never mind on what ultimate goal of the agent the behaviour is based. Indeed, such a requirement of a genuine helping disposition in order to count as a moral agent seems to undermine the case for seeing either psychopaths or autists as morally capable persons. To be sure, there is fairly little research regarding the disposition to help in autists; in fact, I could not find any empirical study regarding this matter.[4] Even if they showed

---

[4] There is at least one study that discusses helping behaviour in children with autism. However, the research did not focus on morally charged situations, in the sense that someone was suffering or in a harmed condition. Rather, the studied situation was about helping others to reach a certain goal of action, namely to obtain an object out of reach (Liebal et al. 2008).

helping behaviour, there is still the question whether this would be of the kind required for normal moral agency. Again, here we face a conceptual problem, which also complicates the assessment of psychopaths' behaviour. After all, psychopaths, even where they do not violate moral codes, hardly seem to genuinely help others in the sense that they have an internal reason – a reason within their moral psyche – that would cause such assistance. They seem to be driven merely by external sanctions or rewards.

Psychopathy can also be interpreted as an impairment of moral patiency, the flip side of moral agency. This reading is in line with some of the findings in the relevant empirical literature. After all, psychopaths seem to be less aware or even unaware of their passive and vulnerable condition; they are apparently self-centred and occasionally feel invincible. They also do not acknowledge the benefits of morality for pursuing even their very own interests. They hence seem to be incapable of acknowledging the specific reasons in favour of the normative pull of moral codes. It is true, of course, that they often complain about being harmed or treated unfairly by others (Cleckley 1982, 63, 77). Psychopaths also show resentment towards the behaviour of others (Deigh 2014), which seems to be a moral reaction. But I doubt that this is evidence of a real understanding of, and caring for, the normativity of morality. After all, resentment alone is an emotion going just in one direction – towards the other. Normal development of moral agency seems to require a capacity to turn resentment against oneself, that is, to feel moral shame, guilt and similar emotions.

I do not want to claim that someone cannot tell a story as to why psychopaths or autists are fully capable moral agents after all. As I have said earlier, it depends on our account of agential morality, and I do not believe that we have clear-cut intuitions regarding this problem. But I find it fairly obvious that psychopaths and autists are impaired in their moral capacity. If that is the case, we might be allowed to assume a constitutive connection between empathy and morality. I use 'constitutive' to describe the role of empathy for morality, but this should still allow for other routes to morality in reality. After all, many capacities that human beings lack can be compensated by other capacities, especially if they are trained. My claim is therefore more about the *normal* development and performance of moral agency. It might be compared to a claim about legs being constitutive of locomotion in humans.

This possibility of other routes to morality, where empathy might play a more restricted role, is made more plausible when acknowledging the fact that there is no single moral capacity, such as a moral sense, or a particular set of capacities that would be restricted in their performance to the realm of morality. Rather, the normal development of one specific capacity on which I have laid my focus, that is, empathy, is an element of a set of capacities that together enable human beings to become social and moral beings. This particular capacity of empathy is impaired in case of certain psychiatric cases and can be linked to deficiencies in moral agency.

Empathy is clearly not simply an important capacity for the purposes of morality but for general epistemological aspects of human agency as well. Understanding other beings has far more areas of application than morality. Neither is empathy the only important capacity when humans become moral agents. To name but one other capacity, it is certainly also important to be able to learn from experience. After all, it is hard to see how we could develop something like stable moral dispositions if we could not remember anything or acknowledge similarities between different situations. So, morality is due to many capacities, some of which we normally do not discuss as specifically moral capacities, though they play an important role. Still, the capacity for empathy seems constitutive in that it is necessary to bring us to see other people as vulnerable beings, which eventually leads us to acknowledge the need for moral codes and to feel the pull of normativity.

One consequence of my account for the philosophical debate is that it undermines the much-cherished distinction between moral sentimentalism and moral rationalism. Such a debate calls for a winner in ultimately explaining morality in terms of either affect or reason. But a winner is not forthcoming. This can already be seen from the problems in explaining empathy either as a cognitive or an emotional phenomenon; it is both. A fully developed capacity of empathy requires shared feeling and perspective taking. Current scientific accounts of several other human capacities also undermine a firm distinction between cognition and emotion (Pessoa 2008). Seeing morality as a set of general human capacities, not as a specialised set of specific moral capacities, further undermines such a rigid distinction between sentimentalism and rationalism. So, I believe empirical-*cum*-conceptual research in moral psychology can indeed help to make progress in moral philosophy.

4. Conclusion

I have stressed repeatedly that philosophers ought to be careful when drawing conclusions that are based partly on empirical data. Still, there is no alternative to an interdisciplinary approach to clarifying the connection between empathy and morality. Mere armchair reflection is not a viable option. In conclusion, even in the light of all sceptical and cautionary notes, it seems that emotional empathy is constitutive for morality insofar as it allows us to understand what it means for us and for others to be harmed. This experience drags us out of a self-centred perspective and eventually leads us, together with other mechanisms and experiences, to develop a genuine moral concern for others. Especially negative affects seem to have motivational force. The motivation to prevent and to redress harm in others seems to be based on empathic affliction. Cognitive empathy also plays a central role, as for a fully developed capacity of morality we need to be able to realise that beings with whom we are not in an emotional relationship also deserve moral respect. Hence, we need to be able to respect persons by whom we are not emotionally afflicted, for instance because they are not physically present. This requires the capacity of inferring mental states of other people, in other words, cognitive empathy, because otherwise we would not be able to see them as persons with their own subjective point of view. Both capacities for emotional and cognitive empathy together (and in combination with other traits) normally lead to the development of sympathy. These elements are the constitutive capacities for moral agency. Now, affective and cognitive empathy can apparently fall apart and may be present in less than fully developed form. This then leads to mental disorders along the autistic spectrum or along the spectrum of antisocial disorders. The fact that these conditions go along with impaired moral agency leads us to the hypothesis that empathy has a constitutive role in the development of the moral point of view.

So, my conclusion is that by gaining access to the minds of others via empathy, we also develop the capacity to care about others. But this is not the end of the story; it is not all that can be said about moral agency. I believe that, in the final analysis, to be moral is to care about morality, or to care about being moral; it means to develop a moral identity. In this chapter, I have argued that empathy in all its complexity, understood as a capacity, plays a constitutive role in becoming a moral agent.

Acknowledgements

I would like to thank Katie Hamilton, Jeanette Kennett, Heidi L. Maibom, Ingrid Robeyns and Neil Roughley for helpful comments on an earlier draft of this chapter. I have profited from discussions at the Universities of Utrecht and Bielefeld, at the Editorial Meeting of the journal *Ethical Theory and Moral Practice* and at the Annual Meeting of the German Bundesverband Autismus Deutschland in Dresden.

References

Aaltola, E. 2014. Affective Empathy as Core Moral Agency: Psychopathy, Autism and Reason Revisited. *Philosophical Explorations*, 17, 76–92.

Baron-Cohen, S. 1995. *Mindblindness: An Essay on Autism and Theory of Mind.* Cambridge, MA: MIT Press.
  2012. *Zero Degrees of Empathy: A New Theory of Human Cruelty.* London: Penguin.
Baron-Cohen, S. and S. Wheelwright. 2004. The Empathy Quotient: An Investigation of Adults, with Asperger Syndrome or High Functioning, and Normal Sex Differences. *Journal of Autism and Developmental Disorders,* 34, 163–75.
Batson, C. D. 2011. *Altruism in Humans.* New York: Oxford University Press.
  2014. Empathy-Induced Altruism and Morality: No Necessary Connection. In: H. Maibom (ed.), *Empathy and Morality.* New York: Oxford University Press, 41–58.
  This volume. Empathy, Altruism, and Helping: Conceptual Distinctions, Empirical Relations.
Bedke, M. S. 2009. Moral Judgment Purposivism: Saving Internalism from Amoralism. *Philosophical Studies,* 144, 189–209.
Bird, G. and E. Viding. 2014. The Self to Other Model of Empathy: Providing a New Framework for Understanding Empathy Impairments in Psychopathy, Autism, and Alexithymia. *Neuroscience and Biobehavioral Reviews,* 47, 520–32.
Blackburn, R. 2009. Subtypes of Psychopath. In: M. McMurran and R. Howard (eds.), *Personality, Personality Disorder and Violence.* Chichester: John Wiley, 113–32.
Blair, R.. 1995. A Cognitive Developmental Approach to Morality: Investigating the Psychopath. *Cognition,* 57, 1–29.
  2008. Fine Cuts of Empathy and the Amygdala: Dissociable Deficits in Psychopathy and Autism. *Quarterly Journal of Experimental Psychology,* 61, 157–70.
Blair, R., R. James, D. R. Mitchell and K. Blair. 2005. *The Psychopath. Emotion and the Brain.* Malden, MA: Blackwell.
Bons, D., E. van den Broek, F. Scheepers, P. Herpers, N. Rommelse and J. K. Buitelaar. 2013. Motor, Emotional, and Cognitive Empathy in Children and Adolescents with Autism Spectrum Disorder and Conduct Disorder. *Journal of Abnormal Child Psychology,* 41, 425–43.
Cleckley, H. M. 1982. *The Mask of Sanity.* New York: New American Library.
Coplan, A. 2011. Will the Real Empathy Please Stand Up? A Case for a Narrow Conceptualization. *Southern Journal of Philosophy,* 49 (Spindel Suppl.), 40–64.
Davis, M. H. 1996. *Empathy: A Social Psychological Approach.* Boulder, CO: Westview Press.
Decety, J., Ch. Chen, C. Harenski and K. A. Kiehl. 2013. An fMRI Study of Affective Perspective Taking in Individuals with Psychopathy: Imagining Another in Pain Does Not Evoke Empathy. *Frontiers in Human Neuroscience,* 7, 1–12.
Deigh, J. 2014. Psychopathic Resentment. In: Thomas Schramme (ed.), *Being Amoral: Psychopathy and Moral Incapacity.* Cambridge, MA: MIT Press, 209–26.

Dziobek, I., K. Rogers, S. Fleck, et al. 2008. Dissociation of Cognitive and Emotional Empathy in Adults with Asperger Syndrome Using the Multifaceted Empathy Test (MET). *Journal of Autism and Developmental Disorders*, 38, 464–73.

Falk, W. D. 1947. 'Ought' and Motivation. *Proceedings of the Aristotelian Society*, 48, 111–38.

Frankena, W. K. 1958. Obligation and Motivation in Recent Moral Philosophy. In: A. I. Melden (ed.), *Essays in Moral Philosophy*. Seattle: University of Washington Press, 40–81.

Frith, U. 1989. *Autism: Explaining the Enigma*. Oxford: Blackwell.

Gert, B. 2011. The Definition of Morality. *Stanford Encyclopedia of Philosophy*. plato.stanford.edu/entries/morality-definition/ (accessed July 2016).

Glenn, A. L., S. Koleva, R. Iyer, J. Graham and P. H. Ditto. 2010. Moral Identity in Psychopathy. *Judgment and Decision Making*, 5, 497–505.

Glover, J. 2000. *Humanity*. New Haven, CT: Yale University Press.

2014. *Alien Landscapes? Interpreting Disordered Minds*. Cambridge, MA: Harvard University Press.

Hare, R. D. 1998. Psychopaths and Their Nature: Implications for the Mental Health and Criminal Justice Systems. In: T. Millon et al. (eds.), *Psychopathy: Antisocial, Criminal and Violent Behavior*. New York/London: Guilford Press, 188–212.

Hitlin, S. 2008. *Moral Selves, Evil Selves. The Social Psychology of Conscience*. New York: Palgrave Macmillan.

Hoffman, M. L. 2000. *Empathy and Moral Development: Implications for Caring and Justice*. Cambridge: Cambridge University Press.

2011. Empathy, Justice, and the Law. In: A. Coplan and P. Goldie (eds.), *Empathy: Philosophical and Psychological Perspectives*. Oxford: Oxford University Press, 230–54.

Ickes, W. (ed.) 1997. *Empathic Accuracy*. New York/London: Guilford Press.

Jaarsma, P., P. Gelhaus and S. Welin. 2012. Living the Categorical Imperative: Autistic Perspectives on Lying and Truth Telling – between Kant and Care Ethics. *Medicine, Health Care and Philosophy*, 15, 271–7.

Kelly, D., S. Stich, K. J. Haley, S. J. Eng and D. M. T. Fessler. 2007. Harm, Affect, and the Moral/Conventional Distinction. *Mind and Language*, 22, 117–31.

Kennett, J. 2002. Autism, Empathy, and Moral Agency. *Philosophical Quarterly*, 52, 340–57.

2010. Reasons, Emotion, and Moral Judgement in the Psychopath. In: L. Malatesti and J. McMillan (eds.), *Responsibility and Psychopathy: Interfacing Law, Psychiatry, and Philosophy*. Oxford: Oxford University Press, 243–59.

Kennett, J. and C. Fine. 2008. Could There Be an Empirical Test for Internalism? In: W. Sinnott-Armstrong (ed.), *Moral Psychology*. Cambridge, MA: MIT Press, vol. III, *The Neuroscience of Morality*, 217–25.

Krahn, T. and A. Fenton. 2009. Autism, Empathy and Questions of Moral Agency. *Journal for the Theory of Social Behaviour*, 39, 145–65.

Lapsley, D. K. 2008. Moral Self-Identity as the Aim of Education. In: L. P. Nucci and D. Narvaez (eds.), *Handbook of Moral and Character Education*. New York: Routledge, 30–52.

Levy, N. 2007. The Responsibility of the Psychopath Revisited. *Philosophy, Psychiatry, and Psychology*, 14, 129–38.
Liebal, K., C. Colombi, S. J. Rogers, F. Warneken and M. Tomasello. 2008. Helping and Cooperation in Children with Autism. *Journal of Autism and Developmental Disorders*, 38, 224–38.
Maibom, H. 2014a. Introduction: (Almost) Everything You Ever Wanted to Know about Empathy. In: H. Maibom (ed.), *Empathy and Morality*. New York: Oxford University Press, 1–40.
   2014b. Without Fellow Feeling. In: T. Schramme (ed.), *Being Amoral: Psychopathy and Moral Incapacity*. Cambridge, MA: MIT Press, 91–114.
Meffert, H., V. Gazzola, J. A. den Boer, A. A. J. Bartels and C. Keysers. 2013. Reduced Spontaneous but Relatively Normal Deliberate Vicarious Representations in Psychopathy. *Brain*, 136, 2550–62.
Minio-Paluello, I., M. V. Lombardo, B. Chakrabarti, S. Wheelwright and S. Baron-Cohen. 2009. Response to Smith's Letter to the Editor 'Emotional Empathy in Autism Spectrum Conditions: Weak, Intact, or Heightened?' *Journal of Autism and Developmental Disorders*, 39, 1749–54.
Noam, G. G. and T. E. Wren, eds. 1993. *Moral Self*. Cambridge, MA: MIT Press.
Pessoa, L. 2008. On the Relationship between Emotion and Cognition. *Nature Reviews: Neuroscience*, 9, 148–58.
Prinz, J. 2007. The Emotional Basis of Moral Judgments. *Philosophical Explorations*, 9, 29–43.
   2011a. Against Empathy. *Southern Journal of Philosophy*, 49 (Spindel Suppl.), 214–33.
   2011b. Is Empathy Necessary for Morality? In: A. Coplan and P. Goldie (eds.), *Empathy: Philosophical and Psychological Perspectives*. Oxford: Oxford University Press, 211–29.
Reader, S. 2007. The Other Side of Agency. *Philosophy*, 82, 579–604.
Roskies, A. 2003. Are Ethical Judgments Intrinsically Motivational? Lessons from 'Acquired Sociopathy'. *Philosophical Psychology*, 16, 51–66.
Rottschaefer, W. A. 1998. *The Biology and Psychology of Moral Agency*. Cambridge: Cambridge University Press.
Schramme, T. 2014a. Introduction. In: T. Schramme (ed.), *Being Amoral: Psychopathy and Moral Incapacity*. Cambridge, MA: MIT Press, 1–39.
   2014b. Being a (A-)Moral Person and Caring about Morality. In: T. Schramme (ed.), *Being Amoral: Psychopathy and Moral Incapacity*. Cambridge, MA: MIT Press, 227–44.
   2014c. Conclusion: The Many Faces of Psychopathy. In: T. Schramme (ed.), *Being Amoral: Psychopathy and Moral Incapacity*. Cambridge, MA: MIT Press, 321–4.
   2014d. Menschen mit Autismus als moralische Akteure. In: autismus Deutschland e.V. (eds.), *Autismus im Spektrum von Forschung und Gesellschaft*, Karlsruhe: von Loeper Verlag, 350–62.
Shoemaker, D. 2014. Psychopathy, Responsibility, and the Moral/Conventional Distinction. In: T. Schramme (ed.), *Being Amoral: Psychopathy and Moral Incapacity*. Cambridge, MA: MIT Press, 247–74.

Sinnott-Armstrong, W. 2014. Do Psychopaths Refute Internalism? In: T. Schramme (ed.), *Being Amoral: Psychopathy and Moral Incapacity*. Cambridge, MA: MIT Press, 187–207.

Skeem, J. L, D. L. L. Polaschek, C. J. Patric and S. O. Lilienfeld. 2011. Psychopathic Personality: Bridging the Gap Between Scientific Evidence and Public Policy. *Psychological Science in the Public Interest*, 12, 95–162.

Smith, A. 1759–90. *The Theory of Moral Sentiments*, edited by K. Haakonssen. Cambridge University Press 2002.

2009. The Empathy Imbalance Hypothesis of Autism: A Theoretical Approach to Cognitive and Emotional Empathy in Autistic Development. *Psychological Record*, 59, 489–510.

Smith, M. A. 1994. *The Moral Problem*. Oxford: Blackwell.

Snow, N. E. 2000. Empathy. *American Philosophical Quarterly*, 37, 65–78.

Sober, E. and D. S. Wilson. 1998. *Unto Others: The Evolution and Psychology of Unselfish Behaviour*. Cambridge, MA: Harvard University Press.

Stich, S., J. Doris and E. Roedder. 2010. Altruism. In J. Doris and the Moral Psychology Research Group (eds.), *The Moral Psychology Handbook*. Oxford: Oxford University Press, 147–205.

Stubblefield, A. 2013. Knowing Other Minds: Ethics and Autism. In: J. L. Anderson and S. Cushing (eds.), *The Philosophy of Autism*. Lanham, MA: Rowman & Littlefield, 143–66.

Svavarsdottir, S. 1999. Moral Cognitivism and Motivation. *Philosophical Review*, 108, 161–219.

Vaish, A., M. Carpenter and M. Tomasello. 2009. Sympathy through Affective Perspective Taking and Its Relation to Prosocial Behavior in Toddlers. *Developmental Psychology*, 45, 534–43.

Watson, G. 2013a. Moral Agency. In: Hugh LaFollette, ed., *The International Encyclopedia of Ethics*. Elsevier, 3322–3333.

2013b. Psychopathy and Prudential Deficits. *Proceedings of the Aristotelian Society*, 113, 269–92

Widiger, T. A. 2006. Psychopathy and DSM-IV Psychopathology. In: C. J. Patrick (ed.), *Handbook of Psychopathy*. New York: Guilford Press, 156–71.

Wong, D. B. 2013. Morality, Definition of. In: H. LaFollette (ed.), *The International Encyclopedia of Ethics*. Amsterdam: Elsevier, 3433–8.

Author Index

Aaltola, E., 315
Ainsworth, M. D. S., 84n1
Aknin, L. B., 197
Allport, F. H., 62
Amir, O., 113
Amsterdam, B. K., 84–85
Anscombe, G. E. M., 250
Apter-Levy, Y., 205
Aristotle, 269–70, 300n8, 303
Avinun, R. S., 203
Ayer, A. J., 257

Bakermans-Kranenburg, M. J., 205
Baron-Cohen, S., 11, 80, 150n5, 202, 276, 311–14
Barrett-Lennard, G. T., 63
Batson, D., 3, 6, 10n2, 10–11, 13–14, 17, 17n7, 19, 19n11, 26–28, 30, 32, 39, 59, 61, 63–65, 71, 73, 84, 109, 111, 123–26, 142–43, 145, 145n2, 153n7, 153n7, 166–68, 203, 216, 220–21, 223, 225, 265, 277n13, 278n15, 309n2, 319
Bavelas, J. B., 63
Beardslee, W. R., 199
Bechara, A., 111n2
Bedke, M. S., 317
Beese, A., 114
Bell, M. A., 231n5
Berberyusz, E., 150
Biderman, G., 114
Bierbrauer, G., 115
Bird, G., 314n3
Bischof, N., 6, 15, 29
Bischof-Köhler, D., 4, 6, 15, 24, 26, 29–30, 33–34, 39, 78, 80, 82, 84n1, 86, 88, 97, 219, 235
Blackburn, S., 286, 315
Blair, J., 10n3, 10–11, 171, 216n1, 314n3, 316–17
Bloom, P., 50n14, 191, 203, 205

Blum, L., 4, 8, 10n2, 20, 24, 43, 48, 143n1, 147n4, 158n11, 165, 294n2
Bons, D., 314
Bräuer, J., 276
Breckler, R., 114
Brentano, F., 38
Broome, J., 266n1, 267n3
Brosnan, S. F., 276, 282
Brunswik, E., 102
Buehler, R., 115
Butterworth, G., 217

Call, J., 276
Cameron, S. B., 169, 205, 207
Campbell, S. B., 197, 202
Campos, J. J., 195, 233
Carlo, G., 171, 173
Carnap, R., 255–57
Caron, A. J., 79
Cartwright, D. E., 14
Castiello, U., 193
Chambers, J. R., 124
Chapman, E., 202
Cheng, Y., 201
Chiarella, S. S., 229
Christensen-Szalanski, J., 114
Cialdini, R. B., 203
Cikara, M., 225
Cleckley, H. M., 320
Clinton, B., 133
Coatsworth, J. D., 207
Cohn, J. F., 197
Coke, J. S., 64–65, 71
Confucius, 136
Constantinescu, M., 202
Coplan, A., 142, 145, 155, 157, 314n3
Cowell, J. M., 187, 193, 196, 205
Cummings, E. M., 194, 199

D'Arms, J., 292, 304
Dahl, A., 233

327

Author Index

Damasio, A., 62, 111n2, 111n2, 111–12
Darwall, S., 7–8, 10n2, 16, 18–19, 26, 39–42, 48, 61, 63–64, 142, 151, 154, 158, 272, 274, 275n11, 277n14, 279–80, 280n18, 289n24, 293n1, 297, 301n10, 301–02, 305n12
Darwin, C., 62, 187, 195–96
Davidov, M., 79, 92, 174, 194–96, 204, 219, 234
Davidson, D., 117
Davis, M. H., 18n9, 63, 109, 117, 124–25, 314
de Sousa, R., 18n8, 18n8, 19n10
de Waal, F. B. M., 4, 31, 62, 66, 69, 133, 222–24, 265, 276, 279, 282
Decety, J., 4, 6, 30, 32, 62–64, 86, 111, 123, 145, 184, 187, 189, 193–97, 199, 201, 205, 218, 221–23, 225, 231, 234, 316
Deigh, J., 8, 40, 48–49, 252, 261, 272, 277n12, 277n12, 320
Dennett, D. C., 117
Descartes, R., 186
DiLalla, L. F., 205
Dimberg, U., 222
Dondi, M., 91, 218
Dziobek, I., 314

Edel, A., 255n4
Eisenberg, N., 4, 6, 13–15, 17, 25, 31–32, 34, 36n13, 62, 101–02, 109, 142–43, 153, 158, 160n13, 165–78, 200, 204, 216n1, 216n2, 216n2, 216–20, 223–24, 226n4, 226–27, 231, 233
Else-Quest, N. M., 198
Englis, B.G., 62, 225
Enoch, D., 252
Epley, N., 115

Fabes, R. A., 109, 167–69, 171–76, 178, 233
Falk, W. D., 317
Fehr, E., 66
Feldman, R., 176
Feshbach, N. D., 166, 171, 218, 223, 226, 230
Fischhoff, B., 115
Flavell, J. H., 79
Fletcher, G., 287n21
Flook, L., 207
Foot, P., 268
Frankena, W., 251, 317
Frankfurt, H., 15
Freud, A., 145–46, 157
Freud, S., 62, 188
Frick, P. J., 171

Friedman, M., 146
Friedman, N. P., 185, 200
Friedman, S. L., 194
Frith, U., 312
Fultz, J., 17, 65, 223

Galinsky, A. D., 126
Gardner, D., 115
Gauthier, D., 271n5
Geangu, E., 218
Gert, B., 309
Gilbert, D., 114–15, 119
Gilligan, C., 146
Glenn, A. L., 311
Glover, J., 311–12
Goffman, E., 298
Goldie, P., 23, 50n14, 274n8
Goldman, A., 10n3, 10n3, 10–11, 61, 64, 109, 112–13, 116, 292–94
Goldsmith, O., 298n7
Goodall, J., 100
Gordon, R. M., 61, 292–94
Grice, P. H., 269–70
Grossmann, T., 231
Gu, X., 224

Habermas, J., 37
Hare, R. M., 42, 45, 268–69, 276
Hare, R. D., 254n3, 276, 315
Hart, T. C., 113
Hastings, P. D., 185, 189, 198, 200, 231
Hatfield, E., 62
Haviland, J. M., 88, 197
Hay, D. F., 195, 233
Heal, J., 117
Hein, G., 234
Hepach, R., 229, 233–34
Hilbert, D., 49, 255, 258, 261
Hitlin, S., 311
Hobbes, T., 186
Hobson, J. A., 201, 227–28
Hobson, P., 227
Hodges, S. D., 124–25, 220–21, 225
Hoffman, M. L., 189–91, 217–19
Hrdy, S. B., 71
Hume, D., 4–5, 15–16, 17n7, 28, 35n13, 42, 49, 62, 133–34, 136–37, 143, 165, 186–87, 216, 245–52, 254, 258, 262–63, 265, 284–85, 293–94, 303
Hursthouse, R., 44
Hutcheson, F., 7–8, 38–40, 45–46
Hutman, T., 201–02

Iannotti, R. J., 226
Ickes, W., 21n12, 313

Author Index

Jaarsma, P., 318
Jackson, P. L., 221–23, 225
James, W., 90
Johansson, E., 147
Johnson, D. B., 83
Johnson, M. H., 189, 231
Jolliffe, D., 173
Jones, N. A., 203

Kaden, S. E., 81
Kahneman, D., 113, 292
Kant, I., 4, 35n13, 37, 42, 46, 50n14, 87, 141, 146n3, 186, 252–53, 254n3, 261–63, 265, 285n20, 286n20, 318–19
Karniol, R., 223
Kärtner, J., 232
Kauppinen, A., 36n13
Kelly, D., 318
Kennett, J., 43, 252–53, 253n3, 254n3, 254n3, 318–19
Kenny, A., 19n10
Kenward, B., 233
Keysers, C., 220
Klimecki, O., 26, 28
Klimes-Dougan, B., 199
Knafo, A., 168–69, 172, 175–76, 178, 185, 192–94, 205–06, 235
Knickmeyer, R., 202
Kochanska, G., 198–99, 232
Kohlberg, L., 37, 186
Korsgaard, C., 265
Krahn, T., 316
Krebs, D. L., 59, 223

Lahey, B. B., 200
Lalande, A., 255n4
Lamm, C., 4, 64, 111, 145, 221–23, 225, 234
Lanzetta, J. T., 62, 225
Lapsley, D. K., 311
Latané, B., 113
Lennon, R., 166, 226
Leslie, A. M., 228
Levenson, R. W., 62
Levi, P., 159
Levy, N., 317
Lewin, K., 66
Lewis, M., 217, 219
Liddle, S. N., 195, 197
Liebal, K., 319n4
Light, S. N., 196–97, 231
Lipps, T., 64
Loewenstein, G., 113–15
Lorenz, K., 102
Luby, J., 199
Luther, M., 141

MacLean, P. D., 188–89
Macnamara, C., 274n7, 274–75
Maibom, H., 4–5, 12–13, 17, 19n11, 22, 109, 111–12, 121, 253, 309, 315
Malti, T., 176
Marsh, A. A., 201
Martin, A., 289
Martin, G. B., 91
Maslow, A. H., 135
Masten, C. L., 230
Mazar, N., 113
McClure, E. B., 198
McDonald, N. M., 202, 205
McDougall, W., 62, 65, 71
McGeer, V., 41, 253, 275n10
McKenna, M., 304
Meffert, H., 316
Mehrabian, A., 171
Meltzoff, A. N., 88
Milgram, S., 113, 115
Mill, J. S., 45
Millikan, R., 18n8
Milner, J. S., 65
Minio-Paluello, I., 314
Moore, B., 31–32, 165–66, 171
Moore, C., 217
Moore, G. E., 255n4, 287n22
Morley, S., 114
Murdoch, I., 147, 157, 158n11, 158n11
Murphy, B. C., 172, 174, 176, 231
Myers, M. W., 124–25

Nagel, T., 271
Negd, M., 124
Neisser, U., 91
Nichols, S., 64, 83, 143n1, 157, 218–19, 253n3, 253n3, 254n3, 254n3, 254n3, 287–89
Nickerson, R. S., 64–65
Nielsen, M., 88
Nisbett, R., 113
Noddings, N., 4, 16, 39–40, 43–45
Nussbaum, M. C., 63

Oakley, B., 220
Obama, B., 155–56, 160
Okun, M. A., 174
Onishi, K. H., 288
Ortiz, J., 200
Osiatynski, W., 115

Panksepp, J., 62
Papousek, H. and M., 91
Perner, J., 80
Pessoa, L., 231n5, 321
Piaget, J., 49, 188, 259–60

Author Index

Pinker, S., 203
Premack, D., 61
Preston, S. D., 4, 62, 222, 224
Prinz, J., 4, 25–26, 31–32, 43, 50n14, 142, 152, 267, 274, 309, 309n2, 311, 317
Putnam, S. K. C., 202

Quoidbach, J., 114

Radke-Yarrow, M., 95, 185, 190–92, 199, 204, 218–19, 229–30, 232
Ramphele, M., 155–56, 160
Rawls, J., 41–42
Raz, J., 267, 267n2
Read, D., 114, 117
Reader, S., 9n1, 311
Rhee, S. H., 168, 185, 192, 200, 202
Ridge, M., 287n21
Robinson, J. L., 168, 192, 197, 201, 204, 218, 232, 235
Rochat, P., 91, 219
Roeser, S., 38
Roskies, A., 317
Rothbart, M. K., 173, 220, 232
Roth-Hanania, R., 195, 219, 229
Rottschaefer, W. A., 311
Roughley, N., 8, 42, 50, 274n9, 277n13, 282n19
Rousseau, J.-J., 186
Ruby, P., 63, 223, 225
Rueda, M. R., 232
Rutter, M., 198

Sagi, A., 14, 29, 33, 62, 88, 218, 278
Sallquist, J., 197
Sayre-McCord, G., 250
Scheeren, A. M., 202
Scheler, M., 11–12, 12n5, 12n5, 14, 22, 30, 64, 144n2, 142–46, 149, 154n9, 153–57, 158n11, 160
Schoen, A., 6, 32, 199, 207
Schoenrade, P. A., 17, 223
Schopenhauer, A., 4–5, 14, 45–46, 143
Schramme, T., 8, 11, 47–48, 315, 317
Seneca, L. A., 122
Setiya, K., 44
Shamay-Tsoory, S. G., 216n1
Shoemaker, D., 318
Sidgwick, H., 47
Sieff, E., 115
Silk, J. B., 69
Simner, M. L., 218
Singer, T., 4, 26, 28, 189, 216n1, 221–22, 225, 231, 234
Sinnott-Armstrong, W., 318
Skeem, J. L., 315

Slote, M., 4, 6, 8, 16–17, 26, 28–29, 32–33, 42–43, 45–46, 133, 151, 277n13, 280n18
Smith, A., 4–5, 15–17, 17n7, 22–24, 29, 33, 42, 62, 64, 74, 143, 143n1, 186–87, 206, 216, 277, 278n16, 278n17, 279n17, 280n18, 280n18, 278–82, 285, 294–96, 304, 310, 314, 317
Smith, K. D., 59
Snow, N. E., 314
Sober, E., 66, 205, 309n2, 314
Sodian, B., 79, 82
Sonnby-Borgström, M., 222
Southgate, V., 288
Spencer, H., 62
Spinrad, T. L., 167–69, 171–76, 178, 219
Staub, E. A., 100
Stel, M., 223
Stern, D. N., 88
Sterzer, P., 201
Stevenson, C., 257
Stich, S., 319
Stotland, E., 59, 63–64, 125, 223
Strawson, P. F., 271–73, 273n6, 275, 282, 296–304
Strayer, J., 4, 62, 233
Stroud, B., 249n2
Stubblefield, A., 313
Stueber, K., 10n3, 11n4, 64
Styron, W., 72
Svavarsdottir, S., 317

Ta, V. P., 21n12
Tappolet, C., 38
Tarski, A., 255
Taylor, Z. E., 175–77
Teper, R., 113
Terry, R., 114
Theimer, C. E., 230
Thompson, R. A., 62, 88
Titchener, E. B., 64
Tomasello, M., 31, 61, 69, 80, 84, 88, 168, 227, 229, 233–34, 276, 277n12, 288n23, 288–89
Trevarthen, C., 88
Trommsdorff, G., 168, 235
Tugendhat, E., 267, 272
Turowicz, J., 150

Underwood, B., 31–32, 165–66, 171

Vaish, A., 6, 15, 25, 31, 34, 36n13, 43, 96, 147, 158, 168, 191, 227–29, 233–34, 289, 314
Valiente, C., 174–75, 177, 220

Author Index

Van Boven, L., 64, 113–15
Van de Vondervoort, J. W., 191
Van Hulle, C., 28, 168, 185, 199
Vetlesen, A. J., 156n10
Vignemont, F., 253
Volbrecht, M. M., 197
Vonk, J., 69
Vorauer, J., 125
Vygotsky, L. S., 288

Wagner, N. J., 200
Wallace, R. J., 272
Waller, R., 200
Walton, K., 30
Warneken, F., 66, 69, 84, 147, 158, 228, 233, 289
Watson, G., 300n8, 304, 311
Weil, S., 147
Wellman, H. M., 80
Werner, H., 81
Widiger, T. A., 315
Wilkinson, A., 138
Williams, B. A. O., 44, 150
Wilson, D. S., 66, 309n2, 314
Wilson, T., 113–15, 119
Wirtz, D., 115
Wispé, L., 158
Wong, D. B., 310
Woodward, A. L., 82
Woodzicka, J., 114, 116

Xu, X., 225

Young, S., 197

Zahn-Waxler, C., 4, 6, 14, 16, 28, 32–34, 47, 69, 83, 100–01, 168, 185, 190–92, 194–99, 201, 204, 207, 218–20, 229–32, 235
Zhou, Q., 171–72, 178

Subject Index

affect transfer, 5–6, 18, 20–21
affect valence, 3, 5, 13–16, 27, 59, 153n7, 175, 224
affective states
    matching of, 62, 222
    mirroring of, 48
    sharing of, 78, 189, 293
altruism, 27, 32, 59, 65–69, 71–73, 133, 139–41, 165, 167, 185–86, 188–89, 203, 220, 267n3, 319
    evolutionary, 66
amygdala, 30, 111, 189, 201, 225
anterior cingulate cortex, 189, 201, 225
antisociality, 171, 198, 200, 216, 219, 315, 322
approbation, 246–48, 249n2
    moral, 246, 309
attitudes
    reactive, 275n10, 282, 296–304
    reciprocal, 296–99, 304
    reciprocating, 41, 296, 303–04
    recognitional, 48, 149–51, 151n6
autism, 11, 33, 47, 198, 201–03, 227–28, 252–53, 254n3, 307–21

blame, 41, 246–47, 250, 297–305
blameworthiness, 199, 300–01
boundary module, 29, 97–99

care, 4–5, 7, 10, 15–16, 29, 33, 38–40, 43–44, 46, 69–70, 99, 142, 159–60, 189, 193, 199, 207, 216, 220, 226, 311, 322
care ethics, 38–39, 43–44
commiseration, 142, 144, 149–50, 158, 160
compassion, 14–15, 17, 46, 60, 63, 65, 74, 83–84, 142–43, 147–50, 155, 160, 187, 207, 216, 294n2
compassion fatigue, 28, 46

concern, 3–5, 7, 10, 13–17, 26–27, 30, 32–35, 38–40, 42–43, 45, 50–51, 83–84, 92, 97, 100–01, 109n1, 139, 142–43, 148–50, 152–59, 159n12, 165–66, 168, 170–71, 174, 184–207, 216–17, 219–21, 227, 229–30, 233, 247, 251, 259, 266, 278, 284, 286, 288, 311, 319
    development of, 185, 191–94
    empathic, 10, 17n7, 27–28, 33, 46, 59–74, 79, 92, 120, 185, 190–97, 200–04, 206, 216–35, 309n2
    moral, 48, 167, 308, 322
    other-oriented, 216n2, 228
    sympathetic, 40, 133, 139, 141, 170, 176
consequentialism, 41–42

deontology, 7, 41–42
depression, 28, 33, 145, 151–54, 197–99, 220
distress
    empathic, 10, 14, 62, 65, 79, 111, 125, 217
    personal, 5, 10, 28, 32, 65, 71, 84, 101, 125, 145, 166–70, 172–78, 190, 192, 204, 216n1, 219–20, 225, 314
    self-, 168, 190, 192, 195–96
    sympathetic, 10, 14

emotion transfer, 6, 16–17, 20, 22, 24
emotional contagion, 5, 10, 14, 17, 62, 78–79, 82–83, 88, 99, 101–02, 144, 166, 217, 222, 228, 293, 296, 313–14, 314n3
emotions
    catching of, 62, 278
    matching of, 62, 314
    mirroring of, 6, 21–22, 24, 31, 40, 196
    modulation of, 226n4
    other-oriented, 60, 70

Subject Index 333

quasi-, 22, 30
  regulation of, 32–33, 36n13, 36–37, 165, 173–75, 177, 194–95, 207, 220, 226, 231, 235
  vicarious, 24, 165, 174, 220
empathic cheerfulness, 33, 196–97
empathy, 3–5, 7–8, 10n3, 10–11, 11n4, 17n7, 14–18, 003190041220–34, 38–43, 0076945–51, 0092359–69, 71–74, 78, 82, 84, 84n1, 86, 0115589–102, 109n1, 109–10, 112–13, 120, 123–27, 01385133–60, 165–79, 184, 187–92, 194, 196–97, 201–03, 205–07, 216n1, 216n2, 216–17, 219–22, 228, 247, 252–53, 253n3, 254n3, 260–61, 265, 277–81, 283–84, 286–89, 292–93, 293n1, 305, 307–22
  affective, 12, 47–48, 109n1, 185
  altruism hypothesis, 3, 27, 0100459–74
  cognitive, 5, 10–11, 21, 30, 47–48, 63, 79, 109n1, 185, 189, 206, 216n1, 229, 278, 308, 313–16, 322
  development of, 33–34, 85, 139, 175, 179, 191–94, 218, 233–34
  egocentric, 33, 79
  expression-mediated, 99
  global, 79, 190, 217
  mature, 48–49
  modulation of, 34, 224–25, 226n4, 228, 230, 234
  other-oriented, 190
  projective, 64, 134
  regulation of, 220–21, 221n3, 224
  situation-induced, 96
  situation-mediated, 97, 99
empathy test, 84

fetal testosterone, 202

guilt, 28, 33, 41, 67, 101, 115, 119, 121, 188, 198–99, 252, 298–305, 320

identity module, 29, 88, 97–98
imagine-other perspective, 11, 28, 63–64, 70–71, 120–21, 123–26, 225, 232
imagine-self perspective, 28, 64, 123–26, 225
impartial empathiser, 50, 283, 285, 287
impartial spectator, 41, 282, 295, 295n4
impartiality, 41, 283, 285, 288
indignation, 50, 281–85, 287–88, 301–02
insula, 189, 201, 225
internalism, 49–50, 255, 317–18

limbic system, 188–89, 231
love, 70, 140

mindreading, 10n3, 10–11, 28, 157
mirror self-recognition, 30, 85, 88, 91–92, 98, 219
Mitleid, 14, 144
moral agency, 4, 6–9, 35, 36n13, 36–39, 43–48, 51, 248, 252, 302, 308, 311–12, 314, 316, 318–22
  development of, 308, 320
moral judgement, 4, 44–50, 143, 171, 245–49, 253n3, 254n3, 254n3, 252–55, 257, 261–63, 267, 285–87, 318
moral obligation, 50, 186, 265–89, 317
moral rationalism, 7, 35n13, 35–38, 40, 42, 321
moral reasoning, 31–32, 169–71, 178, 186–87
moral sentimentalism, 4–5, 7, 35–36, 36n13, 38–40, 42, 143, 143n1, 287, 321
motivation
  altruistic, 28–29, 31, 39, 59–61, 63, 0093865–68, 71–72, 74, 125, 147, 319
  egoistic, 67, 71, 125, 167
  moral, 4, 8, 31, 34, 143, 146, 216, 216n2, 265, 311, 316–17

partiality, 42–43, 248
prefrontal cortex, 34, 111, 188–89, 201, 231
prosociality, 3–4, 6, 30–32, 34–35, 50, 79, 84, 100, 143, 149, 165–71, 173–76, 178–79, 184–87, 189–90, 192–93, 195, 199–201, 203–04, 206–07, 216n2, 216n2, 216–21, 223–25, 227, 229–30, 232–34, 239, 265
psychopathy, 30–31, 33, 47, 50, 69–70, 123, 134, 139, 171, 198–201, 252–53, 253n3, 254n3, 254n3, 254n3, 254n3, 254n3, 254n3, 254n3, 254n3, 254n3, 276–77, 282, 307–22
Psychopathy Checklist, 254n3, 315

quarantine of mental states, 10, 12, 110

reasons
  agent-relative, 7, 41
  moral, 6, 8, 35–38, 40, 43–44, 48, 267n3
regret, 115, 119
remorse, 119, 171
resentment, 18, 25, 50, 274n8, 275n11, 272–77, 277n12, 279, 281–84, 286, 292, 296–99, 301–03, 305, 320
respect, 8–9, 37, 40–41, 48, 148–49, 151n6, 305, 308, 322

self-awareness, 90, 92, 98, 234
self-esteem, 140
self-love, 140, 246, 248
simulation, 10n3, 10–11, 12n5, 12–13, 22, 64, 89, 134, 155, 278, 289, 292, 294
social scripts, 218, 223, 228
sympathy, 3–5, 7, 10, 17n7, 14–19, 19n10, 19n11, 24–29, 31–32, 34, 38–42, 47–48, 50–51, 60, 62, 65, 100–01, 109, 109n1, 125–26, 133–34, 136, 01386139–43, 149–50, 153, 155, 158–60, 165–78, 185–87, 192, 194–97, 204, 216, 216n1, 216n2, 220, 227–29, 233, 247–50, 277, 278n16, 278n17, 281, 284–85, 293–95, 309n2, 322

utilitarianism, 7, 38–39

virtue ethics, 8, 44

Lightning Source UK Ltd.
Milton Keynes UK
UKHW022147130120
356902UK00008B/132/P